EXPLORING CORPORATE STRATEGY

Gerry Johnson
University of Aston Management Centre

and

Kevan Scholes
Sheffield City Polytechnic

Prentice/Hall PHI International

Englewood Cliffs, NJ London New Delhi Rio de Janeiro
Singapore Sydney Tokyo Toronto Wellington

To our students at Aston and Sheffield

British Library Cataloguing in Publication Data

Johnson, Gerry
  Exploring corporate strategy.
  1. Corporate planning
  I. Title   II. Scholes, Kevan
  658.4′012   HD30.28

  ISBN 0-13-295924 0

ISBN 0-13-295924 0

PRENTICE-HALL INTERNATIONAL INC., London
PRENTICE-HALL OF AUSTRALIA PTY., LTD., Sydney
PRENTICE-HALL CANADA, INC., Toronto
PRENTICE-HALL OF INDIA PRIVATE LIMITED, New Delhi
PRENTICE-HALL OF JAPAN, INC., Tokyo
PRENTICE-HALL OF SOUTHEAST ASIA PTE., LTD., Singapore
PRENTICE-HALL INC., Englewood Cliffs, New Jersey
PRENTICE-HALL DO BRASIL LTDA., Rio de Janeiro
WHITEHALL BOOKS LIMITED, Wellington, New Zealand

Typeset by Communitype, Leicester.
Printed in the United Kingdom by A. Wheaton & Co. Ltd., Exeter

10 9 8 7 6 5 4 3

CONTENTS

CHAPTER 4   THE INTERNAL POSITION - RESOURCES   87

CHAPTER 5   VALUES AND POWER   116

CHAPTER 6   EXPECTATIONS AND OBJECTIVES   145

PART III   STRATEGIC CHOICE   167

CHAPTER 7   STRATEGIC OPTIONS   169

CHAPTER 10   ORGANISATION STRUCTURE   270

CHAPTER 11   PEOPLE AND SYSTEMS   310

PREFACE

The Group Corporate Planner of one of the UK's biggest companies explained to us that the main problem he has in his job is to get managers to understand that it is their responsibility to formulate strategy.

'This is my biggest difficulty. First, because they seem to think it's someone else's responsibility and, second, because they think there is some set of techniques which is going to create strategy for the company. I try to get them to understand that if the managers of the business aren't responsible for strategy, then no-one is: and that they already have - or can easily get - any techniques that are necessary. The problem is the inability of managers to think strategically.'

This book aims to provide readers with an understanding of:

* what corporate strategy is;

* why strategic decisions are important;

* approaches to formulating strategy.

It is not a book of corporate planning techniques but rather builds on the practice of good strategic management, as researchers and practitioners in the area understand it. It is a book primarily intended for students of strategy on undergraduate, diploma and masters courses in universities and colleges; students on courses with titles such as Corporate Strategy, Business Policy, Strategic Management, Organisational Policy, Corporate Policy and so on. However, we know that many such students are already managers anyway who are undertaking part-time study: so this book is written with the manager and the potential manager in mind.

Traditionally the study of corporate strategy in organisations has been taught using intensive *case study* programmes. There remain teachers who argue that there can be no substitute for such an intensive case programme. At the other extreme there is a growing school of thought which argues that the only reason cases were used was that there was an insufficient research base to the problems of strategy resulting in a lack of theoretical underpinning. They argue that since the 1960s the strides made in *research* and the development of *theory* make such intensive case programmes redundant. It seems to us that this is a fruitless division of opinion probably rooted in the academic traditions of those involved, rather than a considered view of the needs of students. The position taken here is that case work, or appropriate experiential learning, is of great benefit in the study of strategy for it allows students both to apply concepts and theories and - just as important - to build their own. However, it is also the case that the growing body of research and theory can be of great help in stimulating a deeper understanding of strategic problems and strategic management.

xi

Our approach builds in substantial parts of such research and theory and encourages readers to refer to more: but we also assume that readers will have the opportunity to deal with strategic problems through such means as case study work or projects or, if they are practicing managers, through their involvement in their own organisations. Our view in this respect is exactly the same as the writers of a medical or engineering text and we encourage readers to take the same view: it is that good theory helps good practice, but that an understanding of the theory without an understanding of the practice is very dangerous - particularly if you are dealing with a patient, a bridge or, as with this book, organisations.

In writing the book we have also tried to recognise two important aspects of the subject within the UK which have, perhaps, not been fully recognised in other texts. Firstly, that a study of corporate strategy is equally relevant to the *public sector* of industry and public services as it is to the private sector, and we have many examples of this type in the book. Secondly, that strategic management is a responsibility of *all managers,* and what is more, a responsibility that is becoming more and more important. It is not sufficient for a manager to think of management in some operational or functional context, simply to know his piece of the jigsaw well and trust that others know theirs equally as well. Modern organisations exist in a complex environment with an increasing demand for fast and effective strategic responses. The very least that a manager requires is to understand how his bit of the jig-saw fits into the rest in the context of the strategic problems and direction of the firm. If he does not, then the effectiveness of strategic management and particularly the implementation of strategy can be severely impaired.

But this is not the only reason why the study of strategy and the development of strategic management capabilities are important. There is a growing expectation that managers will be able to take decisions about change and handle situations of change with a great deal more assurance and skill than hitherto. Yet there is evidence to show that managers are not good at handling change, and particularly change of the sort of magnitude often involved with strategic change. One of the reasons for this is that strategic management is not just to do with having a 'bag of management techniques': it is much more to do with the development of a *sensitivity* both to an increasingly turbulent environment and the expectations of those involved in organisations - with employees, with shareholders, with government and with the managers themselves. Here lies one of the fundamental problems of strategic management: the environment organisations now face is increasingly turbulent, so the need for management sensitivity to change is growing. Yet the values and expectations of managers and those influencing major decisions can be very constraining, often very conservative, influences. Since strategic change inevitably brings managers face-to-face with this problem, this book has built into it an explicit treatment of the influence of and management of such value systems. There is an expectation that readers will seek to reconcile 'scientific management' about the complex issues of strategy with an understanding of the human side of strategic management. This is a demanding task but is the challenge of effective strategic decision-making and a fundamental task of all managers in the 1980s.

The book, whilst using up-to-date theory and research, is not primarily an academic treatise, but a book for managers and those who intend to be managers: so a few words about the style of the book are in order. The reader will find that throughout the book there are 'Illustrations' which enlarge upon or give case material related to a point in the text. These illustrations are all taken from actual incidents reported in the press, in journals, from case studies, or from the authors' personal experience and, wherever possible, the organisation or individuals involved are named. Most of these illustrations are based in UK organisations.

The role of references in the book should also be mentioned. References are given throughout each chapter and listed at the end of the chapter. These references provide a source which readers may like to follow up to enlarge their understanding of a particular point where further comment in the text itself seems out of place. References are not used to demonstrate the academic standing of the authors then, but as an aid to the reader. Readers will also find that at the end of each chapter there are recommended readings: these are selected articles and books which are provided so that readers can develop a more thorough understanding of key aspects of the chapter's.

As far as terminology is concerned, we have tried to avoid some of the pitfalls of jargon that management writers often fall into: if we have failed to do so on occasions then it is not for the want of trying. The word 'organisation' has been used frequently but there are times when 'company', 'enterprise' or 'firm' is used: these tend to be where commercial operations are being discussed but it does not mean that the discussion only relates to the private sector. We have also chosen not to make dogmatic distinctions between descriptions of the subject of study such as 'corporate strategy', 'business policy', 'strategic management' and so on.

The structure of the book is explained in some detail in Chapter 1. However, at this stage, it should be pointed out that the book is in four parts. Part 1 comprises an introduction to corporate strategy first in terms of its characteristics and the elements of strategic management (Chapter 1), and then in terms of how strategic decisions actually occur in organisations (Chapter 2). The remaining three parts of the book (Chapters 3-11) deal with the various elements of strategic management as identified in Chapter 1.

There are those whose help and encouragement we would like to acknowledge and whom we would like to thank. Ken Clarke, who was at South West Regional Management Centre and is now at Aston University, George Luffman of Bradford University, John Heath of Leicester Polytechnic, Nigel Slack of Oxford Management Centre, Ken Roberts of North Staffordshire Polytechnic, colleagues at Sheffield City Polytechnic, in particular Tony Wood, Dave Tranfield, Peter Jones and Clive Sutton; and at Aston University, in particular, Bernard Hansom. All read parts or all of the text at different stages and gave vital constructive criticism. Albert Preston ploughed through the text and advised on readability and grammatical accuracy.

Colin Harris and Carole Truman worked patiently, writing and revising illustrations only to find that they needed to change them again as the text developed: they also helped administer the whole process of writing the book and did it cheerfully. We are especially indebted to them. Shirley Wilkes and Ann Healer typed and re-typed the draft chapters and manuscript and our special thanks are due to them. We also thank Giles Wright and Ruth Freestone of Prentice-Hall.

There were also others who encouraged us. The students on Aston's MBA and Sheffield City Polytechnic's DMS and MSc courses were subjected to early drafts of chapters. Staff at the two institutions encouraged us to carry on, as did teaching colleagues at other institutions. And Harry Nicholls, Professor Dudley Jackson and Bernard Hansom who could so easily have made life difficult, made sure they did not. We are grateful to all of them.

Gerry Johnson and Kevan Scholes

PART I

Introduction

1

CORPORATE STRATEGY - AN INTRODUCTION

In 1970, when Sir John Carmichael took over as Chairman of Jute Industries (Holdings) Ltd., the company based in Dundee was still primarily in the business it had followed for fifty years, the importing and processing of jute, mainly for the carpet industry. It is true that the company had widened its activities on the textile side to include the spinning of man-made fibres for carpet pile yarns and there was an engineering division marketing overhead handling equipment. However, the importing and processing of jute still accounted for most of the earnings of the company. By 1981, however, the company had been re-designated 'Sidlaw Industries plc' and the textile operations as a whole accounted for less than half its turnover and none of its £2.5 million profit. Half the turnover and all of the profits were coming from the company's activities in North Sea Oil servicing, a totally different commercial activity from its traditional business

The changes that took place for Sidlaw Industries were dramatic but no more so than for many other organisations during the same period. Sir John and his Board had examined the situation the company faced and decided on a major change in strategic direction. This book deals with why reviews of strategic direction take place and are important, and how such decisions are taken. This chapter is by way of an introduction to this theme and the book as a whole, and the Sidlaw case is used to illustrate the discussion. A review of Sidlaw's developments throughout the 1970s by Sir John Carmichael appeared in Sidlaw's annual report in 1979: it is reproduced here as Illustraton 1. Other such illustrations are used throughout the book to help develop discussion.

This first chapter deals with the questions of what is meant by 'corporate strategy' and 'strategic management', why they are so important and what distinguishes them from other organisational decisions. In discussing these it will become clearer how this book deals with the subject. At the end of this chapter there is a brief discussion of what is special and challenging about strategic decision-making and its study.

ILLUSTRATION 1

Sidlaw Industries Ltd. - A Review of the 1970s

In the company's annual report for 1979, Sir John Carmichael, Chairman of Sidlaw Industries Ltd., reviewed the changes made over the last nine years.

'When I became Chairman in 1970, the Company's business was entirely in textiles and the Company had been a leading employer in Dundee and the surrounding area for many years. During my Chairmanship, the spread of the Company's activities has been broadened so that they now include interests in rapidly expanding businesses as well as a reduced level of textile business. This transformation was achieved by two main strategies:

1. To seek to establish a profitable textile operation at a lower level of activity if necessary, to meet the steadily increasing competitive pressures from synthetic fibres and from imports.
2. To diversify into activities other than textiles and so lessen the dependence on textiles.

These strategies underlay the change in the name of the Company from Jute Industries (Holdings) Ltd. to Sidlaw Industries Ltd. in 1971.

Textiles. Towards the end of the 1960s, diversification within textiles was made in the establishment of the associated polypropylene companies. Polytape Ltd. and Synthetic Fibres (Scotland) Ltd., and in the purchase of Thomas Gill and Sons Ltd., spinners of synthetic fibres. These investments gave the Company a foothold in the industries which were bringing pressure to bear on natural fibre activities. In 1972, South Mills (Textiles) Ltd., was acquired on very favourable financial terms. This company provided some complementary activities in both natural and synthetic fibre fields. The acquisition proved successful. However, the increasing pressures of synthetics and cheap Asian imports on the Company's jute business gave rise to a major modernisation and rationalisation scheme in 1976 which, while resulting in many redundancies gave hope for the production of fabrics with higher margins of profit and continued employment at a higher level than would otherwise have been the case. The financing of this scheme was aided by Government grants and the proceeds from the disposal, in aggregate close to book values, of the associated polypropylene and some other activities in the Textiles Division which were not providing adequate returns.

It was not possible to foresee the magnitude of the continuing rise in oil prices and the effects it would have on the textile business. Because the UK interests in North Sea Oil development, one of the effects of the oil price increase has been the strengthening of the pound particularly with respect to the dollar, but United States policy of maintaining their internal oil prices well below world levels has meant that US chemical manufacturers have received their basic petrochemical materials at more than 22% below those available within EEC countries. This, coupled with greater productivity, has made it possible for American manufacturers to export carpets and yarns to the UK and other EEC countires at most competitive prices into markets already weakened by low demand. Several UK carpet manufacturers have already gone out of business, and since the carpet industry is the main customer of the Textile Division's jute and synthetic yarn spinning production, the inevitable fall in demand has made it necessary to announce the closure of one jute spinning mill and the rationalisation of synthetic spinning operations. Over 300 redundancies have had to be notified.

The fabric element of Sidlaw Textiles has been facing increasingly competitive markets and volume sales were only achieved at the expense of margins. As a result priority was given to a review of the whole fabric strategy and it is inevitable that this will lead to contraction of manufacturing capacity and overhead. The rationalisation will lead to smaller businesses capable of meeting profitable demand and based on plant and equipment of a high standard.

Diversification. For a company which had been entirely devoted to textiles, diversification presented a formidable task because of lack of knowledge and expertise in other activities. Nevertheless, the strategy was rigorously pursued in a number of different directions but with a bias towards new activities which were being created in north-east Scotland to service North Sea Oil developments and for which levels of expertise had still to be developed in the United Kingdom.

The Company has not persevered with diversifications which have no promise of growth within a reasonable time. Attempts to acquire companies involved in hardware and packaging proved to be unsuccessful as did the acquisition of Orkney and Shetland Carriers (a roll-on, roll-off ferry service from Caithness to the Orkney and Shetland Islands) all of which were diposed of with some loss. Investments in Seaforth Maritime Ltd. (owners of supply boats providing onshore services for oil companies and drilling contractors) and interests in two properties in Aberdeen were sold at a sum well in excess of book value. So it is that the two highly successful diversifications in the establishment of the Oil Services Division (composed of: Aberdeen Service Co. (North Sea) Ltd., South Bay Marine Base at Peterhead, Ship Services (UK) Ltd., and Eastern Marine Services (& Supplies) Ltd.) and in the investment in Skean Dhu Ltd. (operator of Skean Dhu hotels) are the only two now remaining. These two new activities have together provided a predominant percentage of the Group's profits in the past two years and have strong growth prospects. The policy of diversification has therefore already been fully justified.

Fortunately, higher oil prices, which have been so harmful to textile activities, have had the opposite effect on these two successful diversified activities. High oil prices have provided greater incentives for exploration in the North Sea and, even before the latest oil price increases, it was clear there would be increased exploration and development throughout the 1980s. The projected activitiy of existing customers and of prospective new customers in the years ahead implies there will be no lessening in the growth of Oil Services Division. The two Skean Dhu hotels astride the Aberdeen airport will also benefit from the consequent increased movement of personnel.

In the 1970s, the Company has been successful in its strategy of diversification, but the formidable pressures which have built up towards the end of the decade have meant that the firm's intention to remain in Textiles can only be justified at a lower level of activity. Since I joined the Company in 1966, many changes have taken place and a different balance of activities has been brought about. Changes create problems and, for some, hardship. I believe problems have been well explained and the understanding shown by employees and their trade union officials has been greatly appreciated. Every effort has been made to deal with problems in a sympathetic manner."

Source: Sir John Carmichael, Sidlaw Industries Ltd., Annual Report, 1979. Reprinted by permission of Sidlaw Ltd.

One other point should be made before proceeding. The term 'corporate strategy' is used here for two main reasons. First, the book is concerned with strategy and strategic decisions in all sorts of organisations - small and large commercial enterprises as well as public services - and the word 'corporate' embraces them all. Second because, as the term is used in this book (discussed more fully in subsection 1.1.2 below), 'corporate strategy' denotes the most general level of strategy in an organisation and in this sense embraces other levels of strategy. Readers will undoubtedly come across, outside this book, terms such as: 'business policy', 'management policy', 'corporate policy' and 'strategic management', all of which deal with the same general area of study.

1.1 THE NATURE OF CORPORATE STRATEGY

Why are Sidlaw's changes throughout the 1970s called 'strategic' changes? What sort of decisions are strategic decisions, and what distinguishes these from other sorts of decision that were no doubt taken in the company at that time? In fact, many of the characteristics of strategic decisions can be illustrated by using Sidlaw as an example.

1.1.1 The Characteristics of Strategic Decisions

The characteristics usually associated with the word strategy and strategic decisions are these:

(i)   Strategic decisions are likely to be concerned with the *scope of an organisation's activities:* does (and should) the organisation concentrate on one area of activity, or does it have many? So for example, Sidlaw, historically rooted in one business area moved into others; and one of these - North Sea Oil Servicing - became its major profit earner.

   The issue of scope of activity is fundamental to strategic decisions because it concerns the way in which those responsible for managing the organisation conceive its boundaries. It is to do with what they want the organisation to be like and to be about.

(ii) Strategy is to do with the *matching of the activities of an organisation to the environment* in which it operates. For most of its early years Sidlaw, or Jute Industries, as it was then, could rely on a strong home-based carpet industry as its major customer, and also enjoyed reliable raw material supplies. However, major environmental changes took place which made both market and supplies much less reliable. Sir John mentions several which illustrate how different environmental changes can combine to threaten the position of a company and yet also create opportunities for the future.

One change was due to an economic influence: the strengthening of the pound as a result of North Sea Oil development and the relative lowering of the dollar made it easier for American producers to import carpets and yarns to the UK. This worsened a situation of decline which had developed throughout the 1960s and 1970s as lower-cost Asian jute producers increased their quality and began to benefit from a lifting of UK quota restrictions on imports. Faced with competition operating at lower costs, the UK carpet industry suffered and threatened the basis of Sidlaw's operation. Another problem was the development of synthetic yarns which threatened the jute operation of Sidlaw. The company responded by adjusting the nature of its business to counter the threats: it moved into synthetic yarn production itself and, more significantly, sought to reduce its reliance on the traditional area of operation. Indeed, Sidlaw saw an opportunity for development in one of the areas that contributed, if indirectly, to their problems - the North Sea Oil industry.

Thus strategy is about matching the organisation's areas of activity to the environment in which it is operating; and since the environment is continually changing, strategic decisions usually involve change, often of a major kind.

(iii) Strategy is also to do with the *matching of the organisation's activities to its resource capability.* Strategy is not just about countering environmental threats and taking advantage of environmental opportunites. It is also about matching organisational resources to these threats and opportunites. There would be little point in trying to take advantage of some new opportunity if the resources needed were not available or could not be made available. Sidlaw might well have been very apprehensive about their resource capability to move into North Sea Oil servicing and would have had to assess the extent to which sufficient resources could be provided to take advantage of the opportunity.

(iv) Strategic decisions often have *major resource implications* for an organisation. These may be decisions to acquire whole new areas of resource, dispose of others or fundamentally reallocate others. So, for Sidlaw, the move from a dominant product interest in jute to a diversified operation in jute, synthetic fibres, hardware distribution and, most significantly, North Sea Oil servicing, had major resource implications. The traditional jute operations were severely cut back and the remainder modernised to make it more competitive. Companies in the field of synthetic fibres were acquired. In association with the Scottish Economic Planning Department, the company redeveloped the harbour at Peterhead as a servicing base for the North Sea and moved into the development of hotels around Aberdeen. These were not small scale changes in resources; they involved a fundamental restructuring of the business in terms of physical, financial and manpower resources.

(v) The strategy of an organisation will be affected not only by environmental forces and resource availability, but also by the *values and expectations* of those who influence strategy. In some respects, strategy can be thought of as a reflection of the attitudes and beliefs of those who have most influence in the organisation. Whether a company is expansionist or more concerned with consolidation, or where the boundaries are drawn for a company's activities, may say much about the values and attitudes of those who most strongly influence strategy. A word sometimes used to describe attitudes and expectations about scope and posture of an organisation is the *mission* for an organisation. Mission may comprise views about the organisation's standing *viz à viz* competition, or in terms of technological advance, in terms of product quality or perhaps in terms of its role in society. It may also be to do with the ownership of a firm particularly in the case of small companies where the desire to perpetuate family ownership may be a very important influence on strategy. Such views are not to do with specific aims so much as conceptions about where the organisation is conceived to be throughout time. In this sense mission is a 'visionary' view of the overall strategic posture of an organisation and is likely to be a persistent and resistant influence on strategic decisions.

(vi) Strategic decisions may well affect the *long term direction* of an organisation. They often have longer time horizons than day-to-day operating decisions. Sidlaw's management knew that their decisions in the early 1970s would take years to put into effect. Throughout the time they were putting them into effect they would have been reviewing them, revising them and planning the next strategic moves that would take the company further into the future.

(vii) Strategic decisions are often *complex in nature,* involving many considerations from within and without the organisation and being likely to have many ramifications. For example, Sidlaw's decision to change the nature of its business involved a 'relearning' of the dynamics of their new industrial base in North Sea Oil servicing. The ramifications of the decision were also very wide, affecting such aspects as manpower planning, the financial structure of the business, the planning of production facilities and plant, negotiations with investors and unions, and changes in organisation structure.

Such are the characteristics associated with the word strategy in an organisational context. They are summarised in Fig. 1.1.[1]

Strategic decisions are concerned with:
* The scope of an organisation's activities
* The matching of an organisation's activities to its environment
* The matching of the activities of an organisation to its resource capability
* The allocation and re-allocation of major resources in an organisation
* The values, expectations and goals of those influencing strategy
* The direction an organisation will move in the long term
* Implications for change throughout the organisation – they are therefore likely to be complex in nature

Figure 1.1 *The characteristics of strategic decisions.*

1.1.2 Levels of Strategy

Strategies are likely to exist at a number of levels in an organisation. An individual may say he has a strategy - to do with his career, for example. This may be relevant when considering influences on strategies adopted by organisations but it is not what is meant by corporate strategy. Taking Sidlaw as an example, it is possible to distinguish at least three different levels of corporate strategy. There is the *corporate* level: here the strategy is concerned with what sorts of businesses the company, as a whole, should be in. Historically it was a one-product (or one type of business) company; it moved to being a company with several different businesses. This decision to spread the range of business interests and the specific decisions concerning the types of business the company should enter are strategic decisions of the most general sort. They are often associated with the senior management of large conglomerates with very many and diverse business interests. It is also the sort of strategic decision that most organisations face when considering the widening of a range of products or services or a move in geographical area.

The second level can be thought of more in terms of *competitive or business strategy*. Here strategy is about how to compete in a particular market. So, whereas corporate strategy involves decisions about the organisation as a whole, competitive strategy is more likely to be related to a unit within the whole. How should the textile division of Sidlaw compete in its increasingly hostile market? How should the new venture in North Sea Oil servicing operations of Sidlaw position itself in relation to competitors to secure their share of the new market they are entering? And again, for example, in the textile division of Sidlaw in 1981, the strategy of modernisation, rationalisation and acquisition of synthetic yarn producers was the response to the need to become more competitive in that industry. It is likely, therefore, that in a large organisation both corporate and business strategy will have to be considered.

The third level of strategy is at the operating end of the organisation. Here there are *operational strategies* which are concerned with how the different functions of the enterprise - marketing, finance, manufacturing and so on - contribute to the other levels of strategy. Such contributions will certainly be important in terms of how an organisation seeks to be competitive. Competitive strategy may depend to a large extent on, for example, decisions about market entry, price, product offer, financing, manpower and investment in plant. In themselves these are decisions of strategic importance but are made, or at least strongly influenced, at operational levels.

The ideas discussed in this book are of relevance to all three levels of strategy but are most specifically concerned with the areas of corporate and competitive strategy - what businesses (or areas of operation) should an organisation be in and how should it compete in each of these.

1.2 STRATEGIC MANAGEMENT

What, then, is 'strategic management'? The easy answer is to say that it is the management of the process of strategic decision-making. However, this fails to make a number of points that are important both in the management of an organisation and in the area of study with which this book is concerned.

Firstly it must be pointed out that the nature of strategic management is different from other aspects of management. In most areas the individual manager is required to deal with problems of operational control,[2] such as the efficient production of goods, the management of a sales force, the monitoring of financial performance or the design of some new system that will improve the efficiency of the operation. These are all very important tasks but they are essentially concerned with effectively managing a limited part of the organisation within the context of some more general guidelines given to the manager. So the production and works managers in charge of Sidlaw's textile operations would have been busy during the 1970s commissioning new plant, negotiating and implementing redundancy schemes and retraining the remaining workforce; and they would be doing this as a result of policies made clear to them from more senior management. This is operational management and it is what most managers spend most of their time doing. It is vital to the effective implementation of strategy but it is not strategic management.

Strategic management is concerned with deciding on strategy and planning how that strategy is to be put into effect. It can be thought of as having three main elements within it and it is these that provide the framework for the book. There is *strategic analysis* in which the strategist seeks to understand the strategic position of the organisation. There is a *strategic choice* stage which is to do with the formulation of possible courses of action, their evaluation and the choice between them. Finally there is a *strategic implementation* stage which is concerned with planning how the choice of strategy can be put into effect. This three-stage approach, summarised in Fig. 1.2, is not dissimilar to the ways in which managers often talk about their strategies, as Illustration 2 shows.

ILLUSTRATION 2

A Chairman's Statement of Strategy is Likely to Contain Within It the Elements of Strategic Management

These quotations are from Godfrey Messervy's 1980 Chairman's review of Lucas Industries. They illustrate how the components of a chairman's statement of strategy correspond to the principles of the strategic framework, see pp. 10 to 17.

STRATEGIC ANALYSIS Position facing the company	STRATEGIC CHOICE Strategies followed by the company	STRATEGIC IMPLEMENTATION How the company is implementing strategies
"For some years, we have seen a fall in UK demand".	"We have increased considerably our overseas business and opened up worldwide markets for our exports ... In this way we have mitigated some of the effects of the decline of our UK operations".	"In Continental Europe, the level of vehicle production has held up fairly well ... our continental factories were able to maintain a good level of output. "In the USA ... we have obtained important new contracts for the supply of diesel fuel injection equipment and for aircraft equipment".
"The state of world trade has brought about mounting competition".	"To remain viable, it is essential that we improve our overall productivity". "We have to slim our organisation to make us more competitive".	"We are determined to increase output per head, and, with full co-operation of our workforce, we shall exploit the benefits of our investment in technology". "We are having to reduce our workforce and we are also closing some uneconomic factories".
"To be successful in the world market place, we must maintain our present position as leader in the technological fields in which we operate".	"We intend to continue our present high commitment to research and development".	"We have increased expenditure on research and development by £10m to £55".
	"We must be quick to respond to new market opportunities".	"Made possible by our aerospace team exploiting advanced technology".

Source: Godfrey Messervy; Lucas Industries Ltd., Annual Report, 1980.

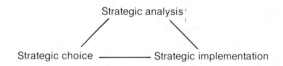

Figure 1.2 *A basic model of the strategic management process.*

Before discussing these stages in detail it is important to make clear how they relate to each other and, therefore, why Fig. 1.2 is shown in the form it is. The figure could have been shown in a linear form - strategic analysis preceding strategic choice, which in turn precedes strategic implementation. Indeed, it might appear that this would be quite logical, and many texts on the subject do just this.[3] However, in practice, the stages do not take this linear form. It is very likely that, far from being separate, the stages are very much involved with each other: it is quite possible that one way of evaluating a strategy would be to begin to implement it, so strategic choice and strategic implementation may be carried out together. It is also very likely that strategic analysis will be an ongoing activity and so will overlap with the implementation of strategy. A linear representation of the process gives the impression that one stage is totally distinct from or precedes or follows another when, in fact, they are part of the same process. The process is examined more fully in the light of research on the subject in Chapter 2 so as to provide readers with a greater 'feel' for the realities of strategic management. It is for convenience only that the process has been divided into sections in this book.

1.2.1 Strategic Analysis

Strategic analysis is concerned with understanding the strategic situation of the organisation: What changes are going on in the environment and how will they affect the organisation and its activities? What is the resource strength of the organisation in the context of these changes? What is it that those people and groups associated with the organisation - managers, shareholders or owners, unions and so on - aspire to and how do these affect the present position and what could happen in the future?

In the late 1960s and early 1970s the managers of Sidlaw examined the environmental changes they saw taking place, or about to occur, and traced the implications of these for their jute-based business. They came to the conclusion that the threats were great and that the sort of resources available within the company in terms of plant, finance and management skills were simply inadequate to deal with this threat. They would also have been well aware, being based in Scotland, of the local opportunities associated with North Sea Oil. They would have considered all this in terms of the performance of the business, its likely future performance and the effects of this on the returns to the shareholders, the aspirations of those managing the company and the livelihood of those whose employment had, perhaps for many years, depended on it. They arrived at an overall conclusion - a view of the strategic position of the firm - that the very existence of the company in its traditional form was under threat but that other opportunities did exist which might be pursued to advantage.

Thus in carrying out the process of *strategic analysis* the aim is to form a view of the key influences on the present and future well-being of the organisation and therefore on the choice of strategy. These influences will be from many sources but they are summarised in Fig. 1.3 and outlined below.

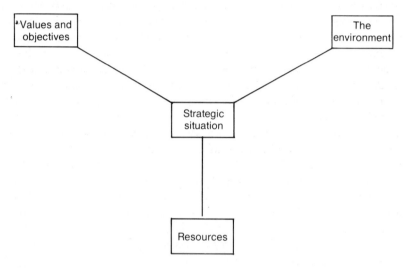

Figure 1.3 *Aspects of strategic analysis.*

(i) The *environment:* the organisation exists in the context of a complex commercial, economic, political, technological, ethical and social world. This environment changes and is more complex for some firms than for others. Since strategy is concerned with the position a business takes in relation to its environment, an understanding of the environment's effects on a business is of central importance to strategic analysis. The historical and environmental effects on the business must be considered, as well as the present effects and the expected changes in environmental variables. This is a major task because the range of environmental variables is so very great. Many of those variables will give rise to *opportunities* of some sort and many will exert *threats* upon the firm. The two main problems that have to be faced are, first, to distil out of this complexity an analytically based view of the main or overall environmental impacts for the purpose of strategic choice; and second, the fact that the range of variables is so great that it may not be possible or realistic to identify and analyse each one. Chapter 3 of this book addresses itself to these sorts of problems.

(ii) The *resources* of the organisation: just as there are outside influences on the firm and its choice of strategies, so there are internal influences. A straightforward way of thinking about the internal strategic position of a firm is to consider its *strengths* (what it is good at doing or what resources it has that are superior to competition or provide it with special competence), and its *weaknesses* (what it is not so good at doing or where it is at a competitive disadvantage, for example). These strengths and weaknesses are usually identified by considering the resource areas of a business such as its physical plant, its management, its financial structure, and its products. Again, the aim is to form a view of the internal influences - and constraints - on strategic choice. Chapter 4 examines resource analysis in detail.

(iii) The *value systems* of those involved with the organisation will affect strategy because the environmental and resource influences are interpreted in the light of these values. Two groups of managers in the same firm may come to entirely different conclusions about strategy though they are faced with the same environmental and resource implications. It is also quite likely that it is not just managers who influence strategy but other groups with an interest in the organisation - sometimes called *stakeholder groups.* Which group's views prevail will depend on which group has the greatest *power,* and understanding this can be of great importance in recognising why an organisation follows the strategy it does. Chapter 5 discusses the influence of values and power on strategy.

(iv) The *expectations* of these different stakeholder groups may also be important in deciding strategy. These may be fairly generalised or take the form of more formal statements of *objectives.* It is likely that the expectations of those involved in this organisation will be closely linked to their values. Managers may value career development and promotion, for example, so they will have expectations of a growing and secure organisation. Their expectations may also take the form of quite specific objectives, such as growth in turnover year after year. Which expectations have the greatest influence on strategy will largely depend on the power of those who have such expectations. Thus the discussion of expectations and objectives in Chapter 6 builds on the discussion of values and power in Chapter 5.

Together a consideration of the *environment,* the *resources, values, expectations* and *objectives* provides the basis for the *strategic analysis* so as to arrive at a view of the organisation's strategic situation. This view is formed by examining the current strategy that is being followed in the light of the strategic analysis. Is the organisation in a situation where it can be confident of dealing with the changes taking place around it? If so, in what respects and, if not, why not? This assessment can then form a basis for deciding on the extent to which a change in strategy is necessary.

1.2.2 Strategic Choice

The strategic analysis provides a basis for strategic choice. This aspect of strategic management can be conceived of as having three parts to it.

(i) *Generation of strategic options.* There are usually many possible courses of action open to a firm. The Sidlaw management, for example, considered (and pursued) diversification into other business activities, the modernisation and rationalisation of the textile business and the development of new textile products. However, it is conceivable that other strategies were considered which were not pursued. A strategy based on the opening up of new markets overseas was perhaps examined; or perhaps selling out altogether or merging with some other company in a related field was considered. One of the dangers of strategy formulation is that managers do not bother to consider any but the most obvious course of action - and the most obvious is not necessarily the best. So an important step in *strategic choice* is to generate strategic options.

(ii) *Evaluation of strategic options.* The strategic options can be examined in the context of the strategic analysis to assess their relative merits.

An organisation may seek for strategies which build upon the strengths of the firm, overcome its weaknesses and take advantage of the opportunities, whilst minimising or circumventing the threats facing the firm - in this book this is called the search for 'strategic fit' or *suitability* of a strategy. Sidlaw would have reasoned that the option of concentrating their activities in their traditional field of operations was to opt for fighting against an increasingly threatening environment. Jute importing and processing and their activities in the threatened carpet industry were not areas in which they could see future growth. It meant that if they wanted to seek growth, they had to examine alternative strategies. It is likely that they would have sought growth opportunities compatible with their then-current strengths. They examined at least two: the distribution of hardware and household goods, which was seen as a growth market; and the activities in the North Sea Oil fields. In neither case could they claim specialist management skills: but they did have rising financial reserves which meant that they could, through acquisition, buy into such skills. Furthermore, in the case of North Sea Oil the opportunity was fairly local.

As well as comparing the suitability of alternative strategies, it is necessary to consider how they could be put into effect. In other words, there is a need to consider the *feasibility* of implementation for strategic options. Sidlaw may well have considered developing an involvement in

North Sea Oil servicing themselves, without resorting to acquisition as a means of achieving it. Such a strategy of internal development may well have been rejected, not because it was unsuitable in terms of the needs of the firm as identified in the strategic analysis, but because it was felt to be less likely to work than the acquisition route.

An organisation will also ask if possible strategies are *acceptable*. For example, would the levels of profitability they would generate be acceptable to shareholders? Would they meet the expectations and ambitions of those with interests in the organisation? A strategy could quite conceivably meet criteria of suitability and feasibility but still not be acceptable. Often, for example, outright closure or dramatic reduction in levels of operation are perfectly sensible as criteria of suitability and feasibility but are not put into effect because of the level of the resistance that would be incurred by employees through their unions.

(iii)   *Selection of strategy.* This is the task of selecting those options that the management is going to pursue. There could be just one strategy chosen or, as in the case of Sidlaw, several. There is unlikely to be a clear-cut 'right' or 'wrong' strategy because any strategy must inevitably have some dangers or disadvantages so, in the end, it is likely to be a matter of management judgment. It is important to understand that a selection of strategy cannot always be viewed or understood as a purely objective, 'rational' act. It is strongly influenced by the values of managers and other groups with interest in the organisation and, in the end, may very much reflect the power structure in the organisation.

Strategic choice is dealt with in Part III of the book. In Chapter 7 there is a discussion of the various strategic options that organisations most typically consider. Chapter 8 moves on to consider more specifically the techniques of evaluation and the selection of strategy.

1.2.3 Strategic Implementation

Strategic implementation is concerned with translation of general directions of strategy into action. A strategy might be the rationalisation of jute weaving and this might then take shape in terms of how many factories there should be, what sort of plant should be used and what the size of the workforce should be. The problem of translating strategy into action is certainly part of strategic management, and at least as problematic as strategic analysis or choice. Implementation can be thought of as having several parts.

Implementation is likely to involve *resource planning* in which the logistics of implementation are examined: what are the key tasks needing to be carried out, what changes need to be made in the resource mix of the operation, by when, and who is to be responsible for them? It is also likely that there will be changes in *organisational structure* needed to carry through the strategy. For example, Sidlaw would have found difficulty in implementing a strategy of diversification into North Sea Oil servicing without setting up a separate division of the company to deal with it and recruiting specialists to develop the operation. There is also likely to be a need to adapt the *systems* used to manage the organisation. What will different departments be held responsible for; what sorts of information systems are needed to monitor the progress of the strategy; and how will employees be motivated to carry through the strategy?

Part IV of the book deals with strategic implementation. Problems of planning resource allocation are discussed in Chapter 9, issues of organisational structure are dealt with in Chapter 10 and the problems of managing the people and systems for strategic change are discussed in Chapter 11.

1.2.4 A Summary of the Strategic Management Process

As stated earlier, there is a danger in thinking of the process of strategic management as a neat sequence of steps; and the description of the process in this chapter may have given the impression of such neatness. The danger is, of course, that readers may not find the same stages described here existing in reality and will therefore argue that strategic management is not taking place. It is for this reason that Chapter 2 deals specifically with how strategic decisions are made in practice.

So it is with some trepidation that a summary model of the influences on, and elements of, strategic management is given in Fig. 1.4. It is not intended as a prescription of what strategic management should be like but as a description or framework which readers can begin with and refine as they progress through the book. It also forms the structure of the remainder of the book.

It was stated earlier that the process cannot be regarded as linear and it should now be clear why this is so. In practice so many elements of the model are expressions of the same thing. For example, a consideration of values and expectations or objectives is not simply to do with strategic analysis. It is also directly relevant to an assessment of the acceptability of a given strategy. Similarly, in considering the planning of resources for the purposes of strategic implementation, a study of feasibility is in fact being undertaken and so too is a reassessment of existing resources, which is normally described as strategic analysis. The point to emphasise is that the elements of strategic management are relevant one to another.

1.3 THE CHALLENGE OF STRATEGIC MANAGEMENT

It should be clear by now that the breadth of concern of strategic management is much greater than that of any one area of functional management. The concern is with organisation - wide issues in the context of a whole range of environmental influences. This gives rise to a number of problems for those who seek to develop their skills in this area.

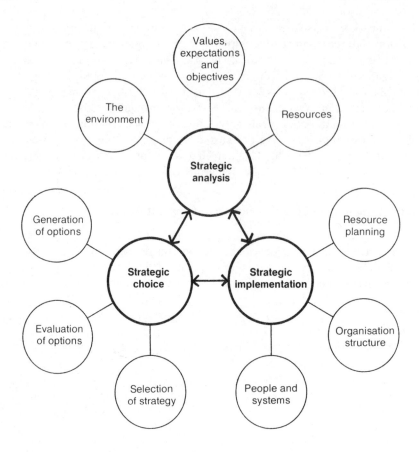

Figure 1.4   *A summary model of the elements of strategic management*

1.3.1 Developing a Strategic Perspective

One obvious problem is that managers have to be able to cope with overall considerations of their organisation and its environment. This is not easy to do, as managers who move from functional responsibilities to general management responsibilities often find. The accountant finds that he still tends to see problems in financial terms, the marketing manager in marketing terms and so on. Each aspect in itself is most worthy, of course, but none is adequate alone. The manager has to learn to take an overview, to conceive of the whole rather than the parts.

It is necessary to develop a facility to take an holistic view of the situation and conceive of major, overall problems rather than dwell on difficulties which, real as they may be, are not of strategic significance.

1.3.2 Coping with Change

To cope with the vast variety and range of environmental inputs in the strategic decision process, managers have to operate within some simplified model of that environment. Essentially managers reduce the 'infinite' to a personally manageable model of reality. More precisely, there is evidence[4] to show that to some extent this 'model of reality' is inherited by the manager in the sense that there exist industry-based 'recipes'. These recipes are the perceived wisdom, for an industry, of the key factors for business success in a particular business environment. The idea of recipes is discussed more fully in Chapter 2: suffice it to say at this stage that their influence can be a significant constraint on change.[5] For example it is quite likely that in Sidlaw in the early 1970s the managers who had gained their experience in the jute industry would tend to see business problems in a fairly similar way. They would expect to operate the business on the basis of past experience and would interpret environmental change in the context of what had gone before.

Readers might care to imagine the problems that faced Sidlaw in reassessing their strategy and eventually changing it. For so many years the company had operated in one business area which was now fundamentally threatened. For years prior to the new chairman the company's profits had declined but management could not see their way out of the decline because they were constrained in the way they saw the business and the influences on it. It took a steadily worsening position and a new chairman to break through such constraints and to enter business areas which would not have been considered in previous years. It is important for those who wish to understand, or develop, skills in strategic management to consider the problems of achieving changes in strategy. To achieve such changes effectively, what is being asked of managers may well be a change in the way they and their colleagues perceive their organisational world. How such changes came about, indeed whether they can be brought about at all, underlies the study of strategic management and is considered in more detail in Chapters 2, 5 and 11 of the book.

1.3.3 Strategy in the Public Sector and Not-for-profit Organisations

The development of concepts and techniques of corporate strategy have, in the past, mainly occurred in the area of commercial enterprises; are they applicable to public sector and not-for-profit organisations? The answer is most certainly 'yes'. There are of course differences in such organisations.[6] The idea of profit may not be central; the expectations of those involved in such organisations and their criteria for success may be different from businesses; the value systems of those influencing such organisations are likely to be more diverse than in commercial enterprises; the structures of such organisations are also often very different. All of this is true but it does not mean that the ideas of strategy and strategic management are not relevant.

ECS–B

ILLUSTRATION 3

Strategic Management and the Public Sector

● In 1972, the Bains Report highlighted the need for local authorities to adopt a strategic approach to their management. The Study Group on Local Authority Management Structures was set up in 1972 to investigate the allegation that 'There undoubtedly exists a body of opinion that infers (sic) that there is very little right with local government management and administration'. Such feeling had grown over the years because the management structures of many local authorities in the early 1970s were still those which had emerged from the development of local government in the 19th Century. Typically, local authorities were highly departmentalised with each department being guided by the relevant committee such as Housing, Recreation, Education and so on. The report of the Maud Committee some years earlier pointed out the 'separateness of the committees contributes to the separateness of the departments and the professionalism of departmental staff feeds on this separateness'. The working group, chaired by M. A. Bains, showed how the dual nature of management only served to exacerbate the problem:

'In the democratic context in which Local Government must operate, there are two elements both trying to 'manage', i.e. elected members and officers too often suspicious and critical of each other's roles which may impair both morale and efficiency.'

The solution to these problems, said the report, was to realise that: 'management skills are as important as professional skills'. One way to overcome the difficulties would be by taking a 'top-down' perspective which would transcend the traditional departmental boundaries. Local authorities would then no longer be limited to seeing their role as the provision of a series of services to the local community, but they should instead be concerned with 'the overall economic, cultural and physical well-being of the community'.

Bains related the importance of taking a strategic perspective:

'Because of this overall responsibility and because of the inter-relationship in the environment in which it is set, the traditional departmental attitude within much of Local Government must give way to a wider-ranging corporate outlook ... We believe that the need for a corporate approach is beyond dispute if Local Government is to be efficient and effective.'

Source: M.A. Bains Study Group on Local Authority Management Structures.

If strategy is to do with reconciling the general direction an organisation takes to fulfil its mission with the environment around it, then the notion is just as relevant to Oxfam, the London Symphony Orchestra, a local authority or the Police Force as it is to Sidlaw Industries. The importance of the different influences on strategy may have different weights; for example, some of the aspects of strategy-making covered in this book which might be regarded as innovative by some business managers - such as the analysis of political influences or of value systems - have long been seen as of central importance in public bodies. The weights of influences may be different but the importance of managing the strategic decision-making process remains just as great. Illustration 3 provides a good example of this.

1.3.4 The Manager as Strategist

Over time organisations do not survive and flourish simply because they are efficient at what they are doing. Decreasing work in progress, cutting wastage rates, controlling working capital and negotiating sensible wage rates are all important to the performance of a business. But to take one example, no amount of this could have turned Sidlaw's declining fortunes into prospects of profitable growth. What is of central and crucial importance to the survival, development and prosperity of an organisation is the extent to which it is able to obtain, allocate and control its resources in such a way as to take advantage of the changes that go on in its environment and avoid or overcome the threats these pose. In short, how effective its strategic management is.

There have been texts which positioned the subject as relevant only to senior managers or those involved in the general management of business units: it is seen as a sort of training course for managing directors.[7] Certainly the subject matter is relevant to senior managers: but strategic management is not their responsibility alone. Chapter 2 will show that strategic changes are seldom made as a result of senior management decisions alone. It is much more usual for strategy to evolve as a result of the activities, perceptions and influence of many other individuals including the different levels of management. Furthermore, when it comes to the implementation of strategy, the chances of achieving success without all levels of management understanding the strategic issues involved is a formula for disaster. It can - indeed often does -result in an inability to formulate or implement any significant strategic changes because those who are responsible for managing them simply do not understand the strategic problems and how they can be dealt with.

1.4 SUMMARY

This chapter has set out to explain the focus, concept and scope of the study and to propose a framework by which to approach the subject. The aim is that by this stage readers will have some idea about the sorts of problems with which the study is concerned. The rest of the book sets out to amplify the different elements of strategic management identified and outlined in this chapter.

However, before this, the next chapter looks at how strategy formulation occurs in practice so that readers can place the discussion in the remainder of the book in the context of managerial practice.

REFERENCES

1. We have chosen not to provide a definition as such of what is meant by strategy, preferring to discuss the characteristics of strategic decisions as a means of explanation. A useful analysis of alternative definitions can be found in C.W. Hofer and D. Schendel, *Strategy Formulation: Analytical Concepts* (West: 1978, pp.16-20).

2. A useful distinction is made by R.N. Anthony and J. Dearden, *Management Control Systems* (Irwin: 1976) between operational levels of management and strategic levels. They identify three levels of management activity:

    (i)   Strategic planning (which) is the process of deciding on the goals of the organisation, on changes in these goals, on the resources used to attain these goals and on the policies that are to govern the acquisition, use and disposition of these resources.'

    (ii) 'Management control (which) is the process by which managers assure that resources are obtained and used effectively and efficiently in the accomplishment of the organisation's goals.'

    (iii) And 'operational control (which) is the process of assuring that specific tasks are carried out effectively and efficiently.'

    Whilst we recognise that the majority of managers are engaged in the third level of activity for most of their time, the first two levels are clearly of great importance and it is with these levels that this book is mainly concerned.

    See for example, W.F. Glueck, *Business Policy and Strategic Management* (McGraw-Hill: 1980) or Y.N. Chang and F. Campo-Flores, *Business Policy and Strategy* (Goodyear: 1980).

4. For a detailed discussion see J-C. Spender, 'Strategy Making in Business' which is a doctoral thesis from the Manchester Business School (1980). Spender's views are also summarised in P. Grinyer and J-C. Spender, *Turnaround: Managerial Recipes for Strategic Success* (Associated Business Press: 1978). Also see Grinyer and Spender, 'Recipes, Crises, and Adaptation in Mature Businesses', *Intl. Studies of Management and Organisation,* Vol. IX, No. 3, P. 113, 1979. The roots of the concept of industrial recipes do, however, stem both from the writings of A. Schutz, *Phenomenology of the Social World* (Northwestern University Press: 1967), and the approaches to psychology advocated by G. Kelly in *The Psychology of Personal Constructs,* Vol. I (W.W. Norton & Co.: 1955).

5. One of the most stimulating papers which addresses itself to the problems arising from an over-constrained view of the scope of a business is that by Theodore Levitt called 'Marketing Myopia' (*Harvard Business Review,* Jul.-Aug. 1960).

6. Chapter 18 in G. Steiner and J. Miner, *Management Policy and Strategy* (Collier Macmillan: 1977) discusses aspects of strategy in 'not-for-profit' organisations. An interesting and brief discussion of the problems and differences in the non-commercial sector can also be found in an article by M. L. Hatten called 'Strategic Management in Not-for-Profit Organisations', *Strategic Management Journal,* Apr.-Jun. 1982.

7.   See, for example, C.R. Christensen, K.R. Andrews and J.L. Bower, *Business Policy, 4th Edition* (Irwin: 1978).

RECOMMENDED KEY READINGS

*   For a discussion of the concept of strategy which incorporates definitions by a number of writers see Chapter 2, C.W. Hofer and D. Schendel, *Strategy Formulation : Analytical Concepts* (West: 1978).

*   As illustrations of the nature and significance of strategic decisions, the reader may care to look at some accounts of strategic change as provided in *Management Today*. For example: *The Retailer's Burden* by Tom Lester (Feb. 1980) and *British Steel's Melt Down* by R. Taylor (Sept. 1982).

2

STRATEGIC DECISION MAKING IN PRACTICE

2.1. INTRODUCTION

In Chapter 1 the idea of corporate strategy was introduced, as were the elements regarded as constituting strategic management - strategic analysis, strategic choice and strategic implementation. It is important to emphasise that these elements are parts of a model, the purpose of which is to help readers think about strategic problems. In this book there is an attempt to reconcile the model to the reality of management by, for example, emphasising the interaction of the elements of this model: nonetheless, its purpose remains as an aid to dealing with the subject of study. It is not intended that the reader should conceive of the model as a direct representation of strategic decision-making as it actually occurs. So before going on to examine the elements of the model in Parts II, III and IV, it is important to have a clearer understanding of the reality of the process of strategic decision-making. This chapter sets out to provide a basis for that understanding.

The first part of the chapter is concerned with the *nature of strategic change*, i.e., the ways in which strategic changes come about in organisations. Such questions are posed as: Do strategic changes always occur as massive changes in direction as they did at Sidlaw or do they take other forms? The conclusion reached is that strategic changes may take different forms but that, typically, they do not occur as major, one-off changes in direction but as more gradual, 'incremental developments'.

The second part of the chapter is concerned with *how strategic decisions are made*. Here the focus is on the process of decision-making: how is a strategic problem recognised and defined; how is a decision to take a course of action actually made? The conclusion reached is that a neat and rational process is not necessarily employed by managers and that some of the aspects of the strategic management model outlined in Chapter 1 are normally not apparent in the processes actually used. However, the study of the process of strategic decision-making also reveals some useful guidelines to the study of strategy which are discussed later in the chapter.

One of the major conclusions reached in the first two sections of the chapter is that, to a very large extent, the strategy of organisations is strongly influenced by the strategic decision-makers themselves. Strategy is not formed by a dispassionate reconciliation of organisational resources with environmental forces, but is intimately bound up with the experience, values and outlook of decision-makers - usually managers. The third part of this chapter examines *strategy as a product of strategists* and concludes that, to understand how strategy comes about, it is essential to understand organisational culture and managerial values and attitudes.

In the final part of the chapter there is a discussion of what can be learned from the practice of strategic decision-making in terms of *implications for the study of strategy.* The overall conclusion is that a good deal can be learned from what goes on in practice: indeed that it would be arrogant not to do so. It is, however, important to sound something of a warning too: just because managers behave in a particular way does not mean it is the 'right' way or the most sensible way. It is important to assess what is 'good practice' and build on that. Our view is that readers will be able to assess a good deal better for themselves which of the techniques and concepts in the book are most useful if they have an understanding of strategic decision-making as it happens.

2.2 THE NATURE OF STRATEGIC CHANGE

In the Sidlaw illustration used in the last chapter the strategic change that took place appeared to have two characteristics which, it might be thought, typify strategic change. In the first place, the change was of a major kind - the move from one product market to an entirely different one. And secondly, it was apparently quite clearly intended and planned. This section of this chapter considers if these characteristics are typical of strategic change.

2.2.1 Strategic Change - Major Shift or Incremental Development

Strategic changes are often conceived of as one-off major changes. However there is increasing evidence to show that strategy is, more typically, formed through a set of decisions being taken which might be considered more operational in nature but which over time, in a piecemeal fashion, build up to form the strategy of an organisation. This is what has come to be known as an *incrementalist* view of strategy formulation.

It is the research and writings of Quinn[1] and Mintzberg[2] in particular which have begun to provide a clearer understanding of the process of strategy formulation in organisations. They have shown that strategy can more accurately be thought of as what Mintzberg describes as a 'pattern in a stream of decisions'. Both writers argue that it is a mistake to think of strategic decisions being made at a point in time and then put into operation. Nor is it sensible to think of strategic decisions always being made at the top of the organisation and, as it were, being handed down to operating management. Rather, what happens more typically can be characterised as follows:

* A continual process of adjustment and modification of existing strategy taking place as environmental changes occur.

* Such adjustment originates in, and is promoted in, what Quinn calls the 'sub-systems' of the organisation. 'Sub-systems' could be the management or operating groups that deal with issues which have an impact on strategy such as acquisitions, financing, research and development or marketing. It is within these sub-systems, which could be functional management groups or teams of individuals working on projects, that initiatives for change are likely to arise.

* Organisations do not tend to make major one-off shifts in strategy. Rather they test out changes first and develop from those small beginnings. A retailer might try out an idea promoted by a group of staff by modifying a number of shops or taking in a limited range of merchandise. An industrial company may test out a proposed diversification by acquiring an interest in a business operating in the area.

* This process needs to be distinguished from what in more traditional approaches has been thought of as the process of 'control'. In a more traditional model of strategy formulation the last stage would be to monitor the performance of the strategy and re-evaluate it on the basis of its performance. The idea is that, within the organisation, there should be systems which ensure that the progress being made is continually monitored and fed back to those responsible for making strategic decisions so as to amend and improve the strategy. The incrementalist view is not the same as this. The incrementalist view is that strategy is normally formulated - not just monitored - by the stream of decisions made within the organisation. It is not a matter of the sub-systems being responsible for 'control' alone but also for strategy formulation itself.

It is tempting to think that this fluid state of affairs must be a complete muddle[3] in which no coherent strategy could exist. However, Quinn argues differently:

> 'The most effective strategies of major enterprises tend to emerge step by step from an iterative process in which the organisation probes the future, experiments, and learns from a series of partial (incremental) commitments rather than through global formulations of total strategies. Good managers are aware of this process, and they consciously intervene in it. They use it to improve the information available for decisions and to build the psychological identification essential to successful strategies. The process is both logical and incremental. Such logical incrementalism is not 'muddling', as most people understand that word. Properly managed, it is a conscious, purposeful, proactive, executive practice'.[4]

ILLUSTRATION 4

Pilkington Brothers Ltd. - Incremental Change

● The Pilkington Organisation has changed dramatically since 1958, not by huge strategic leaps but incrementally.
From Pilkington's inception in 1826 to the introduction of float glass in 1958 their principal interest had been in the production of three different types of flat glass; cast and rolled glass, polished plate glass and sheet glass. Although there had been a few brief, joint ventures with foreign glass manufacturers during this period, Pilkington was still very much a national company.

The development of float glass, a process that produced glass of the same quality as polished plate but without the need for costly grinding and polishing, provided a major opportunity. The strategy that Pilkington formulated to capitalise upon this was aimed at developing a technical dominance in float glass throughout the world. With the protection of its patents and its established businesses, Pilkington reasoned that it would be able to control access to selected growth markets in specific countries. However, this aim was not to be achieved in one go, it preferred to assess the reaction of the markets to its products and improve the flexibility of the process before installing numerous plants worldwide, while at the same time allowing plate competition to settle.

Once this trial period had been completed, float glass generated high growth and, after an initial investment period, high cash flows. This gave the company the necessary funds to diversify both geographically and in product terms, an important task bearing in mind their considerable reliance on flat glass manufacture and the fact that the company was operating in a rapidly weakening British economy. However, the pursuit of diversification by their chosen route of acquisition and joint venture meant that such a strategy could only be implemented when suitable companies became available for sale or developed a product of interest to Pilkington.

Pilkington's rapid growth together with its diversification programme demanded a new professionalism among workers and managers alike, but served to weaken the close relationship between workers and owners. Eventually by 1965, Pilkington's size and complexity had increased to such an extent that the then centralised power structure could no longer cope. The retirement of a key executive provided the opportunity for reorganisation, and following several formal and informal studies, the company was decentralised, although there was a period of reorganisation during which the company was tightened up.

Also in the early 1960s, following changes in the tax environment, age structure and financial fortunes of the shareholders, and as a means of providing a more flexible capital base for the company, it was decided to go public. However, in 1970, just before going public, a strike convinced the owners to ask Lord Pilkington, retiring Chairman, to stay on for three more years before Sir Alistair Pilkington became Chairman. The strike also accelerated the company's move away from paternalistic management to a more professional style.

Pilkington Brothers Ltd., from being basically a privately-owned national company with a limited product range in 1958, had, by the early 1970s, become a public company operating as a multi-national and producing a wide range of glass products. This change came about not by one giant strategic leap, but by the company 'feeling its way' with a new process; strategic change occurred incrementally.

Adapted from: James B. Quinn, Strategies for Change: Logical Incrementalism (Homewood, Illinois: Richard D. Irwin, Inc., 1980) pp.25, 53.© Richard D. Irwin, Inc., 1980.

Quinn does not see the various decisions in the incremental process as necessarily entirely separate. Because the sub-systems (or functions) are in a continual state of interplay with each other, the managers of each should know what the others are doing and should interpret each others actions and requirements. They are in effect learning from each other about the feasibility of a course of action in terms of both resource management and its internal political acceptability. Moreover, the formulation of strategy in this way means that the implications of the strategy are continually being tested out. This continual readjustment does, of course, make a lot of sense if the environment is considered as a continually changing influence on the organisation. It is a process though which the organisation keeps itself in line with such change, as shown in Fig. 2.1(a). Even when there is a major apparent shift in strategy it is quite likely to have come about incrementally. Illustration 4 shows how Pilkington's changed their strategy and the structure of their company fundamentally, but incrementally.

So, the first conclusion is that strategic change may result in major shifts in direction but, typically, these shifts occur in an incremental fashion.

2.2.2 The Incidence of Global Change

The notion of incrementalism does not mean that major shifts in strategy never occur: nor does it mean that there is no such thing as an overall strategy for an organisation. Gradual shifts in strategy may be the norm but it is important to remember that:

* gradual shifts in strategy, over time, may well result in very major changes in strategy (as in Illustration 4);

* there is likely to be an overall strategic direction which exists for an organisation: this may be most clearly seen by considering what the organisation has done in the past and deducing what the strategy is;

* on occasions gradual shifts may not be sufficient; major changes may be needed over a relatively short period of time.

Mintzberg[5] shows that there are different patterns of strategic change. He agrees with Quinn that normally strategy changes incrementally. However, in certain circumstances, strategic change may be 'global' in nature. 'Global' changes are more fundamental strategic shifts in direction which occur occasionally in the history of an organisation.

These briefer periods of 'global' change are often associated with the arrival of a dominant leader who, as a catalyst, brings about a major shift in strategy. (Illustration 5 gives examples of global strategic changes associated with the arrival of dominant leaders.) This pattern of long periods of relative continuity, interspersed with major more 'global' changes makes a lot of sense. No organisation could function efficiently if it were to undergo major revisions of strategy too frequently; however, an organisation, in order to survive, needs to adapt itself continually to what is going on around it. This continual process of adaptation is what incremental change is all about: it is a continuing readjustment to a changing environment. However, environmental change may not always be gradual enough for incremental change to keep apace. If incremental strategic change lags behind environmental change, perhaps because the environmental change is sudden or at a greater rate than normal, then it may well be necessary for strategic change of a more fundamental, 'global' nature to occur. This is represented in Fig. 2.1(B).

It is, however, as likely that global change will be required for a reason other than sudden or major environmental change. A likely reason is the failure of attempts to keep in line with changes in the environment through incremental development. The development has simply not been in the right direction, or has lagged behind the environmental changes taking place over a period of many years.[6] It is then that major change, often through the deliberate assertion of the will and vision of a new leader may take place. Fig. 2.1(C) represents this pattern of strategic change.

2.2.3 Planning and Strategic Change

The words 'strategy' and 'planning' have become so inextricably associated that it becomes necessary to define the role and forms of planning clearly. This necessity stems from a common confusion between 'planning' in the context of strategic decision-making and 'corporate planning' as a formal activity often incorporated into a department within an organisation.

The first point to make is that planning, in the sense of analysing situations, considering the outcomes of proposals and thinking through the sequence of actions required to put change into effect, is part of the job of managers anyway. So, as far as strategic decisions are concerned, planning is not just the task of the corporate planner. Indeed, given an incremental process of strategic change, planning at the managerial level may be a more significant influence than planning at a corporate level.

It is also important to be clear as to the role of corporate planning in an organisation. There is little evidence to support the idea that corporate planning as an activity or corporate planners as managers in organisations are actually responsible for strategic decisions being taken.[7] Rather, the role of corporate planning appears to be to contribute to the strategic management process in three main ways:[8]

Pattern A
The environment changes gradually and organisation strategy develops incrementally with it.

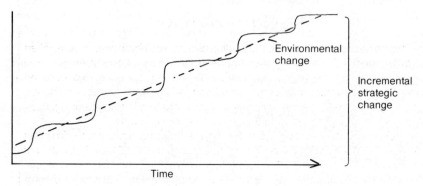

Pattern B
There is major environmental change requiring 'global' strategic readjustment.

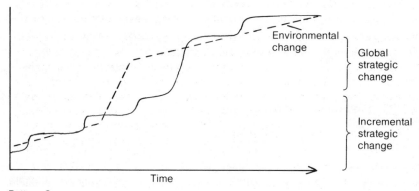

Pattern C
The environment changes gradually but organisation strategy fails to develop in line with it until such time as a major readjustment is needed. This may entail a change in 'global' strategy and is likely to involve a change in leadership.

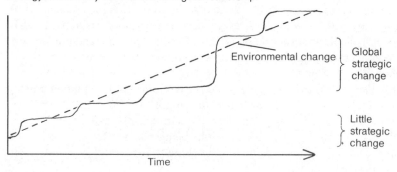

Figure 2.1   *Three patterns of strategic change.*

ILLUSTRATION 5

The Impact of 'A New Leader'

- The appointment of a new managing director or chief executive is often associated with a fundamental change in the organisation's strategy.

Brian Kent at Staveley. Brian Kent's appointment as chief executive on January 1st, 1980 marked the beginning of a period of rapid change, moving the group away from machine tool manufacture and into service engineering, non-destructive testing, precision weighing and spring components.

Achieved in a little over two years, the change involved selling six subsidiaries for £25m, closing nine at a cost of £5m. and acquiring four for £10m. The extent of the change is put in perspective when one considers that Staveley's share capital was only £46m. Staveley strengthened its shareholding in British Salt as a means of providing funds for the newly acquired companies while also changing the role of the subsidiaries' managing directors by getting them involved in corporate planning.

Source: *Financial Times, 19th Nov. 1982, p. 18; Management Today, May 1979, p.82*

Brian Gilbert at Low and Bonar. Founded at the turn of the century, Low and Bonar had, for many years been involved in textiles, primarily as a manufacturer of jute-based fabrics. However, the development of synthetic fibres saw the company fall into decline, a trend that was only reversed following the appointment of Brian Gilbert as managing director in 1973. His first move was to phase out this traditional business, rebuilding the company around specialist engineering and packaging. To complement this change in direction, more than a dozen senior executives were recruited. Gilbert also saw the need to diversify geographically, achieved by expanding their existing Canadian and African operations as well as entering into joint ventures in Sri Lanka, Malaysia and Australia. In order to provide funds for investment in manufacturing operations, Gilbert took Low and Bonar into the service sector with the purchase of Nairn Travel, the retail travel agency and specialist tour operator.

Source: *Management Today, August 1980, p. 26.*

John Bray at Coloroll. Coloroll was originally a manufacturer of plain paper sacks for supermarkets and other retail outlets, a steady business yielding modest profits. John Bray joined the company as sales director in 1970 and immediately replaced the traditional paper sacks with patterned, bio-degradeable carrier bags. Wallpapers, Bray considered, was a natural diversification for Coloroll, though initially involvement was limited to manufacturing 'own brands' for multiple retailers. Following his appointment as managing director in 1977, Bray set about developing and marketing their own collection of wallpapers. This necessitated the recruitment of one of the industry's top wallpaper designers as well as an experienced sales director. Management style was also changed from being highly autocratic to a more participative approach. John Bray brought considerable success to the company: between 1977 and 1980 turnover trebled while profits increased six fold.

Source: *Management Today, March 1980, p. 59.*

(i)   By assisting in the *adaptation* of the organisation to its environment by means of monitoring changes in the environment, formulating environmental and strategic scenarios and acting in a consultancy capacity to parts of the organisation that wish to examine the implications of environmental change. In this sense corporate planning is carrying out a strategic analysis function.

(ii)   By providing an *integration* role in an organisation in the sense of acting as a communication channel between, for example, a corporate head office and its divisions.

(iii)   By providing a *control mechanism* to monitor the performance of parts of the organisation (e.g. divisions) against strategic priorities. So here corporate planning has a role in strategic implementation.

The picture emerges of corporate planning as an aid to, rather than as the means of, strategic decision-making.

It should also be clear that planning, whether in the form of corporate planning or as a task of individual managers, may occur within an incremental process of change just as easily as it may when global change occurs. In an incremental context planning may well take the form of the planning of decisions within parts of the organisation dealing with strategic issues which help form overall strategy. In a global context, planning may be more to do with contributing to more fundametal shifts in strategy originating at a corporate level. For example, in his study of the different patterns of strategy formulation, Mintzberg[9] found what he called 'intended' strategy by which is meant the sort of formalised planning of change of strategy often associated traditionally with strategic planning. Such 'intended' strategy occurs most often where global change is necessary.

Planning is the responsibility of managers and is an important aspect of strategic management. Strategic management is not the property of a corporate planning department but, again, the responsibility of managers and is thus just as much part of incremental change as it is of global change.[10]

2.3 HOW STRATEGIC DECISIONS ARE MADE

If strategic change normally takes the form of a stream of decisions amending and developing existing strategy, how, then, are these decisions taken? This section examines the research evidence which exists to help provide an answer to this question.

There are four stages that can be recognised in the decision process:

(i)   *problem awareness:* the recognition that 'something is amiss', that a state of affairs exists which needs remedying;

(ii) *problem diagnosis:* the collection of information about, and examination of the circumstances of the problem and the definition of the problem;

(iii) the *development of solutions:* the generation of possible solutions to the problem;

(iv) the *selection of a solution:* the means by which a decision about what is to be done is reached.

These stages are amplified in the discussion that follows and represented in Fig. 2.2.

2.3.1 Problem Awareness

The awareness of a strategic problem usually occurs at an individual level. It is individual managers who are likely to get a 'gut feeling' that something is wrong. This awareness is likely to develop through a period of what Lyles[11] calls 'incubation' in which managers sense various sorts of stimuli that confirm and define a developing picture of the problem. These stimuli are what Norburn[12] calls 'signals' or 'ear twitchers' and seem to be primarily of three sorts. First, there are internal performance measurements such as levels of turnover or profit performance. Second, there is customer reaction particularly to the quality and price of services or products. And third, there are changes in the environment, particularly in terms of competitive action, technological change and economic conditions.[13] Together they create a picture of the extent to which an organisation's circumstances deviate from what is normally to be expected. This deviation may not be from a specified set of performance criteria such as profit measures, but could well be a perceived divergence from a normal trading pattern or a change from a typical customer response to some marketing activity for example.

This accumulation of stimuli eventually reaches a point where the amount of evidence is such that the presence of a problem cannot be ignored at an organisational level. This 'triggering point' may well be reached when the formal information systems of the organisation begin to highlight the problem; perhaps the variance against budget becomes undeniable or a number of sales areas consistently report dropping sales. It is at this point that organisational activity takes over from individual consideration of the problem.

It is important to emphasise the importance of this first stage of the individual's role in problem recognition. There is evidence to suggest that successful business performance is associated with management's capability in sensing their environment.[14] This does not mean that the company necessarily needs to have complex or sophisticated means of achieving this sensitivity but rather that managers respond to or take into account a wide range of influences and have an internally consistent view of these influences.

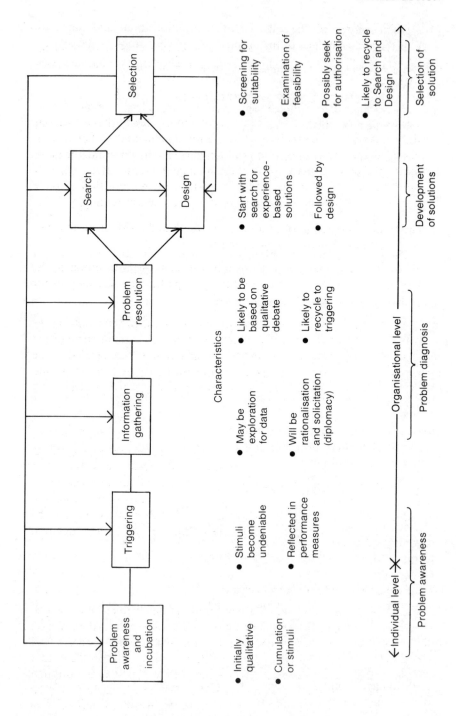

Figure 2.2 *A model of the strategic decision process.*

2.3.2 Problem Diagnosis

At the organisational level there are likely to be two parts to the problem diagnosis stage. The first is *information gathering,* the second *problem resolution.*
Information gathering could take the form of:

*   exploration for information to determine more clearly the facts about the problem. Such information is mainly sought and gathered on a verbal and informal basis[15] and this appears to be the more so the more senior the management. What these managers are, in effect, doing is building up and refining a picture of the strategic position of their organisation by a continual process of environmental sensing.

*   the rationalisation of information and stimuli to do with the problem so as to clarify the picture of the problem;

*   diplomacy and solicitation to establish what those with power in the organisation think about the problem and gather political support for individuals' views of the problem.

The resolution of what constitutes the nature of the problem may prove difficult. This is the attempt to get, through debate and discussion, some sort of organisational view, or concensus on the problem that is to be tackled. Some organisations may well find difficulty in proceeding beyond this stage and continually refer back the problem to the information gathering or triggering stages of the process.

In fact Lyles[11] found that there is considerable recycling within the process anyway. The most common recycling, occurring in 70% of the cases she investigated, was from the problem resolution stage back to triggering: organisations found that the attempt to resolve what a problem was about at an organisational level, triggered different conceptions of the problem at an individual level. Both Lyles and Mintzberg,[7] in their studies of the process of strategic decision-making, also point out that the diagnosis stage may be missed out altogether. Managers may proceed direct from problem recognition to the choice of solutions.

2.3.3 The Development of Solutions

Mintzberg[16] shows how the choice of solution is likely to have two stages; the first is the development of possible solutions and the second is the selection between them. First, then, how does the development of solutions occur?
Managers will first *search* for ready-made solutions to the problems that have been triggered. The indications are that this will first occur through 'memory search', in which the manager seeks for known, existing or tried solutions, or 'passive search' which entails waiting for possible solutions to be thrown up. It is only if these are unsuccessful that the manager will move onto

more active searches, calling upon personal experience as a starting point. There will probably be a number of these 'searches' amongst the known, tried and familiar before any attempt is made to move to the next step, the *design* of a solution. Design is where 'custom-made' solutions are constructed. Here it is not a matter of looking for what is familiar, or what has been done before, but rather of originating a solution.

2.3.4 The Selection of a Solution

It is likely that selection will be made on the basis of the following.

(i) The *screening* of possible solutions in two ways. The first is to 'challenge the appropriateness of alternatives': managers ask themselves if the possible solution is likely to tackle the problems at hand. This criterion of 'appropriateness' is similar to what is called 'suitability' in this book. In practice, managers reduce a range of possible solutions to a lesser number by judging the extent to which each is suitable for dealing with the problems they perceive.

The second criterion is rather different though it is certainly associated with the first. It is the assessment of the 'feasibility' of an alternative. This criterion is concerned with whether a solution is likely to be workable and successful.

(ii) An alternative way of selecting between possibilities is to refer the choice to a more senior level of management - to seek *authorisation*. It should be remembered that this whole process is incremental in nature and therefore is taking place below the most senior levels of management. So referring possible solutions to some higher hierarchical level may be required anyway. Typically, though not always, authorisation is sought for a completed solution after the steps of screening and evaluation have taken place. This raises the interesting question as to whether it is sensible to view this referral as a sort of checking of an incrementally generated strategic solution against some overall strategy. It would certainly be in line with Mintzberg's view that whilst most strategic decisions emanate from a stream of decisions from within the management 'sub-systems' -that they are incremental - it is the role of leadership to maintain some sort of general direction. If this view is taken then the process of authorisation can be thought of as the matching of one strategic decision against an overall, more generalised strategy or mission of the organisation.

2.3.5 The Influence of Judgment and Bargaining

The idea that there is extensive and systematic analysis of data and *evaluation* of possible alternatives using the many tools and techniques that now exist for managers, receives little support from those who have researched the area.[17] There is a much greater reliance on managerial judgment and past experience than the evaluative techniques of the management scientist. If evaluation does take place it is likely to be qualitative in nature, perhaps taking the form of a discussion of alternatives amongst the managers and may well be more an exercise in justifying the choice of a solution rather than really choosing between alternatives. However, Quinn suggests that successful managers actively seek to generate contra-arguments through such discussions and seek for evidence to challenge prevailing strategic inclinations. Certainly it is clear that the selection of alternatives is much more to do with management *judgment* and likely to be bound up in a process of *bargaining* within the organisation. Solutions are not so much likely to be adopted because they are shown to be better on the basis of some sort of objective yardstick, but because they are *acceptable* to those who influence the decision or have to implement it. So there will be a process of bargaining and negotiation taking place which seeks to build up the level of acceptance for a preferred solution arrived at through the screening process or which is developing incrementally within the organisation.

In the early 1960s, Cyert and March[18] published their findings on managerial behaviour in firms and argued that to understand how decisions are made it is important to realise that there are 'coalitions' of interest within organisations. Individuals within a group have different views, different aims and different ways of behaving, but they have to find some means of working together. Within a firm, as in a political party, there could be a number of coalitions which have similar attitudes to issues current in the organisation. Indeed, the firm itself is a coalition of interests in this sense. This proposition of Cyert and March merits comment. The idea of a coalition is important because it affirms the notion that there needs to be some order to what the individuals are pursuing: the firm cannot drift around manned by an anarchic crew. The direction, though, is decided in a bargaining process between individuals and coalitions who are bidding for power: it is essentially a political process.

Thus an organisational objective or course is agreed by 'a process of bargaining among potential coalition members and elaborated over time in response to short-run pressures'. It is easy to dismiss this sort of bargaining process as an irrational means of decision-making, but it can be argued that, during such activity, possible solutions are challenged by different interested parties in a process of 'qualitative evaluation'.

2.3.6 The Role of Objectives

In most texts on management science and corporate or strategic planning there is considerable emphasis on the importance of setting clear, precise organisational objectives. Yet there appears to be little evidence so far in what has been discussed that such objectives, if they exist, play a particularly important role in strategy making. This section of the chapter briefly reviews empirical evidence about the role of organisational objectives.

Do organisations have objectives? The answer appears to be that they do. Norburn[19], for example, found that the companies he studied had many objectives and that managers almost always agreed that one was to increase profits. He also found that there were many other objectives that managers perceived to exist, and that they thought there should be more of them. However, there was little agreement in the firms about what these other objectives were. Managers only really concurred on the existence of profitability as an objective. Even allowing for a much larger number of desired objectives, there was still relatively little concensus on what they should be.

The second question is whether objectives are to be stated in clear and precise terms. After all, Drucker[20] argues that:

'If objectives are only good intentions, they are worthless. They must degenerate into work. And work if always specific, always has - or should have -unambiguous, measurable results, a deadline and a specific assignment of responsibility.'

Yet the uncomfortable fact is that there is evidence to show that many successful companies do not have precise, explicit objectives, and, what is more, their senior executives do not think they should have. Quinn[21] found that 'successful executives announced relatively few goals to their organisation. These were frequently broad and general, and only rarely were they quantitative or measurably precise'. The reasons for this were largely because senior executives saw the need for objectives to be flexible.

It appears that it is not necessarily the formally expressed objectives that are the most significant influences on strategy making. Mintzberg[22] argues that these may be post-rationalised anyway - that they justify rather than influence strategic decisions. It might be more sensible to think of a less formal role for objectives. It is the objectives and expectations of dominant coalitions of interests that are likely to have the most influence on strategy. Such objectives and expectations may not be formally stated but emeshed in the political processes within the organisation. The dominant coalitions of interest may well be different in different organisations or at different times.

It is clear that managers exert a strong influence on strategy. There is ample evidence[23] to show that the strategies of firms can better be understood in terms of objectives which directly benefit managers than other interested parties (e.g., shareholders): such objectives are more likely to be to do with revenue maximisation - or growth - than they are to do with profit maximisation. After all, revenue maximisation means an increase in the size of the firm, and a consequent increase of managerial opportunity - for promotion, status or financial reward. This view of a firm seeking to increase turnover does not, of course, mean that its managers are unconcerned about profits. Rather it casts profits in a different role. Profits become a 'constraint' on management decision-making. The manager seeks to increase turnover *insofar as he can do so at a satisfactory level of profits.*

Objectives, then, do not appear to have the central role that a traditional strategic decision-making model would claim for them. It probably makes more sense to think of objectives, if formally stated at all, as:

*   a product of the expectations and value systems of individuals and groups in an organisation
*   different according to the various interest and influence groups in an organisation, and therefore
*   one of many influences on a strategic decision.

The role of objectives is discussed more fully in Chapter 6.

2.3.7 The Overall Process and Its Iterative Nature

Figure 2.2 outlines diagramatically the process and its characteristics described in this section. There is, however, one feature of the process which needs special emphasis - its iterative nature. It should not be thought of as a sequence of steps followed by managers but rather stages which may be moved through and which are likely to be repeated. It has already been mentioned that recycling from problem resolution to triggering is common. So too is recycling within the development and selection stages of the process. Illustration 6 shows how this recycling from one stage to another might take place and how solutions are eventually developed through the bargaining and negotiation that takes place during this recycling.

What this discussion also shows is how much the individual can influence strategy through problem recognition, definition and as part of the negotiating process through which decisions are made. The next section examines further the role of the individual as a strategist.

2.4 STRATEGY AS A PRODUCT OF STRATEGISTS

Traditionally, strategy has been viewed as the response of an organisation to its environment. The environment changes and the organisation rethinks and adjusts its posture if necessary. However, the organisation has severe limitations on making such readjustments. The constraints that have received most attention from writers have been:

(i)   constraints in the environment itself that hinder change - competitive action, government legislation, economic forces and so on;

(ii) internal organisational resource constraints - a lack of finance or competent management, for example.

This view omits a major influence on strategy formulation to do with the strategy makers themselves. Organisational theorists[24] have pointed out that it is too simplistic to think of strategy as a response to the environment for it is evident that, faced with similar environments, organisations will respond

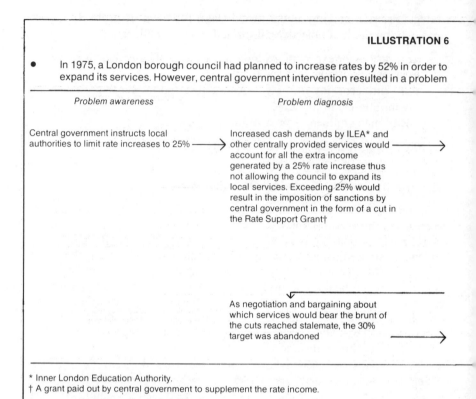

ILLUSTRATION 6

- In 1975, a London borough council had planned to increase rates by 52% in order to expand its services. However, central government intervention resulted in a problem

Problem awareness	Problem diagnosis
Central government instructs local authorities to limit rate increases to 25% ⟶	Increased cash demands by ILEA* and other centrally provided services would ⟶ account for all the extra income generated by a 25% rate increase thus not allowing the council to expand its local services. Exceeding 25% would result in the imposition of sanctions by central government in the form of a cut in the Rate Support Grant†
	As negotiation and bargaining about which services would bear the brunt of the cuts reached stalemate, the 30% target was abandoned ⟶

* Inner London Education Authority.
† A grant paid out by central government to supplement the rate income.

Source: Decision Rates, Granada Television.

differently. Clearly, the response is also influenced by those who decide strategy - most usually the managers. There has recently been some important research which has set out to understand better this managerial influence.

2.4.1 Managerial Values and Ideologies

Research in the USA conducted by Miles and Snow,[25] which will be referred to on several occasions throughout the book, shows that the overall strategic posture of an enterprise, its structure, the sort of people who hold power, its control systems and the way it operates, reflect the dominant ideologies in an organisation. To take two examples, there are organisations in which the prevailing ideology is essentially conservative, where low-risk strategies, secure markets and well tried potential solutions are valued. Miles and Snow call these types of organisation 'defenders'. In contrast, there are organisations in which the prevailing ideology is more to do with innovation and breaking new ground. Here management tend to prefer higher risk strategies and new opportunities. Miles and Snow call these 'prospector' type

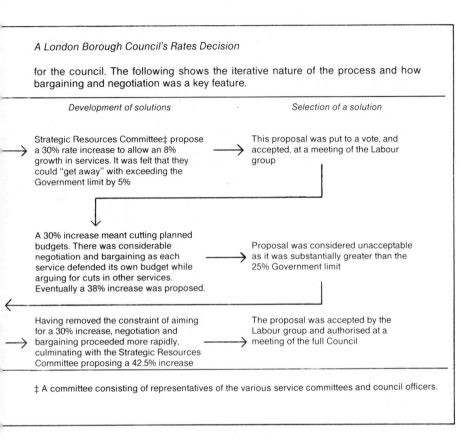

A London Borough Council's Rates Decision

for the council. The following shows the iterative nature of the process and how bargaining and negotiation was a key feature.

Development of solutions	Selection of a solution

Strategic Resources Committee‡ propose a 30% rate increase to allow an 8% growth in services. It was felt that they could "get away" with exceeding the Government limit by 5%

This proposal was put to a vote, and accepted, at a meeting of the Labour group

A 30% increase meant cutting planned budgets. There was considerable negotiation and bargaining as each service defended its own budget while arguing for cuts in other services. Eventually a 38% increase was proposed.

Proposal was considered unacceptable as it was substantially greater than the 25% Government limit

Having removed the constraint of aiming for a 30% increase, negotiation and bargaining proceeded more rapidly, culminating with the Strategic Resources Committee proposing a 42.5% increase

The proposal was accepted by the Labour group and authorised at a meeting of the full Council

‡ A committee consisting of representatives of the various service committees and council officers.

organisations. The point is that prospectors and defenders do not behave in the same way even within similar environments.[26] The strategies that such organisations follow are better accounted for by their prevailing ideologies than by the environmental stimuli. For example, faced with a declining market demand, the defender is likely to follow a strategy of concentration on the market niche in which it specialises and a tighter control of costs, whilst the prospector searches for opportunities to obtain new markets or increase market share.

Miles and Snow have, then, identified how the dominant ideologies of an organisation may affect its strategy. It also appears to be the case that similar sorts of influence exist for managers *within* organisations. A detailed study of a retailing company[27] has shown that the strategies being advocated by managers in the firm can be better accounted for by understanding the managers' personal 'managerial ideologies' than by examining their stated reasons for the strategies.

Such differences in ideology within an organisation are always likely to exist and will play a part in the formulation of strategy. What will determine which set of ideologies has greatest influence will be the dominant organisational ideology that exists. This is likely to have built up over time and be concentrated in the power base that exists in the organisation. For example, Miles and Snow show how in a defender type organisation conservative approaches and an emphasis on efficiency tend to be institutionalised by a dominance over time of managers with personally conservative ideologies, often from managerial functions which emphasise control and efficiency - notably accountants and production management.

Management ideologies can, then, be thought of as an important influence on the overall approach an organisation is likely to take to a strategic problem. However, it is possible to go further and consider how, within this overall approach managers will tackle problems. The idea of 'management recipes' is useful in considering this.

2.4.2 Management Recipes

The basic tenets of the idea of management recipes are that:

* faced with uncertainty or new situations, managers seek to relate such situations to their past experience. This is a tendency which is, at one and the same time, inevitable, understandable, useful and yet potentially dangerous;

* an individual tends to adopt the recipe common within an industry. The commonality between recipes within an industry is greater than between industries;

* the component parts - or 'constructs' - of a recipe are likely to include views about how to cope with the particular business environment. These constructs are, essentially, management views about how to run the operation. Illustration 7 gives examples of the constructs within two such recipes.

This reliance on experience to build up a code of practice has long been recognised by psychologists and organisational theorists.[28] The most specific study of the phenomenon as it relates to strategy formulation has been carried out by Spender[29] who explains them in the following way. In dealing with a strategic problem managers will bring to bear 'an accepted set of beliefs about what is consistent, realistic and which outcomes will follow the commitment of resources to specified actions. These beliefs which comprise the recipe may reflect generally available scientific and technological knowledge but many are specific to an industry'.[30]

Such recipes are not uniform between managers even with the same industry and the concern of this chapter is not so much the extent to which they are uniform but the influence that the recipe has on decision making. The recipe, is important in the construction of strategy because it allows the 'experience gathered over years' to be applied to the situation so as to decide on

ILLUSTRATION 7

Recipes

● The recipe for success in an industry takes the form of managers' views of 'how to succeed' in their business environment.

A fashion retailer
To run a successful fashion retailing operation, management believe that they must:
- look for growth
- continually experiment with new products or ventures
- provide a constant stream of promotion opportunities
- attract new retailing talent
- continually adapt to changes in customer shopping habits
- closely monitor variable costs and centralise control of merchandise distribution.

A milk processor and distributor
To operate a successful milk processing and distribution business, managers believe they must:
- pursue greater volume of sales
- expand territory serviced
- monitor other distribution operations with a view to takeover
- optimise length and sales volume of rounds
- increase sales per customer
- concentrate throughput into ever larger processing plants.

The above views indicate that the managers in the two industries face very different environments and so conceive of their operations quite differently.

The fashion retailer faces a business environment that is dependant on consumer tastes. The emphasis in coping with this uncertainty is to continually test the consumers' reaction to change. Growth is seen as a motivator for existing staff as well as a means of bringing new talent into the company, both of which are thought necessary to generate new ideas.

The business environment faced by the milk processor and distributor is, by contrast, very stable. They operate within a 'set margin', fixed on the one hand by the Milk Marketing Board who set the price at which the company buys, and on the other by the Government who fix the price at which the company sells to the consumer. The method of coping with this situation is more 'internalised', geared towards improving the efficiency of their operations. They seek to concentrate milk processing into ever larger plants to achieve greater economies of scale. However, to be in a position to build these large processing plants, the company must increase the throughput of milk; therefore pursuing greater sales volume by expanding the territory serviced and increasing sales per customer become important criteria for success.

Source: G. Johnson, unpublished reseach in menswear retailing, and J-C. Spender, Strategy-making in Business, doctoral thesis from the Manchester Business School.

relevant information by which to assess the need for change and the likelihood of success of a course of action.

However, the recipe can also be a conservative influence. Faced with the need for change, managers will seek to deal with the situation in ways which protect the recipe from challenge. This notion raises very serious difficulties when thinking about strategic change for it may be that the action required to cope with change effectively is outside the scope of the recipes which predominate. To handle this the members of an organisation would need to reassess and change the norms of their recipe. Desirable as this may be, the evidence is that it does not occur easily.[31] Managers are much more likely to attempt to deal with the situation by searching for what they can understand and cope with in terms of existing recipes. In other words, they will attempt to minimise the extent to which they are faced with ambiguity by looking for the familiar. Figure 2.3 characterises how this might occur. Faced with a stimulus for action, in this case declining performance, managers are first likely to seek for means of improving the implementation of existing strategy: this could be through the tightening of controls. In effect, they will tighten up their accepted way of operating. If this is not effective, then a change of strategy will be considered, but still a change which is in line with the existing recipe. For example, managers may seek to extend the market for their product but retain the same views about the range of products they produce, the main virtues of the products, the nature of what remains as the main markets, and how they should go about operating in those markets. There has been no change to the recipe itself and there is not likely to be until this attempt to reconstruct strategy in the image of the existing recipe also fails. What is occuring is the predominant application of the familiar and the attempt to avoid or reduce uncertainty or ambiguity.

Other students of strategy have found similar sorts of behaviour. Rumelt[32] uses the term 'strategic frame' by which he means the wisdom that 'identifies the critical issues' to allow for the evaluation of strategy. These frames resemble Spender's recipes in that they are codes of successful practice for an industry. Rumelt gives examples such as 'size is vital in the automobile industry, location in retailing, and image in the liquor business'. The point is, again, that they are at one and the same time of great importance in guiding strategy and in creating a resistance to strategic change which challenges the 'frame'.

The point is amplified by another of Mintzberg's findings.[33] He suggests that strategy can be thought of as 'the interplay between three basic forces'. The first, which is dynamic, is the environment. It is continually changing, and occasionally there are bursts of rapid or major change. The second is what Mintzberg describes as the 'organisational operating system, or bureaucracy, which above all seeks to stabilise its actions, despite the characteristics of the environment it serves'. So Mintzberg too finds this organisational pull to what is known and established. However, Mintzberg adds that the mediating agent

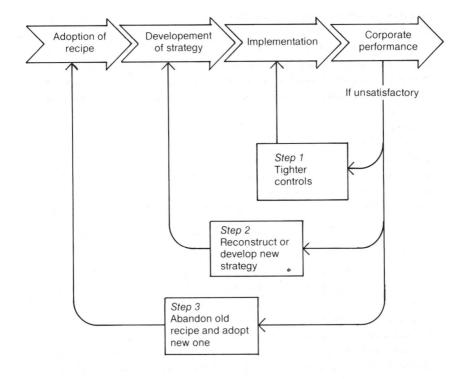

From: P Grinyer and J-C. Spender, *Turnaround: Managerial Recipes for Strategic Success* (Associated Business Press: 1979, p.203)

Figure 2.3 *The dynamics of recipe change.*

between these two forces is leadership. The third force is that 'whose role is to maintain the stability of the organisation's operating system while at the same time to adapt it to environmental change'.

2.5 A SUMMARY OF IMPLICATIONS FOR THE STUDY OF A STRATEGY

This chapter has dealt with strategic management as researchers understand it to occur. It is this book's intention that the subject should be approached in such a way that it builds upon this understanding of reality. In this concluding section of the chapter the basic lessons of what has been discussed are briefly summarised and related to what follows in the rest of the book.

2.5.1 A Summary of the Key Points

First, then a summary of the basic points made in the chapter:

(i)   Strategy usually evolves incrementally: strategic change tends to occur as a continual process of relatively small adjustments to existing strategy through activity within the sub-systems of an organisation.

(ii)   However, there is likely to exist an overall 'global' strategic direction, the change of which is often associated with an organisation getting out of step with a changing environment and the arrival of a new leader.

(iii)   Formal planning (e.g., in the sense of corporate planning) is important as an aid to analysing strategic positions and thinking through options but is not normally a vehicle for the formulation of strategy.

(iv)   The way in which managers assess the need for strategic change is through an essentially qualitative assessment of signals which accumulate from inside and outside the organisation.

(v)   The definition of strategic problems by a manager is not just reliant upon dispassionate analyses of data but, (a) on his perception of what powerful individuals in the organisation see as the problems, and (b) upon the manager's reconciliation of the circumstances of the situation with his past experience and the received wisdom - or recipe - within the industry.

(vi)   The search for strategic options is likely to begin with and be dominated by what managers have experience of doing or observing what others have done in the past.

(vii)   Strategic choice takes place on the basis of examining options against their likelihood of (a) dealing with the problem or threat being faced, (b) being seen as workable, (c) being consistent with the global strategy of the organisation.

(viii) The process of strategic decision-making is characterised by (a) the negotiation of both the perception of problems and their solution between managers and coalitions of interest groups and (b) iteration between stages in the decision making process.

(ix)   Strategy is likely to be strongly influenced by the prevailing ideology of managers within an organisation.

2.5.2 The Implications for the Study of Strategy

There is no reason to discard the traditional framework within which strategy is considered: clearly understanding the strategic position of an organisation through some sort of strategic analysis is important and selecting a strategy and implementing it are prime strategic tasks. However, there are a number of features of this book which have been strongly influenced by the reality of strategic management and which need to be spelled out.

(i)   As has been said in Chapter 1, the idea of a sequential model of strategic management has been rejected. The headings of strategic analysis, choice and implementation are a useful structure for the book but readers are urged to regard these aspects of strategic management as interdependent and an influence on one another. The idea of a systematic, step by step, approach to strategy making as advocated by some writers[34] is not used because it is not the way in which strategy is normally formulated and has not been demonstrated to be of particular benefit to the development of strategy by managers.

(ii)   An understanding of the values and ideologies of those that are, in the most direct sense, able to influence strategy, is vitally important if a sensible view of the strategy of an organisation - past and future - is to be gained. For this reason emphasis is placed on the importance of values in the section on strategic analysis, and on the means whereby these values affect the behaviour of the organisation which is through the political systems of the organisation. It is an emphasis which is the more important given the vital role that Mintzberg points out for the leadership of the organisation as a major influence on strategy and particularly on global strategic change. Understanding the values and ideologies of those in leadership positions is likely to be of particular importance. Later in this book, within the sections on strategic analysis and strategic choice, methods of analysing value systems are discussed and criteria of evaluation embracing value systems and recipes introduced.

(iii)   It is argued in some books that the setting of clear and precise objectives is of central importance to the formulation of strategy. For example:

        'Without realistically established business objectives, strategy is impossible to formulate and thus is totally ineffective.'[35]

        The reader might or might not sympathise with this view but the uncomfortable fact is that there is a growing amount of research which shows that organisations tend not to have clearly defined objectives and yet manage to develop sensible and successful strategies. The view that objectives should be clearly laid down and used as a sort of target or yardstick against which strategy should be evaluated so as to achieve some optimum course of action has to be questioned. There is very little evidence to show that such practice exists even in successful companies. This does, of course, raise the question as to what role objectives have in the formulation of strategy and this is discussed in Chapter 6 in the wider context of the expectations of different stakeholders in an organisation.

(iv)   Since the way a strategic problem is dealt with will, very likely, be strongly affected by the existing management recipes, it is important to understand what these recipes are. One reason for this is because the question needs to be raised as to whether the recipe is capable of dealing with the problem. If it is, it will be a safer way of dealing with the problem than any radical departure from that recipe because it will be in line with how managers are used to operating. However, if the existing recipe cannot provide a means of handling the problem there is a need to understand how far it will be necessary to depart from that recipe so as to implement strategic change. The point is that the greater the extent of the departure, then the greater the risk of the strategy failing because it cannot be implemented without management changing its recipes - a step which is the most difficult of all for individuals to achieve. This understanding of the recipe is, then, important in the analysis of the strategic position of the organisation, in evaluating the feasibility of success of the strategy[36] and in considering the mechanisms by which strategic change is to be implemented. This point is raised again in the sections on analysis, choice and implementation.

(v)   Whilst the reality of judgment and the prevalence of bargaining processes in organisations are accepted and discussed in the text, the book also contains examples of, and references to, many techniques of quantitative and qualitative analysis. This is regarded as important for two reasons. First, because managers often find difficulty in locating suitable techniques of analysis which are workable within a framework of bargaining and negotiation processes. Many of the techniques suggested have been used successfully in such a context. The second reason is because of the recognition of the need for management to challenge the confining and restrictive influence of its recipes. The employment of techniques which 'force' the consideration of alternative perspectives can be of great benefit.

The overall aim is, then, to provide a framework for strategy and strategic management that can be understood in the context of management and organisational practice.

REFERENCES

1.   J.B. Quinn's research involved the examination of strategic change in companies and has been published in *Strategies for Change – Logical Incrementalism* (Irwin: 1980).
2.   Mintzberg and his colleagues at McGill University, Canada have studied the historical development of strategy in several organisations. Their work is published in 'Patterns in Strategy Formation', *Management Science,* 1978.
3.   The logic of incrementalism is not new. In his paper 'The Science of Muddling Through' (*Public Administration Review, American Society for Public Administration,* Vol. 19, Spring 1959), C. E. Lindblom asserted that in public administration, policy decisions are made on the basis of 'successive limited comparisons' rather than major reviews of policy. He points out that this can,

superficially, appear to be a muddle; but that there is a sound logic in the approach.

4. See *Strategies for Change* (reference 1), p.58. © Richard D. Irwin, Inc., 1980.

5. Mintzberg's discussion of the incidence of global changes are in his paper 'Patterns in Strategy Formulation', reference 2 above.

6. This lag in strategic change may often not be perceived by the management in the organisation. It may perceive the need for change as being the result of a sudden change in the environment. In fact, the environment may have been changing quite slowly, unnoticed by the management. Or sudden changes in the environment may, in fact, have been predicted or expected by more perceptive managers in other organisations. Some of the implications of this failure to perceive environmental changes are discussed by G. Johnson in 'Environmental Change: Implications for Organisation and Management Development', *Management Education and Development*, Vol. 12, No. 3, 1981.

7. This is borne out in much of the research into strategic decision-making and corporate planning. For example see Quinn, reference 1 above; H. Mintzberg, O. Raisinghani and A. Theoret, 'The Structure of Unstructured Decision Processes', *Administrative Science Quarterly*, Vol. 21, 1976, 246-275; W.K. Hall, 'Strategic Planning Models: Are Top Managers Really Finding Them Useful?', *Journal of Business Policy*, Vol. 3, No. 2, 1973.

8. The role of corporate planning is based on the research findings in the doctoral dissertation of H. Bahrami entitled 'Design of Corporate Planning Systems' (University of Aston, October 1981). This research was conducted in 14 large, mainly multi-national, UK-based firms.

9. Again, see reference 2.

10. Writers who advocate a step-by-step, formalised planning approach as a basis for thinking about strategic management, recognise the importance of the less formalised management aspect. For example, G. Steiner and J. Miner in *Management Policy and Strategy* (Collier Macmillan: 1977, p.92) say:
'The formal system (of planning) should help managers to sharpen their intuitive-anticipatory inputs into the planning process. At the very least, the formal system should give managers more time for reflective thinking ..... But formal planning cannot be really effective unless managers at all levels inject their judgments and intuition into the planning process.'

11. For a sound and thorough discussion of the problem awareness and diagnosis stages of the decision making process, see M.A. Lyles, 'Formulating Strategic Problems: Empirical Analysis and Model Development', *Strategic Management Journal*, Vol.2, 1981, pp.61-75.

12. The presence and nature of these signals are confirmed and discussed in D. Norburn and P. Grinyer, 'Directors Without Direction', *Journal of General Management*, Vol. 1, No. 2, 1973/4.

13. D. Norburn and P. Grinyer, reference 12, highlight competitive action and technological change as the main environmental signals. However, their research was done in the early 1970s, later research, during a period of greater economic difficulty was conducted by W. F. Glueck who found that economic conditions and changes were also important signals. Glueck's research is summarised in *Strategic Management and Business Policy* (McGraw-Hill: 1980, p.106f).

14. This proposition is supported by the research of P. Grinyer and D. Norburn (reference 12), J.B. Quinn (reference 1), and D. Miller and P. Friesen, 'Archetypes

of Strategy Formulation', *Management Science,* Vol. 24, No. 9, 1978.

15. Researchers who have examined environmental influences on strategy would broadly agree with this. See, for example: P. Grinyer and D. Norburn, 'Directors Without Direction', reference 12; F. Aguilar, *Scanning the Business Environment* (Macmillan: 1967); H. Mintzberg *et al.,* reference 7.

16. This discussion is based on the findings detailed in Mintzberg *et al.'s* research, reference 7.

17. Mintzberg, reference 7, found little evidence of the employment of scientific management tools of evaluation, nor did W.K. Hall, reference 7, or P. Soelberg, 'Unprogrammed Decision-making', *Industrial Management Review,* Spring 1967.

18. The work of R. Cyert and J. March was published in 1963 in *A Behavioural Theory of the Firm* (Prentice-Hall: 1963). However, there have been many researchers who have confirmed the importance of bargaining in strategic decision-making since then. In the references given so far, both Quinn, and Mintzberg *et al.* reference 7, discuss the bargaining process.

19. Again, see 'Directors Without Direction', reference 12.

20. This quotation is taken from P. Drucker, *Management: Tasks, Responsibilities, Practices,* (Harper & Row: 1973, p.101).

21. See (1) above.

22. See Mintzberg *et al.,* reference 7.

23. Much of the evidence for this assertion arises from work by managerial economists. For example, see R. Marris and A. Wood; *The Corporate Economy* (Macmillan: 1971) and W.S. Baumol, *Business Behaviour, Value and Growth* (Harcourt, Brace and World Inc.: 1967).

24. John Child has argued strongly that the manager's strategic choice cannot simply be regarded as a response to environmental stimuli. It is more sensible to think of the process as a two-way decision process: the manager responds to the environment but also seeks to create an environmental context for the organisation through choices about markets and strategic postures within markets. The article which argues this point is 'Organisational Structure, Environment and Performance - The Role of Strategic Choice' *Sociology,* Vol.6, January, 1972.

25. See R.E. Miles and C.C. Snow, *Organizational Strategy, Structure and Process* (McGraw-Hill: 1978).

26. This point is made by A.D. Meyer in 'How Ideologies Supplant Formal Structures and Shape Responses to Environments', *Journal of Management Studies,* Vol.19, No.1, 1982.

27. This is part of a more extensive study conducted by one of the authors (G. Johnson), and is as yet unpublished.

28. For example the concept of 'theories in use' and 'theories in action' is closely related to that of recipes and is fully discussed in Chris Argyris, *Organisational Learning: A Theory of Action Perspective* (Addison Wesley: 1978). Similarly George Kelly, the psychologist, proposed the idea of 'personal constructs' (see *The Psychology of Personal Constructs,* W.W. Norton: 1955) which bears similarity to the notion of recipes.

29. At the time of writing J-C. Spender has not published in detail his research into strategy formulation which discusses the influence of managerial recipes. However, the study is in the form of a doctoral thesis from the Manchester Business School in 1980 entitled 'Strategy-Making in Business'. Also see P.H. Grinyer and J-C. Spender, 'Recipes, Crises, and Adaptation in Mature Busi-

nesses', *Intl. Studies of Management and Organization,* Vol. IX, No. 3, p. 113, 1979.

30.   From P. Grinyer and J-C. Spender, *Turnaround: Managerial Recipes for Strategic Success* (Associated Business Press: 1978, p.83).

31.   Certainly C. Argyris vividly illustrates the extent to which 'theories-in-use', as a code of behaviour, are very resistant to change and challenge, (see reference 28).

32.   R. Rumelt uses the term 'strategic frame' in 'Evaluation of Strategy: Theory and Models' in *Strategic Management,* edited by D.E. Schendel and C.W. Hofer (Little Brown: 1979).

33.   These propositions are put forward by Mintzberg, reference 2.

34.   The systematic step-by-step approach to strategy formulation has its foundations in the corporate planning systems advocated in the 1950s and 1960s. Such approaches continue in the work of many writers on strategy. For example, John Argenti's books on strategic planning, including *Practical Corporate Planning* (Allen & Unwin: 1980); G. Steiner on strategic planning in *Strategic Planning: What Every Manager Must Know* (Collier Macmillan: 1979) or D. Harvey's text *Business Policy and Strategic Management* (Charles E. Merrill: 1982).

35.   See Y.N. Chang and F. Campo-Flores, *Business Policy and Strategy* (Goodyear, 1980, p.76).

36.   R. Rumelt suggests that what he calls the 'strategic frame' (similar to the idea of the recipe) should be used in much this way as one criterion for the evaluation of strategy (reference 32). In this book the idea is built into criteria of suitability, acceptability and feasibility discussed in Chapter 8.

RECOMMENDED KEY READINGS

*   On incremental strategic change: J.B. Quinn, *Strategies for Change - Logical Incrementalism* (Irwin: 1980).

*   On different sorts of strategic change: H. Mintzberg, *Patterns in Strategy Formulation* (Management Science: 1978).

*   On the strategic decision-making process: H. Mintzberg, D. Raisinghani and A. Theoret, 'The Structure of Unstructured Decision Processes' *Administrative Science Quarterly,* Vol.21, 1976; D. Norburn and P. Grinyer, 'Directors Without Direction' *Journal of General Management,* Vol.1, No. 2, 1973/74.

*   On value systems and ideologies and their influence on strategy: R.E. Miles and C.C. Snow, *Organizational Strategy, Structure and Process* (McGraw Hill: 1978).

PART II

Strategic Analysis

The first part of this book has shown how organisations need continually to adjust strategy as circumstances within and around it change. To effect these changes successfully, managers need to form a view of the key influences on their choice of strategy. Strategic analysis is concerned with providing an understanding of the strategic situation which an organisation faces. Such an analysis provides the background against which sensible future choices may be made and also provides some useful insights into the difficulties of implementing strategic change. Readers should remember, however, that this relationship between analysis, choice and implementation is not a simple one in practice and, therefore, strategic analysis should not be viewed as a one-off exercise which precedes choice and implementation. Strategic analysis should be a process of becoming wiser about an organisation's situation, and in some circumstances this wisdom can only be gained by implementing changes (perhaps on a limited scale). Indeed, the process of strategic choice and strategic implementation described in Parts III and IV will constantly challenge the validity of the strategic analysis as well as building upon the analysis.

Analysing an organisation's situation can be a very complex task and, for convenience, it is helpful to divide the analysis into the different types of influence on strategy as described in Chapter 1. The structure of this part of the book follows this division:

* Chapter 3 is concerned with the influence of the environment on an organisation's strategic position, which in itself represents a whole variety of commercial, economic, political and technological factors. The challenge for the manager is to boil down this complexity so as to provide an understanding of the key variables affecting the company perhaps in terms of the major opportunities and threats the organisation faces.

* Chapter 4 looks at the resources which an organisation possesses in an attempt to understand the organisation's strategic capability. These resources will include land, machines, people, money and systems. The manager needs to understand the reasons which underlie special strengths and weaknesses of the organisation.

*   Chapter 5 shows how the values of individuals and groups need to be understood as a major influence on an organisation's strategy. An analysis of values involves understanding the way in which interest groups (coalitions) arise within and around organisations and how they derive power. Power is the mechanism whereby the values of individuals or groups are able to influence strategy.

*   Chapter 6, the final chapter in this part, looks at the role of expectations and objectives within organisations. Objectives are viewed as a product of the values and expectations of those who influence strategic decisions. As such, Chapter 6 discusses the sorts of conflicts of expectations and objectives that arise in organisations and the different forms and roles of objectives.

Although this part is divided into four chapters it should be remembered that there are very strong links between these various influences on strategy. For example, environmental pressures for change may be constrained by the resources available to make changes or the values of people which may lead to resistance to change. The relative importance of the various influences will change over time and show marked differences from one organisation to another. A good strategic analysis must provide an understanding of all these issues.

3

THE STRATEGIC ENVIRONMENT

3.1 INTRODUCTION

Students of strategy, faced with the need to understand the effects of the environment are dealing with a difficult problem. The formulation of strategy is concerned with matching the capabilities of an organisation to its environment. But the word environment encapsulates very many different influences, and the difficulty is understanding this diversity.

There are two typical responses which are dangerous in their limitations. The first is the balance sheet approach which consists of listing all the conceivable environmental influences under what amounts to plus and minus headings. The analyst examines the situation and argues that the organisation has a whole range of things going for it and a range going against it. This is easy: long lists can be generated for most organisations. However, if environmental analysis consists of this and nothing more, then the limitations are significant. No overall picture emerges of what is influencing the organisation and there are likely to be very diverse views about what sorts of influences are most important and why. What is more, there is the danger that attempts will be made to deal with environmental influences in a piecemeal way rather than make more fundamental strategic responses.

The second misleading but typical response is that, faced with a wide range of environmental variables, the analyst dismisses the possibility of understanding the whole and falls back on seeking to understand its significance from just one point of view. Perhaps he takes a marketing point of view, examines the firm in terms of the way the financial institutions have responded to its track record, or considers its adaptation to technological advances. The problem here is, of course, that a strategic situation cannot be understood from only one perspective; it is essential to view the situation as a whole.

In practice, managers cope with this range of influences by evolving, over time, accepted wisdom about their industry, its environment and what are sensible responses to different situations. These recipes were discussed in

55

Chapter 2. The important point to note here is that these recipes are attempts to take an overview of the organisation's links with its environment. They are conceptions of key influences and key requirements for success. The approach in this chapter is similar in some ways, in that it seeks to provide ways in which (a) the environment can be understood in terms of its overall impact; and (b) key environmental factors can be identified from the plethora of other influences.

The rest of the chapter discusses in some detail a series of steps which enable this sort of assessment to take place. However, it is necessary to see the role of each step in relation to the other so they are briefly introduced here and summarised in Fig. 3.1.

(i)   First try to take an initial view of the *nature of the environment* of the organisation in terms of how uncertain it is. In particular, has it been relatively static or does it show signs of change, and in what ways? Is it simple in operational terms or complex? This initial view will help in deciding what focus the rest of the analysis is to take. If the organisation is in a fairly simple/static environment then detailed, systematic historical analysis is likely to be very helpful. If the environment is in a dynamic state or shows signs of becoming so, then a more future orientated perspective is more sensible. This initial view will also highlight some environmental considerations to be examined in more detail later. For example, it may become clear that there are particular aspects of the environment which are changing: it will be necessary to consider if these changes are strategically significant.

(ii)   The second step moves the focus much more towards an explicit consideration of individual environmental influences. The general understanding already begun can be much enhanced by a *structural analysis* which aims to identify the key forces at work in the environment and why they are significant.

From these first two steps should emerge a view of the really important developments taking place around the organisation. It may be that there are relatively few of outstanding significance: or it could be that there are many interconnected developments. What matters is that the analyst should be able to see why these are of strategic significance.

(iii) The next step is to relate this understanding of the environment more specifically to the organisation. Here there is a need to ask to what extent the forces identified so far are *opportunities* or *threats* (or indeed both). This can be done by considering the extent to which the organisation's strategy and structure are matched or mismatched to developments in the environment; and by asking what is the standing of the organisation in terms of these developments -is it strong or weak, safe or vulnerable; is it more or less powerful than competitors? What this analysis seeks to provide is a picture of environmental influences which is clear enough to provide an understanding of opportunities which can be built upon and threats which have to be overcome or circumvented. Such a picture is important when it comes to strategic evaluation.

These steps, briefly outlined here, are developed in the rest of the chapter.

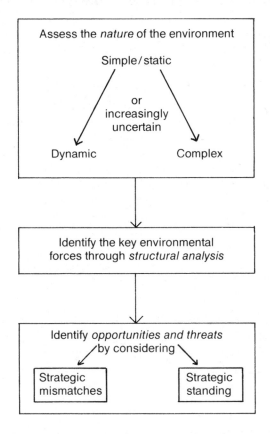

Figure 3.1 *An approach to environmental analysis.*

3.2 ENVIRONMENTAL INFLUENCES ON AN ENTERPRISE

An organisation can be thought of as an open system interacting with the environment. Illustration 8 shows some of the environmental influences important to organisations. The illustration is not intended to provide an exhaustive list but does serve to give examples of ways in which strategies of organisations have been affected by the environment and also indicates some of the ways in which organisations seek to handle aspects of their environment.

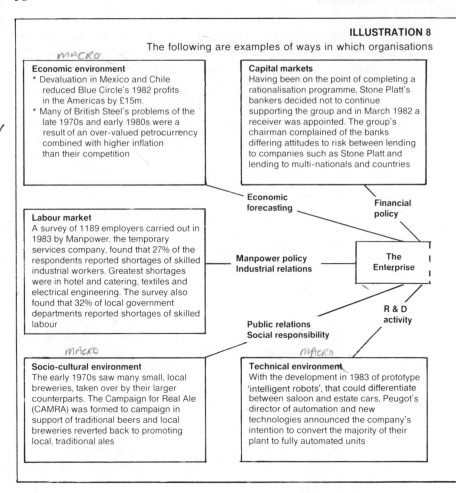

ILLUSTRATION 8

The following are examples of ways in which organisations

Economic environment
* Devaluation in Mexico and Chile reduced Blue Circle's 1982 profits in the Americas by £15m.
* Many of British Steel's problems of the late 1970s and early 1980s were a result of an over-valued petrocurrency combined with higher inflation than their competition

Capital markets
Having been on the point of completing a rationalisation programme, Stone Platt's bankers decided not to continue supporting the group and in March 1982 a receiver was appointed. The group's chairman complained of the banks differing attitudes to risk between lending to companies such as Stone Platt and lending to multi-nationals and countries

Labour market
A survey of 1189 employers carried out in 1983 by Manpower, the temporary services company, found that 27% of the respondents reported shortages of skilled industrial workers. Greatest shortages were in hotel and catering, textiles and electrical engineering. The survey also found that 32% of local government departments reported shortages of skilled labour

Economic forecasting

Financial policy

Manpower policy
Industrial relations

The Enterprise

R & D activity

Public relations
Social responsibility

Socio-cultural environment
The early 1970s saw many small, local breweries, taken over by their larger counterparts. The Campaign for Real Ale (CAMRA) was formed to campaign in support of traditional beers and local breweries reverted back to promoting local, traditional ales

Technical environment
With the development in 1983 of prototype 'intelligent robots', that could differentiate between saloon and estate cars, Peugot's director of automation and new technologies announced the company's intention to convert the majority of their plant to fully automated units

The organisation is not passive in its interaction with the environment. It influences as well as being influenced by the environment. Indeed one of the considerations in corporate strategy is the legitimate boundaries of influence for an organisation. A firm will be someone else's competitor, supplier, customer, even financier: so, in that respect all firms influence their competitive environment just as they are influenced by it. But to what extent does and should it directly influence its macro-environment? In many respects it must do so: the firm is part of the economic structure in which it operates, it may be involved in technologies which have direct links with the world of scientific development. But should a firm seek to influence government; should a firm seek to influence societal expectations; does a firm have responsibilities for the geographic surroundings in which it exists? These are value-laden questions which are becoming more and more significant as the concentration and

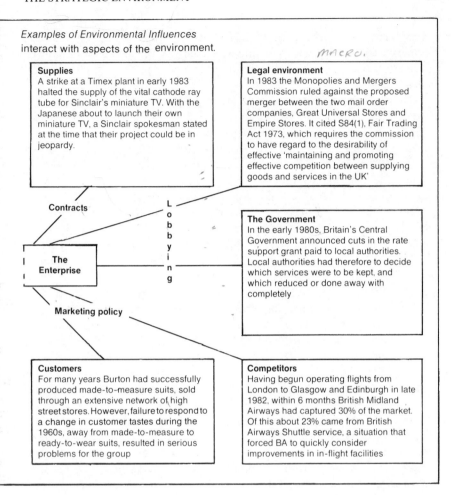

Examples of Environmental Influences interact with aspects of the environment.   MACRO.

Supplies
A strike at a Timex plant in early 1983 halted the supply of the vital cathode ray tube for Sinclair's miniature TV. With the Japanese about to launch their own miniature TV, a Sinclair spokesman stated at the time that their project could be in jeopardy.

Legal environment
In 1983 the Monopolies and Mergers Commission ruled against the proposed merger between the two mail order companies, Great Universal Stores and Empire Stores. It cited S84(1), Fair Trading Act 1973, which requires the commission to have regard to the desirability of effective 'maintaining and promoting effective competition between supplying goods and services in the UK'

Contracts

L
o
b
b
y
i
n
g

The Enterprise

The Government
In the early 1980s, Britain's Central Government announced cuts in the rate support grant paid to local authorities. Local authorities had therefore to decide which services were to be kept, and which reduced or done away with completely

Marketing policy

Customers
For many years Burton had successfully produced made-to-measure suits, sold through an extensive network of high street stores. However, failure to respond to a change in customer tastes during the 1960s, away from made-to-measure to ready-to-wear suits, resulted in serious problems for the group

Competitors
Having begun operating flights from London to Glasgow and Edinburgh in late 1982, within 6 months British Midland Airways had captured 30% of the market. Of this about 23% came from British Airways Shuttle service, a situation that forced BA to quickly consider improvements in in-flight facilities

internationalisation of industry develops and such issues have direct bearings on questions of strategic analysis and evaluation. They are discussed more fully in Chapter 6.

It would be possible to devote the whole of this chapter - indeed of the book - to a discussion of the ways in which different sorts of influences affect organisations. This is not done because the chapter is primarily concerned with how to understand the strategic importance of the influences rather than providing a catalogue of influences. Readers who are anxious to review such influences might usefully consider Illustration 8 which gives brief examples of the way in which different environmental influences have been important in the strategic development of different organisations. In addition, readers will find that references are provided at the end of the chapter which suggest follow up reading on the business environment in general[1], and, as elements of the environment, the market[2], the financial world[3], raw material supplies[4] and suppliers[5], technology and technological change[6], manpower availability[7], government and legislation[8], economic conditions[9] and socio-cultural changes[10].

In environmental analysis for strategic purposes particular consideration needs to be given to the extent to which the environment is changeable. Managers have always had to deal with change; but there are perhaps two ways in which environmental change is becoming more problematic and it is these differences that have influenced the way in which this chapter proceeds.

First, the speed and frequency of change is accelerating. This raises two major problems. The speed of change may be difficult to cope with. For example, the speed of technological change creates the problem of obsolescence. A firm may have been able to conceive of its dominance of a market being dependent on competitive marketing activity in the past: it now has to consider the extent to which it is vulnerable to some new product or process rendering its own obsolete. Investment in plant may have been able to be viewed in the past as having a life of five, ten, even twenty years. Such assumptions are now dangerous, even if plant is not obsolete after a few years, there is a real risk that it could be uncompetitive. Any one change is, at least theoretically, predictable - the oil price rises of 1973 were predicted by many analysts. Few environmental influences should come as shocks to organisations; and yet they often do. Environmental change is not always predicted by organisations and when it occurs may induce a paralysis which prevents managers coping with such change. The reasons for this were introduced in Chapter 2. Organisations usually evolve strategies incrementally, continually adjusting to their environments. This process is effective provided strategic developments can keep abreast of environmental changes. However the speed and frequency of change is such that managers and management systems often cannot cope: what occurs is a sort of internally generated shock which is rooted in managers' inability to see the strategic impact of possible changes and therefore make the changes necessary to adjust the organisation's strategy to its environment.

The second way in which environmental change is particularly problematic is associated with the structure of many modern organisations, which may hinder strategic awareness and capability. Such firms are increasingly likely to be large, perhaps multi-national and probably split into divisions. They are likely to be specialised in structure, with departments to deal with each of the links with their competitive environment. This works well provided the changes that take place can be contained sensibly within these specialisms. Problems occur when changes take place which do not relate to one specialisation, or which are treated as though they do although they are much broader. Problems may also occur simply because specialists, competent to recognise influences from the environment relating to their own function do not recognise, or see the significance of, influences manifesting themselves in their own area, which are actually of wider concern.

It is clear that the ability to sense changes in the environment is important because perceived changes in environmental influence signal the possible need for changes in strategy: they throw up opportunities and warn of threats.[11] The evidence is that organisations which are better at sensing the environment perform better than those which are weak at it.[12] The remainder of this chapter concentrates on the approaches managers can use to improve their sensing abilities. However it is important to stress that techniques of analysis and models of environmental impact are, in themselves, no guarantee that organisations will be able to respond to change. The extent to which an organisation will be successful in adapting to change will depend largely on its flexibility and sensitivity which, in turn, depend on the quality of its management, its organisational culture and its structure. These aspects of change will be dealt with in Chapters 10 and 11.

3.3 UNDERSTANDING THE NATURE OF THE ENVIRONMENT

It has been pointed out that an organisation's environment contains many influences on that organisation. It is, therefore, always tempting to begin an analysis of that environment by reviewing its parts in an attempt to decide how they exert an influence. But such an exercise often provides no more than a detailed knowledge of the parts and lacks any comprehension of what is really significant in strategic terms. This chapter is structured in such a way that the more detailed analysis is postponed until some thought has been given to the overall *nature* of the environment.

Strategic decisions are, by their very nature, made in situations of uncertainty. Uncertainty is a problem for managers to cope with and organisational theorists[13] have pointed out that much management activity is concerned with reducing uncertainty. Strategic analysis can be thought of as just such an activity: the analyst is attempting to reduce the many environmental influences to a pattern which is capable of being understood and acted upon. To do this it makes sense to begin by asking: (a) Just how uncertain is the environment? (b) What are the reasons for that uncertainty? (c) How should the uncertainty be dealt with?

Environmental uncertainty increases the more environmental conditions are dynamic or the more they are complex.[14] The degree of dynamism in the environment has already been considered: it is to do with the rate and frequency of change, and many organisations are finding themselves in a more dynamic environment than they have previously experienced. The idea of complexity perhaps needs a little more explanation. Complexity may result in different ways, for example:

*   Complexity may result from the sheer *diversity* of environmental

influences faced by an organisation. A multi-national company operating in many different countries is an example of this. Whilst it could be that few of the influences are in themselves changing rapidly, the number of influences the organisation has to cope with increases uncertainty.

* Complexity may also arise because of the amount of *knowledge* required to handle environmental influences. A good example of this would be a space agency. The environmental variables it is having to deal with such as advanced technological change are enormously complex.

* A third way in which complexity may increase is if the different environmental influences are, in themselves, *interconnected.*[15] Suppose influences such as raw material supplies, exchange rates, political changes and consumer spending, are not independent of each other but related one to another: then it is much more difficult to understand influence patterns than if they are unconnected.

Lowest uncertainty exists where conditions are static and simple. An extreme example would be a post office in a sleepy English village. There is little change (low dynamism) and relatively few and fairly straightforward influen-

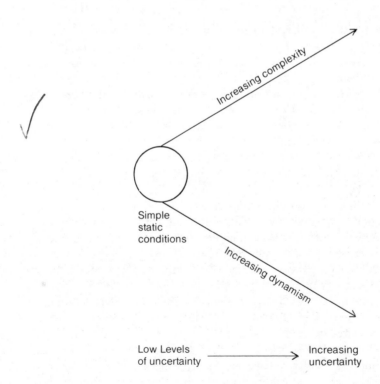

Figure 3.2 *Growing uncertainty according to the nature of the environment.*

ces (low complexity) to cope with. It is as environmental influences become more dynamic or more complex that uncertainty increases. Figure 3.2 summarises this. The significance as far as the chapter is concerned is that differences in the nature of the environment call for different approaches to understanding and responding to the environment. It is not sensible to approach environmental analysis for an organisation in simple static conditions in the same way as would be done for organisations in more uncertain conditions.

3.3.1 Understanding Simple/Static Conditions

In simple/static conditions an organisation is faced with an environment which is not too difficult to understand and is not undergoing significant change. Few organisations would experience the extremes of this that might be typified by the small post office in a sleepy English village, but there are, relatively speaking, environments of this nature. Raw material suppliers and mass manufacturing companies are perhaps examples. Their processes are relatively straightforward, their competition and markets are likely to be fixed over time and there may well be few of them. If change does occur it is likely to be fairly predictable.

How can such organisations cope with understanding their environments? If the situation is both simple and static, then it makes sense to seek for a thorough understanding of the environment on an historical basis. An historical pattern, once identified, might well be expected to continue over time, or at least be sensibly refined systematically. The aim, then, is to understand such complexity and momentum as does exist, in the expectation that it will not vary too much. This can be done by concentrating on detailed analysis of the past, to be used as a basis for forecasting the future. There is also evidence that in static conditions, whether they be simple or complex, environmental scanning is likely to be a more continuous, systematic exercise than in dynamic situations where it is more intermittent:[16] since there is more likelihood of being able to use the past as a predictor of the future it is worth investing management time in systematic scanning.[17]

Another sensible way of dealing with situations of relatively low complexity is to seek for some predictor of any environmental change that might take place. An example of such a predictor might be the way in which the sales of consumer durables have traditionally been thought to be dependent on real income in the UK. This is shown in Illustration 9. Since sales seem to be related to movements in real income it should be possible to predict a rise or decline in market demand according to changes in real income. The danger, as shown in the illustration, is that the influence of real income may not always be unconnected with other influences: and a company that relied on real income as a predictor in the consumer durables industry would have been taken by surprise in 1976.

ILLUSTRATION 9

An Example of an Economic Predictor

● By identifying dependencies, organisations are often more able to predict future changes in their environments. However, there may be dangers. The following graphs show an index of consumer spending on consumer durables against real disposable income in the UK.

Recognising a Dependency

Between 1970 and 1973 there was a gradual rise in RDI (real disposable income) followed by a levelling off. It is clear that expenditure on consumer durables was linked to the changes in RDI, but responded in a much more exaggerated way. A gradual growth in RDI therefore gave rise to a dramatic increase in the sales of consumer durables. As the rate of change in RDI decreased, causing it to level off, from 1973 to 1975 expenditure on consumer durables responded by falling dramatically. This was consistent with the relationship which had been observed for many years previously.

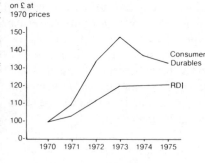

Dependencies may Change

Between the years 1975 and 1979, however, the relationship between RDI and expenditure on consumer durables did not fully hold. In 1976, spending on consumer durables increased even though RDI was in decline. The change in the relationship was brought about:

i)   by a reduction of VAT;

ii) because of the impact of inflation during 1976. Consumers saw the value of any savings they had being reduced, so by investing in consumer durables sooner rather than later they were able to offset future decline in the purchasing power of their savings. Clearly, spending on consumer durables was no longer dependent upon changes in RDI alone.

Whilst identifying dependencies can be useful, there is always the danger of assuming the overriding influence of one environmental impact (e.g. changes in RDI) to the exclusion of other possible future impacts (inflation).

Source: Economic Trends, Central Statistical Office.

Another danger of basing expectations of the future on an understanding of the past is that management become bound by their own recipe. When change of any magnitude does come along, they may not recognise it or fail to handle it. For example, the UK car industry, having evolved for decades on a recipe for success of mass production, growing customer demand and gradual corporate rationalisation, found itself facing a dual attack of foreign imports and decreased overall demand within a matter of years. The change for that industry was truly a shock. For an industry used to a dynamic environment the impact of change would probably have been much less severe.

3.3.2 Understanding Dynamic Conditions

In dynamic conditions the environment is changing. Organisations faced with technological advances, more sophisticated consumers and an internationalisation of markets, find that they can no longer make decisions based on an assumption that what has happened in the past will continue. To cope with this uncertainty there are organisational responses and there are information gathering responses. The organisational responses are discussed more fully in Chapter 10; they involve ensuring that the structure of the organisation is such that it can sense efficiently what is going on in the environment and be flexible enough to respond to such changes.

As for the sensing of the environment and the understanding or analysis of environmental influences, there is evidence that as dynamic conditions increase the interpretation of these conditions becomes more 'inspirational'.[18] Managers sensibly address themselves to considering the environment of the future, not just of the past. For example, retailing in the 1960s and 1970s in the UK underwent a major revolution as firms such as Asda, Tesco, Mothercare, Dixons, Habitat, Fosters, and Fads grew. To a large extent the changes were self-generated, driven by entrepreneurs with the vision and flair to assess and interpret the developments occurring around them to create a view of the future on which to build their businesses.

However, there are more 'structured' ways of trying to understand and deal with the future. Some form of scenario planning approach might be taken, for example. This could involve identifying possible major environmental future changes by a method such as the Delphi technique[19] and based on these projections, building alternative scenarios[20] of the future. In effect, the analyst would construct possible 'alternative futures'. These scenarios might then be considered in terms of the likely behaviour of suppliers, competitors and consumers so that an overall state of possible competitive environments is built up. It is then possible to carry out strategic analysis based on each of the different scenarios: the aim would be to evolve different strategies for different possible futures. It would then be possible to monitor environmental change to see which of the scenarios - and hence which of the contingency strategies - is most appropriate.

Scenario and contingency planning can be done in a highly sophisticated way: but it can also be done in very simple ways. When the entrepreneur acts in an 'intuitive' way, what he is doing is taking a judgment based on his perspective of the future. The principles of future oriented planning as described above can be followed without resort to the more sophisticated refinements of Delphi techniques and scenario planning. The lesson, in straightforward terms, is that in *dynamic conditions it makes more sense to consider the future than rely on the past.*

There are dangers of course. Both a reliance on individuals' sensitivity to trends and the more formal approach of scenario and contingency planning suffer from the risk of myopic perception and response. It is sometimes difficult to get managers to conceive of markedly different scenarios and responses than those already familiar to them - a problem of recipes again. Another danger is that possible scenarios cease to be thought of as possibilities and start to be thought of as 'real'. Managers may build inflexible strategies and organisational structures around mere possibilities rather than creating the flexibility in strategy and structure that would allow speedy responses to environmental change as it actually occurs.

3.3.3 Understanding Complex Conditions

Organisations in complex situations are faced with environmental influences difficult in themselves to comprehend. Organisations facing complexity may also face dynamic conditions. With the growth and application of more and more sophisticated technology, in particular, there is an increasing move to this condition of greatest uncertainty. The computer industry, airlines, the electronics industry are all in, or moving into, this dynamic/complex situation. Furthermore, a multi-national may, as a corporate body, be in a complex condition because of its diversity but find that different operating companies face varying degrees of complexity and dynamism.

How, then, do organisations facing complexity cope with their conditions? Again, there are organiational and information processing approaches. The organisational approaches are dealt with more fully in Chapter 10. They may involve ensuring that complexity as a result of a high knowledge requirement is handled by specialists (e.g. a hospital might handle complexity through its medical staff). Complexity as a result of diversity might be dealt with by ensuring that different parts of the organisation responsible for different aspects of diversity are separate and given the resources and authority to handle their own part of the environment. This is often referred to as differentiation.[21]

As for information processing and analysis, the organisation faces the problem of comprehension. It may have devolved responsibility to specialists or parts of the organisation, but how does it obtain information to make sensible strategic decisions? Typically there may be two responses. The first is, again organisational: the specialists become very powerful in that they are relied upon not only to make operational decisions but are trusted to present information in such a way that a sensible strategic decision can be made, or indeed they themselves become responsible for the strategic decisions. The second is that some attempt is made to model the complexity. This may be done through a financial model, for example, which seeks to simulate the effects on an organisation of different environmental conditions. In its extreme form there may be an attempt to model the environment itself. The Treasury Office might draw heavily on a model of the UK economy and NASA would certainly rely heavily on a simulation of flight conditions and the technology of space flight. However, for most organisations facing complexity, organisational responses are probably more common than extensive model building.

The dangers in complex situations are directly linked to the problems of comprehension. Specialists themselves may not be able to understand the conditions they face, or more commonly, non-specialists, perhaps general managers, fail to create systems which can cope with the complexity. They may fail to give required authority to specialists; create an unsuitable organisation structure; or they may insist upon control procedures that prevent units in the organisation handling their own environments in suitably differentiated ways.

3.3.4 The Nature of the Environment - The Use of the Perspective

Figure 3.3 summarises the discussion on understanding the nature of the environment: the approach has both conceptual and practical uses. Certainly, it should not be taken too literally; it is a conceptual tool and it would be absurd to attempt to bring to bear over-elaborate or rigorous methods of placing an organisation specifically and exclusively in any one situation. However, what the model does provide is a useful checklist of ways of coping with the environment's influences. The key points are these:

* If the organisation's environmental situation is fairly static and simple, then a detailed analysis of past environmental influences may be very sensible.
* The more the situation becomes dynamic then the more a focus on the future is essential, perhaps through some exercise such as scenario building.
* The more complex the environment becomes then, in terms of information processing, the more it may be necessary to move towards more sophisticated techniques such as model-building and simulation.

	Conditions		
	Simple/static	Dynamic	Complex
Aims	• Achieve thorough historical understanding of the environment	• Understand the future rather than rely on the past	• Reduce complexity
Methods	• Analysis of past influences and their effect on organisational performance • Forecasting based on past trends/influences	• Managers' sensitivity to change • Techniques such as scenario planning, contingency planning	• Specialist attention to elements of complexity • Model building
Dangers	• The advent of unexpected or unpredicted change	• Management myopia • Inflexible organisational structures	• Unsuitable organisational structure or control systems

Figure 3.3 *Handling different environmental conditions.*

*   In both dynamic and complex conditions it is important to remember the significance of examining the suitability of the organisation structure (discussed in Chapter 10) and management systems (Chapter 11) as part of the strategic analysis. It may be that many of the organisations problems arise from a structure or control system not suited to its environment.

3.4 ENVIRONMENTAL STRUCTURAL ANALYSIS ✓

Porter

An analysis of the nature of the environment helps to provide guidelines on how to proceed with further analysis and where emphasis should be placed on managing the environment - on formal systems of information gathering or on organisational flexibility, for example. Whichever approach is taken, the aim is to understand the environment in such a way as to generate a credible strategy in relation to the main forces in that environment. A useful guide on the necessary sort of considerations for this is provided by Porter.[22] The section that follows draws on the approach he proposes and is summarised in Fig. 3.5. The approach is essentially a structured means of examining the competitive environment of an organisation so as to provide a clear understanding of the forces at work. Although designed primarily with commercial organisations in mind, it is of value to most organisations which face strategic problems. Illustration 10 is a summary of a structural analysis of one industry environment and might usefully be read in conjunction with this section of the chapter.

Porter argues that 'competition in an industry is rooted in its underlying economics, and competitive forces exist that go well beyond the established combatants in a particular industry'.[23] The task of the strategist is to determine which of these forces are of greatest importance to the organisation. There are four key forces to be considered.

3.4.1 The Threat of Entry

To what extent is there a threat of entry into the strategic group itself? An example is that given in Illustration 10 of the banks witnessing the building societies in the UK becoming more and more involved in current account dealing in the late 1970s and early 1980s. The threat of entry will depend on the extent to which there are *barriers to entry* which most typically are:

*   *Economies of scale.* These will differ by industry. The really important question is not what the optimim scale of operation is, but how damaging it is to operate below that level. For example, in the machine tool industry the optimum scale of production is theoretically very high but the cost of producing at half that level is relatively low: for producers

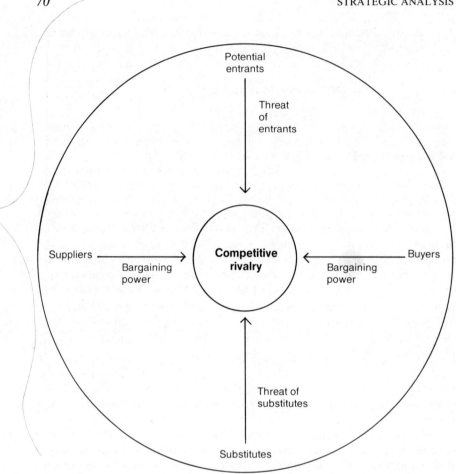

Figure 3.4 *A model for structural analysis*

of nylon, on the other hand, the optimum scale of production is much lower but the cost of producing at half that level is very high.[24] The problem in analysing the significance of this is that economies of scale are difficult to assess precisely, as indeed are the costs of producing below optimum levels of scale. However, some sensible and quite basic questions can be asked. For example, how large is the market and how many competitors are already there? If the market opportunity is small then it is likely to be more difficult to achieve adequate levels of scale than if it is large. In a given market is there any indication that profitability is linked to scale? For example is there a major producer who is profitable whilst there are smaller competitors who are not?

ILLUSTRATION 10

The UK Financial Services Industry - 1983

- A structural analysis highlights the competitive forces at work in the environment thereby providing management with a basis for strategic evaluation.

This is a brief summary of a piece of research which employed structural analysis to study the UK personal financial services industry from the point of view of the UK clearing banks. Particular attention is given to the current account segment because of its importance in being a stepping stone to 'selling' other services such as loans and deposit accounts. Four key sources of competitive forces were examined.

Threat of entry. The main barriers to entry are: strict government regulation, the experience of the industry already gained by the banks, and the large capital requirements. Building Societies are considered potential entrants because of their related experience in operating various savings accounts. However, the barrier they face is whether they can obtain cheque clearing facilities. The capital required to set up a clearing system similar to that already operated by the banks would be considerable.

The power of buyers and suppliers. Buyers (borrowers and buyers of services and advice) and suppliers (depositors) exert little bargaining power over the participants of the industry. Rates of interest remain the same between banks, being determined by macroeconomic factors. The large numbers of buyers and suppliers means that the individual customer will have little bargaining power.

The threat of a substitute service. Substitute services come directly from the state in the form of Girobank and the National Savings schemes. While being a potential threat, they are not intended to capture the market, rather their role is one of funding the Public Sector Borrowing Requirement.

The rivalry amongst existing competitors. Competitive forces that result from internal 'jockeying for position' are low (though growing) because of the lack of product differentiation and the oligopolistic nature of the industry. The main source of competition takes the form of extensive advertising campaigns.

Conclusions. The analysis indicates that the major competitive force facing the industry comes from the possible entry of the Building Societies, especially into the current account segment. Management therefore needs to pay particular attention to monitoring their movements and to prohibiting their entry to the cheque clearing system. Alternatively, the banks may consider allowing the Building Societies to use their cheque clearing facilities providing they could reap some benefit from letting them do so. Competitive forces resulting from internal rivalry were low at the time of analysis but warrant careful monitoring as a potentially significant factor. Substitute services could be a threat if the Government had to finance a larger PSBR.

Source: MBA research project carried out at the University of Aston Management Centre.

*   *The capital requirement* of entry. This is linked to economies of scale. To
     continue the example of banks and the building society competition, for
     the building societies to compete fully with banks in the handling of day
     to day personal financing, they would have to create the facility to
     process cheques, involving enormous capital expenditure to set up a
     clearing system.

*   *Product differentiation.* This might be as a result of a strong brand image,
     product or service quality, efficiency of distribution and so on. Differen-
     tiation will vary by industry, and may change over time. For example,
     many grocery producers failed to realise the extent to which their
     products were becoming perceived by consumers as non-differentiated
     commodity purchases throughout the 1960s and 1970s as supermarkets
     moved into extensive own labelling.

*   Access to *distribution channels.* In the early 1970s in the UK Hygena were
     the market leaders in fitted kitchens. Their early dominance was due to
     the innovation of self assembly kitchen units and a national distribution
     network. The small companies in this distribution network were heavily
     dependent on Hygena to begin with. However, as the market grew, two
     factors reduced Hygena's dominance: the first was the relatively low cost
     of capital required to enter the industry, and the second was the readiness
     of the distributors to accept alternative suppliers to Hygena - there was
     ready access to distribution channels.

*   *Cost disadvantages independent of size.* To a large extent these are to do
     with early entries into markets and the experience so gained. This
     phenomenon is usually known as the 'experience curve' and is dealt with
     in detail in the Appendix at the end of the book.

*   *Legislation or government action.* The Medicines Act in the UK imposes
     strict regulation on the manufacture of pharmaceutical products. The
     government may intervene to prevent a company acquiring another if it is
     not felt to be in the 'public good'. A licence issued by a government
     agency may be required to operate in certain industries. Until the early
     1980s public services in the UK such as the telephone service or postal
     system were operated as monopolies and private companies were
     prevented from competing by law: the removal of such protection meant
     that entry barriers were reduced.

     These barriers to entry differ by industry so it is impossible to generalise
about which are more important than others. What is important is that the
strategic analyst should establish (a) which barriers, if any, exist; (b) to what
extent they are likely to prevent entry in the particular environment concerned;
and (c) the organisation's position in all this - is it trying to prevent entrants or
is it attempting to gain entry. Illustration 11 gives an example of an attempt to
create entry barriers to prevent competition.

ILLUSTRATION 11

Protecting Market Standing

● Faced with the threat of cut-price charter flights, scheduled airlines used their trade association to create a more stable environment in which they could operate.

The early users of international air transport were mostly businessmen, government officials and others whose prime concern was with the convenience of travel rather than its cost. To cater for this need, the world's scheduled airlines formed a trade association, the International Air Transport Association (IATA) which functioned to provide uniformity in such matters as ticketing, operating and pricing regulations between the major airlines.

To a great extent, the conformity that resulted from these agreements helped to increase the popularity of air travel which in turn enabled airlines to offer more scheduled services throughout the world. International tariffs were set through IATA to prevent cost-cutting practices. Because the operating costs endured by an airline are similar whether a plane flies full or half-full, it was important to airline operators that price competition did not develop since any reduction in services would be likely to occur on the less popular routes at the expense of the travellers who used them.

Over the years, however, the scheduled airlines failed to notice the increasing appeal that air travel had to the growing tourist sector, with their needs being catered for by fringe charter operators. Because tourists were more likely to be cost-conscious and less likely to be bound by strict timetable commitments, charter operators were able to capture the mass-market by offering fewer flights where they knew they could sell the majority of seats, but at a lower cost to the customer. Clearly, if charter operations were allowed to grow too much, they would soon be in direct competition with the scheduled airlines.

Because international legislation insisted that all air transport operators belong to the trade association, IATA was able to step in with controls that insisted on the inclusion of hotel accommodation with a cut-price ticket (hence the emergence of package holidays), or membership of a holiday club, which in effect meant that charter flights could only be sold to a certain sector of the tourist trade, leaving the remainder of air travellers to use scheduled services.

Thus controls protected the market standing of scheduled airlines in the face of competition from charter operators.

Source: Management Today, April 1980, p.98.

3.4.2 The Power of Buyers and Suppliers

Porter's next two forces can be considered together because they have similar effects on the competitive environment. Buyers and suppliers influence margins: the greater their power the more likely it is that margins will be low. So it is important to assess the power of buyers and suppliers and any likely changes in it. For example, it has already been mentioned that Hygena failed to recognise the growing power of distributors - their buyers - in the kitchen furniture business. Similarly the power of mutiple retailers has grown enormously since the 1960s. Supplier power may also change over time: the most extreme example is the growing power of OPEC through the 1970s.

There are useful indicators of the extent of this power which can be used by the analyst. Supplier power is likely to be high when:

* there is a concentration of suppliers rather than a fragmented source of supply;
* the 'switching costs' from one supplier to another in the industry are high; perhaps because a manufacturer's processes are dependent on the specialist products of a supplier;
* there is the possibility of the supplier integrating forward if they do not obtain the prices, and hence the margins, they seek;
* the supplier's customers are of little importance to the supplier, in which case the supplier is not likely to regard the long term future of the customers as of particular importance.

Buyer power is likely to be high:

* when there is a concentration of buyers, particularly if the volume purchases of the buyers is high;
* when there are alternative sources of supply, perhaps because the product required is undifferentiated between suppliers;
* if the component or material cost is a high percentage of their total cost, buyers will be likely to 'shop around' to get the best price and therefore 'squeeze' the suppliers;
* where there is a threat of backward integration by the buyer if satisfactory prices or suppliers cannot be obtained.

The interplay of suppliers and buyers may well result in different market structures over time. For example, local authorities in the UK realised throughout the 1970s that they were not optimising their buying power because of their fragmented mode of buying - each authority would put out tenders to suppliers separately. To increase buying power they formed buying groups. For suppliers the implications were significant. This market became increasingly concentrated and competitive. The example also shows that it is important to consider how the organisation can adapt to its market position to achieve the most benefits, and that buyer power can be increased through a structural change of a market. It might also be possible for a supplier to seek out market segments with less powerful buyers, or differentiate products so that buyers become more dependent on that product.

3.4.3 The Threat of Substitutes

The next force which Porter identifies is the threat of substitutes. The question here is to what extent an organisation can legitimately regard itself as operating in a discrete market with a limited number of like competitors, as opposed to having as potential competitors a wider range of substitute products. The threat may take different forms. There would be substitution of one product or another — the calculator for the slide rule is an extreme example, or sugar substitutes for sugar. A substitute may hold down or depress margins: so, for example, the producers of natural fabrics found that the advent of man-made fibres depressed prices and margins. Producers of one product or service may even find themselves competing with unexpected substitutes as, perhaps, recession reduces spending power: for example, package holiday companies and motor car producers may find themselves competing for decreasing amounts of disposable income.

The issues that arise are these: To what extent is there a danger that substitutes may encroach upon an organisation's activities? What steps can be taken to minimise the risk of such substitution, perhaps through differentiation or low cost profiles? And, more positively, is there the possibility that one's own products could find new markets as substitutes for some other product?

3.4.4 The Extent of Competitive Rivalry

Competitors will also be concerned with the degree of rivalry between themselves in their own industry. How intense is this competition? What is it based upon? Is it likely to increase or decrease in intensity? How can it be reduced? All these are questions which need to be thought about in the process of strategic analysis. Porter again provides a useful checklist which enables the analyst to consider these questions. He suggests that the degree of rivalry is based on the following:

* The extent to which competitors in the industry are *in balance*. Whatever their number, where competitors are of roughly equal size there is the danger of intense competition as one competitor attempts to gain dominance over another. To some extent industry concentration may offset this but the most stable markets tend to be those with dominant organisations within them.

* A market in *slow growth* - particularly one which is entering its maturity stage and competitors are keen to establish themselves as market leaders -is likely to be highly competitive.

* *High fixed costs* in an industry, perhaps through high capital intensity,[25] or high costs of storage, is likely to result in competitors cutting prices to obtain the turnover required. This can result in price wars and very low margin operations.

* Again the importance of *product differentiation* is clear. If a product or service is not differentiated then there is little to stop customers switching between competitors, which in turn raises the degree of rivalry between them.

* If the addition of *extra capacity is in large increments* then the competitor making such an addition is likely to create at least short-term over-capacity and increased competition.
* Where there are *high exit barriers* to an industry, there is again likely to be the persistence of excess capacity and consequently increased competition. Exit barriers might be high for a variety of reasons: they may vary from a high investment in non transferable fixed assets such as specialist plant, to the cost of redundancy, to the reliance on one product to be credible within a market sector even if the product itself makes heavy losses.

3.4.5 The Significance of Identifying Market Segments

Although not explicitly singled out for attention within Porter's model of structural analysis, a recurring implication throughout is the importance of identifying the different market segments[26] that are within the competitive environments. The extent to which an organisation has located and exploited a clear market segment is likely to affect its vulnerability to substitutes, its bargaining power with regard to supplies and buyers, the threat of entry into its market area and the degree of rivalry it faces. Segmentation is an important concept for the strategist and warrants particular attention.

As part of a structural analysis it is useful to identify how the market may be segmented and which competitors are concentrating on which segments. It may be possible to do this in a quantified way by establishing market segment values and competitor shares by segment; or it may be that a more qualitative approach is required. In either case what is needed is a breakdown of the market into the segments which are important from a strategic point of view. The importance could arise for a number of reasons. For example, because certain segments are more competitive than others; or by segmenting the market in a particular way new opportunities for product differentiation emerge; or because some segments are growing and others are not; or some segments are much bigger than others.

It is also important to remember that a market can be segmented in various ways: and each different basis of segmentation could give rise to a different assessment of environmental opportunities. Suppose that Fig. 3.5 represents the structure of a retail market worth £100 million, and suppose that all the companies involved are manufacturing much the same sort of basic product. If company C thinks of its markets in overall terms, then it would consider itself to be fairly weak. But suppose the segments shown in the fig. are based on different retailer types: then immediately it is clear that company C is relatively strong in one part of the market - segment IV - and this could substantially affect the strategic opportunities open to it depending on the opportunities and threats in that segment.

Again by looking at the market segmentation in Fig. 3.5 other implications about the competitive environment emerge. Segments I and II are the

Segment	Size £m	Competitor positions			
		A	B	C	D
I	40	Dominant	Weak		No. 2
II	25	No. 2	Dominant		Weak
III	15	Weak		Weak	Weak
IV	10			Dominant specialist	
V	10 (growing)	No one specialising (all weak)			
Total market	100				

Figure 3.5 *Competitor analysis by market segment.*

largest where the competitive battle is at its fiercest. Companies A and B are concentrating on these segments with company D running behind. Company C specialises in Segment IV which it dominates. But what of Segments III and V which are growing? They account for £25 million and no one is really concentrating on them. Even as simple a model as this raises questions about the strategic positions of the various firms and the possible limitations and opportunities they have. Company D, with, say, a 25% share of I (£10 million), a 10% share of II (£2.5 million) and a 10% share of III (£1.5 million), has a turnover of £14 million and is probably having to operate at low margins to try to compete in I and II. Is there an opportunity to concentrate on dominating III and V, achieving perhaps a 40% share of each and sales of £10 million at higher margins? Companies A and B, of course, are probably more concerned with retaining their dominance of I and II respectively. Again, this simple segmentation exercise might point out an opportunity in V which A and B had not previously considered.

3.5 ASSESSING OPPORTUNITIES AND THREATS

What may be an opportunity for one organisation may be a threat to another. The advent of the electronic watch was seen as a threat to Swiss watch makers, who had no major indigenous electronics industry, but as an opportunity for Japanese watch makers who did. A lowering of the value of the pound would be seen as a threat to import agents but an opportunity to home producers. How are the sorts of major opportunities and threats, so important in the formulation of strategy, to be identified? And how is it possible to decide what is an opportunity and what a threat?

The first two stages of environmental analysis - understanding the *nature of the environment* and *structural analysis* - help to identify the general forces at work in the environment that have an impact on the strategy of the organisation. These general considerations need to be understood more specifically in terms of their impacts on the organisation.

3.5.1 Strategic Mismatch

One way of doing this is to consider the extent to which an organisation's strategy is matched - or mismatched - to its environment. Mismatches usually occur in two main ways:

(i) The environment of an organisation may have changed, but the strategy of the organisation itself has not changed with it. It is still behaving as if one set of forces is important when it no longer is. This is typically the case in circumstances where a relatively static environment has become increasingly dynamic. Some organisations get 'left behind'. For example, many of the USA and UK film companies never came to terms with the demise of cinema-going. They persisted in the belief that they were in business to make films for the cinema. Other companies adapted their strategy to become producers of TV movies and still later to produce for the home video market.

(ii) The structure or systems of an organisation are not suited to new conditions. Perhaps there has been a move to dynamic or complex conditions which require a different organisational structure or control systems. There may be resistance to change from within the organisation. For example, with increasing unemployment in the early 1980s, evidence of street unrest and concentration of ethnic groups in particular areas of London, there was a strong argument for a major decentralisation of operational responsibility in the Metropolitan Police. Yet the command structure was essentially one of concentration on very senior officers well removed from the operational levels.

There is, then, a need to examine the environment in terms of existing and potential mismatches. The problem of analysis is that in almost all organisational environments there is some degree of change. What needs to be identified is whether or not the change is of such significance as to affect the strategic position of the organisation. This can be done by reconciling the nature of the organisation and the structural analysis so as to identify the key features which are likely to denote such significance. Such features, giving rise to strategic mismatch if an organisation fails to accept them, include:

*   The degree of *permanence of change:* for example, a market may be cyclical in nature. Such business cycles are of importance but are unlikely to give rise to strategic mismatches because businesses operating in that market will have become used to its cyclical nature. However, what the cycles may hide is an overall decline in the market and this might well be a permanent long term trend of considerable importance.

* The *speed of change:* organisations face more threats of mismatches if there is little time to adapt to them. For example, a gradual decline in market value is not as problematic as a sudden shift in usership patterns away from a product or service.

* The *extent of change:* is the change taking place likely to affect a substantial part of the organisation or its strategy? Are the changes in one sector of the market likely to be limited to that sector alone or might they be indicative of much wider changes which will affect all sectors?

* Linked to this last point may be the extent to which the *structure of the competitive environment* has changed. Are the changes taking place significant in that they modify the major forces in the environment? Are barriers to entry being reduced by a more open access to distribution channels, a reduced capital entry requirement or a pending change in prohibitive government legislation? Has a new market segment of significance developed? Are there threats of vertical integration forward or backward?

3.5.2 Strategic Standing

The identification of strategic mismatch does not necessarily mean that the organisation is under threat. It is only under threat if it fails to, or is unable to, respond. If it is well positioned to change in line with the environment in which it operates then change, significant though it may be, is an opportunity rather than a threat.

The main indicators of whether or not an organisation can turn environmental change into an opportunity rather than a threat are twofold. The first is whether its management, workforce, structure and systems are capable of such change. These considerations will be dealt with in detail in later chapters. The second is the extent to which the organisation is well positioned in terms of its *standing* in relation to the types of change taking place.

By *strategic standing* is meant the relative strength or power that an organisation has in terms of the major environmental changes it faces. Suppose, for example, an organisation is faced with a long term trend in its industry of the replacement of labour with capital equipment, then the extent to which it can respond to such change to its own advantage is likely to depend at the very least on its financial standing in terms of the availability of funds for investment either internally or by borrowing, its standing in relation to the trades unions to avoid costly disruption during de-manning and its relative standing to competition with regard to its margins, because it is quite likely that prices will be reduced in the market.

Analysis of strategic standing will probably reveal that the organisation is strong in some areas and weak in others. In this sense a change is usually both a threat and an opportunity. However what an analysis of strategic standing does provide is a clearer indication of the ways in which the organisation is capable of handling change and the ways in which it is poorly placed to do so. Future strategy could well be designed around taking advantage of the areas of strong standing and improving or overcoming areas of weak standing.

It is not possible to provide a definitive list of the aspects of strategic standing that should be analysed. This must depend on the particular forces at work in the environment for a given organisation. However some examples of the idea and significance of strategic standing might be helpful.

* *Market share:* there is now ample evidence[27] to show that firms with consistently higher market share than their competitors tend to be more profitable. So, in analysing standing of a firm in its environment, its market share provides a perspective of that firm's standing in the market place.

* *Technological standing:* it is likely that throughout the stages of the product life cycle there will be industry-wide differences in the type and role of technology. An example of this is given in Illustration 12. It is important that an organisation is sensitive to how it stands in relation to the application of technology. For example, in the development stage the focus is likely to be on product design and the rate of change here is likely to be high. Companies are most concerned to develop their products to achieve high customer acceptance and market leadership. Thus it is important to assess technological standing in relation both to the speed of innovation in the industry and to assess the organisation's product design capabilities in relation to competitors. In the shakeout and early maturity stages there is decreasing activity in product design. The emphasis switches to developing processes of production which are able to produce products most efficiently and thus provide the most advantageous cost profile in a competitive market which is plateauing. In these circumstances, technological standing would be measured more in terms of capabilities in process development related to improving operating efficiency.[28]

* *External financial standing:* every business is subject to an external financial rating. It may be a fairly informal rating as when a small businessman tries to raise finance from a bank and finds that the bank manager has a high (or low) regard for his business. Or it might be a much more formal rating such as a major study of an industry or firm published by a firm of stockbrokers. The way in which the rating of a public company is often expressed is through its standing in the stock market and the usual measure of this is the price earnings (PE) ratio.[29] A company's strategic options may well be influenced by the company's external financial standing. A company with a high PE ratio is likely to find it easier to raise equity finance than a company with a low PE ratio.

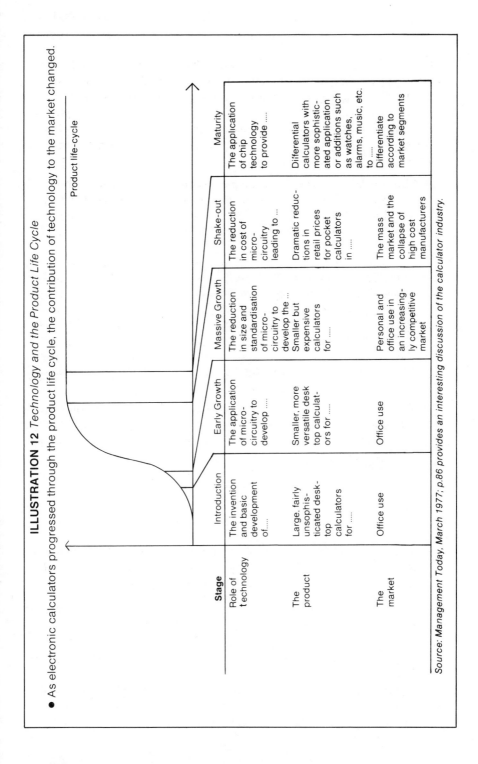

ILLUSTRATION 12 *Technology and the Product Life Cycle*

● As electronic calculators progressed through the product life cycle, the contribution of technology to the market changed.

Product life-cycle

Stage	Introduction	Early Growth	Massive Growth	Shake-out	Maturity
Role of technology	The invention and basic development of.....	The application of micro-circuitry to develop	The reduction in size and standardisation of micro-circuitry to develop the ...	The reduction in cost of micro-circuitry leading to ...	The application of chip technology to provide .....
The product	Large, fairly unsophis-ticated desk-top calculators for	Smaller, more versatile desk top calculat-ors for	Smaller but expensive calculators for	Dramatic reduc-tions in retail prices for pocket calculators in	Differential calculators with more sophistic-ated application or additions such as watches, alarms, music, etc. to ..... Differentiate according to market segments
The market	Office use	Office use	Personal and office use in an increasing-ly competitive market	The mass market and the collapse of high cost manufacturers	

Source: Management Today, March 1977; p.86 provides an interesting discussion of the calculator industry.

A high PE ratio may also be an incentive to acquire other firms because the buyer may be able to obtain the shares of the other company by offering his own shares as bait.

Financial standing is a matter to be considered not only by commercial organisations but also by organisations in the public sector. They may well be competing with other public services for what the government regards as scarce cash or capital resources. Under the Conservative administration in the early 1980s in the UK, it was quite clear that the police force or the armed forces could assess their future strategies with much more confidence of financial support than could educational establishments or local authorities.

* *Political standing:* the view that government takes of an organisation could be important. For example, British Leyland received massive UK government aid for many years because of its importance to the economy. Multinational organisations face the continual task of retaining a high 'standing' in relationships with host governments. Those that fail to do so may face anything from mild disfavour to outright takeover. Other organisations which are part of the public sector may be so enmeshed in the fabric of government that their standing is directly related to the policies of government. In the UK between the mid 1970s and early 1980s, nationalised enterprises and local authorities found themselves regarded first as guarantors of jobs and generators of wealth by the Labour government and then as a potential drain on the national purse by the Conservative government.

It would be possible to provide a much longer list but hopefully the point is made. In terms of the key forces or influences in the environment, a high standing will provide opportunity and a low standing is likely to pose a threat.

3.6 SUMMARY

This chapter has set out to provide a framework by which to understand the influences of the environment on organisations and their strategies. It has sought to do this by:

* showing that a consideration of the nature of the environment can guide further investigation and begin to highlight major influences;
* outlining why an understanding of the economic structure of the competitive environment is important and how analyses of this might be carried out;
* showing how the forces identified in these analyses can be considered as opportunities or threats to the organisation by the examination of strategic mismatch and strategic standing.

In fact, the idea of strategic standing overlaps with the next two chapters since standing depends to a large extent on the organisation's resources and the values of those in and around the organisation. The next two chapters deal with these aspects of strategic analysis.

REFERENCES

1. A sound basic discussion of environmental influences on business is provided in books 1 and 2, M. Glew, M. Watts and R. Wells, *The Business Organisation and its Environment* (Heinemann: 1979).
2. Marketing is considered to be an essential underpinning to the study of strategy. A marketing perspective on environmental analysis is fundamental to this chapter. A good basic text is M. Baker, *Marketing: An Introductory Text,* 3rd Edition (Macmillan: 1979, chapters 1 to 7). Most marketing texts include coverage of the market as an influence on the organisation, e.g. chapters 2 to 7 in P. Kotler: *Marketing Management* (Prentice-Hall: 1980).
3. Not much has been written specifically about how the financial environment of a firm may influence strategy. However a good background to the financial environment in terms of sources of finance and their influence can be found in Part 7, L.J. Gitman, *Principles of Managerial Finance* (Harper & Row: 1976).
4. The issue of scarcity of raw materials was highlighted in the early 1970s by D. Meadows *et al., The Limits to Growth: the First Report of the Club of Rome* (Pan: 1974). Though there have been papers disputing the arguments made in this book, the problem of conflict between ecological considerations and an industrial society remain. For example, for a discussion of the problems of balancing industrial activity and ecological problems see S. Hohn, 'Economic Development and Ecological Equilibrium - A Target Conflict in Modern Industrial Enterprises', *Long Range Planning:* Vol. 15, No. 4, 1982.
5. Various aspects of the way in which suppliers and the availability of supplies affect strategy are covered in the readings in D.H. Farmer and B. Taylor, eds., *Corporate Planning and Procurement,* (Heinemann: 1975).
6. K. Pavitt, ed., *Technological Innovation and British Economic Performance,* (Macmillan: 1980) contains papers which examine the process and impact of technological change on industry. Also A.C. Cooper and D. Schendel discuss the impact of technological change on industry in 'Strategic Responses to Technological Threats', *Business Horizons:* February 1976.
7. Manpower availability and quality of skills as an important aspect of an organisation's environment is discussed in Chapter 2 of G. Stainer, *Manpower Planning: The Management of Human Resources* (Heinemann: 1971).
8. Readers may like to refer to section 13 G.A. Steiner and J.F. Steiner, eds., *Issues in Business and Society* (Random House: 1977). This section includes articles on the role and problems of government legislation and control of business: for example, J.T. Dunlop, '*The Limits of Legal Compulsion'*. Readers may also like to refer to S. Jonsson and I. Petzall, 'Forecasting Political Decisions and their Impact on Business', *Long Range Planning,* Vol. 15, No. 4, 1982.

9. There are no readings which briefly encapsulate the widely different ways in which economic conditions affect strategy. However, there is a useful summary of the economic environment of business in the later chapters (particularly 13) of D.A.S. Jackson, *Introduction to Economics: Theory and Data* (Macmillan: 1982). In addition given the importance of inflation over the last decade, readers may like to refer to D. Hussey, *Inflation and Business Policy* (Longman: 1976).

10. An interesting reading which examines societal expectations and their impact on industry is W.F. Martin and G. Cabot Lodge, 'Our Society in 1985 - Business May Not Like It', *Harvard Business Review:* Nov/Dec 1975.

11. D. Norburn's work supports this and is summarised in: 'Directors Without Direction', *Journal of General Management* Vol. 1, No. 2, 1973/74.

12. Both D. Norburn's findings (reference 11), and Miller and Friesen's (see D. Miller and P. Friesen: 'Strategy Making in Context: Ten Empirical Archetypes', *Journal of Management Studies,* Vol. 14, No. 3, 1977) support this assertion.

13. J.G. March and H.A. Simon, *Organizations* (Wiley: 1958, p.165), point out that one way of reducing uncertainty is through the process of 'uncertainty absorption' by which they mean that 'inferences are drawn from a body of evidence and the inferences, instead of the evidence itself, are then communicated'.

14. R. Duncan's research on which this classification is based can be found in 'Characteristics of Organisational Environments and Perceived Environmental Uncertainty' in *Administrative Science Quarterly,* 1972, pp. 313-327.

15. This notion of interconnectedness was put forward by F.E. Emery and E.L. Trist in 'The Causal Texture of Organisational Environments', *Human Relations,* Vol. 18., 1965. The idea has been developed in the context of the implications on uncertainty by R.H. Miles in *Macro- Organisational Behaviour* (Goodyear: 1980), pp.200-209.

16. L. Fahey and W. King summarise a survey carried out in 12 large business organisations in the USA which shows that it is firms in stable environments that tend to have regular and continuous scanning mechanisms. Firms in less stable conditions tend to have more irregular (ad hoc, reactive, crisis initiated, etc.) scanning mechanisms. This survey is outlined in 'Environmental Scanning for Corporate Planning', *Business Horizons,* August 1977.

17. A good example of a systematic approach to environmental analysis can be found in J. Argenti's books *Corporate Planning* (Allen and Unwin: 1965) and, more recently, *Practical Corporate Planning* (Allen and Unwin: 1980).

18. The term 'inspirational' is used by J.D. Thompson and A. Tuden in 'Strategies, Structures and Processes of Organisation Decision' in *Comparative Studies in Administration* edited by J.D. Thompson (University of Pittsburgh Press: 1958). They argue that as dynamic conditions increase, managers cease to be as reliant on understanding what has gone before and become more concerned with sensing what they expect will happen.

19. For a general text on the Delphi method, see H. Linstone and M. Turoff, eds., *The Delphi Method: Techniques and Applications* (Addison Wesley: 1975).

20. For an example of method and an illustration of the use of scenarios in global economic forecasting see D. Norse, 'Scenario Analysis in Interfutures' *Futures,* Vol. 11, No. 5: 1979. For a brief discussion of the role of scenario analysis see

R.D. Zentner, 'Scenarios, Past, Present and Future' *Long Range Planning,* Vol. 15, No. 3, 1982.

21.   Differentiation is a term coined by P. Lawrence and J. Lorsch in *Organisation and Environment* (Harvard University Press: 1967, and Irwin 1969).

22.   For a detailed exposition of the approach see M.E. Porter, *Competitive Strategy: Techniques for Analyzing Industries and Competitors* (Free Press: 1980).

23.   This quotation is taken from M.E. Porter, 'How Competitive Forces Shape Strategy', *Harvard Business Review* Mar.-Apr., 1979, which is a useful summary of his approach.

24.   For a detailed analysis of differences in economies of scale by industry see C. Pratten: 'Economies of Scale in Manufacturing Industries' *Department of Applied Economics Occasional Papers:* No. 28: Cambridge University Press: 1971.

25.   High capital intensity has been shown to be a major cause of rivalry since, to maintain utilisation of plant, competitors will reduce prices (and margins) to achieve volume. This is discussed more fully in chapter 7 of this book and in S. Schoeffler, 'Capital-Intensive Technology vs ROI: A Strategic Assessment', *Management Review,* Sept. 1978.

26.   Market segmentation as a concept and its relevance will be covered in most marketing texts. For example, P. Kotler: *Marketing Management,* (Prentice-Hall: 1980, Ch.7), or P. Chisnall *Marketing: A Behavioural Analysis* (McGraw Hill: 1975, Ch.15).

27.   For a more detailed understanding of the importance of market share see the work of the Boston Consulting Group and the PIMS research. The Boston Consulting Group's work on the Experience Curve and Portfolio Planning is summarised in the Appendix of this book, but more thoroughly in *Perspectives in Experience* published in 1970 by the Boston Consulting Group. The PIMS (Profit Impact of Marketing Share) project was begun in the USA and consists of the recording of the performances of subscribing companies so as to form a data base for strategic analysis. Its detailed findings are available only to subscribing companies but general findings are published: see, for example, R.D. Buzzel, B.T. Gale and R.G.M. Sultan, 'Market Share a Key to Profitability', *Harvard Business Review,* Jan.-Feb. 1975.

28.   For those who wish to follow up the research on which this is based they should refer to A. Cooper and D. Schendel, 'Strategic Responses to Technological Threats', *Business Horizons,* Feb. 1976.

29.   Most books on financial management will provide an explanation of price-earnings (PE) ratios. For example, see *Principles of Managerial Finance,* (reference 3).

RECOMMENDED KEY READINGS

*   M.E.Porter, *Competitive Strategy: Techniques for Analyzing Industries and Competitors* (Free Press: 1980). Essential reading for those who are faced with the structural analysis of an organisational environment.

For more thorough treatment of techniques of forecasting for management purposes the following are useful:

* S. Makridakis and S. Wheelwright, *The Handbook of Forecasting: A Manager's Guide* (Wiley: 1982).

* T.E. Milne, *Business Forecasting: a Managerial Approach,* (Longman: 1975).

* A useful source of economic, financial, social/demographic and raw material data from 1960-1980 in the UK is Vol. 15, No. 5 of *Long Range Planning.*

4

THE INTERNAL POSITION - RESOURCES

4.1 INTRODUCTION

The preceding chapters have indicated the importance of an organisation's resources in determining the *strategic capability* of that organisation. In Chapter 3 it was emphasised that an organisation's ability to survive and prosper in its environment is strongly influenced by the 'standing' of the organisation, which is, in turn, determined by its resources. This chapter is concerned with understanding the significance of an organisation's *strategic capability* and ways in which resource analysis can contribute to this understanding.

In Chapter 3 the analysis of the environment was separated into two parts. Firstly, an analysis of the past and present environment of the company and how environmental influences had shaped strategy over the years. This was then followed by looking at the future environmental situation. These same two steps will now be used in analysing organisational resources by looking firstly at how the resource position of the company has shaped policy and then at how the resource analysis must take account of the future situation. This latter aspect will be given a fuller discussion in Chapter 9. Illustration 13 shows the importance of various aspects of some companys' resources on the success or failure of those companies.

The discussion which follows will help readers avoid some of the more common pitfalls in resource analysis which are:

* Resource analysis must go beyond simply describing the resources which a company has or has not got. Whereas such a *resource audit* is an important starting point to any resource analysis, it is inadequate as a complete picture of how company resources influence policy. The performance of a company not only results from the intrinsic strength of its resources but also from the way that those resources have been exploited (the *use of resources*) and the extent to which they have been controlled (*control of resources*).

87

ILLUSTRATION 13

The Quality of Resources

● Employers perceive different sorts of resource strengths as a basis for their strategic development.

'In a trading group such as ours, *people* are the most important factor and no individual company can progress without the efforts of the men and women in its organisation'.

Inchcape Chairman's Statement, 1981

'The *names* of Royal Worcester and Spode stand, as for centuries past, at the apex of renown and approbation wherever the highest qualities of workmanship are admired and sought.'

Lyn T. Davies, Chairman, Royal Worcester & Spode, 1981.

'We believe that the *spread of our activities* both in the UK and overseas, the strength of management, strong liquidity, and the large property content in our portfolio will enable us to continue to give as good an account as trading conditions will allow.'

Sir Issac Wolfson, Chairman, Great Universal Stores Ltd., 1981.

'Pulp demand is already reacting to the recession in lost Asian markets but, as there are few major increments in Kraft pulp capacity planned throughout the world, the basic strength of this *product* in the market is likely to bring a quicker recovery.'

Tasman Pulp & Paper Co. Ltd., 1981

'Although the climate for oil shares is currently unfavourable, we believe that our oil *investments* still have great potential - UK oil reserves will always be a valuable insurance policy against trouble in the Middle East which looks like remaining an unstable area.'

Foreign & Colonial Investment Trusts Plc, 1981.

---

* Resources are only one of several influences on company policy and in certain circumstances may not be the major reason for good or bad performance. A company may have first class resources, which are fully exploited and controlled but be operating in highly depressed and unprofitable markets.

* There is a danger that the sheer volume of analysis may result in a failure to draw any valuable conclusions. It is necessary to sort out the important issues from the trivial. In practice this is, of course, what managers' *recipes* are all about, as the discussion in Chapters 1 and 2 suggested. The retail store manager will monitor sales per square foot, the chemical plant manager will assess 'yield' from his raw materials, whilst a manufacturer using production lines might be most interested in 'lost time'. *Recipes* are a useful way of focusing resource analysis into the most important areas. However, there are dangers; the *recipe* may overlook new factors which are of key importance. Managers should always be suspicious of the recipe and question its validity. The purpose of the analytical methods discussed below is to provide a basis on which to challenge the recipe rather than to act as a day-to-day method of making resource decisions.

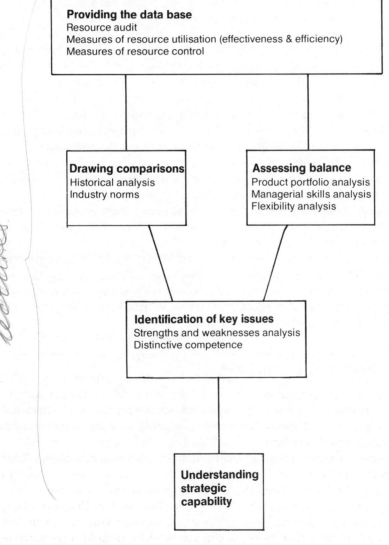

Figure 4.1 *Methods of analysing resources.*

Before reviewing methods which can be used to analyse an organisation's resource position, it is necessary to understand how the various analyses will contribute to the overall assessment of *strategic capability*. These analytical methods can be grouped under four headings, as summarised in Fig. 4.1.

(i) *Analyses which provide the data base.* These methods are largely concerned with a detailed analysis of *individual resource areas* in terms of (a) the intrinsic nature of those resources, (b) the utilisation of the resources and (c) the control of resources. It should be remembered that in terms of understanding the strategic capability of an organisation these data are of little value unless subjected to further analysis. This is an important observation, particularly in relation to the use of financial data in resource analysis. Many managers are capable of producing a wide variety of financial ratios and performance indicators but fail to extract any strategic significance from them.

(ii) *Comparison.* The strategic capability of an organisation is better understood in relation to the company's own past performance or the performance of major competitors, or competitive industries.

(iii) *Balance.* Very often an organisation's strategic capability is impaired, not because of problems with any individual resource area, but because the balance of these resources is inappropriate. For example, there may be too many new products resulting in cash flow problems or a Board of Directors all with similar experience.

(iv) *Identification of key issues.* It has already been mentioned that resource analysis must be capable of identifying those issues which are of particular strategic importance in any given situation. This is best undertaken as the final step in an analysis and draws upon the information from previous analyses. For example, a strengths and weaknesses analysis may be used at this stage once a detailed understanding of a company's resources has been gained by other methods.

4.2 PROVIDING THE DATA BASE

A resource analysis needs to build on a bank of data, much of which will be in quantitative form. As previously mentioned, this part of the analysis must go beyond a simple *resource audit* and, in addition, provide data on how resources have been utilised and controlled. Each of these three aspects will now be discussed more fully.

4.2.1 The Resource Audit

There are many frameworks or checklists which could be used as the basis of a resource audit.[1] For simplicity, the traditional basis - dividing the analysis

	Operations	Marketing	Finance	Personnel	R & D	Others
Physical resources	Machines Buildings Materials Location Stock	Products/services Patents, licences Warehouses	Cash Debtors Stock (Equity)† (Loans)†	Location	Size of R & D Design	Location of buildings
Human resources	Operatives Support staff Suppliers	Salesmen Marketing staff Customers	Shareholders Bankers	Adaptability Location Number of employees Age profile	Scientists Technologists Designers	Management skills Planners
Systems*	Quality control Production control Production planning Purchasing	Service system Distribution channels	Costing Cash management Accounting	Working agreements Rewards	Project assessment	Planning & control Information
Intangibles	Team spirit	Brand name Goodwill Market information Contacts Image	Image in City	Organisational culture Image	Know-how	Image Location

* This area is more fully treated in Figures 4.3 and 4.4.
† Equity and Loans are owed by the company but an understanding of how the company is financed is an important part of a resource audit.

Figure 4.2 A checklist for resource auditing.

into functional areas - is used in Fig. 4.2. For a fuller description of a resource audit in each functional area readers should refer to references.[2] It is important to include in a resource audit some resources which in a strict legal sense do not lie within the boundary of an organisation but are nevertheless, of great importance from a *strategic* viewpoint. Good examples here would be a company's network of customers or outlets, or the Managing Director's personal contacts with suppliers.

Figure 4.2 illustrates a resource audit. Resources which do not neatly fit into one functional area are identified as 'other resources' and include planning, control and information systems which encompass many functional areas. Within each functional area different types of resources are identified:

(i)   *Physical resources.* An assessment of a company's physical resources must stretch beyond a mere listing of the number of machines or the production capacity and ask questions about the nature of these resources such as age, condition, capability, and location of each resource.

(ii) *Human resources.* The analysis of human resources must examine a number of relevant questions. An assessment of the number and types of different skills within an organisation is clearly important but other factors such as the adaptability of human resources must not be overlooked. For example, if a company is likely to face a period of difficulty or retrenchment it is important to know how able the people are to cope with a situation where some of the traditional boundaries and demarcation lines will have to change to ensure economic survival. As with physical resources the location of key human resources could be important. A multinational company may be concerned that all its skilled operatives are in high wage countries making it difficult to compete on world markets.

(iii) *Systems.* A company is far more than a random collection of machines, money and people. These resources are of no value unless organised into a *system* which ensures that the necessary outputs such as a good quality product, are achieved. A resource audit must therefore assess the quality of a company's systems. This would include production, financial, personnel, marketing and general management planning, control and information systems. In certain instances these could be critically important resources. Banks dealing in fast-moving foreign currency speculation rely on these systems; companies manufacturing to and selling from stock need better control systems than those manufacturing to order. These issues will be discussed more fully in Parts III and IV.

(iv) *Intangibles.* A great mistake which can be made in a resource analysis is to overlook the importance of intangible resources. There should be no doubt that these intangibles have a value since when businesses are sold part of that business' value would be 'goodwill'. Illustration 14 makes

---

ILLUSTRATION 14

The Thomas Cook Reputation

- 'Thomas Cook' is such a well established name the world over that it proved to be an invaluable resource when the company was sold to the private sector in 1972.

From the end of World War II up until 1972, Thomas Cook was owned by the British Government. Throughout that time, it had stayed rigidly in the two activities in which it had operated over its 130 years history, namely *travel* (that is, commission on sales of rail and air tickets, and its own somewhat up-market but old-fashioned tours) and *banking* (that is, sales of foreign currency and travellers' cheques). Although this formula had been successful in establishing the Thomas Cook name across the globe from the Victorian era right up to World War II, what Cooks had failed to cater for was the huge demand generated by growing affluence from the late 1950s onwards. The pioneers in this market were newcomers such as Horizon, Clarksons and Thomson. In a similar vein, Cooks' dominance of the travellers' cheques market had also been long overtaken by American Express who had built their reputation on the strength of the dollar and also on the presence of US forces around the world. When the Conservative government issued a prospectus for the sale of Cooks at the end of 1971, it showed how profits had fallen from over £2 million in 1965 to around £200,000 for that year end. Indeed, Cooks' management systems, accounting practices and planning processes were so ossified that no one could say with any certainty where the profit had come from, or therefore, how it could be protected in the future, let alone increased.

Despite the overwhelming presence of this downward spiral, when the bidding opened for Cooks the two interested consortia: Barclays, Grand Met, the State Airlines, and the Midlands Bank or Trust Houses Forte, and the Automobile Association, pushed the bidding up first from £6m to £8m, £15m and finally £22m. The banks naturally had an interest in the foreign exchange and travellers' cheques business as well as the pre-payments on holidays and travel, but the undoubted prop behind all this was the Thomas Cook name. Stronger abroad than at home, the name of Thomas Cook had achieved worldwide recognition and was of inestimable value in an industry like travel where so much depends on good faith and their acceptability of travellers' cheques around the world.

With a core resource as stable as this, Thomas Cook was given a new lease of life to demonstrate how good direction of existing resources might exploit the potential of the growing travel industry.

Source: Management Today, October 1978, p.98.

---

this point. In some businesses, particularly services such as solicitors, retail shops, the catering industry, goodwill could represent the major asset of the company and may result from brand-names, good contacts, company image or many other sources.

Before concluding the discussion of the resource audit, it is important to note that the level of detail needed in such an audit is likely to vary depending on 'who' within an organisation is undertaking the audit. For example, in a large, divisionalised multinational corporation the main board's perspective will differ from that of divisional managers which, in turn, will be different from the management of the individual companies within that division, and so on.

4.2.2 Resource Utilisation

To gain a better understanding of the way the resources have influenced company policy it is necessary to analyse the way that the company's resources have been utilised. It may be that clues to exceptionally good or bad performance lie in this area. To a large extent this is a more detailed analysis of the 'systems of organisation' referred to in the resource audit since these systems will be the major influence on how well a company's resources have been utilised. In other words it is an assessment of how *efficiently* resources have been utilised.

However, care must be taken not to overlook the fact that poor utilisation of resources may have occurred for other reasons; in particular, they may not have been used *effectively*. Certain resources may have been used in totally inappropriate ways; a high capacity cinema may be used to show 'specialist' films; a continuous flow production line may have been processing small batches. In these cases there is a *mismatch* between the resource and the job it is expected to do. For clarity the distinction between these two measures of *efficiency* and *effectiveness* is summarised here:

Efficiency is to do with how well resources have been utilised irrespective of the purpose for which they were deployed.

Effectiveness is to do with whether the resources have been deployed in the best possible way.

Figure 4.3 identifies some useful measures of efficiency and effectiveness against which the utilisation of an organisation's various resources can be assessed.

(i) Assessing Efficiency
There are a number of different measures of efficiency in resources analysis:

* *Profitability* is a broad measure of efficiency for commercial organisations, particularly if it is related to the amount of capital being used to run the business. Other financial measures are concerned with the utilisation of specific resources contributing to this overall picture (e.g. stock turnover, debtors' turnover).

* *Labour productivity* is a measure of how efficiently the human resources are being used. To some extent it combines an assessment of both efficiency and effectiveness since poor allocation of people to jobs

Resource area	Efficiency	Effectiveness
Physical resources		
● Buildings	Capacity fill	Match between production/ marketing resources and nature of work
● Plant & machinery	Capacity fill, unit costs Job design, layout, materials flow	
● Financial	Profitability, use of working capital	Capital structure
● Materials	Yield	Suitability of materials
● Products	Damage (e.g. in transit)	Match between product and market need
● Marketing and distribution	Sales per area Sales per outlet	Choice of channels Choice of advertising method
Human resources	Labour productivity Relative size of departments	Allocation of jobs to people Duplication of effort
Intangibles	N/A	Exploitation of image, brand name, market information, research knowledge, etc. Consumer complaints level

Figure 4.3   *Some measures of resource utilisation.*

(effectiveness) would also result in low productivity. Care needs to be taken in interpreting productivity data since under-utilisation of human resources may be due to other factors such as poor machinery or production systems. Nevertheless, productivity measurements may help managers to identify necessary changes in the way that resources are used.

*   *Yield* can be a very important measure of efficiency in industries where raw materials or energy are a major element of cost. The efficiency of the cutting department in a clothes manufacturing company will be assessed in this way and could determine the cost competitiveness of the company.

*   *Capacity fill* would be viewed as a prime measure of efficiency for organisations whose major cost is overheads. This is particularly important in many service industries where there is often no extra cost attached to satisfying additional customers such as a football club or a dance hall. In some cases the utilisation of this resource may become central to the company's strategy and its ability to survive. Several football clubs are considering the sharing of grounds or the attraction of additional uses such as Rugby League as a means of increasing the efficient use of that resource.

*   *Working capital* utilisation can reveal much about the way in which the financial resources are used strategically. An assessment need to be made of how well the company has managed to achieve an appropriate balance between the *risk* it runs from operating at low levels of working capital and the inefficiency of having too much working capital.

*   *Production systems:* understanding the various aspects of a company's production system such as job design, layout and materials flow are important when assessing a company's efficiency in production terms. It may be found, for example, that excessive costs have been incurred through unnecessary handling and transportation of materials during manufacture or that the company could take advantage of new operational methods. A good example here was the growth of the 'fast-food' industry in the UK during the late 1970s and early 1980s, led by American based franchising companies like MacDonalds.

(ii)   Assessing Effectiveness
     A full understanding of a company's use of resources also requires an analysis of the *effectiveness* with which resources have been used. There are a number of different measures of effectiveness:

*   *Use of people:* there are many situations where a workforce may be used ineffectively. The skilled man may be assigned to unskilled work; the division of work within a sales team may be such that the poorest salesman has been given the toughest area; there may be an inappropriate division of responsibilities between senior managers.

*   *Use of capital:* an analysis of changes in a company's long-term funding (capital structure) may give useful insights. A company may be foregoing the opportunity of additional long-term funds (loans or share issues) and as a result finding difficulty in carrying out necessary investment programmes. Very often an analysis of capital structure would uncover the opposite situation, where a company may be too highly geared for the realities of the markets in which it is operating. Many companies have found that when general levels of profitability are low and interest rates high, as they were in the late 1970s, the conventional wisdom of using gearing to improve profitability has been impossible to achieve.

*   *Organisation structure:* the problems of structuring organisations is fully discussed in Chapter 10. It is sufficient here to point out that an inappropriate organisation structure can cause ineffectiveness due to an inability to respond to external stimuli, failure to coordinate activities or the handling of problems at inappropriate management levels.

* *Use of marketing and distribution resources:* the effectiveness with which a salesforce is being used can often be judged by assessing the volume of sales which each salesman produces. However, expenditure on other items like advertising or distribution may be more difficult to assess. Companies very often use rules of thumb, like percentage of turnover spent on advertising, or attempt more rigorous and expensive analysis such as advertising effectiveness research.[3]

* *Use of research knowledge:* the assessment of how effectively research knowledge is used is equally problematic. Tangible measures are available, such as the number of product and process changes developed internally or the competitive advantage which has been gained from technical improvements resulting in better quality or lower cost. Companies are increasingly trying to cope with their worries about their under-utilisation of the R&D resource by providing better links with the commercial function and improving monitoring and control arrangements. However, because of the long period of time needed before the real impact of new products or process changes can be properly assessed, this type of analysis tends to be very retrospective and not very helpful in understanding how well these R&D resources are being used today.

* *Use of production systems:* poor utilisation of resources may result from the choice of an inappropriate system of production. For example, a hotel may have designed its production systems to cope with the normal summer trade where individual families stay at the hotel. However, these systems are most ineffective in coping with large conferences used as 'fill-in' during the winter months.

* *Exploitation of intangible assets* such as image, brand name, or market information is another measure of effectiveness. The extent to which the image of celebrities such as footballers or TV personalities have been exploited since the 1960s is an excellent example of the effective use of an intangible asset.

4.2.3. Control of Resources

The last criterion against which a company's resource capability needs to be assessed is the extent to which the resources have been properly controlled. Figure 4.4 identifies some controls which should be investigated. There could be situations where good resources have been deployed in the right way and used efficiently, but still performance is poor as the resources are poorly controlled. The following are some of the more important aspects of resource control:

Resource area	Typical Controls to investigate
Physical resources	
• Buildings	Security, maintenance.
• Plant, machinery.	Production control Maintenance system.
• Financial	Costing system Budgets Investment appraisal
• Materials	Supplier control (quantity, quality and cost) Control of stock
• Products	Stock control Quality control Losses (e.g. theft)
Human resources	Control of key personnel Leadership Working agreements Control of outlets (e.g. distributors)
Intangibles	Control of image (e.g. public relations) Industrial relations climate Control of vital information

Figure 4.4   *Aspects of resource control.*

(i)   *Control of key personnel.* Sometimes certain individuals or departments behave in ways which are not conducive to the smooth functioning of the company as a whole. This can be a particular problem with creative and professional people within organisations who often have their own views on what their jobs should entail.

(ii)   *Costing.* This is an area where small, fast-growing, organisations often fall down. The management know what resources are needed to establish the company in the market and how to deploy those resources to good effect. However, they are often unaware of how their method of operating will influence costs and revenue and hence the profitability of the company. In other words they do not understand how they should exert control over their resources.

(iii)   *Quality of materials.* In certain industries the quality of the finished product is highly dependent on the quality of certain materials or components which are bought-in. A car will not function properly if its tyres, or battery, or carburettor are defective and all these items will normally be bought in their finished form from suppliers. Any difficulties which the car manufacturer experiences with customer complaints are traced back to the way in which control is exerted over these important supplies.

(iv) *Marketing outlets.* Many manufacturers can rightly be accused of failing to exert sufficient control over the way in which their outlets present and sell their goods. Retail outlets may sell 5000 to 10,000 different products including many products which are directly competitive with each other. Monitoring and controlling the marketing efforts of outlets is important, but often difficult.

(v) *Stock and production control.* On occasions a company's poor performance can be traced to poor control of stock or the system of production. A poor delivery record often results from ill-developed production control systems relying on high 'buffer' stocks between the various steps in production.

(vi) *Control of losses.* Most companies face the problem of losses, due for example, to theft. Retailers are particularly vulnerable in this respect and euphemistically refer to these losses as 'shrinkage'. Poor company performance may be attributable to lack of control in this area.

(vii) *Control of intangibles.* The company's ability to control its image through its public relations activities is one example. The industrial relations' record can indicate how well 'team spirit' or 'organisational culture' are controlled. In some cases the control of vital information which may be of commercial benefit to competitors would be particularly important to monitor.

The importance of control during the implementation of strategy will be given full consideration in Chapter 11. At this stage it is hoped that readers have recognised that in order to understand the *strategic* importance of a company's resources it is necessary to look at how resources are utilised and controlled as well as the intrinsic nature of those resources.

4.2.4 Financial Analysis

Financial analysis is used at all stages of resource analysis, and not only as part of the data base. It will be seen later in the chapter, for example, that the forecasting of the cash requirements of different activities will be an important measure of how well an organisation's resources are balanced (portfolio analysis). Equally, financial measures such as profitability, gearing or liquidity will be used to compare the performance of a company with its competitors as a means of analysing that company's resource position.

However, in order to perform these later analyses, it is essential that the data base contains an analysis of resources in financial terms. It should be stressed that this is not an analysis additional to those previously discussed

ILLUSTRATION 15

Tizer

• By identifying the important analyses of his company's strategic position, Tizer's managing director was able to identify those areas with the greatest strategic implications.

Tizer Ltd. was founded in 1933 as a manufacturer of soft drinks and by the late 1960s was operating twenty-one depots spread across the country, each of which combined both production and regional sales departments. The company's main products were two carbonated soft drinks, Tizer and Jusoda, each of which had become established household names.

Throughout the late 1960s, Tizer's profits began to show a marked decline, and in an attempt to discover the causes and turn round the operation, the company employed the services of Mr P. Quinn. He immediately perceived Tizer to be in a very challenging situation with some good assets, such as a well known brand name and plenty of cash, that could provide the foundation of a long-term recovery. The first task he set himself was to make a detailed study of available financial reports which helped him to expose and analyse some of Tizer's more fundamental problems - which he hoped would help him to isolate the key strategic areas of the company: 'You cannot accurately evaluate whether your financial resources are adequate for the job until you know what your commitments are going to be.....*one has got to have some criteria for assessment* before looking at the details'.

Quinn therefore set about defining the true nature of the company's business and relating his analysis to this. Since Tizer was a marketing-orientated business, he looked at what successful firms such as Coca Cola or Corona were doing that was giving them success and contrasting them with what small local competitors were doing that was causing them problems. It materialised that, although operating on a nationwide basis, Tizer was operating as a series of twenty or so local operators, rather than as a cohesive national company operating in a similar manner to Coca Cola or Corona. This being the core of Tizer's problems meant that even though the detailed financial analyses revealed a number of shortcomings such as sundry debts being allowed to increase in a period of decling sales, or the presence of high liquid assets which might have been more usefully deployed in reducing operating costs, these might not be of key importance in determining a recovery strategy. On the other hand, Quinn realised that in a light industry such as Tizer's, less capital per £1 of sales is required than in heavier industries. He thus concluded that: 'Tizer's £3 million turnover was not enough from a company with a net worth of £2.3 million - in this business £2.5 million should support at least £5 million and possibly as much as £10 million'.

Quinn therefore concluded that to improve Tizer's performance it was necessary to improve the company's turnover, and to do this marketing became the key area in the development of strategy.

Source: Tizer Case Study by J.M. Stopford and P. Edmonds, from J.M. Stopford et al., Cases in Strategic Management (Chichester, John Wiley: 1980).

(resource audit, utilisation, and control) but simply a means by which parts of these three analyses will be carried out. Financial ratio analysis can be very misleading if not used in the context of information about a company's resources.[4] Financial analysis is included as a separate section here merely for the sake of clarity and because many managers are uncertain about the contribution that financial analyses can make to understanding an organisation's strategic capability.

Financial ratio analysis[5] can be very useful. Figure 4.5 outlines how such an analysis can be done using published financial data. Essentially, it consists of a progressively more detailed look at the separate resources which the company can measure in financial terms and the build-up of profitability. It is important to remember three things about financial analysis as a means of resource analysis. Firstly, that the calculation of financial ratios has no value in itself, it is the *strategic implications* of that analysis which are important. Secondly, it is essential that the analyst can identify which ratios are critical to the situation in hand. For example, the rate of stock-turnover may be important to a high street store, net profit margins to a market-stall trader, or sales volume to a capital intensive manufacturer. Similarly, the key financial measures to monitor will change over time. For example, during the introduction of a new product the key factor may be *sales volume;* once established *profit/unit* might be most important whilst during decline *cash flow* may be the key factor as new replacements are being introduced. These points are highlighted in Illustration 15. Lastly, it should be remembered that the various financial measures identified in Fig. 4.5 are not independent of each other. For example, the level of sales is *not* independent of the amount of stock being carried by the company. A decision to reduce stock levels as a means of improving asset turnover may be unwise because sales revenue could be critically dependent on quick delivery from stock.

In addition to published financial data, the management would normally have access to additional financial information (such as cost data) which would help provide a fairly comprehensive analysis of many of the resource *utilisation* and *control* issues raised above.

Some authors have suggested how financial ratios can be used selectively to answer quite specific strategic questions. For example, Altman[6] developed a composite measure called his 'Z-factor' which purported to be a good predictor of imminent bankruptcy. An interesting review of the use of financial ratios for this purpose is given by Argenti.[7] Sutton[8] presents a model for assessing mergers based upon financial ratio analysis.

4.3 COMPARISONS

Having produced a sound data base, a resource analysis can proceed to use those data to move towards a better understanding of an organisation's

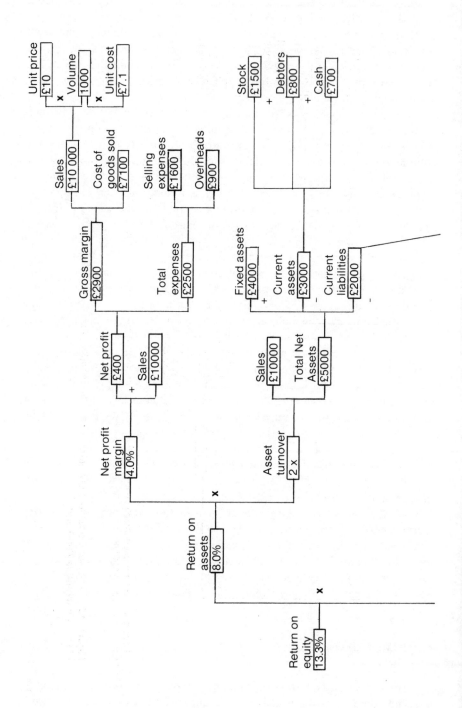

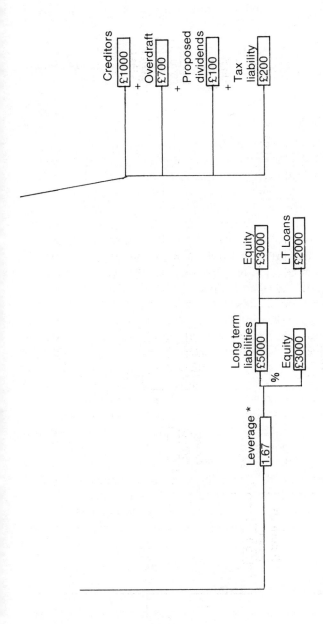

* Leverage is a term used mainly in the USA and is a way of calculating "gearing" which is commonly used in the UK.

Figure 4.5 *The relationship between various financial ratios — The Dupont Model; an example ('000 units).*

strategic capability. An important step in this process will be the comparison of the company's resource position with some useful yardsticks. In particular there are two important bases for comparison:

* identifying trends over time through an historical analysis:
* comparison with competitive or similar organisations (industry norm analysis).

4.3.1 Historical Analysis

An historical analysis looks at the deployment of the resources of a business in comparison with previous years. By doing this any significant changes in the overall levels of resources can be identified. Typically, measures like sales/capital ratio, sales/employees, will be used (as discussed earlier) as well as identifying any significant variations in the proportions of resources devoted to different activities. Although this seems like a fairly straight-forward analysis to perform, it can reveal trends which were not apparent to managers within the company. For example, a manufacturing company which owns its own retail outlets may find that because of the relatively more favourable climate for retailing there has been a slow drift of the business away from the traditional base of manufacturing. It is only when a comparison of the deployment of resources is made with the situation 5 years before that the significance of this slow drift becomes apparent. In some cases it has prompted companies to reassess where the major thrust of their business should be in the future. At Burton the tailors retailing became so dominant in the early 1970s that they chose to expand into other types of distribution (e.g. office furniture) and to view their manufacturing activities as a supplier to their shops.

Although, in some ways, managers are able to assess the resource position in a much less formal way - through the use of the recipe previously described -there are dangers in assuming that all the significant trends are fully understood. For example, the consequences of low investment over a number of years can be starkly revealed by using this historical comparison. It can be an enlightening experience to list the age of plant and equipment and compare the present position with that 5 and 10 years ago. Figure 4.6 outlines a series of questions which might be asked when undertaking an historical analysis of a company's resources.

4.3.2 Comparison with Industry Norms

An historical analysis such as Fig. 4.6 can normally be improved significantly by the additional comparison with similar factors analysed for the industry as a whole: it helps to put the company's resources and performance into perspective and reflects the fact that it is the relative position of a company which matters in determining its performance. The danger of industry norm analysis is that the company may overlook the fact that the whole industry is

	Now	2 years ago*	5 years ago	10 years ago
1. *Asset structure* What is % of total net assets in following categories†				
● fixed assets				
● current assets				
● buildings				
● plant/machinery				
● stocks				
● debtors				
2. *Liabilities structure*				
● capital structure (gearing)				
● creditors				
● short term loans				
3. *Resource deployment*				
(a) What % of assets are deployed in various parts of the business (man-ufacturing, retailing etc.)				
(b) What % of employees are used by each part				
4. *Nature of resources* What is average age of the assets †				
● buildings				
● plant/machinery				
● vehicles				
● people				

* The choice of time scale should vary with the type of company.
† This is not a definitive list but illustrates the type of breakdown needed.

Figure 4.6 *Historical analysis of a company's resources.*

performing badly and is losing out competitively to other countries with better resources or even other industries who can satisfy customers needs in different ways. Manchester United Football Club may have the best resources in the English Football League but may still be unable to prevent its players going to Germany or America or its spectators turning to other forms of entertainment in preference to football.

If an industry comparison is performed therefore, it is wise to make some assessment of how the company's resources compare with those in other countries and industries. This can often be done by looking at a few of the more important measures of resource utilisation. Figure 4.7 compares the *added value per employee* for a number of industries and also a number of different countries over the period 1973-1977.

Industry	Country and year											
	United Kingdom 1973	1975	1977	France 1973	1975	1977	Japan 1973	1975	1977	USA 1973	1975	1977
(A) Footwear and leathergoods	2.44	3.5	4.77	2.98	3.1	4.2	3.9	4.86	8.66	4.53	6.0	8.8
(B) Textiles	2.6	3.45	4.8	3.1	3.63	4.9	4.0	4.38	7.68	5.43	6.67	10.6
(C) Industrial chemicals	6.8	8.95	13.55	14.6	22.0	29.1	12.5	12.7	22.9	17.1	24.8	37.5

Sources: (1) *Yearbook of Industrial Statistics,* Vol.1 United Nations 1978.
(2) Average exchange rates from *CSO Financial Statistics,* Jan. 1978 as follows:
1973 £ = 10.9FF, 665 Yen, 2.45$
1975 £ = 9.5FF, 658 Yen, 2.22$
1977 £ = 8.6FF, 468 Yen, 1.75$

* 'Added-value' represents the difference between the revenue and the costs of materials and services bought-in by the organisation.

Figure 4.7 *A comparison of 'added-value* per employee' for a number of industries and countries 1973–1977 (£000/employee/annum).*

This analysis reveals some interesting issues regarding the utilisation of resources in these industries. For example, the more capital intensive industries, such as chemicals, achieve a higher added value for each employee than do craft industries such as leathergoods. Other conclusions from these data may have to be somewhat more tentative in the absence of further analysis. For example, it is tempting to conclude that the relative performance of UK industry, by this measure, is significantly worse than either Japan or the USA in all three industries. However, the different wage levels in these countries should be taken into account before this statement could be confirmed. If, for example, American wage levels in the footwear industry were double those in the UK, it might be expected that the added value should be appropriately higher. Therefore, when comparisons of this kind are being used in resource analysis it is important to consider whether or not a *fair* basis of comparison is being used.

Some authors[9] have given more emphasis to undertaking a parallel resource analysis of major competitors rather than trying to establish the 'norm' within the industry. In principle, this approach is of considerable value but keeping detailed profiles of competitors' resources may prove very difficult and expensive.

4.4 ASSESSING THE BALANCE OF RESOURCES

So far the discussion of resource analysis has treated individual resources as if they were independent of each other. Of course, this is not the case, so a resource analysis must also look at how well an organisation's resources are balanced as a whole. Three important aspects of such an analysis would be:

* The extent to which the various activities and resources of the organisation complement each other. *Portfolio analysis* is particularly useful in analysing this issue.
* The degree of balance within the *management team* in terms of the collection of individual skills and different personality types.
* Whether the *degree of flexibility* in the organisation's resources is appropriate for the level of uncertainty in the environment and the degree of risk the company is prepared to take.

4.4.1 Portfolio Analysis

Portfolio analysis is dealt with in the Appendix which might be usefully referred to at this stage. It can also contribute to strategic evaluation as will be seen in Chapter 8. At this stage, however, the discussion will focus on the contribution which product portfolio analysis can make to an understanding of a company's resource position. In this context it is particularly useful in as much as it raises some important questions about resources.
For example:

* Whether the mix of products, services or businesses is balanced across the company. The idea of a portfolio of interests emphasises the importance of having areas of activity which provide security and funds (Cash Cows) and others which provide for the future of the business (Stars and Question Marks).
* Drucker[10] has long emphasised the importance of reviewing activities to ensure that the appropriate amount of management, physical and financial resource is being allocated to the activities: that management is

not providing excessive resources to Dogs whilst starving Question Marks and thus reducing the chance of turning them into Stars.

* The BCG emphasise the importance of a sensible flow of funds within the firm (i.e., the extent to which the products or businesses in maturity provide funds for the growth areas) to ensure long-term security.

* Whether the balance of a company's products/markets matches resources available to the company. If a company is particularly good at development and design this may not match the analysis of product/market position which indicates a predominance of mature products in static markets. This may suggest the need to move funds from the development area into a greater emphasis on promotion or market development.

Chairman/team leader
Stable, dominant, extrovert
Concentrates on objectives
Does not originate ideas
Focuses people on what they
do best

Plant
Dominant, high IQ, introvert
A "scatterer of seeds"; originates
ideas
Misses out on detail
Thrustful but easily offended

Resource investigator
Stable, dominant, extrovert
Sociable
Contacts with outside world
Salesman/diplomat/liaison officer
Not original thinker

Shaper
Anxious, dominant, extrovert
Emotional,impulsive
Quick to challenge and respond to
challenge
Unites ideas, objectives and
possibilities
Competitive
Intolerant of wooliness and
vagueness

Company worker
Stable, controlled
Practical organiser
Can be inflexible but likely to
adapt to established systems
Not an innovator

Monitor evaluation
High IQ, stable, introvert
Measured analyses not innovation
Unambitious and lacking enthusiasm
Solid, dependable

Team worker
Stable, extrovert, low dominance
Concerned with individual's needs
Builds on others' ideas
Cools things down

Finisher
Anxious, introvert
Worries over what will go wrong
Permanent sense of urgency
Preoccupied with order
Concerned with 'following-through'

Source: R. M. Belbin, *Management Teams: Why They Succeed or Fail* (Heinemann: 1981) and R. M. Belbin *et al.,* 'Building Effective Management Teams', *Jnl of General Management,* Vol. 3, No. 3, 1976.

Figure 4.8   *Personality types for the effective team.*

4.4.2 Managerial Skills Analysis

A good management team must possess the necessary balance of skills needed to run the business successfully. Companies will need the capability to manage their production and marketing systems as well as controlling the financial and personnel aspects properly. Belbin[11] has looked at another aspect of the balance of managerial resources namely, the extent to which management teams contain an adequate balance of personality types to operate effectively as a team. All the individual managers in a company may be quite able yet as a whole they may lack certain skills or attitudes which would be quite valuable. Some of the more common personality types needed within an effective team are identified in Fig. 4.8.

4.4.3 Flexibility Analysis

Another issue which needs to be assessed is the extent to which an organisation's resources are flexible and adaptable. It is important to assess how far flexibility is balanced with the uncertainty faced by the organisation; flexibility has no strategic significance without an understanding of the uncertainty faced by the company. A manufacturing company facing a highly volatile raw materials market may choose to spread its sources of supply despite the fact that this could prove more costly. In contrast, it may be happy to have a highly inflexible, high volume throughput production system since it is trading in a stable market and this system of production ensures a highly competitive cost structure.

A flexibility analysis need be no more sophisticated than a simple listing of the major areas of uncertainty and the extent to which the company's resources are geared to cope with each of these. Figure 4.9 illustrates a typical analysis which seeks to compare the major areas of uncertainty faced by a company with the degree of flexibility in the related resource areas.

Major areas of uncertainty	Flexibility Required	Actual flexibility (at present)	Comments
1. Demand for product A	Capacity (possibility + 20%) or Stocks	Overtime could cover Low	Probably OK
2. Price of raw materials from present supplier	New suppliers New materials	None known at present Production system cannot cope	Problem area Seek information on new suppliers
3. Major customer may go bankrupt	Replacement customer	No leads	Sound out potential customers
4. Long term loan may not be renewed next year	Other sources of capital	Good image on stock market	New share issue looks favourable
5. Chief design engineer may retire	Design capability for products presently in development	Deputy not suitable Chief may agree to part-time 'consultancy' arrangement	Training and/or recruitment needs urgent attention

Figure 4.9 *Flexibility analysis — an example.*

ILLUSTRATION 16

● The first stage of an analysis of this type is to draw

Strengths	Weaknesses
Company Names - the names of Cadbury and Schweppes are well known and perceived by many as being synonymous with quality	**Saturated Confectionary Market** - together with well entrenched competitors makes expansion in this area very difficult
Effective Advertising - the company has a reputation for stylish, entertaining and persuasive advertising	**Pressure Groups** - various groups have managed to reverse management decisions
Low Gearing - the company's low level of gearing was a considerable strength during the period of high interest rates in the late 1970s	**Intensive Use of Plant** - results in difficulty in adjusting to meet seasonal fluctuations
Image in the City - a favourable image is a considerable strength should the company wish to raise further capital	**Heavy Promotion Costs** - are needed to compete with other well-known brands and with the supermarkets 'cut price' own brands
Broad and Balanced Product Range has enabled the company to survive the recession of the 1970s more successfully than its major UK competitor, Rowntrees	**Automation** - in the past there has been technical difficulty in introducing automated machinery

---

4.5 IDENTIFICATION OF KEY ISSUES

The last major aspect of resource analysis is the identification of the key issues arising from previous analyses. It is only at this stage of the analysis that a sensible assessment can be made of the major *strengths and weaknesses* of an organisation and the strategic importance of these. The resource analysis starts to be useful as a basis against which to judge future courses of action.

Illustration 16 shows the first stage of a strengths and weaknesses analysis. Such a list will need qualifying in several ways before it is useable:

*   Some indication must be made of the reasons why certain factors are

A Strengths/Weaknesses Analysis of Cadbury-Schweppes PLC

up a list of the organisation's strengths and weaknesses

Strengths	Weaknesses
Kenco Coffee - this is the fastest growing brand of ground coffee in the UK	**Plant Location** - capacity is concentrated in the UK where the markets are saturated while there is only a limited capability in the less developed markets
Control Over Resources - there is evidence that the group is very strong in this area. The acquisition of Jeyes in 1972 resulted in an 80% improvement in market share	**US Acquisitions** - there is a question mark over management's abiity to obtain a satisfactory return from the company's two US investments
Industrial Relations - have generally been good and have managed to negotiate flexible working practices	
Plant - the company has up-to-date, efficient, automated machinery	

Source: MBA research project at Aston University Management Centre.

identified as strengths and others as weaknesses; it may be concerned with the instrinsic nature of the resource, or resource utilisation or resource control. This is an important issue since a change of circumstances in the future may require a change of view as to whether a certain factor is still a weakness. For example, a company may have consistently shown high levels of labour turnover because it employed a large number of casual workers. This had been identified as a weakness. However, against a future situation of possible redundancies due to new technology, this position may be considered a strength since adjustment of the workforce size is achievable quickly by natural wastage.

*   The analysis should show the relative importance of the various factors listed. It may be fairly unimportant that the company is weak in design skills if the company already has a number of established products with long product life cycles and access to design consultancy when needed. However, it may be critically important to the success of the small entrepreneurial company that the managing director does not leave as his skills and knowledge are irreplaceable in the short-term.

*   A strengths and weaknesses analysis can be particularly powerful if it incorporates a comparison with competitors. This can be done using the concept of distinctive competence. *Distinctive competence* is concerned with identifying those particular strengths which give the company an edge over its competitors and those areas of particular weakness which are to be avoided. This may require a parallel analysis of competitors' resources as previously mentioned.[9] A supermarket's distinctive strength might be found in its layout, display and control systems which allow for high volume trading at minimal cost. Its particular weakness would be its inability to provide advice to customers. This analysis would help in assessing how viable a move into new product areas might be, such as DIY or furniture.

      This concept of distinctive competence links the area of strategic analysis with that of strategic choice. In Part III it will be explained that traditional approaches to strategic choice have tended to focus on identifying product/market opportunities and then viewing the company's resources as a constraint by assessing strengths and weaknesses in relation to these opportunities. The idea of distinctive competence provides a different focus for identifying and assessing future strategies since strategic choice can also be concerned with seeking out product/market areas which allow the company to capitalise on its distinctive competence. This issue is shown in Illustration 17 and will be given a much fuller consideration in Chapter 7.

    It should be noted that some authors have argued that it is more useful to develop resource analyses specifically designed to detect the onset of important strategic phases in a company's development. In particular, Argenti[12] has concentrated on the identification of companies which are likely to go bankrupt. Although others[13] have not given the same degree of emphasis on resources, there is general recognition that poor resources, badly managed, can be a significant contributing factor to company failure. Porter[14] identifies how the match between resources and the environment will differ in different stages of an industry's development, requiring a reappraisal of the strategic role of a company's resources over time.

ILLUSTRATION 17

The 'Real' Strength of Damart

● Although Damart achieved enormous success making and selling thermal underwear, its managing director believed that its real strength lay in its list of 10 million mail order addresses. Founded in 1966, Damart began to manufacture thermal underwear from a new textile, Thermolactyl, which had been developed in France. At first the company found it difficult to build up production capacity and to find retail outlets through which their products could be sold, since the general opinion in Great Britain was that thermal underwear was on its way out. As a result, Damart had no choice but to sell directly to the public. Response to advertisements in newspapers and magazines gave the company its first mailing lists, which were further built up through word-of-mouth recommendations until, in the early 1980s, Damart's computer files contained nearly 10 million addresses, or about 40 per cent of all households in Britain.

By 1981 turnover had increased to over £30 million, but since the company was owned by two Swiss businessmen who refused to take any dividend, a corporate rule dictated that all after-tax profits must be reinvested in the company. This presented Damart's managing director, David Kemp, with a problem in terms of what he might do with the company's retained earnings. Because of this, he made a crucial corporate decision: whilst Damart was in the thermal underwear business only because that is where it started and that was the market it had grown to dominate in reality, because that strength had been achieved through mail order, that must be the business it was really in.

As a result, Damart decided to use its spare resources in a diversification programme aimed at smoothing out the ups and downs of its highly seasonal sales of underwear. Consequently, the company launched two new catalogues - one selling every day clothes to the outsize women's market and the other aimed at the outdoor activity market for climbers, walkers, riders, joggers and even outdoor spectators. The mailing list for the former catalogue was derived from customers who had ordered larger sizes of underwear, and candidates for the latter catalogue were picked from customers ordering certain types of underwear favoured by climbers, walkers or skiers. Damart's longer term strategy was to produce a series of specialised catalogues which could be aimed at target markets which might be identified from their computer files of addresses.

Source: Financial Times, 9th February 1980, p.2.

4.6 SUMMARY

Resource analysis is an important means of assessing an organisation's *strategic capability* which in turn is necessary if sensible choices of future strategy are to be made. Traditionally, much of the discussion of resource analysis has centred around the idea of strengths and weaknesses. Although this is an important part of resource analysis it is not possible to gain a good understanding of an organisation's strategic capability without using a *variety* of analyses. These include analyses which create a data base, those which are primarily concerned with comparison and others which assess the extent to which an organisation's resources are balanced as a whole. Only after these analyses have been done can the identification of strengths and weaknesses contribute to the understanding of strategic capability.

Equally it should be remembered that strategic capability is just one part of the jigsaw and only makes sense in the context of parallel analyses of an organisation's environment, the values within and around the organisation and the range of options likely to be available in the future. These last two issues form the subject of the next three chapters of this book.

REFERENCES

1. There are a number of papers and standard texts which include traditional resource audits. For example, C.W. Hofer & D. Schendel *Strategy Formulation: Analytical Concepts* (West: 1978, p. 149) and R.B. Buchelle, 'How to Evaluate a Firm', *California Management Review,* Fall 1962, look at resource analysis within funcational areas, the latter, providing extensive checklists.
2. Chapters 4 and 8 in R.G. Murdick *et al., Business Policy: A Framework for Analysis* 2nd edn., (Grid: 1976) look at strategic analysis from a functional viewpoint and, as such, provide some useful guidelines and checklists for functional resource analysis.

   However, we suggest that readers who are unfamiliar with the details of resources in any functional area should consult one of the following texts:

   P. Kotler, *Marketing Management - Analysis Planning and Control,* 4th edn. (Prentice-Hall: 1980, pp. 652-657) for a systematic marketing audit. Kotler's 'audit' also reviews the market and competitive situation together with marketing objectives. He also tries to assess aspects of resource utilisation and control.

   A.G. Cowling, and C.J.B. Mailer, *Managing Human Resources* (Arnold: 1981). Chapter 11 is concerned with manpower planning and illustrates how an analysis of the manpower resources of a company can be undertaken.

   R. Wild, *Production and Operations Management* (Holt, Rinehart & Winston; 1979). Chapter 1 is concerned with the nature of operating systems and the role of operations management. Although the text does not specifically list an 'operating audit' the discussion gives an understanding of how to analyse and assess a company's operating system.

   J.M. Samuels, and F.M. Wilkes, *Management of Company Finance,* 3rd edn. (Nelson: 1980). Chapters 5, 7, 8 and 14 give a full picture of the sources and applications of companies' financial resources.

3. P. Kotler, *Marketing Management - Analysis, Planning & Control,* 4th edn. (Prentice-Hall: 1980). Pages 519-524 discuss approaches to analysing the effectiveness of advertising expenditure.

4. D. Beaven, 'What the Ratios Saw', *Management Today,* July1982, points out some pitfalls of using ratio analysis too blindly.

5. J. Sizer, *An Insight into Management Accounting,* 2nd edn. (Pitman: 1979). Chapter 4 deals in detail with the value of financial ratio analysis and how such an analysis can be done (with examples).

6. E.I. Altman, *Corporate Bankruptcy in America* (Heath Lexington: 1971) explains how his 'Z-factor' can be used to predict the failure of companies.

7. J. Argenti, *Corporate Collapse - Causes and Symptoms* (McGraw-Hill: 1976), is based on research into a number of major British companies (most notably Rolls-Royce prior to the 1971 collapse).

8. C.J. Sutton, *Economics and Corporate Strategy* (Cambridge University Press: 1980, Ch. 7).

9. M.E. Porter, *Competitive Strategy: Techniques for Analyzing Industries and Competitors* (Free Press: 1980, Ch.3).

10. In his book *Managing for Results* (Pan: 1973, pp.67-81), P. Drucker categorises companies' activities under eleven different descriptive headings which attempt to show how company resources can be mismatched with areas of opportunity; and how companies might think about remedying this.

11. R. M. Belbin *et al.,* 'Building Effective Management Teams', *Jnl of General Management,* Vol. 3, No. 3, 1976.

12. See reference 7 above.

13. J. Boswell, *The Rise and Decline of Small Firms* (Allen & Unwin: 1973); Merrett-Cyriax Associates, *Dynamics of Small Firms* (HMSO: 1971); and J. Collins, and J. Roberts, *Reasons Why Small Businesses Have Gone into Liquidation or Bankruptcy* (Bristol Polytechnic: 1971) all provide a useful contrast to Argenti's research by focusing on small companies. However, as a result they tend to emphasise the relationship between the owner and the manager as being of key importance which may, of course, be less so in larger companies.

14. Porter, reference 9, provides an interesting analysis of strategy in the various phases of an industry's development and in different circumstances. Part of this analysis inplies markedly different ways of viewing the strategic role of resources in companies.

RECOMMENDED KEY READINGS

*   An approach to carrying out a resource audit: R.B. Buchelle, 'How to Evaluate a Firm', *California Management Review,* Fall 1962.

*   To understand the value of financial analysis readers should refer to texts such as Chapter 6 in *An Insight into Management Accounting* by J. Sizer (Pitman: 1979, 3rd edn.). This should be read in conjunction with the cautionary words in 'What the Ratios Saw' by D. Beaven in *Management Today,* (July 1982).

*   Chapter 5 of *Corporate Strategy* by I. Ansoff (Penguin:1970), remains an important text for those involved in the 'capability profile' of an organisation. sation.

5

VALUES AND POWER

5.1 INTRODUCTION

In studying corporate strategy there is often a temptation to look for a neat and tidy way of formulating strategy. Such a method might, apparently, be found through the analysis of the organisation's environment (Chapter 3) and the extent to which the company's resources, or strategic capability (Chapter 4) are matched with the environment. This 'economic' analysis of organisations fails to recognise the important role which *people* play in the evolution of strategy as mentioned in Chapter 2. This chapter is concerned with analysing how people's *values* influence the strategies followed by organisations. This third ingredient of corporate strategy is, then, concerned with what people *want* organisations to do. In the discussion which follows, 'values' is taken to mean the aspirations, expectations, attitudes and personal philosophies which people hold. These issues have, in general, been given little consideration in the context of corporate strategy, although Thomas[1] does devote some time to many of the topics raised in this chapter.

The discussion which follows will attempt to illustrate how the values of individuals, both inside and outside an organisation, might succeed in influencing the strategies which that organisation follows. It is the purpose of this chapter to take readers beyond a simple, 'economic' understanding of this process to a position where they are able to analyse a company's position in a 'political' sense. Such a political analysis should be an important part of any strategic analysis.

To understand how the values of individuals can influence the strategy of large organisations, it helps to break the process down into various parts. These are illustrated in Fig. 5.1 which provides a framework for the chapter.

*   Organisations consist of a large number of individuals who represent a *wide variety of individual values.*
*   These individual values are shaped by a number of factors in the *organisation's environment* such as the values of society at large and the

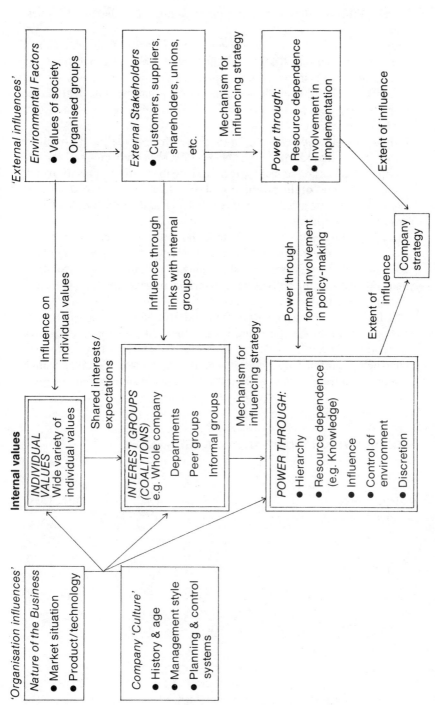

Figure 5.1 *How values influence company strategy.*

membership of external groups (family, church, professional bodies, etc).
* Individual values will also be influenced by the *nature of the business.* For example, the market situation and the type of products and technology.
* In addition, the history of the company and the management style and systems will all influence the attitude of individuals working within that organisation. These factors can be referred to collectively as the *culture* of the organisation.
* Individuals will *share interests* and values with others within the organisation. These shared interests may be concerned with undertaking the company's tasks and reflect the formal structure of the organisation (e.g. the shared values of the production staff). However, interest groups, or *coalitions,* will also arise for other reasons such as identification with peer groups (e.g. graduates).
* These internal coalitions are also influenced through their *contacts with outside stakeholders* - groups who have an interest in the operations of the company such as customers, shareholders or unions. For example, marketing departments will be pressurised by customers to represent their interests within the company.
* The fact that coalitions exist within and around companies and have strongly held values is of no significance unless these various groups have a mechanism to influence company strategies. *Power* is the mechanism by which this influence is achieved and this power can be derived from a number of different sources which will be discussed more fully below.

5.2 FACTORS WHICH SHAPE AND CHANGE VALUES

There are three major sources of influence on an individual's values; external influences, the nature of the business and the company culture. These will now be discussed separately and are summarised in Fig. 5.2.

5.2.1 External Influences

For the purposes of this discussion external influences can be classified under general influences which will be referred to as *values of society* and more specific influences exerted by *organised groups,* including groups who have a direct interest in the company's activities such as customers or unions (stakeholders).

(i)   *Values of society.* Attitudes to work, authority, equality and a whole range of other important issues are constantly shaped and changed by society at large. From the point of view of corporate strategy it is important to understand this process for two major reasons. Firstly,

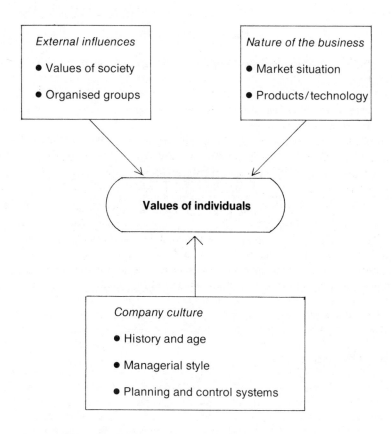

Figure 5.2   *Factors which shape and change values.*

values of society change and adjust over time and, therefore, policies which were acceptable twenty years ago may not be so today. Illustration 18 shows the impact that pressure groups representing different values can have on companies. There has been an increasing trend within the UK for the activities of companies to be constrained by legislation, public opinion, and the media. Secondly, companies which operate internationally have the added problem of coping with the very different standards and expectations of the various countries in which they operate.

Hofstede[2] has undertaken extensive research into how national culture influences employee motivation, management styles and organisational structures. He concludes that individual countries are markedly different from each other. For example, British culture appears to be far more tolerant of uncertainty than do many other societies - notable European examples being France, Spain and West Germany. Terry[3] has undertaken an interesting study of how English culture affects the performance of English managers. He concludes that the biggest single

ILLUSTRATION 18

The Influence of Pressure Groups on Industry

● Pressure groups' activities can lead to changes in policy by companies or legislation by government.
In May 1971 Schweppes found themselves at the centre of considerable controversy following their decision to market their mixer drinks in throwaway containers. After what was to them just one more corporate decision, Schweppes were suddenly faced with a massive campaign directed against the company by Friends of the Earth (FOE), the ecological pressure group.

When FOE decided to dump 1500 of the company's throwaway bottles outside Schweppes' headquarters, the event was seized upon by the media and instantly caught the public's imagination, launching a wave of concern that continued for years afterwards. The initial bottle-dumping campaign was followed up by FOE issuing a report to Schweppes' shareholders. Unwilling to just sit back and let things continue, Schweppes' first response was to launch a series of striking posters with slogans such as 'Don't let them Sch..... all over Britain'.

A second and bigger dump with simultaneous dumps organised on a regional basis at eight of Schweppes' depots finally persuaded the company to enter into discussion with FOE, which resulted in them issuing a joint appeal to the Government to take action.

Subsequent meetings between Government, industry and environmentalists led to the designation of a minister in the Department of the Environment to take responsibility for the recyling of waste and eventually a policy paper, 'War on Waste' was published in 1974. Continued campaigning by FOE led to the setting-up of Bottle Banks in 1977, despite strong initial protests from the packaging industry that recycling of glass was uneconomical.

Since their bottle-dumping days, FOE have launched subsequent campaigns:
Against the importing of whale products for use in the cosmetics and in the pet food industries in order to increase public awareness of the inhumane slaughter of a rare, endangered species and as a protest against the industries involved.
MPs were lobbied to press for a reduction in the level of lead in petrol which has been shown to cause brain damage in children, as well as to pollute the environment.
A Scottish consumer group withheld 20% of their electricity bills since that was the proportion of electricity generated by nuclear reactors in Scotland.
FOE have also commissioned various reports which have exposed official 'cover-ups'; in particular, they presented a case against oil companies' claims that leaded petrol brought about energy savings.

Source: Friends of the Earth Bulletins, 1981/82.

advantage of the English is that they do not panic when things get rough. However, against this he identifies insularity, chauvanism and a low regard for professionalism in business as significant weaknesses.

(ii)   *Organised groups.* Individuals very often have allegiances to other groups which are very influential on their values. These allegiances may be highly institutionalised and directly related to their working situation such as membership of trade unions, or may be more informal and unrelated such as membership of churches or political groups. The membership of professional bodies or institutions can be particularly important in organisations with a high proportion of professional staff. Engineering companies, research and development departments, accountancy sections and many public service departments, are all dominated by professional people who very often have a strong 'professional' view of their role which may not be in accord with the managerial view on how these people can be best used as a resource. At the corporate level the whole organisational ethos of the company may be influenced by its membership of a trade association or similar body. These bodies may exert influence informally but often seek to impose norms of behaviour on member companies through the development of 'codes of conduct'. There are many examples in UK industries such as the Association of British Travel Agents (ABTA), the National House Builders Registration Council (NHBRC) and the British Insurance Brokers Association (BIBA). This process also occurrs on an international scale, the best-known example being the Organisation of Petroleum Exporting Countries (OPEC).

5.2.2 Nature of the Business

There are a number of issues concerning the nature of a business which will also influence attitudes to company policy. These are much more specific to the particular circumstances of a company but are very often concerned with the market situation and the nature of the products/technology within the company.

(i)   *Market situation.* Different companies face quite different market conditions and any one company will face different conditions as time goes on. This is most clearly shown by the difference between recession and boom. As a result of this, the values of the people within the company will also change, often quite markedly, as external conditions change. Policy decisions which can be made in companies facing a highly competitive and depressed market would meet considerable resistance in other companies which face less stringent conditions. In the UK recession of the early 1980s companies, and even whole industries, were subjected to massive changes in scale, working practices, and product/ market strategy. Both the steel and motor car industries were reshaped in this way whilst attempts to follow similar changes in the coal mining industry were halted by strong union opposition.

People's values are also shaped by the position of the company in relation to the life cycle of its products and/or markets. People who have only known a company during a period of rapid growth have developed values and expectations which may be totally inappropriate when its products enter the stage of maturity.

(ii)   *Products/technology.* The influence of technology on values includes a consideration of the technology inherent in the product itself and the systems of production, distribution, etc. Technology influences values in two main ways. Firstly, technology may put a constraint on the way in which the company is able to operate and survive in a competitive environment and therefore dictate methods of operating and the tasks which people perform. The impact of production line working in the motor car industry on the attitudes and antagonisms which have built up within the motor companies has received much discussion.[4]

Secondly, technology changes the mix of skills required by companies which, in turn, may change company values. If a company has developed for a long time with little outside influence , its thinking and values may become very introspective. A change in technology may necessitate the company 'buying-in' outside help and, as a result, introducing new values to the company which can have a profound influence on the way the company views its future policy.

In addition to these two aspects of technology there are those[5] who would question whether or not new technology is necessarily beneficial. In fact, groups like Friends of the Earth actively lobby government and companies on this issue, as was shown in Illustration 18.

5.2.3 Company Culture

There are factors within companies which shape a company's culture and are very influential on the values of individuals within that company. This culture arises from a number of sources such as the history of the company and its systems of management.

(i)   *History and age of the company.* An individual's values will develop and change slowly over time as a result of working in an organisation. Every organisation's history is an important influence on the way that individuals view that organisation as a whole. Thus, the values held by people within an organisation whose senior management have a reputation for being progressive, participative and outward-looking, will be very different from another organisation in the same industry where management has always been parochial, secretive, and discouraged new ideas. History can often be a very considerable problem when attempting to implement strategy, as will be seen in Chapters 10 and 11. A good example was the difficulty faced in introducing new technology into Fleet Street newspapers in the late 1970s whilst many of their provincial counterparts had made the transition some years before.

Stinchcombe[6] found in his research that the way companies were organised and managed bore a strong relationship to the era in which that particular industry had its foundations. So, for example, the pre-industrial revolution industries, such as farming or construction, still retain many of the values associated with craft industries despite modern methods of operation.

(ii) *Management style.* Managers of companies which have a highly special-ised product/market strategy and have always developed new ventures internally, often resist efforts to spread the company's activities more widely. In contrast, managers who have grown up in a company which has developed by a continued process of acquiring diverse companies, are often very tolerant to change. The values of these managers could be very important in terms of shaping new policies.

Miles and Snow,[7] whose findings were introduced in Chapter 2, have shown how managerial values and organisational culture may affect a company's approach to policy-making. They categorise organisations into three basic types in terms of how they behave strategically (see Fig. 5.3).

They suggest that companies behave in these ways because of the philosophies and values of the managers who run them. So, for example, the 'defender' manager who values stability seeks out a market niche that is likely to provide this and orders the company's affairs in such a way that he protects it. In contrast, 'prospectors' welcome change and new

Organisation type	Dominant objectives	Characteristics of policy-making		
		Preferred strategies	Planning and control systems	
1. Defenders	Desire for a secure and stable niche in market	Specialisation; cost-efficient production; marketing emphasises price and service to defend current business; tendency to vertical integration	Centralised, detailed control. Emphasis on cost efficiency. Extensive use of formal planning	
2. Prospectors	Location and exploitation of new product and market opportunities	Growth through product and market development (often in spurts). Constant monitoring of environmental change. Multiple technologies	Emphasis on flexibility, decentralised control, use of *ad hoc* measurements	
3. Analysers	Desire to match new ventures to present shape of business	Steady growth through market penetration. Exploitation of applied research. Followers in the market	Very complicated. Coordinating roles between functions (e.g. product managers). Intensive planning.	

Figure 5.3 *Different types of organisation culture and their influences on policy-making (after R. E. Miles and C. C. Snow, Organizational Strategy, Structure and Process, McGraw-Hill, 1978).*

ECS–E*

ILLUSTRATION 19

Values and the Environment

● Two Public Sector institutions interact differently with the environment because of their contrasting underlying philosophies.

The role of the Pioneer Community Hospital in the United States was described by its Chief Administrator as:

'... a high quality community institution that provides excellent basic health care but refers out cases that are esoteric, highly complex, or require sophisticated medical machinery'.

Similarly, the mission of the Riverside Hospital in California was described by its Chief Administrator as:

'... promoting the health and well-being of the people of the Valley by providing community-orientated primary medicine, either directly or by acting as a catalyst for the development of independently-based health services'.

Although both were in essentially the same business, the two hospitals perceived their environments in different ways, which resulted in contrasts in their approaches to strategy. Pioneer could be categorised as a 'defender' - aiming to do better in its own stable range of operations, and Riverside a 'prospector' - always seeking out new areas of interest.

Pioneer had always emphasised stability which was characterised by a lack of growth in either the number of patient beds or in the scope of medical services offered. This approach had allowed Pioneer to improve efficiency and reduce operating costs, allowing them to generate an operating surplus over the five years leading up to 1975. Riverside, on the other hand, had placed its priority in identifying new needs and developing innovative systems - this led to problems in controlling costs.

Internal change at the Pioneer hospital had, in general, been orientated towards 'fine tuning' for increased efficiency which has resulted in a low turnover of administrative personnel whereas Riverside, with its ongoing organisational change, had found it difficult to achieve staffing efficiency.

Riverside prided itself in coping with environmental changes through its belief that 'given sufficient warning, we can adapt to almost anything'. Pioneer's policy for responding to external change has been 'to wait until it's cast in concrete and then do as little as possible. We don't want to be first - it's a waste of time and money in many cases. We just respond as needed'.

Source: Organizational Strategy, Structure and Process, R.E. Miles and C.C. Snow (McGraw-Hill: 1978).

ventures despite the risks they might involve. So values are likely to influence the purpose and scope of policy and all aspects of operations from choice of product/market to structure, control systems and rewards given to individuals. Illustration 19 shows the contrast between two hospitals with sharply contrasting values.

It is also important to realise that management style within a company can become self-perpetuating since managers in positions of authority very often build a team around them of other similar-minded individuals. This can be a very dangerous situation should the environment change significantly.

(iii) *Planning and control.* Chapter 11 will be concerned with how planning and control systems influence the ability of companies to implement policy successfully (or otherwise). However, at this stage it should be recognised that the way in which planning and control are exercised within a company will have an important influence on the attitudes of individuals towards company policy. In some extreme cases individuals or departments are expected to contribute enthusiastically to a policy change whilst at the same time the system of control is penalising them for doing so.

5.3 COALITIONS

Despite this wide variety of influences, individuals may share many values with others (as a group). A group ethos often develops in one part of an organisation which is quite different from the ethos of another part. This may occur between different departments, different geographical locations, different levels in the hierarchy or different age groups, but any one individual may, of course, 'belong' to more than one of these groups. These groups of common interest are usually referred to as *coalitions.* In order to obtain any influence in decision-making, individuals will need to identify themselves with the aims and ideals of these coalitions. Political parties, of course, represent this process in operation quite clearly, but readers need to recognise that an identical process occurs in virtually every organisation. Notwithstanding these sharp divisions in group values (ethos), the company as a whole (as a coalition) will normally have an ethos which is quite distinguishable from other companies in the same industry and this will be an important influence on policy. In 1981 the shareholders of the Savoy Hotel in London resisted increasingly generous offers to be bought out by Trust House Forte since selling out to what they considered to be a 'down-market' company offended their sense of values as shown in Illustration 20.

This section of the chapter will look at why coalitions arise within organisations, how people and groups outside organisations can influence company decisions, and the way in which these issues can be systematically

---

ILLUSTRATION 20

The Savoy Hotel - Last Bastion of Gracious Living?

- When Sir Charles Forte offered to rescue the Savoy Hotel from its financial difficulties, his takeover bid was met with strong resistance.

The Savoy Hotel in London was once described by one of its shareholders as exuding: 'A sense of history, a feeling that in a tinfoil and plastic world, there was still one last bastion of truly gracious living, a hotel where on could kick one's shoes off, look around, and say: 'Hey, this place is pretty nice'.

For several years leading up to 1980, however, the Savoy had suffered a series of losses which had left it vulnerable to takeover bids. As 'an obvious commercial move' in 1981 Sir Charles Forte made a bid of £58 million to add the Savoy Group to the Trust House Forte chain of restaurants, cafes and hotels. The move was met with indignation from all who were associated with that noble clutch of hotels which had become synonymous with distinction and good tasts. The reason for their resistance to Sir Charles' offer of salvation was not so much on the grounds of commercial wisdom, however, but at the thought of the style and tradition of such a sacred institution being subjected to the rule of the King of the Motorway cafe.

As the squeals of protest echoed around him, Sir Charles retained an air of nonchalance: 'Why are people so excited because I am interested in the Savoy? Do they think I am going to fill the foyer with Coca Cola machines or something?'

Nevertheless, the underlying distress behind the protests were succinctly expressed by the Savoy management's public statement:

'On professional grounds we do not think a vast combine like Trusthouse Forte, which among other things, runs service stations on the main arterial roads, and airport catering, is qualified to run hotels of the quality of the Savoy'.

By mid-1981 the THF offer for the Savoy Group had lapsed, but despite the Savoy's recommendation not to accept the offer, THF had still managed to acquire 61.9% of the Savoy's Equity and a 38.6% voting share.

Source: Sunday Times, 22nd March 1981, p.6.

---

analysed as part of a strategic analysis. To gain a full understanding of how 'value structures' evolve in organisations and their strategic importance, it is necessary to turn to the work of organisation behaviour writers and researchers.[8]

5.3.1 Why Coalitions Arise

Coalitions can arise for a number of reasons, all of which may be present within an organisation at any time.

* *The complexity of an organisation's task* often requires the task to be divided between different groups of people. Such specialisation provides a basis for a potential conflict of values since specialised departments develop a narrow, specialist viewpoint. The production department may be very concerned with maintenance of product quality which is possibly incompatible with the marketing department's desire for more repeat business from customers, and lower prices.

Often the informal systems[9] of an organisation can form the basis of coalitions. People share values and allegiances which do not result from carrying out the company's tasks. For example, a group of graduates who joined a company at the same time may maintain strong links with each other.

* *Relationships with the environment* are important to company survival and therefore the company must, somehow, reconcile the often conflicting demands of suppliers, customers, trade unions, banks etc. This further reinforces the potential divisions of values described earlier. Not only have the marketing department an inherent desire for a lower priced product but they are constantly pressurised by their customers for such a product - often with the threat of placing their orders with competitors. Equally, the financial managers of the company may be pressurised by banks or shareholders. Both these cases show how outside relationships will tend to increase the diversity of values within the organisation.

Previous points in this section have viewed the 'value structures' in a static way. In practice, however, it is usually the case that coalitions arise as a result of specific events or issues. It may take an unexpected crisis such as loss of a major customer, liquidity crisis, or massive increases in raw materials costs to expose fully the extent of division or solidarity which exists within a company. Some organisations will respond to external threat by a grouping together to achieve the common aim of survival, whilst others may find themselves unable to bridge the gaps between their various parts and go under. Clearly this is an important issue to be diagnosed when assessing the strategic significance of the values which exist within a company.

5.3.2 External Coalitions

It has already been mentioned that there are a number of groups or coalitions external to a company which have a vested interest in what the company is doing. These groups are usually referred to as the other stakeholders and include customers, banks, trade unions, etc. Each will attempt to influence strategy, to a greater or lesser extent, through its links with internal groups or individuals as described previously. It is therefore of great importance that an analysis of how values influence strategy includes an assessment of the values held by these external coalitions. It is useful in discussing this issue to think about the concept of company image. This image determines how the company is viewed by its actual or potential suppliers, customers, shareholders etc. in relation to the values that those groups hold. This is an issue of considerable practical importance to strategy-makers in companies. The company's ability to obtain resources of money, supplies and manpower, and to sell its products profitably will be governed not only by the economic equations of profit and value for money but also by the image which the company projects to those with whom it trades. The strategy-makers must, therefore, be aware of and understand the values held by these groups and how they should respond to them. This rather intangible idea of image is a very important ingredient of the 'standing' of a company in its environment -an issue which was discussed in Chapter 3. Several examples are given in Illustration 21.

Precisely how influential these external values turn out to be in practice is largely determined by one of two processes (refer back to Fig. 5.1):

*   the extent of influence and power which external coalitions derive from links with internal individuals or groups (having a 'foot in the door');

*   the power these groups derive for other reasons such as resource dependence.

Both of these issues will receive a fuller consideration in the two sections which follow.

5.3.3 Identifying Coalitions

It is one thing to talk about coalitions and the way in which values influence a company's strategies, but it can often, in practice, be quite difficult to identify coalitions in a way which adds anything of value to a strategic analysis. There is always the danger of concentrating too heavily on the formal structure of an organisation as a basis for identifying coalitions since this can be the easiest place to look for the divisions in values mentioned previously. It is also essential to unearth the 'informal' coalitions and assess their importance.

Other problems in analysis are that individuals will tend to belong to more than one coalition and that coalitions will line up in different groupings depending on the issue in hand. So, for example, marketing and production departments could well be united in the face of proposals to drop certain product lines whilst being in fierce opposition regarding plans to buy-in several items in the product range. To repeat the earlier discussion, it is specific events which tend to trigger-off the formation of coalitions. To overcome this difficulty, the identification of coalitions for the purpose of strategic analysis might sensibly involve following two steps which will now be discussed.

(i)   *Identify the most important coalitions* within and around the organisa-
       tion and the relationships between them.

ILLUSTRATION 21

Image

- Image is capable of saying much more about a company than any of its products or services alone, and once established remains highly durable. The first really large organisations to emerge in the modern industrial and commercial world were the railways. Although all were in essentially the same business, each company intuitively developed its own image which stemmed from its own philosophy and needs. The identity of each of the British Railway Companies was clearly manifested in such things as their architecture, rolling stock, liveries and uniforms - even down to such things as the cutlery in their dining cars. The Midland line was one for comfort and speed, reflected in its rich, gaudy and ostentatious stations, whereas the Great Northern line, with an emphasis on technical advancement had more modest, simple, almost austere stations.

In many cases, a company's image is a direct reflection of its chief executive, as was seen with the late Colin Chapman's Lotus Cars, Laker Airways or Terence Conran's Habitat. The entrepreneurial flair behind Laker Airways and the image that stemmed from that flair was quite inseparable from Sir Freddie.

With older and bigger companies an historically cultivated image can be an asset as Marks and Spencer illustrates: there is an undoubted consistency not only in the way that the company perceives its environment, but also in the way that it is perceived by outsiders. With Marks and Spencers suppliers know what to supply and the type of standards that are expected; customers rely on the image and so the general conformity pervades throughout the company's service, technology, products and appearance serving as both an external and internal influence on company policy.

Image is not an asset, however, if it is not the identity with which the company wishes to be associated. An historical image may be very difficult to shake-off, as F. W. Woolworth discovered when it tried to shed its 'penny bazaar' image. Extensive marketing, new product lines, such as jewellery, even adopting the 'Woolco' name, failed to have the desired impact.

Some industries are seen as generally undesirable despite the fact that there is considerable demand for their products. Betting shops and sex shops often find it difficult to obtain premises to rent or buy, to attract good staff to work for them, and need to be careful in the way that their products are promoted. To a lesser extent the construction industry has suffered from a bad image with the public.

Other companies face a problem of image with their customers because of activities elsewhere in the company. UK companies with subsidiaries in South Africa are often sensitive to how criticisms of their overseas operations might reflect on the UK business.

Source: Management Today, April 1979, p.82.

Reed and Palmer[10] argue that the key to understanding the strategic importance of the values within a company is to be found in the relationship which exists between the various coalitions or interest groups in the company. They are careful to point out that their definition of coalitions would include the whole company, its various parts, and outside stakeholders. They identify three commonly occurring situations:

* *where the parts are more important than the whole* which is well illustrated by the case of many local authorities where people tend to owe more allegiance to the individual committees (service areas) such as recreation, housing or education, than they do to the corporate entity. This can make inter-departmental ventures quite difficult, e.g. use of sports centres by schools;

* *where the whole is more important than the parts* which is often seen in family companies where the maintenance of a strong family identity is often achieved at the expense of the efficient running of the various parts of the company;

* *where external influences are very important,* best typified by many voluntary organisations whose members have strong demands on their time from other sources (home and work), or in organisations in which professionals such as doctors, lawyers or scientists, play an important part and see the maintenance of external codes of practice or standards as of overriding importance.[11] The way in which the organisation operates is dominated by these outside influences.

Figure 5.4 illustrates a systematic method of mapping out the coalitions and their inter-relationships. Each box in the table should be completed to indicate the extent to which the various groups, in general, hold similar or opposing sets of values. In this particular example a number of important observations can be made at this stage in the analysis. For example: the company as a whole seems to have a high degree of commitment to corporate values despite the obvious diversities which exist between the various coalitions. The score of 6+ and 1- in the Total column indicates this. Also, the marketing department (internally) and a major supplier A (externally) seem to have values and aspirations which are shared by a number of the coalitions in the analysis, although there are notable opponents in both cases. And notably the Lincoln plant seems particularly isolated; later analysis will prove this to be an important observation.

The benefit of this type of simple analysis is that it forces the analyst to be explicit about the relationships existing within the company. The analysis shown in Fig. 5.4 indicates a high degree of commitment to corporate values. It follows that a manager would therefore be happier pursuing policies that required a high level of commitment from the various parts of the company.

		A	B (internal coalitions)					C (external stakeholders)			Total
		1 Whole company	1	2	3	4	5	1	2	3	
A	Whole company		+	+	+	−	+	+	+	0	6+ / 1−
B	1 Marketing	+		−	−	0	+	+	+	+	5+ / 2−
	2 Production	+	−		+	0	−	+	−	0	3+ / 3−
	3 Nottingham plant	+	−	+		−	−	+	0	0	3+ / 3−
	4 Lincoln plant	0	0	0	−		0	−	−	0	0+ / 3−
	5 Graduates	+	+	−	−	0		0	0	0	2+ / 2−
C	1 Supplier A	+	+	+	+	−	+		−	−	5+ / 3−
	2 Customer X	+	0	−	−	0	−	−		−	1+ / 5−
	3 Shareholdr. M	−	+	0	0	0	0	0	0		1+ / 1−

Note: + = shared values; — = opposing values ; 0 = neutral.

Figure 5.4 *Identifying coalitions (interest groups) in and around a company.*

However, there are also dangers with an analysis of this kind. It is a statement of the value structure in relation to the present situation and policies and so may overlook the emergence of new coalitions and/or the redefining of relationships between interest groups both of which might occur in different circumstances. It is for this reason that the second part of the analysis needs to be undertaken.

(ii) Speculate on the *degree of unity or diversity* between these various groups if faced with a number of possible future events (in this respect it is also a tool of strategic evaluation).

To some extent this process could be viewed as strategic evaluation since it is necessary to speculate on how the coalitions would react to specific future changes. Nevertheless, it is also part of strategic analysis as this speculation may well uncover potential alliances or rifts which will be significant in the process of strategic choice.

Pfeffer[12] provides a very interesting example of how this step in the analysis can be performed. Figure 5.5 shows an analysis of how the various interest groups of Figure 5.4 might react to possible future events or strategies. There are several points which can be gleaned from this analysis:

* There will always be some events over which the majority of interest groups can unite. Such solidarity tends to occur during the early stages of development of new companies or when survival is threatened by such events as a possible takeover by a major competitor.

Possible changes	A Whole company	B (internal coalitions) 1 Market-Dept	2 Productn.	3 Notts plant	4 Lincoln plant	5 Grads.	6 Clerical staff	C (external stakeholders) 1 Suppl A	2 Cust. X	3 Shr. hdr. M	4 Local comm.
1.Sell out to competitor	-	-	-	-	-	-	-	0	-	0	-
2. Introduce computerised systems	+	+	?	+	0	+	-	0	+	+	0
3. Close Lincoln plant	?	+	-	+	-	0	0	0	+	0	-
4. Develop new EEC markets	?	?	-	+	-	0	0	+	-	+	0
5. Sub-contract production	?	+	-	-	-	0	0	-	0	-	-

Note: + = support; 0 = neutral; - = oppose; ? = divided opinion.

Figure 5.5 *The attitudes of various 'interest groups' towards possible future changes.*

* New interest groups may become important in certain of the situations envisaged. For example, the proposal to close the Lincoln plant would meet resistance not only from the employees there but also from the local support which they were able to muster. Equally, computerisation would be resisted by clerical staff who had hitherto never been viewed as a cohesive group.

* In some cases there would be *divided views* within one of the coalitions. For example, the export section of the marketing department might be delighted by plans to expand sales in the EEC but not so their UK counterparts. Thus these would need to be viewed as separate interest groups in such circumstances.

* At this stage it is important to identify potential alliances between interest groups regarding any of these future alternatives. In this example a particularly significant observation is that the possibility of closing the Lincoln plant could well see an alliance between the Nottingham plant and the marketing department with strong support from the major customer X. In any such move the Lincoln plant could only rely on production staff and local community action; others seem to be broadly indifferent.

This section has been concerned with 'mapping-out' the way in which values are structured within and around any organisation. In practice such a map is only useful alongside a parallel analysis of the power which individuals or groups possess. Power is the mechanism by which values are able to influence policy, and in most organisations power will be unequally shared between the various coalitions or stakeholders. In other words, policy-making tends to be dominated by one of the stakeholders, usually by the management of the company.[13]

5.4 POWER

To understand the importance of power in relation to corporate strategy, it is helpful to look at sources of power within organisations and for external stakeholders, and methods of assessing that power. Before proceeding it is necessary to understand what is meant by power in the way that it is used in this chapter.[14] In particular, a distinction needs to be drawn between the power which people or groups apparently have as a result of their position within the organisation as against the power they actually possess due to other reasons. For the purposes of strategic analysis, power is best understood as *the extent to which individuals or groups are able to persuade, induce or coerce others into following certain courses of action.* This is the mechanism by which one set of values will dominate policy-making or seek compromise with others. An analysis of power must, therefore, begin by an assessment of the sources of power.

5.4.1 Sources of Power Within Organisations

Power within companies can be derived in a variety of ways, any of which may provide an avenue whereby the values of an individual or group may influence company policy. The following are the normally recognised sources of power (see Fig. 5.6).

(i)   *Hierarchy* provides people with formal power over others and is one method by which senior managers will influence policy. In particular, if strategic decision-making is confined to top management this can give them considerable power. However, it is important to remember that this type of power has a very limited effect if used in isolation. Many industrial disputes illustrate the impotence of management if they rely only on formal power.

(ii) *Influence* can be an important source of power and may arise from personal qualities (the charismatic leader) or because a high level of *consensus* exists within the group or company (i.e., people are willing to support the prevailing viewpoint). It is important to recognise, however,

A. Within organisations	B. For external stakeholders
1. Hierarchy (formal power) e.g. autocratic decision-making	1. Control of strategic resources e.g. materials, labour, money
2. Influence (informal power) e.g. charismatic leadership	2. Involvement in strategic implementation e.g. distribution outlets, agents
3. Control of strategic resources e.g. strategic products (coal)	3. Possession of knowledge (skills) e.g. subcontractors
4. Possession of knowledge/skills e.g. computer specialists	4. Through internal links e.g. informal influence
5. Control of the environment e.g. negotiating skills	
6. Involvement in strategic implementation e.g. by exercising discretion	

Figure 5.6 *Sources of power.*

that the extent to which an individual or group can use their influence is determined by a number of other factors. For example, in 1982 Joe Gormley, then president of the National Union of Mineworkers, was accused of 'unfairly' influencing the miners' vote on strike action by making public statements in the media. This illustrates how access to channels of communication are an essential requirement. In many situations prior commitments to principles or specific courses of action can give individuals influence. Some of these principles may be quite central to the organisation's mission. For example, the 'no-redundancy' policy of many Labour-controlled local authorities can be used by individuals or groups within that authority to challenge courses of action proposed by senior management (such as productivity deals).

(iii) *Control of strategic resources* is a major source of power within companies. It should be remembered that the relative importance of various resources will change over time and hence power derived in this way can show dramatic changes. The power of organised labour is most potent when demand for output is high and labour supply short. The decline in the position of car workers in the wages-league between 1970 and 1980 is evidence of the erosion of this source of power. In the case of the coal industry, the union's power arose from the *strategic nature of the product.* Within any one company the extent to which the various departments are seen as powerful will vary with the company's circumstances. Design or R&D departments may be powerful in companies developing new products or processes, whereas marketing personnel may dominate companies which are primarily concerned with developing new markets.

(iv) *Knowledge/skills:* the logical extension of the previous point is that individuals can derive power from their specialist knowledge or skills. Certain individuals may be viewed as irreplaceable to the company, and some will jealously guard this privileged position by creating a mystique around their particular job. This can be a risky personal strategy since others in the organisation may be spurred to acquire these skills or to devise methods of bypassing them. The power of the organisation's computer specialist is very much threatened by the advent of micro-computers which provide others within the organisation with a means of bypassing those specialists.

(v) *Control of the environment:* most employees are conscious of the fact that events in the company's environment are likely to influence company performance. However, some groups will have significantly more knowledge of, contact with, and influence over the environment than others. This can become a source of power within the company. It is probably for this reason that financial and marketing managers have traditionally been seen as dominant in policy determination whilst production managers have taken a back seat.[15] This source of power becomes most important when the environment is hostile or unpredictable. Then most of the factions will unite behind those who are seen to be best able to protect the company, despite the fact that the 'medicine' which might be doled out might represent a denial of many of their values. Many would argue that Sir Michael Edwardes derived much of his power within British Leyland in this way.

(vi) *Exercising discretion:* this is a most significant source of power within all organisations which is very often overlooked. Individuals derive power because they are involved in the decision processes of the company by the very nature of their jobs. The execution of strategy, by its very complexity, cannot be controlled in all its minutest detail by one person or group and hence many other people within the company will need to interpret and execute particular parts of that policy and, in doing so, will use their own personal discretion. This is a major source of power for middle-management in organisations. An example will illustrate the point.

   A local authority council had publicly committed itself to 'improving the level of care in the community', which the Social Services Committee had interpreted as increasing the number of needy cases which they would seek out and cater for. They identified the elderly as a priority category. The senior managers of the Social Services department then had to use their discretion as to how their resources could be best utilised to achieve this result. Their particular problem lay in defining what represented needy. Should they give preference to those who were needy in a financial sense, or those who were particularly infirm, or those who had no other source of support (e.g. family)? The senior managers decided that the major need was for those who were partially infirm, and instructed social workers to pay particular attention to that group. The social workers themselves needed to use discretion in the execution of this policy and would have varying priorities. For example, one social worker considered that those who were bed-ridden should receive priority whilst others were more concerned with the blind or mentally deficient.

Although this is a very simplistic example, it illustrates how the overall policy (improved care) became progressively refined by the groups and individuals responsible for executing policy,and through this process the values of these people were very influential on the final outcome. The extent to which discretion is allowed to influence policy is obviously related to the types of control systems within the organisation. These will be discussed in Chapter 11.

5.4.2 Sources of Power for External Stakeholders

As with internal groups, those outside the organisation may have a number of sources of power which help them influence the organisation's strategies. These are also summarised in Fig. 5.6.

(i)   *Resource dependence* is the most common source of power. For example, major suppliers, banks and shareholders all derive power from this source. The short-term survival of the company may be critically dependent on one or more of these stakeholders.

(ii) *Involvement in implementation* can be an important source of power for companies involved in the marketing of a manufacturer's product. In fact, one of the major changes since the 1960s in many industries has been the extent to which power has shifted from the manufacturing sector to the distribution sector. The greater knowledge that distribution companies have of trends in consumer tastes has allowed them to dictate terms to manufacturers rather than simply being outlets for goods designed and planned by manufacturing companies.

(iii) *Knowledge and skills* critical to the success of the company may be a source of power. A subcontractor for example, may derive power in this way.

(iv) *Internal links* can provide a route for external stakeholders to influence company strategy. This is related to the policy-making processes within the organisation. At one extreme a highly authoritarian organisation is likely to be hostile to any attempts by outside stakeholders to be formally involved in formulation of strategy, and therefore any influence on policy must be derived in other ways. In contrast, some organisations, e.g. some small cooperatives, actively seek to involve a wide variety of stakeholders in strategic decision-making. This issue of policy-making processes and their relationship to 'values' will be discussed separately in

Section 5.5 and will include a discussion of industrial democracy. In the context of this chapter, industrial democracy is usefully seen as being concerned with the extent to which stakeholders can be *formally* involved in policy-making.

5.4.3 Methods of Assessing Power

The discussion in the previous subsection should have indicated how difficult it is to get a clear picture of the power of any one group or individual within a company. There are so many different sources of power and influence, and they are so dependent upon circumstances, that many managers find this type of political analysis quite bewildering. However, it is important to incorporate a political analysis into any strategic analysis and this section provides readers with some simple guidelines on how this can be done.

The analysis will, once again, rely heavily on Pfeffer[16] who argues that the best way to cope with this complex situation is by stepping back from the detail and looking for *indicators of power*. This is a useful approach since it is this failure to understand the subtle symbols and behaviours within companies which students of traditional corporate strategy approaches have been accused of. For simplicity, it is suggested that there are four major indicators of power:

(i)   The *status* of the individual or group. One measure of status might be position within the hierarchy, but others are equally important, for example, an individual's salary, or job grades of groups. Equally, the reputation which a group or individual holds with others will be very relevant.

(ii)   The *claim on resources* as measured by the size of a department's budget, or the number of employees within that group. In particular, trends in the proportion of resources claimed by that group may be a useful indicator as to the extent to which their power is waxing or waning. The least powerful groups invariably see their resources eroded by the more powerful. A useful comparison can be made with similar groups in comparable organisations.

(iii)   *Representation in powerful positions.* The best example of this is the composition of the board of directors and their particular specialisms. The weakness of the production function may result from lack of representation at board level. Within less hierarchical organisations representation on important committees could be a measure of power, although a simple head-count in this type of analysis would overlook the extent to which the individuals are influential. Here individual status should be taken into consideration.

(iv)   *Symbols of power.* Internal division of power may be indicated in a variety of ways. Such physical symbols as the size and location of people's offices, whether they have a secretary, carpets, a private telephone, or newspapers delivered each morning, are all important clues. Whether individuals are addressed by their first or second names, even the way they dress, may be symbols of power. In more bureaucratic organisations, the existence of 'distribution lists' for internal memoranda and other information can give some clues to the power structure. Surprisingly, these lists do not always neatly reflect the formal hierarchical structure and may provide some useful pointers as to who really is viewed as powerful within the organisation.

It should be remembered that none of these four indicators of power by itself is likely to uncover fully the structure of power within a company. However, by looking at all four it may be possible to identify which people or groups appear to have power by a number of these measures. Figure 5.7 illustrates how such an analysis might be performed to assess the relative power of the marketing and production departments, and the Nottingham and Lincoln plants, using the previous example (Figs. 5.4 and 5.5). It is clear from this simple analysis that the marketing department is seen as powerful by all measures and the production department universally weak. Equally, the Nottingham plant looks particularly powerful in relation to Lincoln.

Alongside this internal assesment of power a similar analysis of the power held by *external stakeholders* needs to be carried out. The indicators of power are slightly different.

(i)   The *status* of an external party such as a supplier is usually indicated in the way that they are discussed amongst company employees and whether they respond quickly to the supplier's demands.

(ii) *Resource dependence* can often be measured directly. For example, the proportion of a company's business tied up with any one customer, or a similar dependence on suppliers can normally be easily measured. Perhaps the key indicator is the ease with which that supplier, financier or customer could be replaced at short notice.

(iii) *Negotiating arrangements:* whether external parties are treated at arms length or are actively involved in negotiations with the company. For example, a customer who is invited to negotiate over the price of a contract is in a more powerful position than a similar company who is given a fixed price on a take-it-or-leave-it basis.

(iv) *Symbols* are equally valuable clues. Whether the management team wine and dine some customer or supplier, or the level of person in the company who deals with a particular supplier. The care and attention paid to correspondence with outsiders will tend to differ from one party to another.

Again, none of these measures by itself will give a full understanding of the extent of the power held by external people, but the combined analysis will be very useful. Part 2 of Fig. 5.7 illustrates how an analysis of power of external stakeholders can be performed (using the previous example from Figs. 5.4 and 5.5).

1. Internal coalitions

Indicators of power †	1 Marketing dept.*	2 Production*	3 Nottingham plant*	4 Lincoln plant*
A. *Status*				
1. Position in hierarchy (closeness to board)	H	L	H	M
2. Salary of top manager	H	L	H	L
3. Average grade of staff	H	M	H	L
B. *Claim on resources*				
1. Number of staff	M	H	M	M
2. Size of similar company	H	L	H	L
3. Budget as % of total	H	M	H	L
C. *Representation*				
1. Number of directors	H	None	M	None
2. Most influential directors	H	None	M	None
D. *Symbols*				
1. Quality of accommodation	H	L	M	M
2. Support services	H	L	H	L

2. External stakeholders

Indicators of power †	Supplier A*	Customer X*	Shareholder M*
1. Status	H	H	L
2. Resource dependence	L	H	H
3. Negotiating arrangements	M	H	L
4. Symbols	H	H	L

* These are examples — the list will clearly vary from one situation to another.
† H = high; M = medium; L = low

Figure 5.7 *Assessing the relative power of coalitions.*

This extended example has been used to illustrate how an analysis of both the 'value structures' and 'power structures' in an organisation can be undertaken as part of a strategic analysis. Such a 'political' analysis is very often far from being scientific yet is nevertheless valuable in terms of understanding the context within which any new strategies will be developed. To gain maximum benefit from this type of analysis and to understand how values influence company policy, readers need to look for a combination of *strongly held values and the power to exercise these values*. For example, customer X may well pose a significant problem to a strategy of entering new EEC markets - the company may lose X's business on which they are highly dependent. Furthermore, the survival of the Lincoln plant looks even more precarious when this analysis of power is added to the previous assessment of coalitions. Not only does Lincoln appear to be isolated (from the previous analysis) but the most powerful coalitions (marketing and customer X) would welcome closure. In contrast, both Lincoln and its major potential ally (production), have little power themselves.

5.5 VALUES AND POLICY-MAKING PROCESSES

The discussion so far has concentrated almost entirely on how the values of individuals and groups influence the strategies that organisations pursue. However, values can also influence the process by which strategic decisions are made. There are two aspects: firstly, the way in which the changing values of society have affected the processes by which all organisations formulate policy, and secondly, how values and decision-making are related within any one organisation.

5.5.1 Changing Values of Society

Since the Second World War there has been a marked and steady change in the way in which society values its business organisations. As well as influencing the type of policies (discussed earlier), these changes have also changed the process by which policies are formulated. Some of these changes have been forced on companies through legislation, others have been adopted as codes of conduct, whilst others are simply norms of behaviour. Good examples are in the area of disclosure of information and the need to justify the company's actions in advance. This ranges from government requirements such as planning permission, price codes, monopolies investigations, and accounting standards, to disclosures to employees. Whereas this increased openness could be argued to be of great benefit to society, it does have a considerable impact on the way in which companies are able to carry out policy-making. Entrepreneurs complain that red-tape is responsible for reducing their competitiveness in the market place. By this they normally mean that their natural inclination to develop policy by a fast, judgmental process is impaired by the need to disclose and justify their plans to others. In some cases it has been argued that this very process of disclosure has given vital information to competitors.

Another important change in the values of society has been the desire to shift the balance of power in the policy-making process as mentioned in the previous section. Most notable have been the pressures for *industrial democracy* culminating in the Bullock report[17] of 1977. Bullock was essentially concerned with shifting some of the formal power in policy-making towards organised trade unions through the appointment of Worker Directors, a system which has been widespread in other countries e.g. West Germany, for some years. Industrial democracy attempts to ensure that a wider set of values should come to bear on companies' policies by altering the formal policy-making processes.

5.5.2 Differences Between Organisations

Within the UK there is a wide variety of ways in which policy is formulated by organisations as was mentioned in Chapter 2. Many of these differences can be traced back to the values which exist within and around the company. For example, Cyert and March[13] argue that the most common way in which values influence corporate strategy is for the dominant coalition (normally management) to impose its values on others within the constraints of the political process discussed in the previous section. They talk about strategy proceeding by the 'quasi-resolution' of conflict, by which they mean that the aims and values of less dominant groups are coped with by partially satisfying them or by satisfying them some of the time.

Very often, the *objectives* of an organisation will have a strong influence on the policy-making process. For example, many small, family companies have a strong desire to establish a thriving business to be handed on to the children. This tends to require tight family control of all aspects of the business which, in turn, leads to a highly autocratic management style with little disclosure or discussion of policy issues. In contrast, at the other extreme, there are organisations whose objectives incorporate strongly-held principles of democracy. Thus local authority decision-making processes exclude the full-time senior managers (officers) despite the fact that they are likely to be the most knowledgeable on the issues under discussion. Strategic decision-making is carried out by the political arm of the organisation, whilst the executive arm is there to operate in an advisory role and to be responsible for the implementation of policy once decided. Of course, even in such an overtly democratic process the values of the executive arm do have a considerable influence due to the power they derive from their knowledge and control over implementation of policy as discussed in the previous subsection.

The *culture* of an the organisation will reflect the values of people within the company and in turn dictate policy-making processes. Small cooperatives are an interesting example. Decision-making procedures here are often quite different from 'typical' commercial organisations. It is quite common for policy changes to be decided only on the basis of consensus amongst all members of the cooperative. Policy-making processes are often very different in a culture which expects detailed, rational explanations, such as a research laboratory, rather than companies which survive by the 'seat of their pants'. Equally, an organisation which has many people on the same level in the organisation (such as polytechnics) will require a more overtly democratic policy-making process than an organisation with a traditional pyramid structure.

5.6 SUMMARY

This chapter discussed how the values of individuals and groups might influence an organisation's strategies. It has been necessary to look at the values of people both inside and outside the organisation (e.g. customers, suppliers, financiers). The strategic importance of values can only be understood by a parallel consideration of the power structure within and around the company since power provides the mechanism by which the values of a group or individual are able to influence strategy.

So, what people *want* to do will influence strategy. This has long been thought of in strategic terms under the more formalised label of 'objectives' - the next chapter examines the role of objectives in the light of this discussion of values and power.

It is important to remember that values are only one of a number of influences on policy. The extent to which values can be pursued is constrained by the realities of the environment and the limitations of the company's resources. Strategy-making must respond to all these pressures.

REFERENCES

1.   In *Business Policy* (Philip Allan: 1977), R. Thomas devotes a good part of the book to a discussion of policy from a political rather than a rational economic stance. In particular, Chapters 5 and 11 are of interest to our discussion of values.
2.   G. Hofstede, *Cultures Consequences* (Sage Publications: 1980). An abridged version of the findings relevant to this chapter can be found in his article 'Motivation, Leadership and Organisation: Do American Theories Apply Abroad?', *Organisational Dynamics* (Summer 1980).

3. P.T. Terry, 'The English in Management', *Management Today,* November 1979.
4. For example: Huw Beynon, *Working for Ford* (Allen Lane and Penguin Education: 1973). Republished by E.P. Publishing Ltd., 1975.
5. For example: C. Hines and G. Searle, 'Automatic Unemployment', *Earth Resources Publication,* 1979, discusses the impact of microelectronic technology on UK employment and possible responses which it demands.
6. A.L. Stinchcombe, 'Social Structure and Organisation', in *Handbook of Organisation,* J.G. March, ed. (Rand McNally: 1965).
7. R.E. Miles and C.C. Snow, *Organizational Strategy, Structure and Process* (McGraw-Hill: 1978).
8. I.C. Macmillan, *Strategy Formulation: Political Concepts* (West: 1978, p.65) identifies a number of writers whose work has influenced how we view the structure of values in organisations. The following four references should be useful for the readers who are interested in pursuing this area most fully:
    R.M. Cyert and J.G. March, *A Behavioural Theory of the Firm* (Prentice-Hall: 1964).
    D. Katz and R.L. Kahn, *The Social Psychology of Organisations* (Wiley: 1966).
    J.G. March and H.A. Simon, *Organisations* (Wiley: 1967).
    J.D. Thompson, *Organisations in Action* (McGraw-Hill: 1967).
9. This section on 'informal systems' is based on the discussion of the issue in B.D. Reed and B.W.M. Palmer, *An Introduction to Organisation Behaviour* (Grubb Institute: 1972). This is also a useful reference work for readers who wish to know more about the relationship between organisation behaviour writings and strategy
10. Reed and Palmer, see reference 9, also discuss the importance of coalitions in their book.
11. For a discussion of the influence of the professional on the values and practices of management see the work of R.H. Hall in 'Professionalisation and Bureaucratisation', *American Sociological Review,* 1968, pp.92-104, and *Organisations: Structure and Process* (Prentice-Hall: 1972).
12. J. Pfeffer, *Power in Organizations* (Pitman: 1981, pp.37-43) includes an example concerned with educational planning at New York University which is useful in understanding the approach.
13. R.M. Cyert and J.G. March, see reference 8, argue that management is usually the dominant stakeholder and its values (often growth) tend to influence strategy most strongly.
14. I.C. Macmillan, see reference 8, p.15, provides some useful definitions of the words 'power, 'influence' and 'authority'. Readers should note that in *our* book the word 'power' is used in a much wider sense than Macmillan's definition, in fact much nearer to his definition of 'authority'. The choice was made since it more closely resembles the normal usage of the word 'power' within the UK. The central point to remember is that formal lines of authority do not always describe the *actual* power structure - a point made by M. Dalton, in *Men who Manage* (Wiley: 1959).
15. Certainly this was found to be the case by J.M. Godiwalla, W.A. Meinhart and W.D. Warde, in their research documented in *Corporate Strategy and Functional Management* (Praeger: 1979), though Miles and Snow, see reference 12, do point out that in 'defender' type companies, production managers may also exercise considerable influence.

16.   J. Pfeffer's (reference 12) Chapter 2 is a most interesting discussion of the problems and approaches to assessing power in organisations.

17.   *Bullock Report: Report of the Committee of Inquiry on Industrial Democracy.* Chairman: Lord Bullock (HMSO: 1977).

RECOMMENDED KEY READINGS

*   A useful text which further examines the relationship between organisation behaviour and corporate strategy is B.D. Reed and B.W. Palmer, *An Introduction to Organisation Behaviour* (Grubb Institute: 1972).

*   Readers should be familiar with the political context of organisational decision-making. We recommended either I.C. Macmillan, *Strategy Formulation: Political Concepts* (West: 1978), or J. Pfeffer, *Power in Organizations* (Pitman: 1981).

*   The book which deals most thoroughly with strategy as a product of value systems is R.E. Miles and C.C. Snow, *Organizational Strategy, Structure and Process* (McGraw-Hill: 1978).

6

EXPECTATIONS AND OBJECTIVES

6.1 INTRODUCTION

Chapter 5 has made the point that strategy is not just the outcome of matching organisational resources to the environment; what those who control or influence the organisation *want* from the organisation, or what they want it to be like, is also very important. It is possible to think of such wants in terms of formally expressed objectives, and argue that these act as a focus for decision-making in the organisation by providing a yardstick against which to measure performance or assess alternative proposals. This view of the role of objectives is not taken in this book for three reasons.

* First, as seen in Chapter 2, there is little evidence that formalised objectives actually have this central role in strategic decision making processes.
* Second, it does not take account of how objectives arise. This chapter sets out to show how they do arise and to demonstrate that, quite sensibly, they take different forms.
* Third, it is an over-constrained view of the roles that objectives play in organisations. This chapter argues that they can and should be conceived of as having different roles to play in the analysis and formulation of strategy.

The idea that objectives are somehow 'given' in formulating strategy, that they are received by an organisation in the same sort of way as environmental change or exist like physical plant, is obviously fallacious. Objectives are set by somebody or some group of individuals. Figure 6.1 is a simple model of what is likely to influence objective-setting. It proposes that objectives are normally set by those directly influencing strategic decisions; usually this would be management though it could be the owners of a business, the management of a parent company or financial institution, perhaps a consultant, or in the case of a public body, civil servants or politicians. These objectives are likely to be shaped by the expectations of different coalitions of interest, including those of the strategic decision makers themselves, and also by how the strategic decision makers perceive the power structure in the organisation.

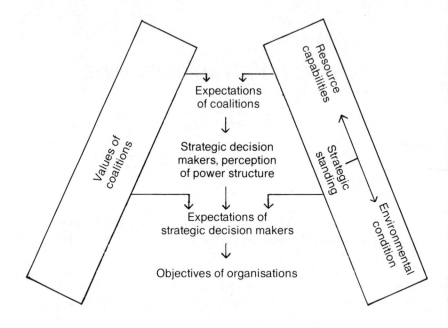

Figure 6.1   *Influences on objective setting*

    As described in Chapter 5, coalitions influencing the organisation may be from within the organisation - groupings of managers, for example - or from outside - shareholders and financial institutions, government departments, and so on. Such coalitions of interest are sometimes referred to as stakeholders in an organisation. Their expectations of an organisation will be influenced by their own values in relation to the organisation (discussed in Chapter 5) and by their perception of the strategic position of the organisation, which is to do with the resource capabilities of the organisation in terms of its environment (discussed in Chapters 3 and 4). Another way of putting this is to say that their expectations are a function of what they want and what they see as possible or necessary. However, the objectives are dependent on one other influence, and that is the perception that the strategic decision makers have of the power structure with regard to the coalitions themselves. Illustration 22 is an example of the variety of stakeholder groups that existed for an organisation - a theatre in this instance. Here, objectives would be set by the management but they would be influenced in so doing not only by their own expectations but by the

ILLUSTRATION 22

The Crucible Theatre, Sheffield

- In a subsidised theatre, policy is influenced by a wide range of different groups (stakeholders) who have differing views on the objectives which the theatre should pursue.

In 1972, only ten months after the opening of a brand new, £1m theatre complex, the Crucible Theatre was being criticised by Sheffield Corporation for failing to cover its costs to the tune of £130,000 and for catering almost exclusively to middle class audiences. The theatre management defended their position by claiming that the level of financial subsidy from the Local Authority and the Arts Council was insufficient to prevent an erosion of artistic standards. Disagreements over theatre policy and how its performance should be measured were no new thing - ever since the Sheffield Theatre Company received its first Arts Council grant in 1960/1, there had been arguments about the types of plays produced and the extent to which they appealed to the people of Sheffield. Such arguments continue to the present day.

Peter James, Theatre Director between 1974 and 1981, was very conscious of the need to respond to a wide variety of interest groups (stakeholders). The problem, he said, was trying to strike a balance and to try to satisfy everybody at least once a year.

The following shows the major stakeholders and the way in which they might try to influence theatre policy:

Stakeholder	Reason for interest	Expectations
1. Arts Council	Provide revenue grant	Artistic standards Financial viability
2. Local Authorities - Sheffield MDC S. Yorks CC	Provide revenue grants 'Voice' of local community	Breadth of appeal - (including events other than drama) City's prestige e.g. attracting new employers Financial viability
3. Present theatre-goers	Customers	Quality plays at reasonable prices
4. Directors of plays and actors	Employees	Job satisfaction (e.g. new plays)
5. Writers	Need plays to be adopted by theatres	Prefer a lot of new and different productions rather than a few long runs

Like all organisations, the Crucible Theatre survived only because the management gave sufficient consideration to *all* these varied demands in formulating theatre policy.

Source: Crucible Theatre, Sheffield, case study by K. Scholes. Available from the Case Clearing House, Cranfield.

ECS–F

expectations of other stakeholder groups. To be more precise, they would be influenced in particular by the expectations of the stakeholder groups they perceived to be most powerful - for example, the Arts Council on whom they were financially dependent.

The model proposes then, that the influences on objective setting are much the same as those on the strategy of an organisation. Indeed, objectives are conceived by some writers[1] not as a step in the strategy formulation process, but as an element of strategy.

The view of objectives as expressed in Fig. 6.1 is developed in the first section of this chapter which makes the point that objectives need to be interpreted in the wider context of expectations and power. The first section also includes a brief discussion of the issue of social responsibility, an issue which raises significant questions about expectations about the social role of organisations. The second section of the chapter is a discussion of the nature of the objectives as they are likely to be found in organisations: and the chapter concludes with a review of the different roles played by, and uses of, objectives.

6.2 EXPECTATIONS AND RESPONSIBILITIES: PROBLEMS OF CONFLICT

Since the expectations of coalitions are likely to differ, and there are likely to be differing perceptions of the strategic standing of the organisation, it is likely that there will be a conflict of objectives within the organisation. Indeed researchers have cited that, even where they exist, formally stated objectives do not necessarily represent the views of strategic decision makers; also that the objectives proposed by strategic decision makers may differ within the same organisation.[2]

6.2.1 Conflicts of Expectations and Objectives

The idea of conflicting expectations and objectives existing in an organisation is important. In analysing the strategic position of an organisation it is not necessarily the formally stated objectives that are of prime importance: it may be just as important to understand the conflicts that exist, and out of which emerge concensus or compromise views. This section considers some of the typical expectations and objectives that exist and how they might conflict.

Small owner controlled businesses may well reach a point where there is a conflict between the desire to remain small and slim so that control can be retained in the hands of the owner, and the need to grow to combat competition

---

ILLUSTRATION 23

Chevron Foods Ltd

● The owner of a small company faces a conflict between personal prefer-
ences and competitive threats.

A small business, two years old in 1977, had been successfully and profitably
established importing fruit juice and a dispensing system from the USA and
marketing it to hotels, mainly in London. The business had been run as a
marketing-only operation, relying on subcontract distribution of juice and servicing
of the dispensers. Because the operation was limited to London, direct personal
control was retained by the owner of all operations. However, by the end of 1977, he
faced a dilemma.

'I have no particular desire to create a multi-million pound company, nor go
for growth for its own sake. I suppose that the main reason I'm in business is
because I enjoy what I'm doing and it makes me quite a nice living.
But I am concerned about some things. My objective is to keep a slim
operation: I don't like the idea of lots of levels of management and increasing
overheads; and some of the developments could point that way. For instance,
I just cannot get some business simply because we're not national.
Trust House Forte and British Transport, two of the largest hotel groups,
require a national service - and I can't give it. If I do, what will it do to my ideas
of a slim operation? And if I don't -well, they have to get juice from someone
and although no one else is distributing post-mix now, that is not to say
someone won't in the future.'

On the one hand is the objective of remaining slim, arising from personal
values concerned with ownership and control. On the other is the owner's
perception of the threat of competition if he does not expand geographically.

*Source: Chevron case study by G. Johnson. Available from the Case Clearing House,
Cranfield.*

---

or meet the demands of customers.[3] Illustration 23 gives such an example of
this conflict between personal values and environmental influences. Anyone
who chose to take the stated objectives of the owner to remain slim and small
would be failing to understand the complexity of the underlying dilemma he
faces. This is an instance of the conflict that could be faced between values and
perceived standing.

Another sort of conflict important in considering strategy is that arising
from the values and expectations of managers. Galbraith[4] argues that large

corporations are now controlled by what he calls the 'technocracy' whose interests are largely to do with their own career development rather than other stakeholder groups. It is a view not shared by all[5], but few would dispute that managers have a key influence on strategy. It was pointed out in Chapter 2 that managerial economists[6] have shown that it is not profit maximisation, but revenue maximisation - the generation of increased turnover - that best describes the basis of strategic decision making: that managers will tend to take decisions and follow courses of action which benefit themselves. They argue that this means that managers will aim for growth as a means of increasing managerial opportunity and reducing the risk of takeover. Certainly growth appears to be of major importance to managers, though reasons for this may be rather wider and different than some of the managerial economists have argued, as shown by the reasons for growth stated by managers in a retail company given in Illustration 24.

A desire for growth is likely to lead to conflicts of expectations and objectives too. For example, the managers whose reasons for growth are given in Illustration 24 express potentially conflicting reasons which take form in different expectations for the company. Some want to grow to provide a personal challenge; others because they see it as a way of countering competition. The research from which these statements are taken found that such differences expressed themselves in different views about what is meant by growth. Those who want to counter competition tend to see growth in terms of expanding the existing network of shops. Those who see growth in more personal terms tend to favour diversifying away from the existing operation.[7] Within the management of an organisation, there is likely to exist different coalitions between which there may be a conflict of expectations too; so to take at face value objectives that might be publicly or formally stated is inadequate.

The growth expectations of managers may also conflict with other stakeholder groups. Managers of a division may desire growth whilst their parent company may see the division's role as one of consolidation. The growth expectations of the managers of a family-owned company may conflict with those of the family shareholders, whose expectations may be to do with maintaining family control and minimising external influences on the firm.

What emerges is the need to understand the expectations of different stakeholder groups and weigh these in terms of the power that they exercise. For example in the public sector, government departments may be a powerful influence; they may seek to achieve their own objectives of reduced public spending, as the Conservative administration in the UK did in the early 1980s by expecting nationalised industries and local government to reduce expenditure. Here government cash limits on expenditure for nationalised industries became dominant objectives for such organisations. Financial institutions such as banks may not have a shareholding in a company but may well have a direct interest through the funds which they loan: their main expectation is to achieve a secure return on their investment in terms of interest and a company with high borrowings may well discover that meeting the bank's expectation

---

ILLUSTRATION 24

Reasons for Growth

● An objective to pursue growth is shared by many comapnies. Reasons for growth are many and varied: here are some given by managers in a major UK retailer.

Growth is natural, normal, 'instinctive' state of affairs:
'A businessman will look to see how much more he can make one year over another: a general with a small army wants a big army: I want a bigger house and a bigger car: it's all the same'.

Growth is for personal gratification:
'People want to be associated with a successful company. They want to be part of that growth ... it satisfies my ego to be associated with something that is growing'.

Growth provides personal challenge and satisfaction:
'... there is a challenge in growing that isn't there in standing still. If you are looking at a set of figures that show no growth, where is the satisfaction in that?'

Growth provides opportunities both for managers and to those they manage:
'Growth for me is growth of responsibility ... I want to end up running something'.
'How are we going to retain good staff if there are no promotional prospects for them'.

Growth is seen as a means of keeping ahead of competition:
'You can't stand still because there are firms which, as soon as they see an opening which we are not looking to move into, will be ready to fill the gap'.

Growth is seen as giving rise to increased profits - even if indirectly:
'Growth means getting bigger, and bigger means more investment and you want a return on your investment, don't you?'.

Growth is a means of avoiding takeover:
'If you do not grow, the City will down-rate you and you become easier to pick off'.

Growth may provide Corporate Benefits such as economies of scale:
'A company of our size has clout: whether it is in advertising or buying'.

Source: Statements taken from unpublished research by G. Johnson.

---

becomes a dominant requirement. In local government there is an excellent example of the influence of a variety of stakeholder groups which are likely to have differing expectations, all of which are likely to influence the strategy that will be followed. The electorate are able to influence the situation by allocating power to political parties. They in turn are likely to be subject to their own internal pressures from groupings with differing expectations and must reconcile their policies with the views of opposition parties and the administrators in the local government departments.

The idea of a conflict of expectations and objectives can be usefully thought of in terms of expectations and constraints: the expectations of one stakeholder group can be thought of as a constraint on those of another. Managers in a company may wish to pursue growth but are able to do so only insofar as they can achieve profits acceptable to shareholders. A political party may wish to cut local services drastically to achieve its stated aim of reduced rates but is likely to be opposed by opposition parties, local pressure groups and even council officials interested in maintaining their jobs. Some stakeholder groups do not seek to impose objectives as such on an organisation but they do insist on imposing constraints. A local authority may not have the power or desire to impose any objectives as such on a company in its area: it can, however, impose constraints on such matters as pollution control and planning permission. The influence of the stock market on companies may be regarded as a constraint: if a company does not perform to expectations then it is likely to suffer a reduction in share price. National government may argue that it is not its intention to influence the policies of private companies but may impose sanctions if that company defies a trading embargo for example.

Given that objectives arise out of these differences of expectations, it is unwise to regard objectives as permanent or pre-ordained. They are a product of the sort of bargaining process discussed in Chapter 5 and should be regarded as such in the analysis and formulation of strategy. This approach is discussed more fully in the last section of the chapter.

6.2.2. Social Responsibility[8]

In the past twenty years or so there has been an increasing acceptance by the management of organisations that there is a diversity of stakeholder interests and expectations to be accommodated in the conceiving of objectives and strategy. This has given rise to the notion of *social responsibility*, by which is meant the acceptance by management of organisational responsibilities of a social nature wider than the legal minimum which it is bound to fulfill. It is particularly relevant to this discussion because it raises a fundamental conflict about what is expected of an organisation in terms of its social role. There is a wide variety of issues[9] which can be considered to fall under this broad heading. These issues are summarised in Fig. 6.2.

How organisations respond to these issues varies considerably and may be summarised as shown in Fig. 6.3. There are, however, four broad groupings of response, each of which may give rise to conflicts of objectives and policy.[10]

*   At one extreme there are organisations which largely conform to Milton Friedman's maxim that 'the business of business is business', and that the 'only social responsibility of business is to increase its profit'.[11] These are in categories 1 to 3 in Fig. 6.3. The holders of these beliefs argue that not only is it not the duty of business to be concerned about social issues but that in doing so they would detract from the primary way in which they

Should organisations be responsible for

Employee welfare
. . . providing medical care, assistance with mortgages, extended sickness leave, assistance for dependents, etc?

Working conditions
. . . enhanced working surroundings, social and sporting clubs, above minimum safety standards, etc?

Job design
. . . designing jobs to the increased satisfaction of workers rather than economic efficiency?

Internal aspects

Pollution
. . . reducing pollution below legal standards if competitors are not doing so?

Product safety
. . . danger arising from the careless use of product by consumers?

Marketing practices
. . . curtailing advertising which promotes products which harm health (e.g. tobacco and sweets)?

Employment
. . . positive discrimation in favour of minorities?

Community activity
. . . sponsoring local events and supporting local good works?

External aspects

Figure 6.2   *Some questions of social responsibility.*

should be contributing to society, that is by operating businesses which are economically efficient. Social responsibility, they argue, is the domain of government which should prescribe, through legislation, the constraints which society chooses to impose on business in their pursuit of economic efficiency. Expecting companies to exercise these duties can, in extreme cases, undermine the authority of government and give business organisations even more power. Somewhat paradoxically, however, it is often devotees of this school of thought that most resent government 'interference' in business affairs.

* The next group are in categories 4 to 7 in Fig. 6.3. Here social responsiblity is exercised in a careful, selective way and usually justified in terms of economic commonsense. Sponsorship, or welfare provision would be rationalised as sensible expenditures akin to any other form of investment or promotion expenditure. Many companies recognise that this careful attention to aspects of social responsibility could be in the long term interests of the company. For example, the avoidance of 'shady' marketing practices will prevent the need for yet more legislation in that area. They argue that if managers wish to maintain discretion in the long run over issues such as marketing practices, they are wise to operate responsibly in the short term. Within this category lie companies who would agree with an industrial journalist[12] who, when asked why

Behaviour and attitude / Role	Economic	Social	Political
1. Profit maximiser	Profit dominates	Regarded as an impediment to profit	Actively avoids involvement with political system
2. Profit satisficer	Growth dominates	Reacts against societal and social pressures as incursions	Avoids interaction with political system
3. Defender of free enterprise	The business of business is business	Reacts against social component as being not within firm's proper scope	Stands up for "free enterprise"
4. The lone wolf	Prime emphasis on profit	Voluntarily but unilaterally assumes responsibility	Avoids involvement unless cornered
5. Societally engaged	Prime emphasis on profit	Interactively engaged	Engaged only in negotiation of the rules of the game
6. Societally progressive	Prime emphasis on profit	Interactively engaged	Positively involved in formulation of national industrial policies
7. Global actor	Prime emphasis on profit	Interactively engaged	Assumes a responsibility to foster a balance between national and international economic policies
8. Developer of society	Financial self-sufficiency	Produces changes in the lives of mankind through innovation	Positively involved with emphasis on planned development of social infrastructures
9. Social servant	Secondary to societal obligations	Provides essential but non-economic goods and services	Positively involved in formation of national industrial policies with emphasis on social matters
10. Employment provider	Subsidised operation	Provides jobs	Subsidised and supported by government

Figure 6.3   *Social responsibility, ten roles of the firm (from: Facing Realities — The European Societal Strategy Project — Summary Report, produced jointly by the European Foundation for Management Development and the European Institute for Advanced Studies in Management, 1981, p.14).*

some companies behave more responsibly than others, replied 'because some companies are smarter than others'! They would argue that management ignores social influences at their peril and 'smarter' companies are those which recognise and cope with these issues in policy-making. The sorts of conflicts of responsibility which arise here are, for example, between pollution control and job provision. Extra costs of pollution control could mean uncompetitive costs and thus threaten plant closure and the loss of jobs.

*   The third category is the 'progressive' organisation which regards a wide variety of social responsibility issues as an important influence on policy-making. These are in category 8 in Fig. 6.3. The Quaker companies of the last century are a good example and, to a considerable extent, the attitudes of these companies have remained more progressive than others into this century. Companies in this category might argue that they would retain uneconomic units to preserve jobs, would avoid manufacturing certain products or not deal with certain suppliers or customers on ethical grounds. Here a company might be prepared to bear reductions in profitability for the social good. But to what extent would it be prepared to do so? At some point there could be a conflict between social responsibility and survival or between social responsibility and the expectations of shareholders.

* There are also organisations which are quite specifically founded and run as a response to community needs. Societal needs are paramount and profits or financial surpluses secondary or a constraint. These are categories 9 and 10 in Fig. 6.3 and include many public services, charities, the church and so on. The problem these organisations face may be to do with how 'commercial' they are prepared to be in order to carry out their social role. For example, charities are often accused of spending too high a percentage of their funds on internal administration.

The issue of social responsibility provides a good example, then, of the way in which the expectations of one stakeholder group may conflict with or be constrained by the expectations of another.

6.3 THE NATURE OF OBJECTIVES

The preceding section has argued that objectives need to be seen in the context of the expectations of different stakeholders of the organisation. This section reviews the sorts of objectives that are likely to be found in organisations and why they are expressed in the way they are.

Illustration 25 shows the sort of formal objectives stated by companies. Just a brief glance shows that there are differences in their content and in the extent to which they are specific. They all have two things in common: they all express in some way desired ends to be achieved, and they are all expressed as formal organisational aims. However, they are different types of statements about desired ends. These differences can be thought of as reflecting a hierarchy of objectives.[13] Objective 1 is an expression of what might be called *mission;* 2 and 3 are expressions of *corporate objectives;* and 4 and 5 are expressions of *unit objectives.* The discussion which follows is summarised in Fig. 6.4.

6.3.1 Mission

The mission of an organisation is the most generalised sort of objective and can be thought of as an expression of its *raison d'etre.* Richards[14] writing on objectives calls it the 'master strategy' and says it is 'a visionary projection of the central and overriding concepts on which the organisation is based'. He goes on to say that it 'should not focus on what the firm is doing in terms of products and markets currently served, but rather upon the services and utility

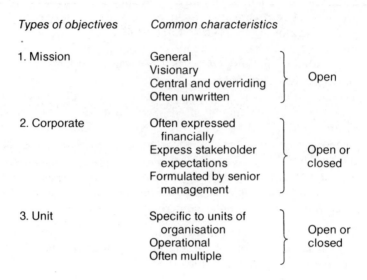

Figure 6.4   *The nature of objectives.*

that the products provide'. It is essentially a conception of what the organisation is about as a whole.

Mission has some key characteristics. It is *visionary* in the sense that it is not a statement of where the organisation is now, or is expected to be at a point in time, but a statement of where the organisation is conceived to be throughout time. There may be an historical element to it in the sense that the mission has been developed and refined over time: but essentially it is a vision of what the organisation will be aiming to achieve or be like on an ongoing basis. It is likely to be *central and overriding* in that it tends to persist even when shorter term objectives change or strategy changes. Conversely, if the mission does change then the ramifications on strategy - and indeed all aspects of the business - can be great. One of the clearest examples of the influence on changes in direction of strategy as a result of changes in mission takes place, of course, in local and national government. One political party will be elected with a mission and will pursue its strategy: four or five years later another may be elected with a different mission and will pursue what may be a totally different strategy.

Mission is not necessarily the property of any one party within the firm. It may be an unwritten concept of a founder or a Chairman. It may be a written 'creed' (as in the case of 1. in Illustration 25) that is handed down to generations of managers. It may be as imprecise as a generally accepted view of what the firm is about that is accepted by most of those working in the company. It may not exist at all or be a matter for disagreement or conflict

ILLUSTRATION 25

Types of Objectives

● Companies' objectives are of different kinds and vary in the extent to which they are specific.

1. Mission:	'The supreme purpose of the whole organisation is to secure the fairest possible sharing by all the members of all the advantages of ownership - gain, knowledge and power. That is to say, their happiness in the broadest sense of that word, so far as happiness depends upon gainful occupation'.
	- As stated in the John Lewis Partnership 'gazette' in 1975.
2. Corporate : Closed	In his 1980 report, the Chairman of the British Transport Docks Board referred to:
	'The quinquennial target of 20% return on capital by 1980 as agreed with the Government'.
3. Corporate : Open	'Amongst our most important tasks over the next few years is to simplify the business portfolio and to concentrate our attentions on those traditional businesses in the Group which provide us with ample opportunity for growth'.
	- BOC International Group Executive's Report.
4. Unit : Closed	'It is hoped that plant modifications undertaken to improve integration of the plant steam systems will result in savings equivalent to 5,000 tonnes of fuel per year.'
	- Esso Report, 1980.
5. Unit : Open	'One of the main aims for one of the business areas in which the Company is involved is to play a leading role in meeting the requirements of the widening and expanding home entertainments industry'.
	- Sir Richard Cave, Chairman, Thorn EMI, 1980.

within the firm. However, if there is substantial disagreement within the organisation as to its mission, it may well give rise to real problems in resolving the strategic direction of the organisation.

6.3.2 Corporate Objectives

Corporate objectives and unit objectives are distinguished in this chapter because there are different 'levels' of objectives with different characteristics in organisations. *Corporate objectives* are often expressed in *financial* terms. They could be the expression of desired sales or profit levels or rates of growth, dividend levels or share valuations. Increasingly, however, organisations have corporate objectives of a non-financial nature, such as employee welfare or technological advance, but it is rare for these to be unaccompanied by financial objectives. They are frequently formal *statements of stakeholder expectations.* Traditionally, this may have meant the shareholders, so the corporate objective may have been a statement about the required return to shareholders. However, as it is becoming increasingly recognised that stakeholders might also be employees, customers, suppliers, the local community and so on, there could be formal statements of objectives to be met on their behalf.

Corporate objectives are usually formulated by senior members of the board or even the chairman or chief executive. They are more likely to be handed down to lower levels of management than to be formulated by such lower levels of management. In a divisionalised company, for example, corporate objectives may be set by the board at head office and then translated into divisional objectives which become financial targets for the division.

Having said that such characteristics tend to define corporate objectives, it is important to say that corporate objectives may not exist at all; or if they do, may not be at all precise. Some organisations may see it as the role of head office to hand down corporate objectives: other firms may see as the role of head office the acceptance of whatever their operating units (divisions, for example) set as their objectives. Of course, some organisations are single unit businesses with no such thing as a head office and separate operating units. In such cases corporate objectives and business objectives may be mixed together.

6.3.3 Unit Objectives

Unit objectives are here distinguished from corporate objectives insofar as they are likely to have the following sorts of characteristics:

(i)   They relate to the individual units of the organisation. For example, they may be the objectives of a division or of one company unit in a holding company. In the case of public sector organisations, the unit could be a department of a local authority or a hospital in a particular health authority. In the case of a company which is a single business unit, then unit and corporate objectives are likely to be one and the same anyway.

(ii) They may be financial objectives stated in much the same way as corporate objectives, but at a unit level. A corporate objective of a given growth in profit after tax might be translated into an objective for each business unit. They are likely to be more operational in nature than corporate objectives. They might address themselves to the financial operations of a business - objectives about liquidity or profit margins for example. They might be concerned with marketing operations - objectives about market share or relative price levels for example. They might be concerned with operations management - objectives about capacity utilisation or production costs for example. In this sense they are to do with the planning of operational activity, which is discussed in the next section.

(iii) Multiple objectives might well be more common at the unit level than at the corporate level. This is likely to be the case if objectives are conceived of in operational terms since the operations of a business are multi-faceted. Indeed, Drucker[15] has said that business level objectives should be drawn up for market standing, profitability, productivity, physical and financial performance, the performance and development of managers, the attitude and performance of the workforce, innovation, and social responsibility, since in his view all of these areas are crucial to the success of the business.

Unit level objectives may, of course, be in conflict with other unit objectives and with corporate objectives. For example, in public sector operations there are often competing unit objectives; one committee of a local authority, will quite likely have aspirations for the provision of services which conflict either with other committees or overall constraints of local authority spending.

6.3.4 The Precision of Objectives

Illustration 25 may be looked at in another way. Some (numbers 2 and 4) are objectives which can be measured: it is possible to say they can be achieved at some future time. These are 'closed' objectives. Others (numbers 1, 3 and 5) are objectives which can never be achieved since they will always persist. They are like the individual who might say his aim is to make more money; he can always make more money no matter how much he makes. These are 'open' objectives .

Many writers[16] have argued that objectives are not helpful unless they are capable of being measured and achieved - unless they are closed. This view is not taken here for three reasons. First, because open statements may in fact be just as helpful as closed statements. For example, mission may be a very important influence on strategy: it may concentrate the manager's perception of his operation on the needs of his customers and the utility of his service, for example, and at the same time set the boundaries within which he sees the business developing. But statements of mission are very difficult to make in closed terms. The role of this sort of objective is very much to do with focusing strategy rather than deciding when it has been 'achieved'. Second, there may be some objectives which are important but are difficult to quantify or express in measurable terms. An objective such as 'to be a leader in technology' may be highly relevant in today's technological environment, but may become absurd if it has to be expressed in some measurable way.

Third, there is ample evidence to show that many very successful companies do not have precise, explicit objectives, and that their senior executives do not think they should have. As Quinn[17] found: '... successful executives "announced" relatively few goals to their organisation. These few were frequently broad and general, and only rarely were they quantitative or measurably precise.' Objectives tended not to be announced for four reasons. First because the effect would be to over-centralise the organisation. Second, that announced objectives could become a focus for opposition from outside the firm or from within. Third, because once an objective is set, it could be very difficult to change: there is a fear of creating rigidity and an out-of-date or inappropriate stance. And fourth, the danger that competitors will get to know too much about the intentions of the organisation.

However, it also became clear to Quinn that there are times when specific objectives are required. These are times when immediate or urgent action is required, such as in a crisis, or at times of major, usually strategic, transitions essential to focus the attention of management onto a limited number of essential requirements. An extreme example would be in a turnaround situation. If the choice is between going out of business and surviving, then there is no room for latitude through vaguely stated requirements: intentions and requirements have to be specific — this is discussed more fully in subsection 6.4.2. Quinn also found that objectives tended to be specific after a crisis when there was still a need for a clear focus. It is also helpful to have closed objectives for planning purposes. Here the objective becomes a target to be achieved. Suppose a company is seeking to develop and launch new products for example: it is helpful for managers to have some yardstick, of profitability perhaps, against which to judge the success of the new venture.

6.4 OBJECTIVES AND STRATEGIC MANAGEMENT

This chapter has shown that there are likely to be a considerable variety, and probably diversity, of expectations and objectives in an organisation. The aim of this concluding section is to relate the discussion of this diversity to the practice of strategic management. The general point that needs to be made is that, for those who set out to analyse or formulate strategy, objectives have different roles in different circumstances. These different roles are summarised in Fig. 6.5.

Objectives in:	Can be considered
Strategic analysis	— as an historical influence — in the context of the expectations and power of stakeholders

Strategic evaluation	— as one of many influences in steady state conditions
	— as of central importance if:
	
	   ● management heighten their significance
	   ● the organisation is in crisis
	
	— as a yardstick in the selection of strategy

Stategic implementation	— as a yardstick against which to assess project viability — as a control mechanism in monitoring progress — as a means of management motivation — as a means of coordinating activity

Figure 6.5 *The roles of objectives in strategic management.*

6.4.1 Objectives and Strategic Analysis

In carrying out a strategic analysis of an organisation it is important to build up an understanding of the objectives that have historically influenced strategy. The analyst is in effect asking: 'Why is this organisation in the position it is in?' One reason for its position may well be the objectives it has followed. Here it is important to differentiate between what is stated or explicit and what is deduced by the analyst. It may be that there are no stated objectives and never have been. Or there may be a good deal of difference between the direction the organisation has supposedly been following according to its stated objectives, and that which it has been following if its track record is studied.

As the early part of this chapter argued, in order to understand the role of objectives it is also important to think about the expectations of various stakeholder groups in line with the sort of political analysis discussed in Chapter 5. It should not be assumed, for example, that the objectives given by management are necessarily the ones that are most significant because management may not be the most powerful stakeholder group. Linked to this idea, since objectives should be thought of as the product of what is likely to be a conflict of expectations, they should not be considered as fixed but as capable of amendment in the same way as strategy in order to cope with a changing environment and different stakeholder expectations.

6.4.2 Objectives and Strategic Evaluation

Objectives are likely to have different roles in the evaluation of strategy according to the circumstances of the organisation and the evolving strategic or management needs which emerge. First, consider a situation in which a firm's market is mature and the relative standing of competitors pretty well fixed. There might be a possibility of strategic change but it is unlikely to be much more than an adjustment to what has gone before. In such a situation it is likely that the role that the objectives will play is as one part, one element, within all the other influences on strategy. In taking a decision on choice of strategy, objectives might not be considered as of greater consequence than an organisation's strengths, its weaknesses, or the opportunities and threats it faces in its environment. Indeed it might be that in such circumstances the objectives are much more flexible than environmental or resource influences on strategy, and in this sense they are less of a determinant of strategy than these other influences. Here, objectives are likely to be more use as a means of sifting possible strategic choices or considering ways of implementing strategy: they may well be more important as constraints on freedom of choice than as reasons for choice.

On the other hand, even in this steady state situation some objectives may be seen as a dominant influence in evaluation. Suppose management believe it is important that an objective is of overriding importance: suppose they are not content to accept an emerging consensus view of the objectives of the firm: then the role of objectives is likely to become more dominant. Senior management might feel that the firm is becoming too complacent, too ready to accept the *status quo:* a way of challenging this could be to emphasise certain centrally determined key objectives. Here it is management taking a deliberate decision to emphasise the role of objectives to make them more central in the strategic decision-making process. The objectives might then become more specific and explicit.

There are situations when certain objectives, particularly formal corporate or unit objectives, become a central focus for strategic decision-making. Typically, in times of crisis the need for explicit, specific objectives becomes of much greater importance. It is in such situations that objectives become elevated to a primary role in strategic evaluation and implementation. A strategic analysis of the strengths and weaknesses of the organisation and its opportunities and threats is likely to be useful in assessing strategic position, but the initial choice of strategic direction is in effect, defined by the impact of the crisis itself and the objectives arising from that. Suppose, for example, that a firm, well established in a mature market and largely reliant on its sales in that market for its profits, learns that an impending technological advance, which it is not involved in, is likely to take over the traditional market within two to three years. This is a crisis: the very existence of the firm is challenged and the time available to do anything about it is short. In less critical circumstances management might have considered future strategic directions by weighing up what the firm is and is not good at doing, avoiding weakness areas and building on strengths. That comfortable option will not now solve the problem. The objective is survival and there may be limited possibilities. Means have to be found to put a strategy into effect with the objective of survivial. If this means drastic pruning of overheads to maintain short term viability then it has to be, even if it means a lowering of morale. If board members who disagree or who are not able to commit themselves to the policy have to go, then it has to be, even if it means skilled managers are lost. If the business has to accept reduced profit margins in a new venture to get itself established in a new market then so be it. All of these considerations would normally be strong reasons for not going ahead with a strategy or modifying it: but in times of crisis it is the end -the objective - that becomes paramount.

Objectives may also be of use in the selection of strategy. Managers may use stated objectives as a yardstick against which to choose between possible strategies. For example, it may be stated that a particular return on capital employed is expected in a company and strategies might be selected on the basis of the extent to which they are likely to meet this criterion. It is this role of objectives that has received particular attention from a number of writers on corporate planning. For some of these writers, objectives then take on a central role in strategy-making. To take one example from the corporate planning literature of the 1960s, Argenti[18] argued that the objective of a business must be an expression of its 'permanent unalterable *raison d'etre':* and that there should only be one type of objective - and no other - and that this was to make a profit, measured as return on shareholders' funds. A logical flow of decision-making routines could emanate from this central focus so as to achieve the optimum strategy judged on the basis of the extent to which it meets the objective. Indeed, Argenti went further and argued that if a strategy could not be found which would be likely to achieve the objective, then a search for such a strategy must continue: the objective must remain unchanged because it is an expression of the 'unalterable *raison d'etre'* of the firm.

6.4.3. Objectives and Strategic Implementation

Objectives are part of the strategic implementation stage: they are used to facilitate the management process. Objectives may serve several purposes in the planning, management and control of strategy implementation:

* An objective may be essential to provide the yardstick or target against which to assess the viability or acceptability of a particular project in much the same way as an objective acts as a yardstick for assessing possible strategies. For example, an objective may take the form of a required return on capital for project planning purposes.

* In managing the implementation of strategy, it may well be helpful to have objectives against which to monitor the progress being achieved. This often takes the form of budgeted sales or profit figures and provides a means of controlling the implementation of strategy.
* Setting objectives for managers or parts of organisations might also be a useful means of motivating them to achieve improved performance. This again might be achieved through the performance levels agreed in their departmental budgets.
* When there is a need to implement change, the translation of strategic objectives into departmental and management objectives can be an important means of focusing attention on the key requirements to make that change successful. Here objectives become a means of ensuring that the various parts of the organisation are pulling in the same direction. This system of management is known as 'management by objectives'.[19]

All of these uses of objectives are, then, to do with the translation of strategy into operational activity and the control of performance. These are particular roles of objectives which are somewhat different from those discussed hitherto. Strategy may have evolved over time or been the subject of a bargaining process: it may be lacking in the precision required for management purposes. By converting strategic intent into more precise, more explicit statements of objectives, it is possible to plan the process of strategic change efficiently.

This is an important point to make because the objectives that managers or observers of organisations often see are the objectives that are used for the planning of strategic change. Whilst such objectives may be thought of as a determinant of strategy, it is quite likely that, in fact, they are the product of strategy. Again, then, the point has to be made that objectives have different roles and need to be considered as such by those who seek to understand their significance.

6.5 SUMMARY

This chapter has examined the expectations and objectives that play a part in influencing strategy. The conclusion is that it is too simple to think of such influences solely in terms of formalised corporate objectives. Rather, it is more useful to consider objectives in the context of the expectations and power of various stakeholders. In doing this it becomes clear that objectives take different forms and can be considered and used in different ways. They are important to understand as part of a strategic analysis, as an influence on the strategic problem of the organisation: they are likely to be useful in the choice of strategy, which will be discussed in the next part of the book, and they have a role to play in planning, coordinating and controlling the implementation of strategy, which is discussed in the last part of the book.

REFERENCES

1. Writers on strategy who have conceived of objectives as part of strategy as distinct from strategy, or a step in formulating strategy, include H. Uyterhoeven, R. Ackerman and J. Rosenblum, *Strategy and Organisation: Text and Cases in General Management* (Irwin: 1973); K. Andrews, *A Concept of Corporate Strategy* (Irwin: 1980) and C. Hofer and D. Schendel, *Strategy Formulation: Analytical Concepts* (West: 1978).
2. An interesting account of the variety and differences of the objectives of managers may be found in D. Norburn and P. Grinyer, 'Directors Without Direction', *Journal of General Management,* Vol. 1 No. 2, 1973/74.
3. This conflict is reported by J. Boswell *The Rise and Decline of Small Firms* (George Allen & Unwin: 1973) to be of particular importance for the owners of small firms.
4. See J.K. Galbraith, *The New Industrial State* (Hamish Hamilton: 1967).
5. S. Nyman and A. Silbertson, 'The Ownership and Control of Industry', *Oxford Economic Papers,* Vol. 30, No. 1, show how in the UK the control of shareholders and family stakeholder groups has been prematurely dismissed. They argue that even with relatively low shareholdings these shareholder groups can, and do, still exercise considerable influence.
6. See R. Marris and A. Wood, *The Corporate Economy* (Macmillan: 1971); and W.S. Baumol, *Business Behaviour, Value and Growth* (Harcourt, Brace & World Inc: 1967).
7. This discussion of managerial attitudes to growth arises from an unpublished study by one of the authors of this book (G. J.).
8. For a fuller discussion of the issues of social responsibility see K. Davis, 'The Arguments For and Against Corporate Social Responsibility', *Academy of Management Journal,* Vol. 16 No. 2, 1973.
9. See, for example, D. Clutterbuck, *How to be a Good Corporate Citizen: Managers' Guide to Making Social Responsibility Work - And Pay* (McGraw-Hill: 1981). A brief summary is also given in *International Management,* May 1981, pp. 38-40.
10. Many of the problems arising from differing conceptions of the social roles of organisations in a changing environment are discussed in the report 'Facing Realities' published by the European Societal Strategy Project (see Key Readings at end).
11. This argument is well illustrated in an article by Milton Friedman entitled 'The Social Responsibility of Business is to Increase its Profits', reported by D.J. McCarthy, R.J. Minichiello and J.R. Curran in *Business Policy and Strategy* (Irwin: 1979, 3rd edn.).
12. These comments were made by F. Wright, Business Editor of the Morning Telegraph, Sheffield, on a video documentary entitled 'Social Responsibility of Companies', made by H.K. Scholes and A. Wood and produced by Sheffield City Polytechnic Education Services Department, 1975.
13. The idea of a hierarchy of objectives has been used by many writers. For an early example of its use see C.H. Granger, 'Hierarchy of Objectives', *Harvard Business Review,* Vol. 42, No. 3, 1964.
14. See M. Richards, *Organisational Goal Structures* (West: 1978).
15. See P. Drucker, *The Practice of Management* (Pan Management Series: 1968).

16. So, for example, I. Ansoff, *Corporate Strategy* (Penguin:1965) p.44 says:
'We define an objective as a measure of efficiency of the resource conversion process. An objective contains three elements: the particular attribute that is chosen as a measure of efficiency, the hardstick or scale by which the attribute is measured and the goal - the particular value on the scale which the firm seeks to attain.'

17. Quinn's work is discussed more fully in Chapter 2 of this book. His particular findings on the role of objectives can be found in Chapter 3 of *Strategies for Change, Logical Incrementalism* (Irwin: 1980).

18. See J. Argenti, *Corporate Planning* (George Allen & Unwin: 1968).

19. For further reading on the ideas behind management by objectives, it is probably as well to return to the earlier work of John Humble, *Management by Objectives in Action* (McGraw-Hill: 1970). A more recent exposition of the ideas can be found in G. Odiorne, *Management by Objectives II: A System of Managerial Leadership for the Eighties* (Pitman: 1979).

RECOMMENDED KEY READINGS

* As an overview of organisational goals: M. Richards, *Organisational Goal Structures* (West: 1978).

* A more traditional approach to the idea and use of corporate objectives might be useful. The following will help: I. Ansoff, *Corporate Strategy* (Penguin: 1968, Chs. 3 and 4), or chapters on objective setting in books by J. Argenti such as *Practical Corporate Planning* (George Allen & Unwin: 1980) or *Corporate Planning* (George Allen & Unwin: 1968).

* For a more detailed understanding of the role of goals in practice see J.B. Quinn, *Strategies for Change: Local Incrementalism* (Irwin: 1980, Ch. 3).

* On social responsibility: *Facing Realities: the European Societal Strategy Report,* available from the European Institute for Advanced Studies in Management (1981).

PART III

Strategic Choice

In many ways strategic choice is the core of corporate strategy. It is concerned with decisions about an organisation's future and the way in which it needs to respond to the many pressures and influences identified in the strategic analysis. In turn the consideration of future strategy must be mindful of the realities of strategic implementation which can be a significant constraint on strategic choice.

Chapter 2 showed that organisations are continually attempting to re-adjust to their environment and one of the major criticisms which can be made of managers concerns their inability or unwillingness to consider the variety of strategic options open to the company. Rather they tend to remain bound by their recipes and resistant to change. It is for this reason that this part of the book presents a systematic way of looking at strategic choice. The primary benefit of this systematic approach is that it helps to put in context the choices which are being made. So even where managers are making choices largely by judgment, a more analytical approach will at least provide an assessment of the consequences of those choices and some of the opportunities which the company is foregoing in pursuing its chosen strategies.

The discussion of strategic choice has been divided into two chapters:

*   Chapter 7 looks at the strategic options which are available to organisations and the reasons why some strategies might be viewed more favourably than others. There are important links with Part II on strategic analysis since the pressure to change strategy and the possible alternatives available can arise from many sources related to the environment, resources, or values within and around an organi-sation.
*   Chapter 8 examines more detailed principles and methods of evalua-tion of strategic options, not from the narrow viewpoint of seeking the "right" answer but as a means of providing a better picture of the future within which choices can be made. For example, evaluation should

normally include an assessment of contingencies - alternatives which are not preferred but may well be needed - and an understanding of when such contingencies should be implemented. This chapter also discusses the means by which options are selected for implementation.

This division into two chapters has been made for convenience and readers should remember that there may be no such division between the generation of options, evaluation, and selection in practice.

7

STRATEGIC OPTIONS

7.1 INTRODUCTION

Traditionally much of the discussion of strategic choice has been built around the assumption that organisations are concerned with growth as a major objective. Clearly, if organisations wish to grow they invariably need to seek out new opportunities. Whereas this justification of strategic choice is undoubtedly relevant to a large number of companies, there are also many organisations who, either by choice or circumstances, would not feature growth as a major objective. In fact, during periods of recession many managers will be mainly concerned with the process of managing the organisation through a period of retrenchment.

The approach in this chapter, therefore, is to argue that the process of strategic choice must address itself to a wide variety of different situations. Growth is not the reason for strategic choice being necessary; rather the need for strategic choice lies in the fact that an organisation's internal and external circumstances are constantly changing.[1] Put another way, an organisation needs to change even to stand still. Change is an absolute prerequisite of long term survival. The emphasis in this chapter is, therefore, on *development strategies* rather than the narrower growth strategies discussed in many other texts.

7.1.1 The Two Aspects of Development Strategies

In reviewing the alternative development strategies available to companies it is important to distinguish between two separate aspects of any strategy both of which need consideration:

(i) the alternative *directions* in which the organisation may choose to develop;

(ii)   the alternative *methods* by which that direction of development might be
        achieved.

Figure 7.1 illustrates this point and also provides a structure for this
chapter. Whereas decisions on *direction* and *method* are not totally independent
of each other, they do benefit from separate discussion. For example, an
organisation may make a decision to develop by market development.
However, this still leaves a further choice as to whether that is best achieved by
a process of acquiring companies already operating in the chosen markets or
whether these new markets should be developed through the company's own
efforts.

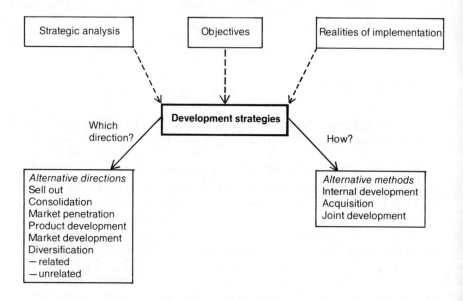

Figure 7.1   *Development strategies*

7.1.2 A Framework for Identifying Alternative Directions of Development

There are many directions in which companies may choose to develop and
therefore it is normally helpful to have some rationale or framework to help
with the identification of strategic options. There is a problem, however, in
developing a systematic approach, namely, that of coping with the great
differences which exist between organisations. In particular it needs to be
recognised that some companies are highly specialised in terms of their product
range and the markets which they serve whilst others are very diverse. The
starting point for analysing alternative directions of development for a supplier

of a highly specialised product like British Steel is quite different from that of a diversified company like Unilever or the Rank Organisation. For simplicity, this chapter in the first instance will focus attention on situations where the product/market strategy is narrow, that is, where a high degree of specialisation exists. This is not because the majority of companies are in this situation (research in fact shows quite the opposite), but because it helps illustrate the principles of identifying alternatives which are of universal applicability. Chapter 8 will pay more specific attention to additional analysis which might be useful in the case of multi-product, multi-market companies.

The framework for identifying strategic options is shown in Fig. 7.2 and concentrates on strategic options relating to product/market strategy. It should help readers identify alternative directions of development by progressively moving away from the type of products/markets in which a company is involved at the time of the analysis.

7.2 ALTERNATIVE DIRECTIONS FOR DEVELOPMENT

This section will set out the strategic directions an organisation could take. The methods by which any of these alternatives might be developed (e.g. acquisition, internal development) will be discussed in Section 7.3 below. Figure 7.2 summarises the various altertnatives.

7.2.1 Selling Out

This is an option which is often overlooked. There could well be circumstances where, in fact, selling out is the most appropriate course of action. The obvious one is when the internal and external situation has deteriorated to such a degree that the possibility of survival is remote. Voluntary or forced liquidation may be the only alternatives open to the company. However, these are not the only circumstances in which selling out would be a sensible course of action. For example, in certain markets the value of a company's products or assets are subject to considerable movements over time and a central issue in policy-making may be the astute purchase and disposal of these products and assets and the timing of purchases and disposals. This is particularly important for companies operating in markets which are essentially concerned with speculation such as strategic resources (energy, metals, commodities) or land and property.

Very often the objective of a small entrepreneur would be to 'make his million' and then retire. In these circumstances he may well follow policies which are concerned with 'fattening the goose' - making the company an attractive proposition to buy rather than being guided by longer term considerations. In family companies this can often be a source of considerable

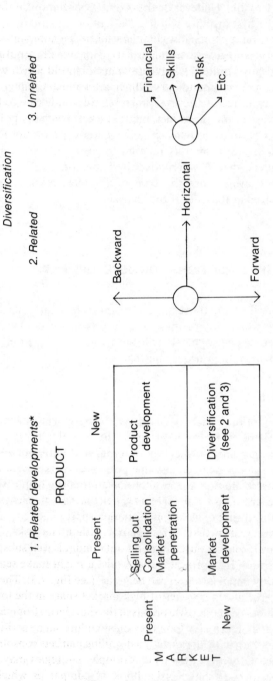

Figure 7.2 *Alternative directions for development.*
* Adapted from H. Igor Ansoff, Corporate Strategy (Penguin: 1968, p.99).

conflict between those who hold this view and others who may be more concerned with providing a lower risk, more stable company for their children to inherit.

Large, diverse companies may view their subsidiary companies as assets to be bought and sold at regular intervals as part of an overall corporate strategy. There are a variety of reasons why ventures may be sold which will be given more consideration towards the end of this chapter and in Chapter 8. This type of strategy is often called *divestment* or *disinvestment* and needs to be carefully planned.[2] The use of divestment as a central part of company policy in some multi-national companies has proved to be a source of friction between the company and host governments.[3]

7.2.2 Consolidation

Consolidation should not be confused with the 'do nothing situation' which will be discussed in the next chapter. It will be seen that 'do nothing' represents the situation where the company simply pursues current policies with complete disregard of important changes occurring both outside and inside the company. In contrast to this, strategies of consolidation may imply quite considerable changes in the specific way the company operates, but nevertheless the range of products and markets remains unchanged. (Illustration 26 is an example which makes the point.) Consolidation is equally relevant to growing, static, or declining markets and may take on several forms:

(i)   *Maintaining share in a growing market.* A company which is operating in markets showing high levels of growth may wish to maintain market share, i.e. a consolidation strategy. In fact the Boston Consulting Group's work (see Appendix) shows that the pursuit of growth to achieve dominant market share makes strategic sense: the failure to grow in line with competition is likely to mean that the firm ends up with a disadvantageous cost structure and, when the market reaches maturity, a very difficult task in increasing its market share.

However, growth is certainly not without its risks. The Boston Consulting Group themselves point out - and it is well substantiated by data from the PIMS project[4] - that whilst it might make sense to go for growth, the cost of doing so can be great[5] (see Fig. 7.3). The dilemma is clear: to reap the advantages of high market share in the longer term it may be necessary to sacrifice profits in the short term. For many firms the problem is to gauge how long they must endure such sacrifices.

(ii) *Competing in a declining market.* In declining markets consolidation may require significant changes.[6] For example, strategies may need to be developed to buy-up the order book of companies which leave the market; distributors may need to seek new sources of supply; new internal agreements may need to be developed to ensure continuing cost competitiveness in the smaller market.

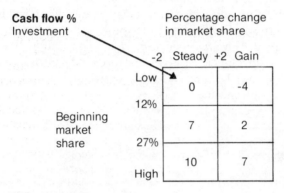

The figures in the boxes show the cash flow generated as a % of the investment which has been made. This is greatest when a company already has a high market share which it is consolidating (10%) and lowest where the investment has been used to gain market share from a low starting position (-4%).

Figure 7.3 *The cost of growth in market share (From: Valerie Kijewski, "Market-share Strategy: Beliefs v Actions", Pimsletter No. 9, The Strategic Planning Institute. Reprinted with the permission of the SPI).*

(iii) *Improving quality.* Another common consolidation strategy is the upgrading of product or service quality. The evidence is that quality is of very real significance in the improvement of profit performance[7] (see Fig. 7.4). The best situation appears to be a combination of high share and high product quality, but even firms with low market shares demonstrate significantly higher profit performance if they have products of superior quality. Often, companies trading internationally may be forced into quality improvement as a means of defending their market share overseas where competition has increased due to shifting exchange rates.

(iv) *Increasing marketing activity.* A reliance on increased marketing spending as a consolidation strategy in itself does not appear to be a satisfactory way of improving performance. Heavy marketing expenditure (as a percentage of sales) may actually damage ROI for firms with low market shares (see Fig. 7.5). This does, of course, pose a problem for a firm that is trying to improve or maintain its standing within its existing product/market: there is little evidence that it will succeed through increasing marketing expenditure other than by reducing profitability.

Marketing expenditure and product quality are also related.[7] High

---

ILLUSTRATION 26

Consolidation Does Not Mean Standing Still

- When protective patents expired Rank Xerox had to take positive steps to retain its position as market leader in the photocopying business.

For over two decades, up to the early 1970s, the basis of the Xerox Corporation's fortunes had been with photocopying technology, which they had developed and fully patented. When the patents ran out, Xerox, and with it Rank Xerox, its UK subsidiary, faced stiff competition from large multi-nationals such as Kodak, IBM, and various Japanese companies who had been patiently waiting with their own machines to capitalise on Xerox's success. It was clear that if they were to remain market leaders, Xerox would have to re-examine its strategies in the light of this new threat and take action accordingly to consolidate its position.

Xerox had always rented out its machines to companies up until the patents expired, but a change in marketing tactics in 1976 to sell machines as well as rent them proved to be an effective method of strengthening their market position. Coinciding with this selling strategy, reorganisation of the sales force around nine business areas in the UK was aimed at improving the responsiveness of the service and sales force to the customers' needs. Additional selling programmes included experimenting with telephone sales which could be followed up by salesmen and the introduction of high street showrooms where a whole range of office equipment could be sold off the shelf. Copy bureaux undertook a wide range of light printing jobs which could be performed on Xerox machines.

The Japanese always sold copiers through dealers who were able to offer various trade discounts to customers. Because Xerox sold from price-lists, their various discounts were generally only for large customers, and although they aimed to remain price competitive, they hoped to gain their edge over the Japanese by providing an unrivalled back-up service to customers. This was done by operating a decentralised field service force which aimed to carry out repairs to rented machines within an average of 4 hours of any breakdown.

By improving their sales techniques and service back-up, Xerox and Rank Xerox were able to consolidate their position as market leaders and remain ahead of competitors at that time.

Source: Management Today, June 1980, p.90.

---

marketing expenditure is not a substitute for quality: indeed it appears that high marketing expenditure damages ROI when quality is low (see Fig. 7.6). It must be concluded that simply gearing up marketing expenditure as a means of consolidating a company's position is not sufficient.

(v)   *Improving productivity through capital investment.* Another approach is through improved productivity - the mechanisation of routine tasks for

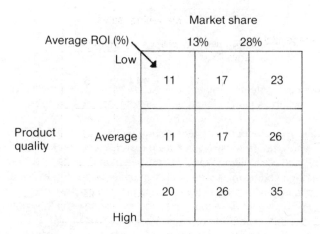

Figure 7.4 *Quality, market share, and return on investment (From: R. D. Buzzell, 'Product Quality', Pimsletter No. 4, Strategic Planning Institute. Reprinted with the permission of the SPI).*

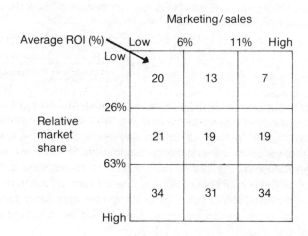

Figure 7.5 *Heavy marketing is not profitable for low share business (From:The Strategic Planning Institute, 'A Programme of ... The Strategic Planning Institute', 1977. Reprinted with the permission of the SPI).*

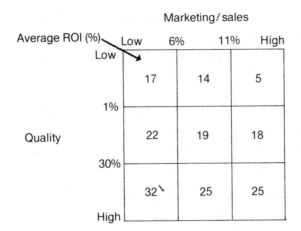

Figure 7.6 *High marketing expenditures hurt profits especially when quality is low (From: The Strategic Planning Institute, 'A Program of . . . The Strategic Planning Institute', 1977. Reprinted with the permission of the SPI).*

example. This has become so much a part of accepted 'management wisdom' that it might come as something of a shock to learn that there is very little evidence to support the notion that increased capital intensity generates greater profits and a good deal of evidence to show the reverse[8] as shown in Fig. 7.7.

The reasons for this are important to understand. What often happens is that analysts project reduced costs through mechanisation and reduced labour input but assume that revenue will remain constant or rise. However, in capital intensive industries, companies are especially keen to ensure that capacity is fully loaded and may cut prices to keep volume, thus reducing overall margins, or undertake uneconomic production runs to keep customers happy; or even raise marketing expenditure to wrestle volume from competition. Since these companies have probably already had to raise wages[9] to recompense a depleted workforce, the overall result can be a very substantial drop in profits. In fact, the required level of savings in manpower may never take place. Reductions in direct labour are partially offset by increased administrative staff and expensive specialists.

High capital investment is also a barrier to exit. The result is that those suffering from low profits are reluctant to get out so they continue to battle on and make the situation worse. Indeed, raising capital intensity as a method of consolidation is most likely to be successful for companies who already have a strong position in the market, are unlikely to meet fierce price competition, and who are able to make real reductions in labour and production costs.[10]

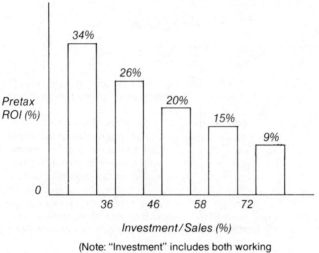

Investment/Sales (%)

(Note: "Investment" includes both working
capital and fixed capital at net book value.
The figures are four-year averages.)

Figure 7.7   *Investment intensity and ROI (From: S. Schoeffler, "The Unprofitability
of 'Modern' Technology and What to do about it", Pimsletter No. 2, The Strategic
Planning Institute. Reprinted with the permission of the SPI).*

7.2.3 Market Penetration

The previous section has been concerned with options which would
maintain a company's market share in its present markets. Opportunities often
exist for gaining market share as a deliberate strategy and this is normally
referred to as market penetration. Much of the previous discussion is relevant
to this option since, for example, improving quality or productivity, or
increasing marketing activity could all be means of achieving market
penetration. Equally the arguments concerning the long term desirability of
obtaining a dominant market share are relevant. However, the ease with which
a company can pursue a policy of market penetration will be dependent on the
nature of the market and the competitive position which prevails.

When the overall market is growing or can be induced to grow, it may be
relatively easy for companies with a small market share, or even new entrants,
to gain market share fairly rapidly. This is because the absolute level of sales of
the established companies may still be growing and indeed, in some instances,
those companies may be unable or unwilling to meet the new demand. Import
penetration into some industries can be traced back to the early 1970s when
companies were unable to supply the peak demand occurring during booms
and their customers had to seek alternative sources overseas. Once established
with overseas suppliers many UK users were reluctant to revert to UK

sourcing. When the boom was over the importers held on to their market share.
In contrast, market penetration in static markets can be much more difficult to achieve. The lessons of the experience curve (see Appendix) would, of course, emphasise the difficulty of market penetration in mature markets since the advantageous cost structure of market leaders should prevent the incursions of lower market share competitors. In declining markets it is difficult to generalise on the difficulties of pursuing a policy of market penetration. A company which is determined to confine its interests to one product/market area and unwilling to permit a decline in sales will need to gain market share. If other companies are leaving the market, penetration could prove easy although the wisdom of the strategy may be in some doubt.

7.2.4 Product Development

Often companies will feel that consolidation in their present products/ markets does not present adequate opportunities and will search for alternatives which build upon the company's present knowledge and skills. In the case of product development the company maintains the security of its present markets whilst changing and developing new products. Some examples will illustrate the many reasons why companies might show a preference for product development. Companies in retailing will follow the changing needs of their customers by a continuing policy of introducing new product lines. In the same way local authorities need to shift their pattern of services as local needs change. Sometimes product development is preferred because the company is particularly good at R&D or because it has structured itself around product divisions. When product life cycles are short - as with consumer electronics -product development needs to be a central part of company strategy.

Nevertheless, product development raises uncomfortable dilemmas for firms. New products may be absolutely vital to the future of the firm. The problem is that the process of creating a broad product line is expensive and potentially unprofitable. For example, it is often the capital intensive firms with the lowest rates of new product introduction that perform best.[10] Product development is likely to require a commitment to high levels of spending on R&D. Figure 7.8 shows that high market share companies may benefit in profit terms from relatively high levels of R&D expenditure, companies in a weak market position with high expenditure may suffer badly.[7]

7.2.5 Market Development

In the case of market development the organisation maintains the security of its present products whilst venturing into new market areas. Market development can include entering new *market segments,* exploiting *new uses* for the product or spreading into new *geographical areas.*

Just as companies have good reasons to prefer product development, other companies might have a strong preference for market development. In

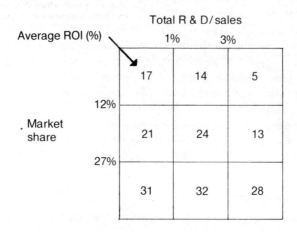

Figure 7.8   *R & D expenditure, market share and ROI (From: S. Schoeffler, 'Market Position: Build, Hold or Harvest?', Pimsletter No. 3, The Strategic Planning Institute. Reprinted with the permission of the SPI).*

capital intensive industries many of the company's assets (money, plant, skilled people) will be specifically devoted to the technology which produces a particular product or products. These assets cannot easily be switched to produce any other products. In this situation the company's *distinctive competence* lies with the product and not the market and hence the continued exploitation of the product by market development would normally be preferred. Most capital goods companies have developed this way by opening up more and more overseas markets as old markets become saturated. A similar argument applies to organisations whose distinctive competence is in R&D. The rapid worldwide exploitation of microelectronic technology is a good example.

Exporting is an important method of market development. There are a variety of reasons why organisations might want to develop beyond exporting and *internationalise* by locating some of their manufacturing, distribution or marketing operations overseas. Figure 7.9 summarises some of these reasons and the importance assigned to each in a survey of managers.[11] Illustration 27 gives examples of both product and market development.

7.2.6 Diversification

Diversification as a description of strategy is used in different ways by different people. In this chapter the word will be used in a fairly general way to identify all directions of development which take the company away from its present products and its present market at the same time.[12] However, it is

The reasons	The frequency with which this reason was mentioned (key at foot of table)▼
1. Defensive Strategies	
A company is operating abroad to defend its existing business as a result of:	
1.1 Government action in establishing or increasing:	
(a) tariff barriers	A
(b) the subsequent lowering of tariff barriers	B
(c) import controls	D
(d) legislation (at home or abroad) against monopolies or trade agreements	C
(e) legislation for import substitution, usually by enforcing part local manufacture or assembly	D
1.2 Demands for local manufacture and other problems of nationalism in overseas markets	C
1.3 Transport costs and delays	A
1.4 Difficulties with agents and licensees	A & B
1.5 Troubles with after-sales service and other technical difficulties abroad	C
1.6 The need to protect patents	C
1.7 The need to ensure supplies of raw materials and components	C
1.8 The need to go international when competitors, suppliers or customers do so	B
1.9 The need to protect shareholders at home from trade recessions by:	
(a) a geographical spread	C
(b) product group diversification (which may involve geographical as well)	D
2. Aggressive Strategies	
The search for:	
2.1 More profitable uses for underemployed resources at home in:	
(a) capital and equipment	C
(b) personnel	D
(c) know-how	C
2.2 The search for lower factor costs, including those for:	
(a) capital (availability as well as cost)	C
(b) labour	C
(c) supplies	D
2.3 The more effective use of opportunities by the development of global plans and strategies for resources and markets	C
2.4 Access to foreign knowledge or methods	D
2.5 The need to expand, when this can only be abroad, and the possibility of escaping from constraints at home	E
3. Other Pressures	
3.1 Influence of governments, for example:	
(a) by general encouragement to foreign investment	D
(b) tax concessions	D
(c) cheap loans	D
(d) grants or guarantees	D
(e) buildings	E
3.2 Influence of other companies, e.g. approach for know-how	C
3.3 Internal to company, such as pressure groups advocating overseas manufacture because of the expertise and insights of members	C

Note on the frequency:
A. Mentioned by virtually all respondents
B. Mentioned by over half of respondents
C. Mentioned by less than half of respondents
D. Mentioned once or twice only by respondents
E. No mention

Figure 7.9 *Why companies expand overseas (Source: M. Z. Brooke and H. Lee Remmers, The Strategy of Multinational Enterprise, 2nd edn. (London: Pitman: 1978, p. 162). Reprinted by permission of Pitman Books Ltd., London).*

ILLUSTRATION 27

Directions of Growth

- Growth may be achieved in several ways: Mothercare offered a greater product range to its existing customers, Fads spread its DIY shops across Britain, and Hunting Plastics which had specialised in industrial products diversified into the leisure market.

Product Development. Back in the 1960s, Mothercare was conceived to provide shops which would cater for all the needs of the mother-to-be and her baby under one roof. Mothercare built a solid reputation upon this specialised image but at the risk of diluting this specialisation, decided to extend its product range into older children's clothes, so continuing to serve the same 'baby boom'. Mothers of the 1960s were able to continue using the Mothercare service even as their children got older.

Market Development. One of the commonest forms of taking existing products into new markets is by expanding business interests over a wider geographical area. Operating solely in the south for several years, this is exactly what the DIY chain Fads did when, in 1976, it took the decision to open up in the north of Britain the same sorts of shops that had proved so successful in the south. Again, this was a successful move, and after two years, Fads broke even on their investment.

Diversification. A company which specialised in glass reinforced plastic products such as cladding, lorry cabs, and urinals, found that a move into the leisure market paid dividends. Hunting Industrial Plastics, part of the Hunting Organisation - the engineering, aviation and oil field services group set up Skiddale Leisure Products to diversify into speedboats, motorised surf boards and hover-craft. This diversification enabled the company to still use their original competence in the glass-reinforced plastic (GRP) industry, but offset the fall in their present markets due to a resistance to lorry cabs made of GRP and restraints on council spending affecting the market for cladding and urinals. Because GRP was found to be ideal for boat hulls a two-year diversification drive costing £250,000 developed new ideas, and designs aimed at the leisure industry. Although the company continued to make its original products, its managing director saw the potential for production of leisure products to treble over two years.
Source: Management Today, February 1978, p.70.

---

convenient to divide the consideration of diversification into two broad types:

* *related diversification* which represents development beyond the present product and market but still within the broad confines of the industry within which the company operates;

* *unrelated diversification* is development beyond the present industry into products/markets which, at face value, bear no clear relationship to the present product/market.[13]

Subsections 7.2.7 and 7.2.8 discuss diversification, its different forms, and the advantages and disadvantages of developing by diversification.[14] It should be remembered, however, that many organisations are already very diverse and may sensibly be needing to ask the reverse question, namely how far should they specialise their activities. It is not intended to give separate discussion to *specialisation* as an alternative since the arguments are simply the reverse of those used in diversification. Readers should bear this in mind when reading the sections which follow, and view them as a discussion of the relative merits of specialisation and diversification.

7.2.7 Related Diversification

Referring back to Fig. 7.2, it can be seen that even though related diversification takes a company beyond its present products and markets, it still keeps the company in areas where it has some knowledge. The new alternatives are within the industry in which the company presently operates. It is important to be clear what is meant by 'industry' and to understand some of the terminology which is commonly used:

* *industry* refers to all the steps of manufacturing, distribution and servicing which go into the production and marketing of a company's products and any other products of which they form a part. This is a very broad definition in some cases since, for example, a manufacturer of nylon cloth might be viewed, for this purpose, as being in the same industry as chemical companies, synthetic fibre producers, clothing manufacturers, designers, retail outlets, to name but a few.
* *backward integration* refers to development into activities which are concerned with the inputs into the company's present business (i.e. are further back in the industry). For example, raw materials, machinery and labour are all important inputs into a manufacturing company.
* *forward integration* refers to development into activities which are concerned with a company's outputs (i.e. are further forward in the industry). Transport, distribution, repairs and servicing are examples.
* *vertical integration* is a broader term used to describe either backward or forward integration (or both together).
* *horizontal integration* refers to development into activities which are either competitive with, or directly complementary to, a company's present activities. A lending library's extension into a tourist information service or video cassette material would be examples.

To simplify the reasons why companies might view related diversification favourably, the case of a manufacturing company can be considered. There are many activities which are inputs to, and outputs from, a manufacturing company and therefore candidates for related diversification. These are shown in Fig.7.10. Illustration 28 is an example of related diversification. Figure 7.11 summarises the major advantages and disadvantages of the concept.

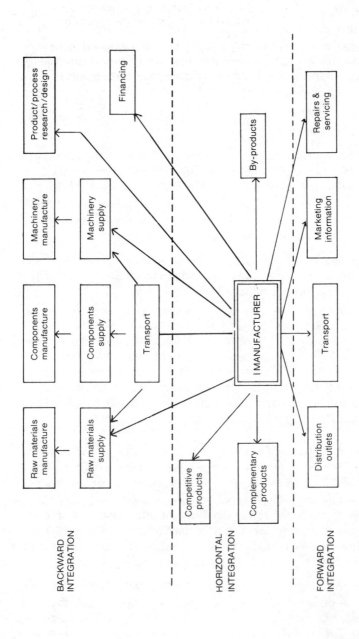

Note: (1) Some Companies will manufacture components or semi-finished items. In those cases there will be additional integration opportunities into Assembly or Finished Product Manufacture.

Figure 7.10   *Alternatives open to a manufacturer to develop by related diversification.*

A. Possible advantages	Examples/comments
1. *Control of supplies*	
— quantity	Tyre manufacturers own rubber plantations (Dunlop) to secure continuity of supply
— quality	Components for motor cars may need to be manufactured by the company
— price	Design facility (fashion clothes), can be cheaper if 'in house'
2. *Control of markets*	Unilever bought Mac-fisheries to help sell products of Hebrides fishing fleet
3. *Access to information*	
— technological change	Shoe manufacturers involved in machinery companies to keep abreast of developments
— market trends	Manufacturers concern at being isolated from market trends
4. *Cost savings*	Fully integrated steel plants save cost on re-heating and transport
5. *Profit or growth*	All sectors of the same industry are not equally profitable at any time
6. *Indirect competition*	Manufacturer who owns a raw material supplier may also supply competitors
7. *Spreading risk*	Avoids over-reliance on one product/market but builds on related experience.
8. *Resource utilisation*	British manufacturers act as consultants to overseas clients — capitalising on the 'know-how'
B. Possible disadvantages	
1. *Management control*	The 'recipe' for success in managing a manufacturing company may not be transferable to a supplier or distribution company
2. *Inefficiencies*	In declining industries companies may need to dis-integrate (specialise) as the scale of production declines

Figure 7.11 *Some reasons for related diversification.*

ILLUSTRATION 28

Related Diversification

* Clarks' success may be largely attributed to the growth it achieved through
  its forward and backward integration within the shoe industry.
Shoemakers since the mid-1800s, C. & J. Clark grew to become the largest shoe
manufacturer in Britain, and possibly in Western Europe, by the late 1970s. From a
cottage industry using sheepskin off-cuts to make slippers, Clarks have pursued
both forward and backward integration to achieve involvement in almost every
aspect of shoe manufacturing and retailing.

   One of Clarks' earliest backwards investments came in 1877 when a leather
board and leather components business was founded to use the original shoe
factory's scrap leather. Over the years the importance of this factory has grown as it
became the major supplier of leather board not only to Clarks but also to other shoe
manufacturers. Acquisitions of a rubber solution and rubber factory, and of a
company making non-rubber soles, heels, lasts and trimmings further increased
Clarks' control of their supply. Clarks also manufacture shoe machinery for both
internal and external sale.

   Up to 1946, Clarks had only 20 shops, with the majority of their shoes being
sold through independent retail outlets. By 1970, however, their 280 shops formed
a major retail chain in its own right, and also gave Clarks' research unit a first-hand
view of the market which not only helped to direct their manufacturing operations,
but could also be used as a service to independent retailers whom they supplied.

   This complete involvement in the shoe industry has allowed Clarks to benefit
from many of the advantages of vertical integration as described in the text, whilst
some of the associated disadvantages such as management control have been
minimised through Clarks remaining a family firm.

Source: Management Today, February 1969.

Figure 7.11 shows the great variety of reasons why companies might
choose to develop through related diversification. Equally, highly diversified
companies might see any of these as reasons to increase their degree of
specialisation. For example, it may be decided that supplies of raw materials
have become available from a reliable low-cost source and this provides a good
reason to cease the manufacture of those materials within the company.

7.2.8 Unrelated Diversification

Unrelated diversification refers to options which lie beyond the
boundaries of the industry within which the company presently operates. At
face value these options may bear no logical relationship to the company's
activities. (Illustration 29 is an example of unrelated diversification.)

ILLUSTRATION 29

Unrelated Diversification

●   Gill and Duffus have grown since 1907 by a continuing process of diversified acquisition.

In 1907, Mr F.G. Gill and Mr A.S. Duffus began trading in edible nuts and other raw materials used in the confectionary and baking business. The progress of the company since then has been a history of continuous growth through diverse world trading in commodities, manufacturing, produce, chemicals and energy, futures market services, insurance, securities and money broking.

In the 1920s a newly formed export department started to trade in cocoa butter for shipment to chocolate factories throughout the world. This led to the start of raw cocoa bean trading in 1929.

The company's first manufacturing venture grew from their early success in cocoa trading. In 1940 two cocoa mills were opened in Britain, followed by one in Ghana and another in Brazil after the war.

The group became a public company in 1950, and the acquisition of Pacol in 1962 added coffee and rubber to its trading activities and also strengthened its international network.

Subsequent trading in metals bolstered the Group's 'soft' commodity trading activities, and by 1977 a chemical trading division was formed, prompted by an increasing proportion of world trade being represented by chemicals.

Because all commodity traders are dependent on efficient and highly specialist insurance services, Gill and Duffus developed their own insurance capability within the Group by acquiring two insurance interests which they merged to form one company.

As a natural consequence of the Group's involvement in commodity markets worldwide, Gill and Duffus have made their services available to selected clients via companies in New York, Hong Kong and London through their futures market services. This then paved the way for involvement in the world-wide money market, securities and money broking.

From origins in nuts, Gill and Duffus became a group involved in a very diverse range of activities.

Source: Gill & Duffus annual reports.

Synergy[15] is a commonly quoted reason for unrelated diversification. Synergy can occur in situations where two or more activities or processes complement each other to the extent that their combined effect is greater than the 'sum of the parts'. Although the success of product and market development strategies can also depend upon synergy, it is a particularly important idea in the case of unrelated diversification. Synergy may result for financial reasons where, for example, one activity generates a short-term positive cash flow and another needs such a source of cash. Equally the good image of a company may be used as a platform to develop into a new line of business which might have proved very difficult without such a support. The estimation of the likely benefits which synergy can bring can be a method of evaluation of strategy and is discussed in Chapter 8.

Other reasons for unrelated diversification may be related to the values and aspirations of decision-makers, the opportunity to employ existing under-utilised resources in a new field, or the desire to move into a different area of activity perhaps because the present one is in decline. These and other reasons are summarised with brief examples in Fig. 7.12.

Reason	Examples/comments
Need to use excess cash or safeguard profit	Buying a tax loss situation (Trafalgar House purchase of Cunard)
Personal values or objectives of powerful figures	Personal image locally or nationally may be a strong motive. Many successful businessmen sink their fortunes into football clubs. Some business ventures are described as "buying a knighthood"
Exploiting under-utilised resources	Farmers use fields for camp sites. Local authorities use plastic-waste for new materials. Coal industry makes building materials from coal waste
Escape from present business	A company's products may be in decline and unrelated diversification presents the only possible 'escape'.
Spreading risk	Some companies believe that it is good sense not to have all their 'eggs in one basket' and so diversify into unrelated areas
To benefit from synergistic effects	See text

Figure 7.12 *Some reasons for unrelated diversification.*

Strategies of diversification can raise many of the problems previously discussed for product development (see Subsection 7.2.4). Illustration 30 shows some of the difficulties experienced by EMI in developing their body scanner. The same illustration also serves to show that categorising diversification as 'related' or 'unrelated' is not a straightforward matter: the body scanner was related in terms of technology but unrelated to their existing products in terms of its market.

ILLUSTRATION 30

The EMI Body Scanner

- Despite its technical brilliance, EMI's Body Scanner failed to bring the company success because it was incompatable with their traditional business activities.

Throughout the 1960s and early 1970s, the main interests of EMI were in electronics, music, television and leisure, with the majority of its revenue being earned by the music division's sales of popular records.

In the late 1960s, a researcher in the electronics division of the company drew upon recent technological innovations to produce an advanced form of X-ray device which proved in trials to be a cost-effective method of scanning the brain. It also had the advantages of being less painful and time-consuming than existing methods, whilst at the same time gave superior results.

Vigorous internal lobbying by highly-placed supporters in the EMI management secured the go-ahead for the project's development and subsequent marketing, despite the fact that the company had no market expertise in that field.

Production commenced in 1972/73 and orders were received at a rapid rate: since EMI were the only company engaged in that field of technology. They estimated that they would be at least two years ahead of any competition that would inevitably come from existing medical electronic companies. In any case, EMI were confident that their other business divisions would be able to provide financial support for the brain scanner when the competition did arrive.

Although in the first four years of activity in the medical electronics field, EMI reaped operating profits of £38 million, by 1975 with orders still way ahead of production, the company gradually realised that they lacked the management expertise to maintain this momentum in the face of rising competition. Firstly, the company lacked the close ties with radiology departments that their competitors had, and also suffered the disadvantage of having no existing service division to maintain their scanners. EMI also found that their unfamiliarity with medical electronics meant that their management were ill-equipped to evaluate and implement new product strategy. Also, because of their newness to the field, existing managers from other medical electronics firms were wary of joining this newcomer before it had become established.

As a result, EMI's management became increasingly over-stretched and under-staffed when they tried to introduce the technically brilliant but cost-ineffective Body Scanner in the mid-1970s. As traditional medical electronics companies begain to gain a firmer hold on the market, EMI's weaknesses were only amplified. As profits fell in their other operating divisions, the group found that by the late 1970s, they could no longer afford to finance the research and development that was needed to keep their Body Scanners competitive and in two years profits of £14.7 million on a turnover of £93.2 million turned into a loss of £13.2 million on a turnover of £66.5 million.

Source: Management Today, February 1979, p.66.

7.2.9 Diversification and Performance

There have been a number of attempts to assess the extent to which diversification is related to company performance. The evidence from the USA[16] and UK[17] summarised in Fig. 7.13 suggests that:

(i) The more diversified businesses grew faster than less diversified businesses. Indeed, the greatest growth comes from firms with diversified interests of an unrelated nature.

(ii) The USA research, 1960 to 1969, suggests that the most profitable strategy, in terms of measures of return, is diversification of a related nature constrained to the core skills of the business.

(iii) Notably, however, the more recent research on UK firms shows that it is companies which rely on a product of 'dominant' importance rather than on a strategy of diversification that are most profitable in terms of return on capital employed.

Care must be taken in interpreting these results. The data base is not directly comparable since it comes from different countries and at different times. However, it is possible that the results reflect the trading conditions of the time. Related diversification might be more suited to firms when there are opportunities for expansion in a growing economy: on the other hand, in terms of little or no economic growth, a strategy of concentration on mainline products rather than the spreading of interests might make more sense.

The balance of evidence does warn against unconstrained diversification.[18] As with product development, it is one thing to show that diversified companies can be profitable but it also has to be pointed out that the process of diversification can be very difficult and costly.[19] A firm that follows a strategy of launching new businesses is likely to suffer a major drain on its cash resources: the average length of time it takes to move into profits is eight years and severe losses can be expected for four years.

7.2.10 Development Strategies in Practice

In the preceding discussion the implicit assumption has been made that a company's product/market strategy should be the focus of attention when reviewing strategic options for the future. The extent to which these various options are viewed as 'sensible' can then be reviewed by looking at the constraints under which these options would be pursued. In particular during this second stage, which is called evaluation and discussed in Chapter 8, the resources of the company and the values of people in and around the company will be viewed as major constraints on new product/market strategies.

There is a danger in assuming that this product/market focus is the only way of looking at strategic options. In practice it is very often the case that the company's *resources* or *values* would more sensibly form the focus for identifying alternatives and product/market opportunities (or lack of

USA 1960-1969†	Company product strategy*			
	Single product	Dominant product	Related products	Unrelated products
Sales growth (% p.a.)	7.2	8.0	9.1	14.2
Earnings growth (% p.a.)	4.8	8.0	9.4	13.9
Earnings growth per share (% p.a.)	3.9	6.0	7.6	7.9
P/E	14.6	15.7	19.2	15.8
Return on investment (%)	10.8	9.6	11.5	9.5
Return on equity (%)	13.2	11.6	13.6	11.9

UK 1970-1980‡	Company product strategy*			
	Single product	Dominant product	Related products	Unrelated products
Sales growth (% p.a.)	1.0	1.5	1.3	2.1
Profit growth before interest & tax (% p.a.)	0.09	0.75	0.67	1.31
Share growth (capital value % p.a.)	-3.65	-3.54	-3.58	-3.44
Return on capital employed (%)	18.1	19.1	16.9	16.7

*These product groups describe strategies which are progressively more diversified. So, for example, the "dominant product" situation refers to companies which have 70% or more of their sales in one product area and "related" to companies with less than 70% in one product area. In Rumelt's research, highest profit returns were found for related strategies where diversification remained associated with core skills of the business (termed "related constrained").

Sources: †From: Richard P. Rumelt, Strategy, Structure and Economic Performance, Boston, Mass.: Division of Research, Harvard Business School, 1974 (Table 3-1, p.91). Used with permission.
‡ R. Reed and G. Luffman (see reference 17).

Figure 7.13 Financial consequences of product strategies.

opportunities) would be seen as a constraint on these alternatives. Some of the options already discussed are perhaps better understood this way.

Organisations operating in very stable environments may be mainly concerned with *resource utilisation* and this will become the focus of attention for the identification of alternative strategies. The idea of *distinctive competence* discussed in Chapter 4 is seen as the main issue steering company strategy. Product/market opportunities and values become constraints upon the company in attempting to capitalise on this distinctive competence. Some of the options already identified in Fig. 7.12 as unrelated diversification are only described as unrelated because a product/market focus has been taken. They are not unrelated to the company's present strategy if resource utilisation becomes the focus. The strategy of an organisation which diversifies into new businesses in order to capitalise on a distinctive strength such as financial management skills or under-utilised machinery is perhaps better understood in this way.

Similarly, there are many circumstances when the dominant values of an organisation are the best focus of attention for the identification of alternative strategies. *New business ventures* tend to be dominated by the values of the founder, which are not always expressed in product/market terms. The desire to be independent or to be successful can be very important values which dominate new ventures. A similar situation can recur in an organisation at a later date, triggered off by unexpected or difficult events such as the loss of a major customer or supplier when short term survival, almost at any cost, dominates company strategy. Very often the need to halt the steady decline of a company dominates strategy formulation. In such a *turnaround* situation alternative courses of action are assessed primarily by this measure.

Figure 7.14 summarises this idea of *focus*. The issue of central importance is that the process of strategic choice must recognise the importance of a variety of factors (environment, resources and values) but that the sequence in which these factors are considered may vary. One factor is used to identify alternatives whilst the other factors are viewed as constraints and introduced during the process of evaluation. The dominance of a product/market focus in the literature has probably occurred because of the dominance of growth as a business objective which inplies the need to seek out new product/market opportunities. For similar reasons a situation of retrenchment would also tend to be dominated by the need to adjust product/market strategy to fit new environmental circumstances.

Another assumption which has been made for reasons of simplification is that developments tend to occur as isolated events. In reality, of course, strategy develops as a combination of various strategic changes which can involve the abandonment of certain alternatives as others are developed. This more dynamic view of how strategy evolves has been described as zig-zagging.[20] Figure 7.15 shows how a company manufacturing and selling freezer baskets to the consumer market gradually developed into a manufacturer of plastic bags and cardboard boxes for industrial companies.

Focus	Options concerned with:	Constraints	Most applicable to situation of:
1. Environment (Product/market)	Satisfying market opportunities	Resource utilisation Values	Growth Retrenchment
2. Resource utilisation	Capitalising on the company's distinctive competence	Environmental opportunities Values	Stability
3. Values (Mission)	Meeting the needs of powerful individuals or groups	Environmental opportunities Resource utilisation	New companies Turnaround Sudden change

Figure 7.14 *Different focuses for generating strategic options.*

Step	Strategic change	Manufacture	Distribute	Type of customer
Start	—	Baskets	Baskets ⟶	Householders
Step 1	Product development into freezer packaging (bags) bought-in	Baskets	Baskets ⟶ Bags	Householders
Step 2	Backward integration Into bag manufacture	Baskets Bags	Baskets ⟶ Bags	Householders
Step 3	Market development Selling bags to industrial companies	Baskets Bags	Baskets ⟶ Bags ⟶	Householders Companies
Step 4	Product development Buy-in cardboard boxes for sale to companies	Baskets Bags	Baskets ⟶ Bags ⟶ Boxes	Householders Companies
Step 5	Backward integration Into box manufacture	Baskets Bags Boxes	Baskets ⟶ Bags ⟶ Boxes	Householders Companies
Step 6	Backward disintegration Discontinue manufacture of baskets — buy in	Bags Boxes	Baskets ⟶ Bags ⟶ Boxes	Householders Companies
Step 7	Divestment Sell consumer goods distribution division		Bags ⟶ Boxes	Companies

Figure 7.15 *Development strategies in practice – an example of zig-zagging (After: J. Kreiken in, "Business Policy and Strategic Management", W.F. Glueck (ed.), McGraw-Hill 3rd edn., 1980).*

7.3 ALTERNATIVE METHODS OF DEVELOPMENT

The previous section has been concerned with alternative directions in which organisations might develop. However, for each of these alternatives a further choice is also needed, namely, the *method* by which that direction is to be developed. These methods can be divided into three 'pure' types:

* Internal development
* Acquisition
* Joint development

Like most strategic decisions the choice between these methods is essentially a trade-off between a number of factors such as cost, speed and risk. How this trade-off is viewed in any one situation will depend not only on the circumstances of the company but also on the attitudes of those making the decision. This should be apparent since companies within the same industry often have quite different, and long standing, approaches to development - some always preferring to develop internally, others by acquisition. Illustration 31 shows a situation where all three approaches - internal development, acquisition and joint developments-were explored. Before reviewing these alternatives in more detail it is worthwhile looking at the information that is

---

ILLUSTRATION 31

Thorn and the Video Disc Player

- Keen to compete in the newly emerging UK video market, Thorn explored three ways in which it might achieve its strategy of product development.

When the newly formed Thorn-EMI Group saw the potential to diversify into the field of video disc players in the late 1970s, it was very conscious that, should a move materialise, it could easily become a mere satellite of Japanese technology because of Japanese domination. Keen to retain control of its own UK market place, it was clear that to exploit successfully its own strengths in the area of video discs, Thorn would have a lot of ground to make up in the technological development of video disc players. So whilst a great opportunity was materialising for Thorn to exploit the EMI activities in the film and music world by offering a highly comprehensive library of 'software' for these video disc players, the Group was faced with the problem of acquiring the technological experise required for 'hardware' development.

Three possible options were explored by Thorn:

Firstly, they could develop their own technology - but of the estimated £1 billion spent on research and development by other manufacturers worldwide on video disc systems, not one penny had been invested by Thorn. Thus, from a financial aspect alone, internal development would have been quite impractical -even if the market could actually have tolerated further variants.

Secondly, Thorn might have attempted to acquire technological expertise by purchasing a company which had developed its own system. Because most of the innovations in developing video disc players had stemmed from large (especially Japanese) corporations, acquisition would also have been impossible, if only because of the sheer size of a takeover bid.

The final option for Thorn was to attempt to enter into joint agreement with one of the large corporations and to cooperate in producing a complete video system. Thorn were ultimately able to form such a contract with the Japanese Victor Company whereby both parties sought to benefit: whilst Thorn could live and prosper off the JVC technological expertise, JVC were able to utilise Thorn's knowledge of the UK market and gain a far larger market share than they might otherwise have expected.

Source: Management Today, June 1981, p.82.

---

available concerning the popularity of these alternatives as methods of development.

Both Channon[21] and Sutton[22] provide a detailed picture of the role of acquistion/mergers as a means of strategic development in British industry. Their major conclusions are that development by acquisition tends to go in waves (for example, 1898-1900, 1926-29, 1967-1973) interspersed with long periods where most development (as measured by new investment) occurs internally. Moreover, these merger booms tend to be selective in terms of industry sector. For example, in the UK the 1960s boom was particularly important in brewing, electrical engineering (GEC) and textiles (Courtaulds). Similar patterns of activity have been observed in the USA and other developed countries. Although joint development is an increasing trend within the UK, particularly in service industries like catering, or household services, etc., there has been little written about its extent. The discussion which follows will attempt to cast some light on the advantages and disadvantages of development internally, by acquisition, or jointly.

7.3.1 Internal Development

For many organisations internal development has always been the primary method by which strategy has developed and there are some compelling reasons why this should be so. Very often, particularly with products which are highly technical in design or method of manufacture, companies will choose to develop new products themselves since the process of development is seen as the best way of acquiring the necessary *skills and knowledge* to exploit the product and compete successfully in the market place. A parallel argument would apply to the development of new markets by direct involvement. For example, many manufacturers still choose to forego the use of agents within the UK and export markets since they feel that the direct involvement (which they gain from having their own salesforce) is of considerable advantage in terms of understanding 'what makes the market tick'.

Although the final cost of developing new activities internally may be greater than by acquiring other companies the *spread of cost* may be more favourable and realistic. This is obviously a strong argument in favour of internal development for small companies who simply do not have the resources available, in the short term, to develop in any other way. A related issue is that of *minimising disruption* to other activities. The slower rate of change which internal development brings usually makes it favourable in this respect.

It is often forgotten that a company may, in reality, have *no choice* on how new ventures are developed. Companies that are breaking new ground are not in a position to develop by acquisition or joint development since they are the only ones in the field. But this problem is not confined to such extreme situations. On many occasions, organisations that would prefer to develop by acquisition cannot do so since they cannot find a suitable company who is willing to be bought out. This has been cited as a particular difficulty for foreign companies attempting to enter Japan.[23] Internal development avoids the often traumatic *behavioural problems* arising from acquisition.[24] The cultures of the acquiring and acquired companies may be incompatible.

There are also many reasons why companies find it difficult or inappropriate to develop new strategies internally. These reasons will be discussed in the next section since the shortcomings of internal development are very often the reasons for preferring acquisition as a method of development.

7.3.2 Acquisition

Perhaps the most compelling reason to develop by acquisition is the *speed* with which it allows the company to enter new product/market areas. In some cases the product and/or market are changing so rapidly that this becomes the only way of successfully entering the market since the process of internal development is too slow in comparison. Another common reason for acquisition is the lack of *knowledge or resources* to develop certain strategies internally. For example, a company may be acquired for its R&D expertise, or its knowledge of property speculation, or a particular type of production system.

The *overall cost* of developing by acqustion may, in certain circumstances, be particularly advantageous. Companies going in to liquidation may be a good buy. An extreme example is asset-stripping where the sole motive for the acquisition is short term gain by buying up undervalued assets and disposing of them piecemeal.

The *competitive situation* may influence a company to choose acquisition. In markets which are static and market shares of companies reasonably steady, it is often a difficult proposition for a totally new company to enter the market since their presence would upset this equilibrium. If, however, the new company chooses to enter the market by acqustion, the risk of competitive reaction is reduced. The same arguments also apply when an established supplier in an industry acquires a competitor either for the latter's order book (market share) or in some cases to shut down their capacity to help restore a situation where supply/demand is more balanced and trading conditions are more favourable.

Sometimes there are reasons of *cost efficiency* which would make acquisition more favourable. This cost efficiency could arise from the fact that a company which is already established and running may already be a long way down the learning curve and have achieved efficiencies which would be difficult to match quickly by internal development.

Many of the problems associated with acquisition have been hinted at in the discussion of internal development. In essence, the overriding problem with acquisition lies in the ability to *integrate* the new company into the activities of the old - an issue which will be given much fuller consideration in later chapters.

The performance characteristics of firms in the UK that develop by acquisition are interesting. The rate of sales growth is likely to increase and there may be a more stable profit position, perhaps because of a wider product base.[25] Although stock market valuation of the acquired firm is likely to rise prior to takeover, the stock market rating of the acquirer almost always suffers. The implication is, of course, that the stock market has little confidence that the enlarged company is likely to perform as well, at least in the short term, as it did before the acquisition. In fact, there seems to be little overall profit performance gain or loss after acquisition.[26] It might be concluded that an important impetus for takeovers is management's desire to increase the size of the firm.

Despite the fact that the majority of research[27] would confirm the widespread failure of acquisitions to achieve promised economic benefits, it still remains popular with management.[28]

7.3.3 Joint Development

Joint development of new products/markets has become increasingly popular in the UK since the early 1970s largely as a result of North American influence. The advantages of joint development can best be illustrated by describing some of the different types of joint development which occur.

*   *Franchising* is perhaps the best known and most common type of joint development. The details of a franchise agreement can vary considerably but the underlying rationale is the same. The advantages of franchising arise from the fact that each of the parties to the agreement only has a particular strength or interest in part of the development process and that these two interests are complementary. Perhaps the best known franchising system internationally is Coca Cola. Here the Coca Cola company's part of the development is through the product, its unrivalled brand-name, and the mass consumer advertising. Against this, franchise holders will be responsible for manufacturing, bottling, distribution and selling of Coca Cola (or just some of these activities). By this means, both parties benefit since it allows them to use their own limited resources to greater overall effect.
*   *Licensing* arrangements are a form of franchising which is common in science-based industries such as chemicals. The R&D department of a chemical company may develop and patent more products than the company is able to manufacture itself. Licences are, therefore, granted to other manufacturers who pay a fee (percentage of turnover) to the patent holder. Licensing is also used as a means of developing overseas markets without being involved in local manufacture or exporting from the UK.
*   *Agents* have been used in joint developments for many years. Many UK companies develop overseas markets by use of local agents not only on the grounds of their better local knowledge but also because this is the most cost efficient way to operate. This is particularly true in markets where levels of sales are relatively low and hence do not justify the full-time attention of even one sales representative.

The attractiveness of joint ventures could, arguably, increase as environmental change accelerates. For example, given the rate of obsolescence of plant due to technological innovation, it could well be advantageous for a company to consider becoming a marketing and distribution operation working on a joint venture basis with a manufacturer who is more specialised in the necessary field of technology.

7.4 MARKET SHARE, COMPANY SIZE AND COMPANY PERFORMANCE

Sections 7.2 and 7.3 have commented on the research findings which relate development strategies (e.g. diversification) *or* methods of development (e.g. acquisition) to company performance. The chapter will finish with a review of the relationship between market share, company size and company performance which is clearly relevant in guiding an organisation's choice of strategy.

There is an increasing amount of evidence that market share and profitability are related. The Boston Consulting Group argue this (see Appendix) and this assertion is also supported by the findings of the PIMS study, as shown in Fig. 7.16. Return on investment rises steadily in line with market share.[29] It should be pointed out that these results are based on the performance of firms in relevant market segments *not* in terms of a total market. For example, in comparing the performance of British Leyland and Ford in the UK in the 1970s the major criticism of British Leyland would be their excessively wide product range at the time which included many models which competed in the same market segment. In contrast, Ford had a much smaller product range but dominated the market segments in which they competed. Where British Leyland did dominate market segments (e.g. Land Rover, Jaguar) their profits were greater.

The PIMS researchers suggest a number of main reasons[30] why market share and ROI should be linked. The purchase to sales ratio differences between high and low market share firms are startling - in simple terms, high market share companies seem to be able to buy more competitively. Also some economies of scale benefit firms with high market shares. For example, marketing costs tend to decline as a percentage of sales with increased share. The indications are also that high market share firms develop strategies of higher price/higher quality than low share competitors. This phenomenon may, in fact, be somewhat circular. High share firms tend to be more profitable, thus providing the cash resources for R&D to improve and differentiate products, thus enhancing their market position and also justifying higher prices which in turn increase profits. It must be remembered that high market share and size are not the same. There are large firms which do not dominate the markets in which they operate; and there are small firms which do.

The most frequently cited reason for *size* being a benefit is that economies of scale give rise to increased levels of profits over smaller firms. In fact the evidence on the relationship between size and profitability is rather confused

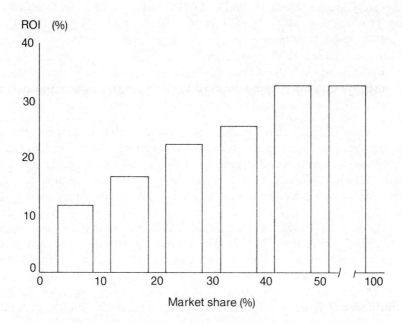

Figure 7.16 *The relationship between market share and ROI (From: B. T. Gale and B. Branch 'The Dispute About High-Share Businesses', Pimsletter No. 19, The Strategic Planning Institute. Reprinted with the permission of the SPI).*

but it points to two broad conclusions. Firstly that profits and size are inversely related: that is, the mean profitability for smaller firms is higher than that for large firms.[31] Secondly, however, large firms demonstrate less variability over time in their levels of profitability; their profits tend to be more stable.[32]

These findings imply two main strategic alternatives for smaller businesses. The first is to recognise the lessons about the importance of market share and the crippling effects of high marketing and R&D costs for small share firms and adopt the *follower* approach. This essentially means watching what the market leaders do and then copying them but with a lower cost structure - minimal marketing overheads, for example - and a slim operation. Companies that specialise in own-label products for supermarkets are a good example of this strategy. The second approach takes note of the PIMS project findings and the arguments of the Boston Consulting Group. This strategy involves concentrating on a market segment - perhaps one that the bigger companies have neglected – and dominating that. In effect, it is the 'big fish in the little pool' strategy.

7.5 SUMMARY

This chapter has been primarily concerned with the strategic options which are available to organisations both in terms of new directions for development (product development, diversification, etc.) and the different methods by which companies might develop (internal development, joint development, acquisition). It should be remembered that, in practice, strategic changes of the type discussed here are likely to occur slowly within organisations, perhaps through a process of 'testing the water', rather than as sudden changes in direction. This issue was fully discussed in Chapter 2.

In reviewing the strategic alternatives open to companies it has proved necessary to discuss the relative merits of the different development strategies and therefore an element of evaluation has inevitably crept in. However, it is in the next chapter that strategic evaluation will be explored in more detail, alongside a consideration of how alternative strategies might be selected for implementation.

REFERENCES

1. M.E. Porter, *Competitive Strategy: Techniques for Analyzing Industries and Competitors* (Free Press: 1980). Chapters 10, 11, and 12 compare some of the different features of growing, mature and declining industries and the opportunities which each presents to companies.
2. R. Cohen and S. Slatter, *Management Today,* May 1983, argue that selling off a business needs to be planned and managed just as carefully as running it.
3. J.C. Sachder, 'Disinvestment: A New Problem in Multi-national Corporation/ Host Government Interface', in *Management International Review* (1976) reviews disinvestment activities amongst multi-national companies.
4. The PIMS programme originated as an internal project of the GEC in the USA in the 1960s and was developed through the 1970s by the Harvard Business School. Its European arm is now the Strategic Planning Institute in London. It is a project which analyses data from a wide range of subscribing companies in an attempt to discover 'general laws' of business performance. The references given below will help readers who wish to follow up the PIMS findings (ref. 5,7,8,10,19).
5. These data are further discussed in B.T. Gale, 'Planning for Profit', *Planning Review,* January 1978.
6. M.E. Porter, see reference 1, Chapter 12. Also K.R. Harrigan, 'Strategies for Declining Industries', Lexington Books, 1980, on which parts of the chapter are based.
7. This is discussed in one of the major articles describing the PIMS findings - S. Schoeffler, R.D. Buzzell and D.F. Heany, 'Impact of Strategic Planning on Profit Performance', *Harvard Business Review,* Mar.-Apr. 1974.
8. For a more thorough discussion of the impact on profit performance of capital intensity see S. Schoeffler, 'Capital-Intensive Technology -vs- ROI : A Strategic Assessment', *Management Review,* September 1978.

9. This finding is borne out by the research of G. Newbould and G. Luffman to be found in *Successful Business Policies* (Gower Press: 1979).

10. This is dealt with in another article dealing with the issue of capital intensity, B.T. Gale, 'Can More Capital Buy Higher Productivity', *Harvard Business Review*, Jul.-Aug. 1980. Also: 'Make Ready For Success' (NEDO: 1981) - a report on the UK printing industry between 1974 and 1981 - draws similar conclusions.

11. M.F. Brooke and H.L. Remmers, *The Strategy of Multi-national Enterprise*, 2nd edn. (Pitman: 1978).

12. Our use of the term 'diversification' is similar to that used by I. Ansoff in *Corporate Strategy* (Penguin: 1968). In Chapter 7 Ansoff identifies general reasons why firms might choose diversification as a method of development.

13. Our use of the terms 'related' and 'unrelated' in the context of diversification follow those of the 'strategy/structure' school of researchers. For example, see the definitions by R. Rumelt in *Strategy, Structure and Economic Performance* (Harvard Press: 1974).

14. For further reading about the logic of diversification see I. Ansoff, *Corporate Strategy* (Penguin: 1968); R. Rumelt *Strategy, Structure and Economic Performance* (Harvard Press: 1974); C.J. Sutton, *Economics and Corporate Strategy* (Cambridge: 1980); or M.E. Porter, *Competitive Strategy* (Free Press, Ch.14: 1980).

15. The idea of synergy is well explained by I. Ansoff in *Corporate Strategy* (Penguin: 1968).

16. These findings are from the work of R. Rumelt, *Strategy, Structure and Economic Performance* (Harvard Press: 1974) also summarised in an article by Bruce Scott entitled 'The Industrial State: Old Myths and New Realities', *Harvard Business Review*, Mar. 1973. Readers should be careful about drawing fine distinctions between Rumelt's categories since the sample size of 100 is small and such distinctions would not be statistically significant.

17. R. Reed and G. Luffman - private communication 1983 (part of forthcoming doctoral thesis, Bradford University Management Centre), used a much larger sample than did R. Rumelt, reference 16. Their results were derived from inflation adjusted data for British industry over the period 1970 to 1980. The top 1000 UK companies were used to produce a sample of 349 who had not changed their product market base over the ten years. The sample included manufacturing and service companies. Significant deletions from the top 1000 included non-British companies, those subject to takeover or liquidation during the period, financial institutions, non-public companies and those which government owned or controlled.

18. R.A. Bettis and W.K. Hale, 'Diversification Strategy, Risk and Return', *Academy of Management Journal*, 1982; D.F. Channon, 'Strategy, Structure and Financial Performance', *Manchester Business School Review*, 1979; P.H. Grinyer *et al.*, 'Strategy Structure, The Environment and Financial Performance in 48 UK Companies', *Academy of Management Journal*, 1980.

19. An interesting study of the profit impact of diversification is given in R. Biggadike, 'The Risky Business of Diversification', *Harvard Business Review*, May-Jun. 1979. Biggadike's work was part of the PIMS study.

20. J. Kreiken, in *Business Policy and Strategic Management*, 3rd edn., edited by W.F. Glueck (McGraw-Hill: 1980).

21.   D. Channon, *Strategy and Structure of Business Enterprise* (Macmillan: 1973), based his research on an analysis of the *'Times* Top 500' companies in an attempt to replicate earlier studies in the USA, notably by Chandler (1962). His findings on the relationship between strategy and structure will be discussed in Chapter 10. At this stage his observations of how acquisition and merger has been part of the development of UK companies is interesting.
22.   C.J. Sutton, *Economics and Corporate Strategy* (Cambridge University Press, Ch. 7: 1980).
23.   J. Capito, 'Joining with Japan', *Management Today,* April, 1983, reviews many of the difficulties which foreign companies can face in attempting to acquire Japanese companies. However, he also cites successful examples of such acquisitions.
24.   For an interesting example of the turmoil that can result from acquisition see M. Fenton, *Management Today,* September 1979.
25.   These points are supported by G. Newbould and G. Luffman, reference 9.
26.   These points are supported by the research of M. Firth in an article entitled 'The Profitability of Takeovers and Mergers', *The Economic Journal,* June 1979.
27.   See A. Buckley, 'A Blueprint for Acquisition Strategy', *Accountancy,* September 1979.
28.   J. Thackray, *'The American Takeover War', Management Today,* 1982, reports the continuing fashion for acquisition despite firm evidence of the economic benefits.
29.   These data are taken from the article by B.T. Gale, reference 4.
30.   See R.D. Buzzell *et al.,* 'Market Share - a Key to Profitability', *Harvard Business Review, Jan.-Feb. 1975.*
31.   See J. Samuels, 'Size and Growth of Firms', *Review of Economic Studies,* Vol. XXXII, 1965.
32.   The relationship between size and profitability is discussed in detail by R. Singh and G. Whittington in 'Growth, Profitability and Valuation' *Department of Applied Economics Occasional Papers* No. 7, (Cambridge University Press: 1968).

RECOMMENDED KEY READINGS

*   For an interesting discussion of strategies appropriate to companies in differing market environments see, M.E. Porter, *Competitive Strategy* (Free Press: 1980), Chs. 10,11,12.

*   An excellent discussion of the logic of diversification is given in I. Ansoff, *Corporate Strategy* (Penguin: 1968) Ch. 7.

*   The early work of the PIMS project and some of the general findings are summarised in R.D. Buzzell *et al.,* 'Market Share: A Key to Profitability', *Harvard Business Review,* Jan.-Feb. 1975.

CHAPTER 8

EVALUATION AND SELECTION OF STRATEGIES

8.1 INTRODUCTION

Whereas most managers will see strategic evaluation as an important means of deciding which of the many alternative strategies should be pursued, this search for the 'best strategy' is only one way in which evaluation can help policy-making. In an uncertain world, evaluation should aim to give a better insight into the likely consequences of pursuing each of a number of different strategies. In other words the evaluation process should provide managers with a sound understanding of how they might respond to a range of different situations which might arise in the future.

The previous chapter discussed the range of strategic options available to organisations in their continual efforts to survive. That discussion inevitably began the process of *evalutaion* by reviewing the pros and cons of these various alternatives and the circumstances in which any one alternative might prove most suitable. This chapter will contains a much fuller discussion of how strategic options might be evaluated. The chapter begins with the criteria which can be used to assess alternative strategies; these criteria are developed from the understanding of the ways in which strategy is evaluated by managers in practice (as discussed in Chapter 2). The chapter then moves on to discuss the various steps which a systematic evaluation can follow, the techniques available for evaluation and the factors which are likely to influence the choice of evaluation method in any given situation.

The process of evaluation is concerned with gaining a better understanding of what the future holds and how the company can survive and prosper. This is important to the way that options are evaluated:

* Although an evaluation may list options in a league table of *priorities* it may still be necessary to evaluate some options which are low down on this list. This is a recognition of the fact that, in reality, low priority options may have to be followed in practice and therefore should be ready as contingencies. For example, most public services have well formulated strategies to cope with all sorts of catastrophes despite the fact that everyone hopes they will be unnecessary.
* The process should also try to identify the likely consequences should plans not work out quite as planned. It is useful to know how *sensitive* the forecasts of success/failure are to the assumptions which have been made, i.e. the risks implicit in each alternative as well as its most likely outcome. For example, a company may choose an investment programme consisting of a step-by-step build-up of capacity in preference to a major one-off project despite the fact that the latter is forecasted to give a lower unit cost of production. The reason for this choice is that the step-by-step build-up is lower risk as it gives the company more flexibility to adjust its thinking during the build-up in the light of new circumstances. The company's *attitude to risk* has had a dominant influence on the evaluation.

8.2 CRITERIA FOR EVALUATING ALTERNATIVES

Perhaps the major difficulty faced in evaluating strategy is the need to use a number of different measures or criteria that cannot all be satisfied simultaneously. A simple way of looking at evaluation criteria is to view them as falling into three categories:

* Criteria of *suitability* which attempt to measure how far proposed strategies fit the situation identified in the strategic analysis. Does the strategy, for example, capitalise on the company's strengths, overcome or avoid weaknesses and counter environmental threats?
* Criteria of *feasibility* which assess how any strategy might work in practice. For example, whether the strategy is achievable in resource terms.
* Criteria of *acceptability* which try to assess whether the consequences of proceeding with a strategy are acceptable. For example, will it be profitable or generate the growth expected by senior management, shareholders or other stakeholders? One important measure of acceptability is the level of risk involved in any strategy.

Chapter 2 has already mentioned that managers, in practice, do use these sorts of criteria in evaluating company strategies. The review of evaluation techniques later in the chapter will show that different methods tend to focus on one or perhaps two of these criteria so it might be important to use more than one technique. Firstly, however, a little more needs to be said about these evaluation criteria.

8.2.1 Suitability

One of the prime purposes of strategic analysis is to provide a clear picture of the organisation and the environment in which it is operating. A useful summary of this situation might include a listing of the major opportunities and threats which faces the organisation its particular strengths and weaknesses and any objectives which seem to be a particularly important influence on policy.[1]

One important measure of evaluation is the extent to which any strategy addresses itself to the situation described in the strategic analysis. Does the strategy fit the situation - does it seem suitable? Some authors[2] have referred to this as 'consistency'. Certain questions need to be asked about any alternative strategy such as:

* How far does it overcome the *difficulties* identified in the strategic analysis (resource weaknesses and environmental threats)? For example, is the strategy likely to resolve the company's liquidity problems, or cope with aggressive new competitors, or decrease dependence on a particular supplier?

* Does it exploit the company *strengths* and environmental *opportunities?* For example, will the proposed strategy provide appropriate work for skilled craftsmen, or help establish the company in new growth sectors of the market, or utilise the present, highly efficient distribution system?

* Does it fit in with the organisation's *objectives* and *values?* For example, would the strategy entail trading with countries which the company would prefer not to, or imply loss of control for the owner/manager, or require dropping present products?

8.2.2 Feasibility

An assessment of the feasibility[3] of any strategy is concerned with how it will be done. For example, the scale of the proposed changes needs to be achievable in resource terms. As suggested earlier, this process will already have started during the identification of alternatives and will continue through into the process of assessing the details of implementation. However, at the evaluation stage there are a number of fundamental questions which need to be asked when assessing the feasibility of any strategy:

* Can the strategy be *funded?* This can be examined by producing a future funds flow forecast showing estimated sources and uses of funds.

*   Is the organisation *capable* of performing to the required level (e.g. quality level, service level)?
*   Can the necessary *market position* be achieved and will the necessary marketing skills be available?
*   Can *competitive reactions* be coped with?
*   How will the organisation ensure that the required *skills* at both managerial and operative level are available? (Training and recruitment)
*   Will the *technology* (both product and process) to compete effectively be available?
*   Can the necessary *materials* and services be obtained?

This is not a definitive list but does illustrate the broad range of questions which need answering.

8.2.3 Acceptability

Alongside the analysis of suitability and feasibility is the third measure, acceptability. This is concerned with an assessment of whether the consequences of proceeding with a strategy are acceptable. This can be a difficult area since acceptability is strongly related to people's values, and therefore the issue of 'acceptable to whom' requires the analysis to be thought through carefully. Some of the questions that will help identify the likely consequences of any strategy are:

*   What will be the financial performance of the company in *profitability* terms?
*   How will the *financial risk* (e.g. liquidity) change?
*   What will be the effect on *capital structure* (e.g. gearing or share ownership)?
*   Will any proposed changes be acceptable to the general *cultural expectations* within the organisation (e.g. attitudes to greater levels of risk)?
*   Will the *function* of any department, group, or individual change significantly?
*   Will the company's relationship with outside *stakeholders* (e.g. suppliers, government, unions, customers) need to change?
*   Will the strategy be acceptable in the company's *environment* (e.g. will the local community accept higher levels of noise)?
*   Will the proposed strategy *fit existing systems* or will it require major changes?

Since the issue of acceptability is so strongly linked with values readers may have recognised that the above questions in fact identify the range of issues and *coalitions* which might influence an organisation's strategies.

Illustration 32 shows how the criteria of suitability, feasibility and acceptability can be used to help evaluate a strategic option.

ILLUSTRATION 32

• In order to evaluate strategic options, it is useful to consider if they are

George Bassett Holdings Ltd. was founded in 1842 as a manufacturer of confectionery. By 1976 the company commanded around 10% of the sugar confectionery market in the UK, and was especially well known for its liquorice confectionery, in particular 'Liquorice Allsorts', which were marketed in boxes and accounted for over half the company's sales. The remainder of the company's product range was composed of other sugar confectionery products such as 'Jelly Babies' and 'Wine Gums', marketed under one of the company's three house-names, Barratt, Bassett and Wilkinsons.

The company's salesforce consisted of three selling units: one a small group of two salesmen who sold to large retail charge accounts such as Marks and Spencer, and two other groups which consisted of about 50 salesmen each, and who sold the company's product according to the house-name attributed to each item: either Bassett/Wilkinson or Barratt. Because all products were sold through similar outlets, this arrangement often led to duplication of sales calls, but the company's chairman did not believe that it was possible for salesmen to sell products effectively operating under three house-names at once.

1. *Consolidate current positions in present markets and develop sales through supermarkets*

Suitability

Bassett might be able to maintain growth and profits in short terms by (a) increasing efficiency in their current markets; (b) expanding their outlets of catering for supermarket requirements. However, these would not deal with their other problems of:

    (i)   being heavily susceptible to fluctuations in the sugar market;
    (ii) the threats presented by savoury snacks;
    (iii) incursions of chocolate manufacturers;
    (iv) worries about tooth decay which cause market demand to fall.

Feasibility

Internally, would Bassett have the skills to sell to supermarkets — could they cope with the development of merchandising techniques required for supermarket trading?

Acceptability

Would consolidation and concentration on supermarkets actually provide a sound enough basis for long term improvement? Would the management be prepared to integrate the separate identities of Bassetts and Barratts to consolidate separate salesforces?

Source: George Bassett Holdings Ltd., case study by R.M.P. Green (available from the Case Study Clearing House of G.B.)

George Bassett Holdings Ltd.

suitable, feasible and *acceptable.*

Over the years Bassett had achieved good profits and grown steadily by a process of vertical integration into wholesaling and by consolidating its product range. In 1976, the future presented a number of threats such as the instability of sugar prices, an increasing concern about tooth decay caused by sweets, an increase in the popularity of savoury snacks, and the possibility of incursions into sugar confectionery from chocolate manufacture. Similarly, there was an increasing concentration of confectionery in supermarkets, at the expense of small shops which had been Bassett's traditional outlets. Supermarkets demanded pre-packed sweets in a form Bassetts found difficult to comply with.

Faced with such threats, Bassetts Board of Directors viewed the future stability of the company as requiring steady expansion. Of the options open to them, two might be used to show the importance of considering *suitability*, *feasibility* and *acceptability*.

---

2. Adopt a programme of product development, e.g. chewing-gum, medicated or savoury snacks.

By spreading out from their present base, Bassetts would no longer be as susceptible to the threats to their current markets. The possible new areas also appeared to be growing faster than their traditional activities. And such new products would be compatible with their existing market outlets.

There was no evidence that Bassetts would be able to find the R&D expertise needed from their own resources. If they tried to acquire this expertise by buying a company it would be likely to be a problem-child company since they would be unlikely to acquire a market leader. In this case, would Bassetts have the skills to develop such a company?

Would they be able to gain a substantial foothold in markets such as chewing gum which were already mature?

Given the problems of feasibility, would Bassetts be able to make the profits they were looking for? Would a company with such traditional roots as Bassetts be prepared to move the focus of their business away from *Liquorice Allsorts* after being in that market for over 100 years?

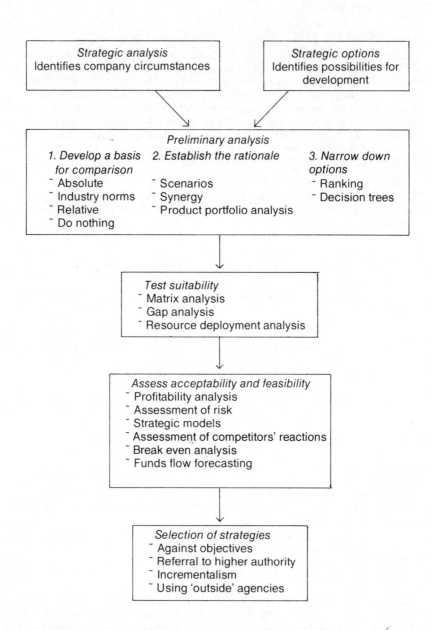

Figure 8.1   *A framework for evaluating strategic options*

8.2.4 A Framework for Evaluating Alternatives

Whereas the analytical techniques which will be discussed below can help with measuring alternatives against the criteria outlined above, the sheer number of considerations involved in evaluating a range of options against these criteria can be quite bewildering. For this reason, evaluation of options might usefully begin with a number of preliminary analyses which attempt both to establish the underlying rationale behind each option and to assess whether that option then warrants a more detailed appraisal. In addition, this preliminary analysis should provide a sensible basis for comparison against which the other alternatives can be measured.

Figure 8.1 summarised the proposed framework for undertaking a strategic evaluation. The steps are outlined below and explained in more detail in the rest of this chapter.

* The first step is a *strategic analysis* in order to gain a clear understanding of the circumstances affecting the organisation's strategic position as discussed in Part II of this book.

* The second step is to produce a *range of strategic options* as discussed in Chapter 7.

* Next a *basis of comparison* needs to be developed. This may already be available from the strategic analysis (e.g. company performance vs. competition) or may need to be specially produced (e.g. the 'do nothing' situation discussed later).

* It is helpful to *establish the underlying rationale* for each strategy by explaining why the strategy might succeed. This is often done in qualitative terms and techniques such as scenario building, product portfolio analysis and the assessment of synergy can be very useful at this stage as will be seen below.

* It will be important to *narrow down* the large number of alternatives before a more detailed analysis is undertaken. Ranking can be a particularly useful technique for this purpose.

* The next step would be to test the *suitability* of each alternative. It will be seen below that there are a number of analytical techniques which can help in this process. The specific choice of technique will depend upon the circumstances. For example, a company facing a number of clearly identified changes in its environment may choose matrix analysis, whilst a single product company operating in a declining market may use gap analysis to test the suitability of various market development alternatives.

* The next stage in Fig. 8.1 consists of assessing the *feasibility* and *acceptability* of strategies which appear reasonably suitable from the previous analysis. Again the choice of any specific technique should be dictated by the company's circumstances.

* Lastly, the company will need some system for *selecting* future strategies as a result of these various evaluations.

Each of these steps will now be discussed separately in order to review the methods of analysis which can be used for strategic evaluation. Readers should remember that many techniques will, in practice, contribute to more than one of the steps in Fig. 8.1 and that they have, therefore, been 'boxed' for convenience of discussion. In other words, this approach should be used as a flexible framework for evaluation and not used too pedantically.

8.3 PRELIMINARY ANALYSES

8.3.1 Bases for Comparison

Many of the methods of evaluation which follow are only of value if the analysis of any given strategy has some appropriate basis for comparison. The chapter on strategic analysis of company resources (Chapter 4) has already discussed the importance of establishing an appropriate basis for comparison. Several alternatives exist such as an *absolute scale* (e.g. expressing likely future return on capital at 20%, or 25%, etc), or comparison with *industry norms.* Alternatives can also be compared with *each other* or with the *do nothing* situation.

There are problems in using absolute measures and industry norms as bases for comparison. They assume that alternatives are independent of each other: and more importantly, they do not address themselves to a central problem in strategic evaluation, namely the need to identify the *incentive to change* from the present strategy to a different strategy. An example will help make the point.

If a completely new company was being formed as a distributor of sports goods then one of the strategic decisions it would need to make would be that of location. Having analysed the likely costs and probable revenue from operating in a number of different towns the entrepreneur would be likely to ask two basic questions. Firstly, whether this business is worth entering at all? (This is the *absolute* basis for assessment mentioned above.) Secondly, if he did enter this business how would the various locations compare against the norm for sports distribution and against each other? Some locations will appear more favourable than others. (This is the *industry norm* basis.)

However, whereas this process of deciding whether or not to set-up from scratch is clearly relevant to this entrepreneur, it is quite different in nature from the strategic decision that faces companies which are already established. The circumstances of an established distributor are quite different in several important ways. Since they are already established and trading in one location they need to be convinced that the benefits of changing will outweigh the disruption - they need some real *incentive* to change. They are unlikely to be interested in changing location unless the new location appears significantly more attractive. They also have to have the *desire* to change. Evaluation is not usually concerned with finding the best strategy but very often about finding a satisfactory strategy. The company may be quite happy with their trading position and the fact that they could do even better elsewhere is of no particular interest to them.

Since strategic evaluation is concerned with assessing whether or not companies should change their present activities it is often helpful to use the *do nothing* situation as a basis for comparison since this helps assess the company's incentive to change from present strategies. Like so many simple but useful ideas 'do nothing' is difficult to define rigorously. In this book the term represents the situation whereby a company continues to follow, in broad terms, its current strategies whilst events around the company change. So, for example, the 'do nothing' situation for a company facing a declining market would assume no major response to this change such as developing and launching new products. It would, however, allow for the normal operational changes which occur in any business like replacing operatives who leave or continuing to advertise at the same level and in the same manner as before. The easiest way to incorporate the 'do nothing' situation into an evaluation is by including it as an alternative strategy to be evaluated alongside others, as will be seen in the later discussions of techniques such as ranking, gap analysis or matrix analysis.

8.3.2 Establishing the Rationale of Strategies

One of the reasons why strategic evaluation can be so difficult is because people often start the process by using detailed analyses of options. It is usually very helpful to establish first the rationale behind an option. For example, a simple statement of *why a strategy should succeed* can be a good starting point. One strategy may be mainly concerned with moving the company's emphasis into higher profitability market sectors, another with the reduction of distribution costs and a third with achieving highly competitive standards of service. This rationale provides a useful focus for more detailed analyses.[4] There are some evaluation techniques which can be very helpful in the process of establishing a rationale, although this is not their only use.

(i)   *Scenarios:*[5] are attempts to describe in detail, a sequence of events which could plausibly lead to a desired result (often described in terms of company performance). The approach is essentially qualitative and is used as a means of addressing some of the less well structured or uncertain aspects of evaluation. They are often used to forecast the likely impact of possible environmental changes as Illustration 33 shows in the case of Shell UK Ltd. Although scenarios are usually qualitative they are, nonetheless, detailed. They should identify the key elements which could influence company performance such as competitive, economic, technical, social or political forces.

The type of scenario used will differ depending on their level within

---

ILLUSTRATION 33

One Use of Scenario-building

● By taking a conceptual or qualitative approach to planning, management can base its decision on a series of possible future outcomes, rather than on centrally set forecasts.

Scenario-building has been used on several occasions by Shell UK Ltd. where it has had to take into account societal and political analyses, as well as economic and technical analyses of the environment, and how these could influence long-range planning.

In 1980 Shell used scenario-building to examine possible trends in the growth of the UK GNP and to use this information to link up what might be the likely demand for oil in the event of these outcomes.

1. **Unresolved conflicts scenario.** A 'muddling through' scenario in which policy is largely determined on the basis of expedient compromise in response to short term pressures, rather than tackling the country's underlying problems. Since the economy would be behaving in much the same way through the 1980s as it did through the 1960s and 1970s, it might be assumed that demand for oil would increase only marginally, since economic growth would be dependent upon oil revenues.

2. **The revival scenario.** This would give the highest growth in the long-term. It implies a change in attitude and a restructuring of industry away from the older, declining fields and concentrating on areas of growth. The eventual upturn after restructuring has taken place may vary in its time scale depending upon the consistency of government direction, but in any event the trend would be similar. Under this scenario, it is likely there would be increased energy efficiency with greater development of less energy intensive industries, and so the demand for oil would not increase in direct proportion to the GNP.

3. **Rake's progress scenario.** This would be the result of an extrapolation of the social, political and macro-economic trends for the UK for the years leading up to 1980. It could materialise if the Government persistently changes its policies so no one strategy is given enough time to work. Although in terms of GNP, this scenario represents the other extreme to the revival scenario, the resultant energy demand may show a similar increase over the years since industry would probably remain energy intensive and hold less energy-efficient equipment.

Source: P.W. Beck, Corporate Planning in an Uncertain Future, Shell UK: 1981.

---

an organisation. For example, in a multi-national organisation like Shell the highest levels of management will be most interested in 'global scenarios' - world-wide developments - while the focus becomes narrower for the purposes of specialised divisions, functions or business sectors.

Some aspects of global scenarios may, nontheless, be relevant to more localised decision-making - for example, developments in the Middle East will inevitably have an influence on the local energy situation.

Scenarios are essentially a qualitative forecast of events but (unlike traditional forecasting) based on the belief that the future is very difficult to measure and control.

(ii)   *Synergy.* The previous chapter introduced the concept of synergy[6] as a means of explaining why organisations might choose to take on new activities through market development, diversification and so on. Synergy was seen as a measure of the extra benefit which could accrue from providing some sort of linkage between two or more activities. The estimation of this extra benefit is an important means of assessing how successful any new strategy might be.

Figure 8.2 gives an example of how synergy might be assessed in the case of a single-outlet grocery retailer wishing to increase the overall size of his business. The company wants to assess the degree of synergy between the present business and three alternative methods of development: buying more grocery shops, expanding the product range into alcoholic drinks, and opening a cash and carry wholesaler. The factors identified in the figure are intended to illustrate the possible areas where synergy might occur (use of cash, stock, premises or in purchasing, etc). This analysis attempts to assess the contribution of each of these factors towards the relative merits of each alternative. For example, the fact that the retailer has a good name in the locality should reduce the launch cost of new shops compared with a totally unknown retailer setting up in the area. The detailed assessment of how much these savings might be would then evolve from a consideration of the advertising and promotional campaign details (at a later stage).

(iii) *Product portfolio analysis.* Most of the discussion so far has been concerned with the analysis of competitive strategies or activities of single organisational units. However, much of the strategic evaluation which goes on at the centre of large, diverse organisations takes a somewhat different perspective from that at the level of the individual business unit. American literature[7] in the field of corporate strategy draws strong distinctions between the former which they call 'corporate strategy' as against the latter which they refer to as 'business strategy'. In a large and diverse organisation a prime concern of evaluation at the corporate level is that of achieving a balanced range (or portfolio) of businesses or activities. The product portfolio concept has already been mentioned in Chapter 7 as a possible justification for unrelated diversification. The idea evolved from the work on experience curves by the Boston Consulting Group (BCG) which is explained more fully in the Appendix.

Degree of synergy with present activities	Strategy 1 Buy more shops	Strategy 2 Expand into alcoholic drink	Strategy 3 Open cash and carry wholesaler
1. Use of cash	- produces profit from idle cash	- produces profit from idle cash	- produces profit from idle cash
2. Use of premises	- none	- more turnover / floor space	- none
3. Use of stock	- perhaps small gains from moving stock between shops	- none	- reduction of stock in shops as quick delivery guaranteed
4. Purchasing	- possible discounts for bulk	- none	- reduced prices to shops
5. Market image	- good name helps launch (i.e. cost of launch reduced)	- none	- little

Figure 8.2   *The assessment of synergy for a grocery retailer.*

Figure 8.3 (A) illustrates the simple BCG matrix which is used to indicate where each business activity lies in relation to two factors: market growth rate and market share. It should be remembered that this type of analysis can be used to look at whole businesses (e.g. within a group) or to look at business activities (e.g. products) within any one company. Future alternatives can be plotted onto the matrix in the same way. This matrix can then be used as a guide on a number of important strategic questions relating to the evaluation of future strategies:

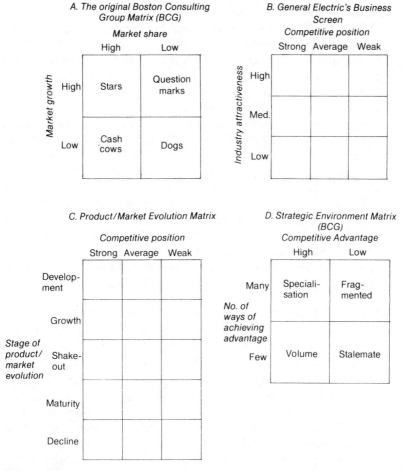

Figure 8.3 *Product portfolio matrices. (Parts A and D from research by the Boston Consulting Group. Part B adapted from Strategy Formulation: Analytical Concepts by Charles Hofer and Dan Schendel, copyright © 1978 by West Publishing Company; all rights reserved. Part C from C. Hofer, Conceptual Constructs For Formulating Corporate and Business Strategies (Boston: Intercollegiate Case Clearing House, no. 9-378-754: 1977, p.3), and adapted by C. Hofer and D. Schendel, Strategy Formulation: Analytical Concepts (St. Paul, MN: West Publishing Co.: 1978 p.34)*

*   How far will the proposed new strategy improve the company's portfolio of interests? For example, will it help develop business growth areas whilst removing the Dogs that drain cash flow for no long term reward?
*   Since Stars generally require an investment of funds will there be sufficient Cash Cows to provide this necessary investment? This is an important question about the balance of the portfolio. For example, a major reason for company bankruptcies is that a firm may be investing heavily in the promotion and stocking policy for products in rapid growth without profitable and well established products from which it can fund these new ventures.
*   There are some situations where Dogs may need to be kept since they provide a necessary platform for the successful development of the Stars. A car manufacturer might argue that it needs to be involved in the low profitability bulk market if it wishes to operate in the more specialist, profitable sectors of the market. It is in the former activity that the skill of making cars is learned and improved.
*   The long term rationale of product or business development can be highlighted by the matrix. Which strategies are most likely to ensure a move from Question Marks through to Stars and eventually Cash Cows? In short, is the company likely to dominate its particular markets?
*   The matrix can also help in thinking about acquisition strategy. Companies that embark on acquisition programmes often forget that the most likely targets for acquisition are not the Stars and Cash Cows of the business world but the Question Marks or Dogs. There may be nothing wrong with acquiring a Question Mark provided the resources are there to move it towards Star-dom bearing in mind the real costs and difficulties of acquisition as pointed out in Chapter 7.

There have been a number of refinements and modifications to the original BCG matrix, three of which are also illustrated in Fig. 8.3. These matrices are used in the same way as described above.

*   *General Electric's business screen*[8] which introduces a three by three matrix to allow for a medium category. It also uses 'industry attractiveness' as a much broader measure than the simple market growth and substitutes 'competitive position' for market share. Hofer and Schendel[9] give a useful explanation of how industry attractiveness and competitive position might be measured.
*   The *product/market evolution matrix*[10] attempts to expand on the thinking behind BCG's assumptions that industry attractiveness and need for investment funds are related to growth. The authors argue that the real issue is the stage in the product/business life cycle and hence substitute this for market growth. The BCG 'high growth' situation is effectively divided into the 'development' and 'growth' stages, whilst BCG's 'low growth' markets become 'shake-out', 'maturity' and 'decline'.

* The BCG itself has made many amendments to its matrix notably its *strategic environments matrix*[11] which replaces market share with competitive advantage and business growth rate with the number of ways of achieving advantage. This is not really a substitute for the original BCG matrix but an additional tool.

     However, there are clear relationships between the two. For example, the rationale behind the Cash Cows was that of high volume low cost output which the new matrix also recognises to be key to strategy in situations of high competitive advantage and few competitive weapons (e.g. a bulk steel manufacturer). Similarly Dogs are usually viewed unfavourably because they represent a stalemate situation where achieving profitability is difficult. The virtues of Stars are very often explained in terms of product or market specialisation leading to a dominant and (eventually) lucrative business as recognised in this new matrix and also well established ideas like market segmentation.[12]

There is a danger that product portfolio analysis is seen as a panacea or comprehensive evaluation technique. This is *not* the case. In fact as an evaluation technique its scope is limited.[13] It is a preliminary step in any evaluation and helps to identify the underlying rationale of any strategy. More detailed techniques of evaluation need to be used to assess the overall desirability of any strategy which seems to fit the product portfolio.

8.3.3 Narrowing Down Strategic Options

Preliminary analyses also need to narrow down the number of options which are to be considered in more detail in order to make that task more manageable. This does not mean that some of the alternatives which are eliminated may not eventually need a fuller evaluation since subsequent analyses may show some alternatives to be less favourable than might have first appeared. Readers are reminded that strategic evaluation should help provide managers with a map and therefore 'unfavourable' alternatives may warrant a detailed evaluation if, for example, they need to be thought through as possible contingency plans. There are two methods particularly useful in narrowing down alternatives: *ranking* and *decision trees.*

(i)   *Ranking.* The criteria by which the number of options will be reduced are the same as will be used for evaluating options more fully. Ranking relies heavily on a qualiative assessment of the suitability or fit of any strategy with the picture gained from the strategic analysis. Each alternative strategy is assessed against a number of key factors which the strategic analysis identified in the organisation's environment, resources, and values. Illustration 34 is a simple example of how such a ranking might be performed. One of the major benefits of ranking is that it helps the analyst to think through mismatches between a company's present position and the implications of the various strategic options. This is

ILLUSTRATION 34

Ranking options — an example, Chevron Foods Ltd.

Chevron Foods began trading in 1976 and grew rapidly in its first two years of operation to an annual turnover of about £0.5m by 1978. This small private company imported orange juice under licence from Florida and distributed the frozen juice to hotels in the UK together with a dispensing system which was installed and serviced free of charge. The key to the company's successful growth lay in this system which allowed hotels to serve high quality juice, at the right temperature, very quickly and efficiently during periods of high demand (breakfast). The company's sales had been largely confined to the larger hotels in the London area (with the exception of national chains which required a national service). The distribution of juice and installation/servicing of dispensers were subcontracted to independent operations.

In 1978 the company needed to decide to which of the many development alternatives they should give more detailed consideration, and a preliminary ranking of alternatives against a number of strategic factors was made (shown in the table)

Alternatives	Desire for small company	Need to control quality of service	Dependency on supplier – licence – credit	Threat of competition	Need for 'big' outlets (To 'pay' for cost of installation)	Need for high margins	Ranking
1. Do Nothing (i.e. current strategy)	√	√	Supplier wants growth(X)	X	√	√	C
2. Seek new suppliers	√	√	X	X	X	?	C
3. More customers of same type (in London)	X	√	√	Already large market share(X)	Best outlet already serviced(X)	√	A
4. Expand nationally (in hotels)	X	Could lose X control	√	√	√	√	A
5. Expand product range (e.g. other juices)	√	X	√	X	X	√	B
6. Seek new outlets (restaurants)	X	X	√	May spread effort too widely(?)	Few large enough(X)	√	A
7. Seek new outlets (hospitals)	X	X	√	X	√	X	B
8. Diversify (frozen foods)	?	X	X	X	X	?	B
9. Take over distribution and/or servicing	X	√	?	X	X	?	C

Key   √ = Favourable influence   X = Unfavourable influence   ? = Uncertain or irrelevant
       A = Appear most suitable   B = Moderately suitable   C = Appear least suitable

The ranking process is used to group the various options into three categories (A, B, C) in relation to their suitability. It should be noted that each strategic factor may not carry the same weight or importance: the need for growth to counter competition was in fact of over-riding importance, so options 4 and 6 were identified as most suitable despite their lack of fit with other factors.

Source: 'Chevron Foods Ltd.', Case Study by G. Johnson (1980). Available from the Case Study Clearing House of G.B.

a useful preliminary step for a more detailed consideration. For example, one mismatch might be the lack of adequate production facilities to meet the output implied by a strategy. This would identify the need to assess the feasibility of a capital investment programme to bridge this gap using some of the techniques discussed below.

(ii) *Decision trees.* Although decision trees[14] have been widely used in operational decision-making, their use in strategy formulation has not, in general, received a great deal of attention. A typical strategic decision tree is illustrated in Fig. 8.4. It can be seen that the end-point of the tree, a number of discrete development opportunities, is the same as would be developed by the approach used in the previous chapter. However, the difference lies in the way in which these options are ranked for evaluation. Whereas previous methods have assumed that all alternatives have equal merit (in the first instance), the decision tree approach will rank options by the process of progressively eliminating others. This elimination process is achieved by identifying a few key elements or criteria which future developments are intended to incorporate such as growth, investment and diversification.

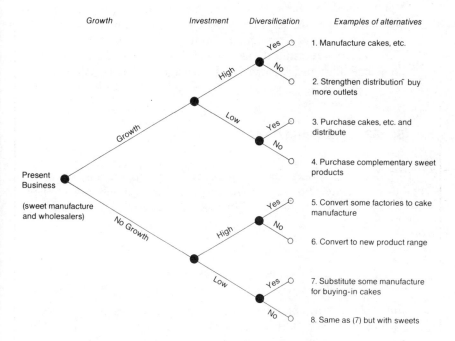

Figure 8.4 *A simplified strategic decision tree for a sweet manufacturer.*

For example, in Fig. 8.4 choosing growth as an important aspect of future strategies would automatically rank options 1-4 more highly than 5-8. At the second step the need for low investment strategies would rank 3 and 4 above options 1 and 2 and so on. Decision-trees combine the identification of options with a simultaneous ranking of those options.

Perhaps the greatest limitation of decision tree analysis is that the choice at each branch on the tree can tend to be somewhat simplistic. For example, answering yes or no to diversification does not allow for the wide variety of alternatives which might exist between these two extremes (see Chapter 7). Nevertheless as a starting point for evaluation, decision trees can often provide a useful framework.

Although the discussion of decision trees has been confined to that of a 'preliminary analysis' technique readers should note that decision trees can also be used to evaluate specific aspects of strategic decisions. Historically, most emphasis has been placed on the assessment of the pay-off or profitability of alternative strategic decisions such as investment programmes or major R&D exercises. Such an analysis usually relies on forecasts of the profitability of various outcomes or performance levels being achieved. For example, probabilities must be assigned to the successful launch of a new product, the degree of market share gained, or the level of sales. It is not intended to discuss this particular use of decision trees more fully but to remind readers that the use of any evaluation technique at a strategic level is always limited by the difficulties of forecasting the factors which are used in the analysis. This is sometimes forgotten when using neat techniques like decision trees.

8.4 ASSESSING SUITABILITY

In effect, the process of ranking options, begins the analysis of the suitability of strategic options. However, there are a number of methods which can be used to analyse suitability in a more systematic and quantitative way.

8.4.I Matrix Analysis

A more systematic approach to assessing suitability can be achieved by constructing an opportunity analysis matrix.[15] Strategic options can be assessed against any number of factors relating to the future environment, company resources, and company values. Illustration 35 gives an example of how such an analysis might be performed.

ILLUSTRATION 35 *An Opportunity Analysis Matrix*

A company was considering three strategic options; launching a new product, extending into new markets or diversifying into a new business. They wished to consider the suitability of each of these alternatives alongside the possibility of continuing their present strategy ("do nothing"). The strategic analysis had identified a number of critically important factors which were likely to influence strategy in the future. The strengthening of the sterling exchange rate against the American dollar and the likely upgrading of competitive products due to new technology were key environmental issues. On the resource front, the company had available cash but envisaged difficulties with raw materials supplies. In terms of values, the imminent retirement of the chairman and recently strengthened unionisation were considered to be important.

The analysis began by assessing the likely impact of these factors on each proposed strategy using a scale of +10 (highly favourable) to -10 (highly unfavourable). The following opportunity analysis matrix was produced:

Strategic options	Environment		Resources		Values		Strategy scores	
	Exchange	Competition	Cash	Materials	Chairman	Unions	+	-
Do nothing	0	-8	0	-7	-6	-5	0	26
A. Launch new product	0	-6	+6	-5	+3	+2	11	11
B. Extend into new markets	-8	-5	+2	-5	+3	+5	10	18
C. Diversify into new products	+2	0	+4	0	+3	-5	9	5
Impact scores	+2 / -8	0 / -19	+12 / 0	0 / -17	+9 / -6	+7 / -10		

Influence on strategy

It can be seen that each of the influences is expected to affect the various strategies in different ways. For example, strengthening exchange rates makes extension into new markets look unfavourable whereas diversification might be assisted (through lower cost of imported materials). In contrast, the retirement of the chairman is identified as favouring all three strategies! The 'do nothing' situation looks particularly worrying providing a considerable incentive to change.

Matrix analysis is essentially a more detailed form of ranking and, as such, its limitations must be considered. The analysis in Illustration 35 has assumed that each of the influences is of equal importance. The value of the analysis can be increased by assigning different weights to each of the factors to take account of this point. There is also a danger of jumping to the conclusion that the strategy with the highest score (most positives and least negatives) should necessarily be the chosen strategy (strategy C in the example). This need not necessarily be a sensible conclusion. For example, a single negative score (e.g. union resistance) could represent an insuperable hurdle despite a host of positive scores elsewhere.

Matrix analysis can be extended to test how sensitive any strategy might be to the assumptions made about these factors. This can be done by changing the weightings given to factors to see if this would change the outcome of the analysis.[16] Used in this way matrix analysis combines some elements of sensitivity analysis which will be discussed more fully in Subsection 8.5.2.

8.4.2 Gap Analysis

Gap analysis[17] is used to identify the extent to which existing strategies will fail to meet the needs/requirements of the company in the future. This shortfall or gap becomes a measure of how far new strategies are needed in order to achieve long term performance objectives.

This approach fits in nicely with the earlier comment that most organisations will choose not to seek new strategies until the *incentive to change* is great enough. Viewed in this way, gap analysis attempts to assess the organisation's incentive to change. Traditionally, discussion of this technique has centred around quantitative financial measures such as profitability. Figure 8.5 outlines the analysis for a single product/single market situation. Of course, this is a highly simplified example and readers must bear in mind that like any other forecasting process, gap analysis can be difficult and time consuming. In addition, it is usually necessary to apply measures other than profitability. Some of these may be quantifiable such as productivity or volume of sales, whereas others may be subjective but nonetheless very important, such as levels of quality or service. Gap analysis underlines the advantage of evaluating the do nothing situation as a basis against which the desirability of other strategies can be judged. For example, a company which identifies a large gap will be more urgently in need of new strategies than one foreseeing little shortfall from desired performance levels.

8.4.3 Resource Deployment Analysis

Chapter 4 discussed how the analysis of organisational resources on an historical basis and in relation to competitors could yield a picture of what was called the *distinctive competence* of the company. Such an analysis,[18] if

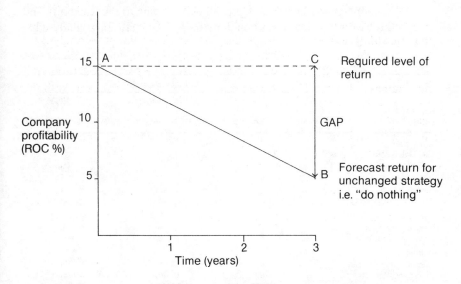

The company is currently operating at 15% Return on Capital and wishes to maintain that level. Increased competition, escalating labour costs and deteriorating machinery underlie the forecast of declining profitability unless current strategies are revised. BC represents the gap which is likely to exist in the 3 years time between required performance and actual performance. This gap needs to be 'filled' by new strategies.

Figure 8.5 *Gap analysis.*

extended into the future, will provide a more detailed means of assessing the suitability of a strategy in resource terms as shown in Fig. 8.6.

The resource requirements of alternative future strategies should be laid out indicating what the key resources would be for each strategy. For example, an extension of the home market would be critically dependent on marketing and distribution expertise together with the availability of cash to fund increased stocks. The resource analysis of the company should then be matched with the resource requirement for possible strategic options. In the example it is clear that the company's resources are specifically geared towards the current product/market strategy and may represent a constraint to any change.

There is a danger that resource deployment analysis will simply result in organisations choosing strategies which most closely fit the configuration of their present resources. It should be remembered that the real benefit of such an analysis should be the identification of those necessary changes in resources which are inferred by any strategy. For example, in Fig. 8.6 both strategies B and C would require quite significant changes in resources. To this extent there is some attempt to highlight possible problems relating to the feasibility and acceptability of that strategy - although neither of these criteria is analysed in detail by this technique.

(a)	(b)	Resource implications (c)		
Key resource areas	Present company situation	Strategy A (extend product range)	Strategy B (extend home market)	Strategy C (sell overseas)
Financial				
- available cash	2	3 (1)	4 (2)	4 (2)
- high stocks	3	2 (1)	4 (1)	4 (1)
Physical				
- modern machines	5	5 (0)	3 (2)	3 (2)
- distribution network	0	1 (1)	5 (5)	5 (5)
Human				
- skilled engineers	5	5 (0)	1 (4)	2 (3)
- marketing expertise	0	2 (2)	5 (5)	5 (5)
Other				
reputation for quality	5	5 (0)	5 (0)	5 (0)
overseas contacts	0	0 (0)	0 (0)	4 (4)
Degree of mismatch		(5)	(19)	(22)

Notes (a) This would be produced from a strengths and weakness analysis (see section 4.5 of Chapter 4).
(b) From previous resource analysis 0 = major weaknesses, 5 = major strength (see Fig 4.6 in Chapter 4).
(c) 0 = unimportant, 5 = critical to success of strategy.
Figures in parentheses refer to the degree of mismatch between that strategy and current resources.

Figure 8.6   *Resource deployment analysis.*

8.5 ASSESSING ACCEPTABILITY AND FEASIBILITY

There are a number of analytical techniques that can contribute to an assessment of the likely acceptability and feasibility of strategic options. Some techniques are solely concerned with one criterion whereas others can be used to assess both. So, for example, analyses of profitability and risk are concerned with the acceptability of alternatives and funds flow analysis with feasibility. In contrast, strategic modelling or breakeven analysis can be used to assess both acceptability and feasibility. This section will review the contribution which each method can make during strategic evaluation. A more in-depth discussion of techniques can be found in the references.[21]-[28]

8.5.1 Profitability Analysis

Profitability is a most important measure of financial acceptability.[19] For profitability measures to be useful they must relate back to a sensible basis for comparison. In strategic evaluation the most useful measures are those which

1. Return on Capital Employment

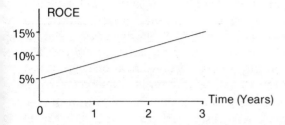

2. Pay-back period

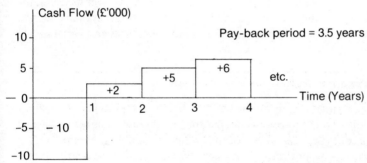

3. Discounted Cash Flow (DCF)

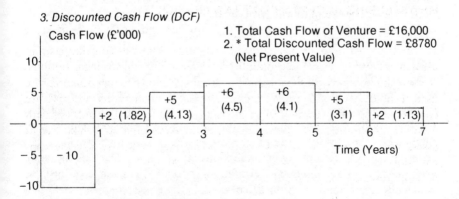

* Using a discounting rate of 10%
Figures in brackets are discounted by 10% annually

Figure 8.7   *Some useful measures of profitability for strategic evaluation.*

relate anticipated earnings to the amount of capital needed to generate those earnings.

A useful evaluative measure is the anticipated *return on capital employed* x years after a new strategy is implemented (e.g. the new strategy will result in a return on capital of 20% by 1987) - see Fig. 8.7. Care must be taken to establish whether this measure is to be applied to the whole company or simply to the extra profit related to the extra capital required for a particular strategy. The former is more relevent to a company undergoing slow strategic changes whilst the latter would normally be applied to large investment programmes.

When new strategies involve large amounts of capital investment then there are better measures of this relationship between earnings and capital expenditure. *Pay-back period* analysis assesses the period of time required to pay back the invested capital.

Perhaps the most useful technique is *discounted cash flow analysis* (DCF) which seeks to measure the nett cash generated by a venture over its useful life whilst giving more value to cash which is generated earlier rather than later. All of these techniques are explained more fully in the references and illustrated in Fig. 8.7.

8.5.2 Assessment of Risk

The degree of risk is an important measure of acceptability. A strategy may potentially be quite profitable but may be too risky in a number of ways. It may reduce a company's *liquidity* to a level which is too tight for comfort. This could be assessed by projecting the likely liquidity ratios[20] over the future period. For example, a small retailer eager to grow quickly may be tempted to fund the required shop-fitting costs by delaying payments to suppliers and increasing bank overdraft. This reduced liquidity increases the financial risk of the business. The extent to which this increased risk threatens survival depends on the likelihood of either creditors or the bank demanding payments from the company.

The *capital structure*[21] of a company may alter when long term loans are taken out to fund development strategies. The case of Laker Airways in 1982 was a reminder of the dangers of funding capital investment exclusively through long term loans (in the case of Laker, to the tune of £150m) particularly if market demand does not develop as forecasted. The level of financial risk created by funding a proposed strategy from long term loans can be tested out by re-examining the likelihood of the company reaching the break even point and the consequences of falling short of that volume of business whilst interest on loans continues to be paid. In this respect there is a clear link between the assessment of risk and the feasibility of alternative strategies.

Another method of assessing the degree of risk is to look at the level of uncertainty in the expected performance should that strategy be adopted. It is helpful to speculate what is likely to happen to performance if some of the assumptions behind the forecasts are ill-founded. *Sensitivity analysis*[22] is a simple and effective method of performing this task. So, for example, the key assumptions underlying a strategy might be that market demand will grow by 5% p.a., or that the company will stay strike-free, or that certain expensive machines will operate at 90% loading. Sensitivity analysis asks what would be the effect on performance (in this case profitability) if, for example, market demand grew at only 1% or as much as 10% - would either of these extremes alter the decision to pursue that particular strategy? A similar process is repeated for the other key assumptions. This process helps management develop a clearer picture of the risks of making certain strategic decisions and the degree of confidence it might have in a given decision. Illustration 36 shows how sensitivity analysis can be used in strategic evaluation. *Risk analysis*[23] is a more sophisticated way of incorporating uncertainty into strategic evaluation.

8.5.3 Strategic Model Building

In the 1960s there was great enthusiasm for the possibilities which global strategic models could bring to policy evaluation. Models of this kind attempt to measure and predict all the complex relationships which shape a company's future. For example, a model would include all the relevant environmental factors and the way they affect company performance, together with internal factors such as cost structure, deployment of assets and so on. In other words, strategic models attempt to encompass all the factors considered by the separate analyses discussed in this chapter into one quantitative simulation model of the company and its environment.[24] It should be no surprise that such global models have been virtually impossible to build. Nevertheless the principle of *simulation modelling* is a useful one in strategic evaluation and is often used in parts of the evaluation of acceptability or feasibility which lend themselves to this qualitative view.

Financial models are often used to assess the likely effects on profitability and/or cash flow of different strategic alternatives. Figure 8.8 shows an example of such a model. Due to the inherent complexity of strategic evaluation financial models are often most useful when they are simple in construction. The model in Fig. 8.8, for example, does not include any dependencies between factors like price and demand: these dependencies need to be discussed outside the model. Strategic models are not normally used as a direct means of providing answers but help managers to better understand the situation.

One of the limitations on the use of strategic modelling is the need for large amounts of high quality data concerning the relationship between environmental factors and company performance. In this respect the recent work of the Strategic Planning Institute (SPI) using the Profit Impact of Market Strategy (PIMS data base[25]) has been interesting. Research at SPI has tried to build a number of quantitative causal models (multiple regression) which

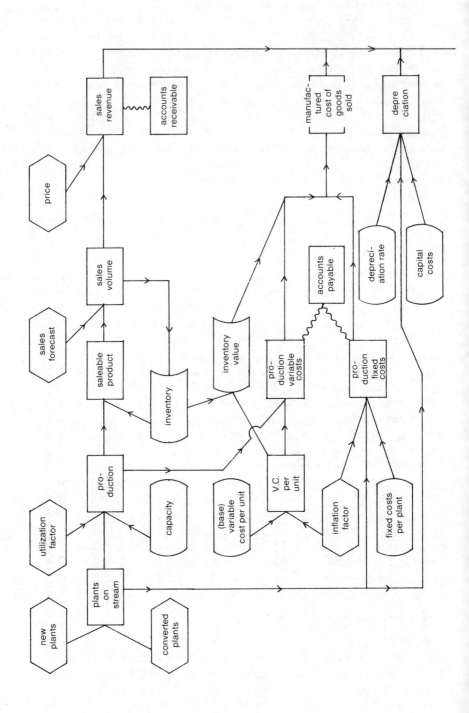

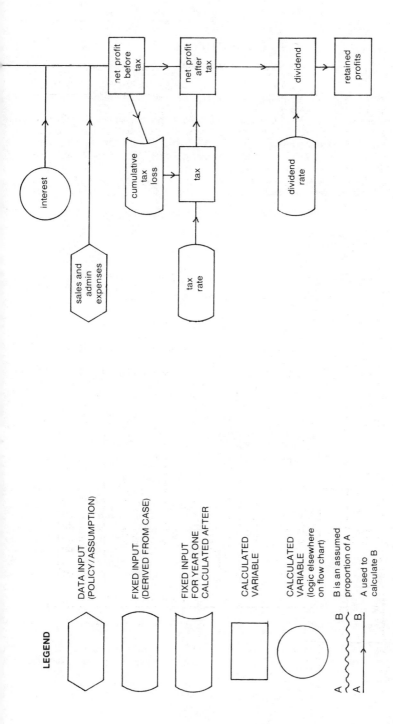

Figure 8.8 *A financial model - the P&L account (by kind permission of Peter H Jones, Principal Lecturer in Management Studies, Sheffield City Polytechnic)*

ILLUSTRATION 36

Sensitivity Analysis

● Sensitivity analysis is a useful technique for assessing the extent to which the success of a company's preferred strategy is dependent on the key assumptions which underly that strategy.

In 1982 the Dunsmore Chemical Company was a single product company trading in a mature and relatively stable market. It was intended to use this established situation as a Cash Cow to generate funds for a new venture with a related product. Estimates had shown that the company would need to generate some £4m cash (at 1982 values) between 1983 and 1988 for this new venture to be possible.

Although the expected performance of the company was for a cash flow of £9.5m over that period, (the *base case*), management were concerned to assess the likely impact of three key factors:

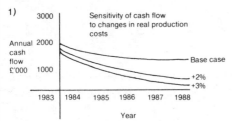

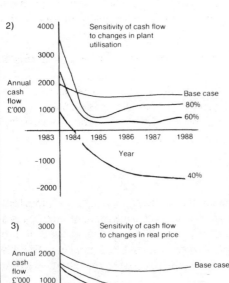

1) Possible increases in *production costs* (manpower, overheads, and materials) which might be as much as 3% p.a. in real terms.

2) *Capacity-fill* which might be reduced by as much as 25% due to ageing plant and uncertain labour relations.

3) *Price levels* which might be affected by the threatened entry of a new major competitor. This could squeeze prices by as much as 3% p.a. in real terms.

It was decided to use sensitivity analysis to assess the possible impact of each of these factors on the company's ability to generate £4m. The results are shown in the graphs.

From this analysis the management concluded that its target of £4m would be achieved with *capacity utilisation* as low as 60% which was certainly going to be achieved. Increased production costs of 3% p.a. would still allow the company to achieve the £4m target over the period. In contrast, *price* squeezes of the order of 3% p.a. would result in a shortfall of £2m.

The management concluded from this analysis that the key factor which should affect their thinking on this matter was the likely impact of new competition and the extent to which they could protect price levels if such competition emerged. They therefore developed an aggressive marketing strategy to deter potential entrants.

Source: The Dunsmore example is from the authors. The calculations for the sensitivity test utilise computer programs employed in the Doman Case Study by P.H. Jones (Sheffield City Polytechnic).

explain how companies' performance have been influenced by up to two dozen different factors.

8.5.4. Assessment of Competitors' Reactions

Since an understanding of the competitive situation and the development of competitive strategies would usually be an important element of any strategic evaluation, *game theory*[26] should, in principle, have some use as an evaluation technique. However, the difficulties of coping with the complexity of the strategic situation have limited the use of game theory to largely qualitative applications. Perhaps the biggest difficulty with using game theory lies in the assumption that the strategic competitive behaviour of companies can be predicted by using simple rules. Readers should refer to the references for a fuller discussion of this technique.

8.5.5 Break Even Analysis

Break even analysis[27] can be a useful and simple method of combining a parallel assessment of the acceptability and feasibility of a strategy. An example is shown in Illustration 37.

The value of such an analysis is not that it makes the decision but that it focuses attention on some key issues of feasibility. In this example questions would need to be asked about:

*   The likelihood of ever achieving such high levels of market penetration in a static market.
*   Whether the competitors reactions would allow profitable entry.
*   Whether cost and quality assumptions are, in fact, achievable.
*   Whether funding would be available to provide the required capacity, and skilled manpower to operate the plant.

8.5.6 Funds Flow Forecasting

The assessment of financial feasibility would normally be an important part of any strategic evaluation. A simple and valuable piece of analysis is a *funds flow forecast,*[28] which seeks to identify the funds which would be required for any strategy and the likely sources of those funds. For example, in Fig. 8.9 the evaluation of a proposed strategy (X) would proceed by the following steps:

*   An assessment of the capital investment needed (e.g., new buildinqs, machines or vehicles) - £13.25m.
*   A forecast of the cumulative profits earned over the period 1983-1985. *'Funds from operations'* of £15m are calculated from an estimate of future profits plus the adding back of any non-fund items such as depreciation, and represent the real flow of funds into the company forcasted for that period.

ILLUSTRATION 37

Using Break Even Analysis to Examine Alternative Strategies

A manufacturing company was considering the launch of a new consumer durable product into a market where most products were sold to wholesalers who supplied the retail trade. The total market was worth about £4.4m (at manufacturer's prices) -about 630,000 units. The market leader had about 30% market share in a competitive market where retailers were increasing their buying power. The company wished to evaluate the relative merits of a high price/high quality product sold to wholesalers (Strategy A) or an "own brand' product sold directly to retailers (Strategy B). The table below summarises the market and cost structure for the market leader and these two alternative strategies. The important conclusion is that the company would require about 22% and 13% market share respectively for Strategies A and B to break even.

Market and cost structure	Market leader	Strategy A	Strategy B
Price to retailer	£10	£12	£8
Margin to wholesaler	30%	30%	-
Wholesaler buys at	£7	£8.40	-
Variable costs/unit:			
raw material	£2.50	£2.90	£2.50
marketing/selling	£0.50	£0.60	£0.20
distribution	£0.20	£0.20	£0.20
others	£0.30	£0.30	£0.20
total	£3.50	£4.00	£3.10
contribution/unit	£3.50	£4.40	£4.90
Fixed cost	£500,000	£600,000	£400,000
break even point (units)	£500,000 / 3.50 = **142,857**	£600,000 / 4.40 = **136,363**	£400,000 / 4.90 = **81,633**
Market size	630,000	630,000	630,000
Break even point (market share)	**22.6%**	**21.6%**	**13%**
Actual share	30%	0	0

Source: Authors

£'000

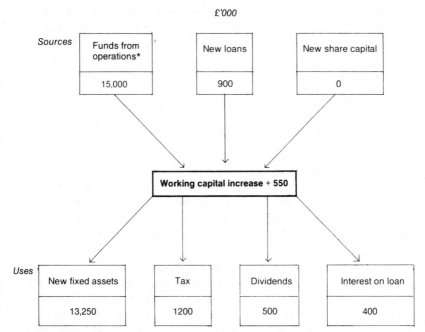

* Funds from operations = Profits corrected for non-fund items such as depreciation.

Figure 8.9   *A funds flow forecast for strategy X (1983-1985), £'000.*

* An estimate of the necessary increases in *working capital* required by the strategy can be made by the separate consideration of each element of working capital (stock increases, increased creditors, etc.) or by using a simple *pro rata* adjustment related to the forecasted level of increase in sales revenue. For example, if the present revenue of £30m requires a working capital level £10m then a forecasted increase in sales revenue to £31.65m would account for the anticipated increase in working capital of £0.55m. This type of *pro rata* adjustment would only be valid when looking at future strategies which are similar in nature to the present company activities.

* *Tax* liability and expected *dividend* payments can be estimated (in relation to the anticipated profitability). In this case £1.2m and £0.5m respectively.

* The calculation so far leaves a *shortfall* in funds of £0.5m. The forecast is then finalised by looking at alternative ways of funding the shortfall and this is where the critical appraisal of financial feasibility occurs. In the example shown this shortfall is to be funded by an additional short term loan of £0.9m (which in its turn will incur interest payments of £0.4m over the three year period assuming simple interest at 14.8% p.a.).

It should be remembered that funds flow analysis is a forecasting technique and is subject to the difficulties and errors of any method of forecasting. Such an analysis should quickly highlight whether the proposed strategy is likely to be feasible in financial terms and could normally be programmed on to a microcomputer should the model be repeatedly required during evaluation.

8.5.7 Other Assessments of Acceptability and Feasibility

There are certain aspects of acceptability which would not necessarily be covered by any of the methods discussed so far. For example, a new strategy which required a substantial issue of new shares might be unacceptable to some important groups or individuals since it might *dilute their voting power*. Plans to merge with other companies or to trade with new countries might be unacceptable to the unions, the government, other customers or any of the stakeholders discussed in Chapter 5. It is, therefore, important that the evaluation of strategy must address itself to the political realities of change. These issues have been discussed at length in Chapter 5 and, therefore, will not be repeated here. However, readers are urged to look again at the extended example from Chapter 5 (Fig. 5.5 and 5.7) in the context of this discussion of the acceptability of alternative strategies.

Equally, the example of break even analysis in Section 8.5.5 highlighted the fact that the feasibility of any proposed strategy can only be judged by a detailed consideration of all the *resources* which would be required to operate this strategy. This issue is the subject of Chapter 9. This once again underlines the difficulty of dividing a discussion of strategic choice from that of strategic implementation. Assessing feasibility is an important part of evaluation but, by necessity, requires a detailed consideration of the resource implications of implementation.

8.6 SELECTION OF STRATEGIES

Before closing this chapter on evaluation there are two issues which need consideration. Firstly, the way in which an organisation's *circumstances* will dictate which methods of evaluation are most useful when selecting future strategies. Secondly, the *process* by which selection of strategies occurs since this illustrates how the information from evaluation is used in strategic decision-making.

8.6.1 Influences on Choice of Evaluation Methods

There are a variety of factors which might influence the way in which different methods of evaluation are used. For simplicity they can be looked at under two headings; factors *internal* to the organisation and *external* factors.

(i)   *Internal factors.* The *size* of the organisation will affect the extent to which skills and money are available for some of the more detailed evaluation methods. For example, it is highly unlikely that sophisticated strategic models will be used in small companies where less time consuming approaches (scenarios or resource deployment analysis) may prove valuable. The *diversity* of the organisation's activities as measured (for example) by product/market spread is likely to dictate whether more emphasis is required on techniques like product portfolio analysis (for diverse companies) or gap analysis (for individual product/market strategies).

    The *internal political climate* of the organisation will be important, as discussed in Chapters 2 and 5. The role of rational analysis techniques is very much determined by the power structure of the company and the level of agreement between different factions. In situations where judgement tends to be the dominant process of strategic decision-making the more global techniques like scenarios, product portfolio analysis and synergy will be used most often since they perform a useful function of giving insight into the situation without requiring detailed, quantitative, justification. At the other extreme, extensive use of detailed quantitative methods would tend to dominate where there is a high degree of agreement on objectives and a strong desire to follow the best course of action.

    The *degree of change* anticipated (which is also influenced by external factors) will influence the choice of methods. For example, gap, matrix, and resource deployment analyses are most suitable in situations where the future is expected to have strong links with the present shape of the company whereas scenarios and decision trees are particularly valuable for analysing situations where considerable change might be needed. Capital intensive companies often need to make a few large capital investment decisions which, clearly, require more careful, detailed analysis than equivalent decisions in organisations which have more flexible resources, and where strategic changes can evolve more steadily.

(ii)   *External factors.* The *nature of the environment* will be very influential on how future strategy is evaluated. Discussions in Chapter 3 emphasised how the stability and complexity of the environment influenced the way that organisations analysed their situation. This same approach applies to strategic evaluation. Organisations in simple, stable environments may well benefit from detailed techniques which build on historical data. Strategic model building and gap analysis are good examples. At the other extreme in complex unstable environments the most useful techniques will be those which provide insight into the nature of the decision in hand. For example, sensitivity analysis helps managers think about risk; scenarios and synergy help in understanding the underlying rationale of different strategies.

Sometimes the need to follow new strategies is thrust upon companies quite suddenly when they enter a period of crisis. Perhaps the owner dies or a new technology unexpectedly undermines the market for the company's product. In these circumstances the company may have insufficient *time* to indulge in lengthy evaluations and often must rely heavily on one man's judgement of what the best course of action might be.

Relationships with other bodies may affect the choice of evaluation techniques and, certainly, the method of presentation. In general, more detailed, formal techniques will tend to be used by organisations who are overseen by other bodies. This may occur formally, e.g. between a subsidiary and parent company and (extensively) within the public sector. It may, however, be less formal, e.g. the need for the company to keep its bank manager or shareholders happy. More formal techniques may build the confidence which these other bodies have in the management of the company.

8.6.2 The Selection Process

It is important for readers to recognise that the selection of one or more strategies for the future may occur by a number of very different processes. This final section of the chapter will list some of the more common methods of selecting strategies and indicate what contribution evaluation methods would normally make in each case. Readers are also referred back to Chapter 2.

(i)   *Selection against objectives.* This is a common view of how a rational choice of future strategies should occur, although it is normally impracticable to proceed in this way. This method of selection uses the organisation's objectives, quantified where possible, as direct yardsticks by which alternatives are assessed. Evaluation methods are therefore central to the decision-making process and are expected to provide quantified answers regarding the relative merits of various alternatives and to indicate the right course of action. In practice, however, even where this rational selection process occurs it is very often the case that objectives need to be adjusted as the evaluation proceeds and become what is often called post-rationalised. The objectives, therefore, fit the strategy and vice versa.

(ii) *Referral to a higher authority.* A common method of selecting future strategies in many companies is by referring the matter to a higher authority.[29] Those managers responsible for evaluation may not have the authority to give the go-ahead to the solution. Equally those senior managers who must decide on strategy may not have participated in the evaluation of alternatives. This is a very important observation which should have a strong influence on how the results of evaluation are conveyed to senior management. In particular, it is very unlikely that senior managers will have the time or inclination to unravel all the detailed implications of an evaluation. They are more concerned with using their judgement of the situation on the available facts and also seeing how well different strategies fit the overall strategy of the company. Thus the evaluation process is best seen as a means of raising the level of debate which occurs amongst senior managers when they are using their judgement on the selection of strategy.

(iii) *Incrementalism.* It has already been mentioned in Chapter 2 that many strategic decisions are made in small steps, in isolated parts of an organisation and as a reaction to events (usually outside changes). This process has been called incrementalism. In these circumstances selection of strategy tends to result from experimenting with strategic changes in parts of the organisation (e.g., a division or area). It may well be that the initiative for such activity comes from decisions made in the various parts of the organisation and through the political processes occurring between those parts.

In these circumstances it is likely that evaluation methods are used in two quite different ways. Firstly, the senior (or corporate) management will evaluate the overall practice in a quite general way in order both to satisfy themselves that the tide is drifting in the right direction and to make appropriate interventions. The board of a holding company, for example, might look at their businesses using product portfolio analysis and buy or sell them to keep the portfolio properly balanced without any detailed understanding of how each business operates. At the same time the management of the parts of the business will be evaluating alternative strategies to convince their corporate masters that they should be given more resources to try out some new ideas. In other words, evaluation is used to strengthen their political position *vis-a-vis* other parts of the organisation.

(iv) *Using outside agencies.* Sometimes within organisations there are potential disagreements on strategy between parties who have similar amounts of power within the company. This may be between management and unions, or between two different managers. In these circumstances it is not unusual for an outside agency, such as a consultant, to evaluate the situation for the company. Very often this process of evaluation is described as an objective, rational process by virtue of the consultants detachment from the situation. In practice, of course, all good consultants are aware of the political reasons for their involvement. To a large extent their role is one of an arbitrator and the evaluation must reflect those circumstances.

8.7 SUMMARY

Strategic evaluation has often been presented as an exact science - a way of deciding what organisations should do. In fact, the analytical methods discussed in this chapter are only useful as a *source of information* to managers in making strategic decisions. It has been seen that the contribution which various techniques make to improving the quality of strategic decision-making will differ quite considerably. Some methods of analysis are valuable because they are eye-openers - they help managers to see the logic or rationale behind strategies rather than assessing those strategies in detail. Other methods are more detailed and are useful ways of understanding how suitable, acceptable or feasible a strategy might be.

However, even the most thorough strategic evaluation cannot possibly anticipate all the detailed problems and pitfalls which might be encountered in the implementation of a strategic change. So it is necessary to recognise that strategic decisions will be refined or even reversed as their implementation is planned and executed. It is this stage of strategy implementation that is discussed in the final part of the book.

REFERENCES

1. Some sort of SWOT (strengths, weaknesses, opportunities and threats) analysis is a useful basis for considering suitability: it is discussed in Chapter 4. The idea of SWOT as a commonsense checklist for use in strategic analyses and evaluation has been used by writers on strategy for many years: for example S. Tilles in 'Making Strategy Explicit' which was written in 1966 and is reproduced in *Business Strategy* edited by I. Ansoff (Penguin: 1968).

2. The idea of consistency of strategy was used by S. Tilles ('How to Evaluate Corporate Strategy', *Harvard Business Review*, Jul.-Aug. 1963) to describe 'the efficiency of policies with respect to the environment'. He also referred to the extent to which strategy was appropriate in terms of resources available. These ideas of consistency and appropriateness are encapsulated in the term 'suitability' used in this book.

3. The term 'feasibility' has much the same meaning as Tilles' (see reference 2 above) criterion of 'workability', i.e., is there a likelihood that the strategy can be made to work?

4. This idea that establishing the underlying rationale is an important preliminary analysis is similar to Rumelt's idea of the 'strategic frame' discussed in Chapter 2. Rumelt describes this step as follows: 'Before one can decide whether or not a given strategy will "work" some indication that the right issues are being worked on is needed'. See: 'Evaluation of Strategy: Theory and Models', in *Strategic Management* edited by D.E. Schendel and C.W. Hofer (Little Brown: 1979).

5.   The following references provide useful discussions of scenarios: P.W. Beck, *Corporate Planning for an Uncertain Future* (Shell UK: 1981); J.H. Grant and W.R. King, 'Strategy Formulation: Analytical and Normative Models' *Strategic Management,* edited by D.E. Schendel and C.W. Hofer (Little Brown: 1979, p. 111); G. Steiner, *Strategic Planning* (Free Press: 1979, p. 235).

6.   The idea of synergy was discussed in Chapter 7 and more extensively by I. Ansoff in *Corporate Strategy* (Penguin: 1968).

7.   For example C.W. Hofer and D. Schendel, *Strategy Formulation: Analytical Concepts* (West: 1978) structure their chapters around this distinction between 'corporate level' and 'business level' strategies.

8.   General Electric's business screen is discussed in Hofer and Schendel (see 7 above) page 32.

9.   Hofer and Schendel (see 7 above) pp. 72-79 explain how 'industry attractiveness' and 'competitive position' can be measured. Readers should also bear in mind the discussion in Chapter 3 on 'structural analyses' and the work of M. Porter, *Competitive Strategy: Techniques for Analyzing Industries and Competitors* (Free Press: 1980).

10.   Hofer and Schendel (see 7 above) p. 34 illustrate a product/market evolution matrix in more detail.

11.   The Strategic Environments Matrix - BCG's New Tool' *'Financial Times,* 20 November 1981 explains the use of this matrix.

12.   Market segmentation is a central idea in marketing theory and practice and is discussed in most marketing texts. For example see: P. Kotler, *Marketing Management: Analysis, Planning and Control,* 4th edition (Prentice-Hall: 1980, Ch. 8).

13.   Reservations about the use of the Boston Consulting Group's concepts and proposals are to be found in S. Slatter, 'Common Pitfalls in Using the BCG Product Portfolio Matrix', *London Business School Journal,* Winter 1980.

14.   Decision trees are discussed in many books on management science and operational research. For example: P.G. Moore and H. Thomas, *The Anatomy of Decisions* (Penguin: 1976, Ch. 4 and 6); R.D. Harris and M.J. Maggard, *Computer Models in Operations Management,* 2nd edn. (Harper & Row: 1977) - Exercise 4 (p. 55) describes a computer package called *Decide* which uses a decision tree.

15.   A fuller discussion of the 'opportunity analysis matrix' can be found in F.F. Neubauer and N.B. Solomon, 'A Managerial Approach to Environmental Assessment', *Long Range Planning,* Vol 10, April 1977; and G. Johnson, 'The Strategic Workshop', *Management Today,* October 1980.

16.   This extension of the technique is called 'strategy mapping' by G. Johnson and illustrated in his article detailed in reference 15.

17.   J. Argenti, *Corporate Planning: a Practical Guide* (George Allen & Unwin: 1968) describes an approach to corporate planning which is essentially focused around the idea of gap analysis.

18.   Hofer and Schendel (see 7 above) pp. 36-39 discuss the resource deployment matrix as a method of historical resource analysis. We have extended this idea into an assessment of the future (i.e. evaluation).

19.   Most textbooks on financial management will include sections relating to the techniques discussed in the text. We would recommend J.M. Samuels and F.M. Wilkes, *Managment of Company Finance,* 3rd edn. (Nelson: 1980) pp. 172, 217 & 218.

20.   See for example Chapter 12 on liquidity and working capital management in Samuels and Wilkes, reference 19.

21.   Again, see for example Samuels and Wilkes, reference 19, Chapter 10.

22.   B. Taylor and J.R. Sparkes in *Corporate Strategy and Planning* (Heinemann: 1977, pp. 48-52) discuss the use of sensitivity and risk analysis as do Samuels and Wilkes, reference 19, p.233, as methods of incorporating uncertainty into strategic evaluation.

23.   A long-standing article on risk analysis is D.B. Hertz, 'Risk Analysis in Capital Investment', *Harvard Business Review,* Winter 1964.

24.   The use of corporate simulation models is discussed by J.H. Grant and W.R. King, reference 5, p.109.

25.   The PIMS project is organised by the Strategic Planning Institute, the UK arm of which is based in London. The project collects and analyses data from subscribing companies to discover indicators of performance. An example of one such study employing multiple regression techniques is described in P.W. Farris and R.D. Buzzell, 'Why Advertising and Promotional Costs Vary: Some Cross Sectional Analyses' *(American) Journal of Marketing,* Vol. 42, Fall 1979.

26.   The application of game theory is discussed in a number of texts. For example: J.H. Grant and W.R. King, reference 5, p.113; P. Kotler, reference 12, p.622; M.E. Porter, *Competitive Strategy* (Free Press: 1980, pp. 88-107).

27.   Break even analysis is discussed in J. Sizer. *An Insight into Management Accounting,* 2nd edn. (Pitman: 1979).

28.   Again, most books on financial management will include a section on funds flow analysis. For example see J.M. Samuels and F.M. Wilkes, reference 19, pp.280-283.

29.   H. Mintzberg, *et al.,* in their article 'The Structure of Unstructured Decision Processes', *Administrative Science Quarterly,* Vol. 21, pp. 246-275, 1976 make the point that referral to some higher authority is a common means of decision-making on strategic issues.

RECOMMENDED KEY READINGS

*   The most extensive discussion of approaches to strategic evaluation is C.W. Hofer and D. Schendel, *Strategy Formulation : Analytical Concepts* (West: 1978). Also, S. Tilles, 'How to Evaluate Corporate Strategy', *Harvard Business Review,* Jul./Aug. 1963 is still worth referring to.

*   Readers should be familiar with the financial evaluation techniques discussed in the chapter. If they are not they should read relevant chapters of a financial management text. For example: J.M. Samuels and F.M. Wilkes, *Management of Company Finance,* 3rd Edn. (Nelson: 1980) or L. J. Gitman, *Principles of Managerial Finance* (Harper & Row: 1976).

PART IV

Strategic Implementation

Strategic analysis and choice are of little value to an organisation unless the proposals are capable of being implemented. Strategic change does not take place simply because it is considered to be desirable; it takes place if it can be made to work. There are many examples of strategies which have come unstuck when being implemented; for example, Laker's attempts to provide low cost air travel, the introduction of new technology in the newspaper industry, or plans for pit closures in the mining industry.

This part of the book deals, then, with the vital problems of implementing strategy and with the planning of that implementation. Chapter 1 made it clear that one of the major characteristics of strategic decisions is that they are likely to give rise to important changes in the resources of an organisation. Chapter 4 explained that such resources do not simply mean physical materials, plant and finances but also include the people in the organisation and the systems used to manage those people. So when thinking about how strategic change affects the resources of an organisation it is necessary to think about all these sorts of resources.

*   Chapter 9 is concerned with the planning of how resources will have to be re-allocated given strategic change; for example, with issues such as the phasing in of production, the addition or deletion of new products, the raising of finance or the retraining of part of the workforce. Typically an organisation will have managerial functions to handle such problems and there has grown up a whole literature of management science to aid such functional managers. However, strategic changes usually involve and affect many resource areas: they may be implemented on a day-to-day basis through the functions, but they need to be thought through as a whole to see if they form a coherent package. It may be for example that what the marketing department view as desirable and feasible for a product launch would create major company wide financial difficulties. In Chapter 9 the approach is not simply to regard the implementation of strategy through resource management as a matter of functional planning but to look at the overall strategic planning of resources.

*   A major resource of any organisation is the people who work for it. How these are to be managed is obviously important: it is also clear that changes in strategy are likely to give rise to the need to reorganise how people are managed. The last two chapters of the book examine this problem. Chapter 10 concentrates on how people are to be organised in terms of who will be responsible for what: it is therefore concerned with structural questions - what shape should the organisation take and at what level should different sorts of decision be taken. Chapter 11 then considers the systems by which the organisation is managed, both formal control and reward systems and less formalised systems of managerial control. The focus here is on the problems of managing strategic change through the people in the organisation.

Throughout Part IV of the book it is important to remember the distinction between the planning of implementation and actually carrying out the tasks of implementation. As the three chapters proceed they move progressively from planning to the harsher realities of implementation.

9

PLANNING THE ALLOCATION OF RESOURCES

9.1 INTRODUCTION

Strategic change needs to be put into effect through the operations of the organisation. It is one thing to decide upon a strategy of product development but the success of its implementation is likely to depend on the phasing-in of production, the addition or deletion of new products, the raising of finance, the retraining of part of the workforce and so on. These are changes in the resources of an organisation and it is the planning of such changes that is the subject of this chapter.

Strategic changes usually involve and affect many resource areas: in the end they may be implemented on a day-to-day basis within individual functions, but they need to be thought through as a whole. The approach in this chapter is not to regard the implementation of strategy through resource management as simply a matter of planning within functions but to raise a series of questions, the aim of which is to guide the overall resource planning of the organisation. This is achieved by raising a set of basic questions about resource planning at the beginning of the chapter and then discussing their significance in terms of the main resource areas of an organisation. In this sense the chapter treats this level of operational strategy as the product of more generalised levels of strategy - what has previously been referred to as 'corporate' and 'business' (or 'competitive') levels of strategy. Finally, in the chapter, there is a review of some planning aids which will help the reader consider how resource can be examined and planned as a whole.

It is also important to emphasise again that in thinking through how strategy will be put into effect, detailed thought is in fact being given to the feasibility of its implementation. As such, the planning of resource allocation is part of the evaluation of strategy. There is no sense in proceeding with the implementation of a strategy if, in planning how it should be done, it becomes clear it is unrealistic. Indeed, given the often generalised nature of strategic decision-making as it occurs in reality, it may be that really detailed consideration of a strategic course of action does not actually take place until the planning of implementation begins. Managers should then realise that they are not simply planning how something is to be done but also whether it is possible or sensible to do it.

9.2 CENTRAL QUESTIONS IN RESOURCE PLANNING

There is always the danger that the resource implications of a given strategy are not thought through as a whole; that implications are overlooked in the day-to-day management of the organisation for example, or that consideration is given to one set of resource requirements - finance perhaps - whilst another such as manpower needs is neglected. This section of the chapter raises some basic questions designed to help avoid this trap. The questions are stated in such a way that implementation has to be considered in detail. The first three questions identify the sort of resource issues that have to be dealt with in implementing strategy; the fourth with the identification of key influences or constraints on implementation; and the last two questions deal with the planning steps themselves. The questions are summarised in Fig. 9.1.

1. Exactly what resources will a strategy require for its implementation? (Resource identification)
2. To what extent do these required resources build on or are a change from existing resources? (Fit with existing resources) — The identification of planning issues
3. Can the required resources be integrated with each other? (Fit between required resources)
4. What are the priorities and key tasks?
5. What should be the plan of action? — The planning steps
6. What are the key assumptions on which the plan is based? — Assumption testing

Figure 9.1 *Central questions in resource planning.*

9.2.1 Resource Identification

The most basic requirement is the precise *identification* of what resources are required to carry out the strategy. Effective planning of resources must depend on the extent to which the planner is clear abour resource needs. The danger is that resource requirements will be overlooked or that it will be assumed that the resource needs of the past will cope with the strategies of the future. The powerful influence of recipes[1] on the views and practices of managers has already been pointed out: it is likely that both at an individual level and at a corporate or even industry level, managers manage very much on the basis of past experience. There is the danger that new strategies will be considered in the context of old expectations or existing bases of operating rather than in terms of what is required in the future. Illustration 38 shows how one such company - Sinclair - built on the undisputed innovative skills of its founder, faltered at one stage in its development because it did not adequately consider the resource implications of its own development.

The requirement is for a detailed consideration of what is needed to make a strategy work. To take an example, a company manufacturing a limited range of disposable paper products mainly for industrial use decided to add new paper products to its range with a view to providing a more complete range. Its aim was to attract wider users, in particular public authorities and retailers. The strategic logic was that its existing product base was too limited, that it was over-reliant on products now in mature and declining markets, so it needed to develop product lines in markets showing signs of growth. The company intended to do this through internal development of new products because it had a R&D department of proven ability in improving and up-dating existing products. In considering the implications of this strategic move the checklist of resources given in Fig. 4.1 as a resource audit doubles as a checklist for resource identification.

In terms of *physical resources,* although it did not require additional factory space, it did need new plant and different sorts of base materials to develop the required products. It was possible to identify the *funding level* required to finance the project and the products and their associated costs were estimated in detail. The *human resource* requirements could also be identified. Internally, there was the need for additional general management to coordinate the project, as well as production, development and marketing management. There was also a requirement for more operatives and staff, and for sales-people who could operate in new markets. Externally, the company needed new suppliers and the services of outside technologists and advertising personnel.

The *systems* requirements were identified in particular as different forms of quality and production control, a costing system that could distinguish between the products in the wider range, and agreed working and manning arrangements in the factory. In addition, the distribution channels for selling to the retail and public authority markets needed to be set up, as did sensing mechanisms for assessing market needs and demands. *Intangibles,* such as product image and the reputation of the company both in its existing markets and with financial institutions, were seen to be important. Most of all the company saw the need for a range of new skills of management at the development and at the operating level.

ILLUSTRATION 38

Sinclair Radionics

- Clive Sinclair would have liked to see his company continuously launching his latest inventions, but in the 1970s the resources were not there to realise his dreams.

As founder, chairman and chief executive of Sinclair Radionics, Clive Sinclair found himself faced with trying to exploit his talent for invention without becoming embroiled in the problems of managing an enterprise. His undoubted skill, said those who knew him best, was his eye for a market opening - but despite building up a turnover of £8 million through pioneering the development of the pocket calculator, Sinclair failed to maintain a consistent momentum to finance the development of later innovations.

Sinclair launched his pocket calculator in 1973, soon followed by the digital, 'black watch'. However, the watch failed to make the desired impact, while at the same time Sinclair's share of the calculator market was being rapidly eroded by cheap imports from the Far East. The effect was to considerably reduce profitability, leaving Sinclair without a source of finance for future research and development. The first of Sinclair's subsequent projects to suffer from inadequate funding was the pocket-sized television, which although might have received considerable public interest, left Sinclair with no choice but to seek outside financial help or abandon his ideas altogether.

Although lack of *financial* resources may have appeared to be the reason that Sinclair got into difficulties, this may only have been a symptom of the underlying problems of insufficient *management* resources. Sinclair needed to build up a stable company with scope for long-term growth to achieve his desired ends of launching new products. The failure to achieve this, Sinclair realised, was very much his fault.

'I have no great desire, or experience of management - I don't think you can be chairman and chief executive, and do research - I'm experienced in research'.

As a result, the company was unable to develop the mass-consumer marketing skills which were needed to give the company the stability that it required in order to fulfill Sinclair's innovatory aims. Ultimately Sinclair's solution was to establish a business that just undertook research and the inventions that came from this were subcontracted out for production and marketing to other companies. For example, the Timex corporation manufactured his micro-computer, the ZX81, while W. H. Smith undertook a considerable amount of the marketing for it.

Source: Management Today, March 1981, p. 62.

9.2.2 Fit With Existing Resources

Assuming the resources required to implement the desired strategy are identified, then it is possible to move to the next stage, which begins to clarify just how problematic implementation is likely to be. Strategic change may well entail important *changes* of resources. Since major resource changes will inevitably raise problems both of operational logistics and probably of conflict within an organisation, it is important to be clear of the extent to which existing resources can cope, will need to be changed or added to, or perhaps will need to be replaced altogether. The likelihood is that some will be adequate and some will become redundant. For example, it could be that the venture into new paper products in a new market might need totally new plant but that this could be located in an existing factory. It could be that the existing process engineering capability is sufficient and that the production workforce could provide a basis for the new operation if they were retrained. However, the marketing and selling skills required to move into the retail market may not exist at all, and would need to be obtained from outside the firm. It may be that the values of people required in a new venture are not compatible with those in the organisation as it now exists: this is often the case with the acquisitions of companies.

What has been done, even in such a simple example, it to highlight the need to spell out which existing resources are adequate and which are not. Of course, the analysis would be a good deal fuller than this but the point is that this approach has four useful benefits.

(i)   It identifies the extent to which intended strategy builds on what exists or demands new resources.

(ii)   It helps identify just how extensive the new resource requirements are.

(iii)   It helps in thinking through the implications of obtaining few, or many, new resources. In this way it is possible to get a clear picture of the extent of the difficulties in implementation. It is one thing if the new strategy in the main builds on what the company already has: there may be reasonable confidence of its success perhaps. It is another if it demands extensive resources of which the company has no experience: this is much more difficult and risky.

(iv)   The identification of changes in resources leads on to a consideration of the extent to which the 'resource mix' that exists is adequate for the future. It could be that an analysis of fit with existing resources leads to the conclusion that previously perceived strengths are not really strengths at all when it comes to the problems of strategic implementation. Suppose, for instance, it becomes clear that in order to break into the retail market, fundamentally different R&D skills are necessary. The strength of R&D that the company perceived in their strategic analysis becomes a problem - it is not a strength as far as required implementation goes. In effect the requirements of implementation have given rise to a re-evaluation of company resources.

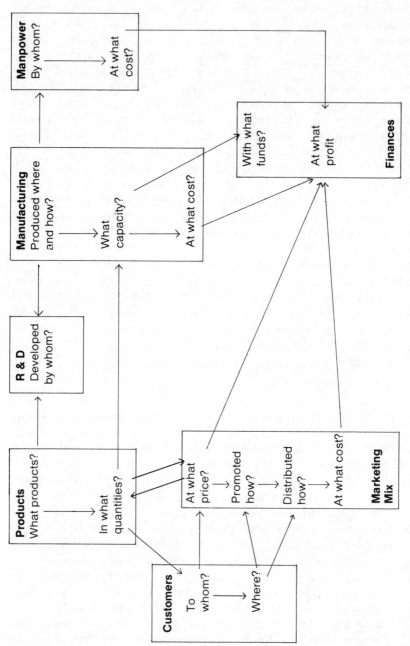

Figure 9.2 *Some implications for resource integration in a product launch.*

9.2.3 Fit Between Required Resources

Underlying much of what has been said is the assumption that the resources needed to carry out the proposed strategy are capable of working together. The point has already been made that resource areas interact: this interaction needs to be considered explicitly. Figure 9.2 shows some of the ways in which resource interaction occurs using the example of a new product's launch.

Suppose the company decides that a new division is required: this involves consideration of manpower availability, control systems and probably the structure of the whole company. A decision to adopt a penetration pricing policy and run the new product range on a marginal basis in its early years to gain market share, could substantially affect the marketing of existing products, the policy on retained earnings and dividends and, almost certainly, the control systems used for monitoring the progress of the product. The purchase of plant, the research and development of products, the setting up of the new division, retraining, launch marketing costs, indeed all the development activity for the new venture has financial implications. So the project will need to be investigated in terms of what funds are required, by when: what might be generated by the profits from the new venture itself and by when: what might be available from present trading operations: and what needs to be raised externally? What is necessary is a 'model' of the new venture to judge whether the parts of that model can actually work together.

9.2.4 Priorities and Key Tasks

The first three questions help identify what resources will be needed, what change in existing resources will be needed and what the future resource mix needs to look like. It is now necessary to plan *how* things will happen. A sensible way to start is to extend the analysis of the extent of the change from the existing resource mix by identifying *key tasks* and *priorities*. Indeed, it is their identification that provides the basis for not only a resource plan but, more widely, for the management and control of the whole implementation of the strategic change: and this will be discussed more fully in Chapter 11.

Key tasks and priorities are different from each other. Key tasks are to do with the major areas of attention that the strategic change depends on. It could be that management determines that the new venture will depend on the construction of an effective marketing and selling effort no matter how good it becomes at producing the new product. Think of key tasks as the few central things that the venture crucially depends on.

Priorities on the other hand are more to do with timing: they are the actions that need to be tackled to get the project underway: so the design and commissioning of plant or ensuring that financial resources are available might be priorities in this sense. There is little point pedantically trying to define what is a key task and what is a priority; it is likely that some areas of required action will be both anyway. What is important is to distinguish and to be clear about those things that the strategy vitally depends upon from those that are important simply because they are 'first in the queue'.

The identification of priorities and key tasks also provides a basis for the allocation of responsibilities. Who is to be responsible for each of the key areas? Where key areas interlink, who is responsible for coordination? It is also worthwhile to be explicit about what is *not* so important. What are the things that should or can be left until later or, more likely, which of the different priorities being advocated around the building are to be followed up and which are not.

9.2.5 The Plan of Action

A plan is the output of the series of questions raised so far. It sets out what resources need to be obtained and which disposed of. This may well be in the form of a budget, but might also be usefully expressed as a sequence of actions or a timetable in a written plan. To take the example of the paper products company, some planning of timing would clearly be necessary: on-the-job production line retraining cannot begin until a production facility exists; until the company has examined in detail the timing of development, installation, commissioning and completion of plant, it is not possible to examine fully the flow of funds required to finance the venture; until it knows at what rate production is to be geared at, it cannot take a sensible view about the extent of the product launch; that in turn means that it will not have a clear idea of expected revenue flow, so again it cannot think sensibly about the requirement for funds.

The circularity of the problem is quite usual in developing a plan of action and raises the question of where to start - with a market forecast, an available level of funds, a production level constraint or what? The answer is that it may not matter too much where the starting point is since the plan will have to be reworked and readjusted several times. A useful guideline is to enter the problem through what appears to be the major change area. For example in the paper products company the executives might see the major change as the necessity for very different sorts of products to be added to the range. This would mean that they might sensibly begin to think about the plan of action in terms of projected sales volumes by product type.

A plan of action will provide the basis for understanding the impact of changes in the sequencing of activities. What would be the effect of a delay in one part of the programme on the rest of the programme? Are some areas of activity less sensitive to delays or change than others? It might be found that delays in the installation of plant do not have major impacts on the retraining programme or even on the recruitment and activity of the marketing team since both are fairly flexible. However, such a delay may have very serious marketing consequences if it means that the launch is delayed giving the competition time to react. The plan of action will also provide a means of monitoring and controlling the development of the project. It helps identify points in the programme at which certain key stages should be completed for example.

9.2.6 The Recognition and Testing of Key Assumptions

All plans are based on assumptions. They may be assumptions about resource availability, the capacity of the organisation to adapt existing resources or coordinate the resource requirements of a new strategy. Assumptions may also be to do with the environment; that a market will grow, that funds can be raised or that suppliers will deliver on time. The questions raised so far in this chapter help identify the main assumptions upon which a plan is based and these assumptions should be made explicit as part of the planning process.

The danger is that when a plan is drawn up the assumptions built into it take on the appearance of fact and become unquestioned. It is dangerous if this occurs because the vulnerable areas of the plan are then disguised and reasons for shortfalls or failures may not be recognised. If assumptions are made explicit the plan can be used as a model to help both in the evaluation of strategy (as discussed in Chapter 8) and also in the investigation of alternative means of implementation of strategy. Different assumptions about market conditions, price acceptability, competitive action, cost levels and so on, can be tested out to see how vulnerable plans of action are to different assumptions. So too can different assumptions about timing be tested out: what effect would delays in a construction programme have on capital requirements for example? A common way of carrying out this sort of sensitivity analysis is to build 'best', 'worst' and 'most likely' assumptions into budgets, models or a break even analysis to see what the implications are. The 'best' view would be a budget based on a relatively optimistic set of assumptions, the 'worst' on a pessimistic set, and the 'most likely' on what might be, for example, a consensus view of most reasonable assumptions. The resulting plans can be examined to see the implications of the differing assumptions.

9.3 RESOURCE PLANNING AT THE OPERATIONAL LEVEL

It is at the operational level of an organisation that the management of strategy implementation takes place. Illustration 39 shows how a change of strategy may have major operational implications in an organisation.

Without consistency between corporate or business strategies and operating strategies both levels of strategic decision are likely to be ineffective. For example, if a company wishes to follow a strategy of extensive product development, it will have to decide:

ILLUSTRATION 39

National Cash Registers

- Implicit in a change in strategy is often the fact that there will have to be many changes in the organisation's resources. The case of National Cash Registers highlights the number of changes that may be necessary.

Traditionally NCR's main business had been the manufacture of electro-mechanical cash registers and accounting machines. Although they were involved with computers, the computing division was isolated from head office and considered relatively unimportant.

As electro-mechanical technology became outdated, NCR's profits declined, culminating in a $60 million loss in 1972, a loss that brought home to the Board that a change in strategy was imperative. They appointed Bill Anderson as president, his immediate task being one of taking NCR into the manufacture of electronic data processing equipment, a move that necessitated many changes to the company's resources.

In terms of human resources, changes spanned the whole spectrum of employees; 28 out of the 35 'corporate officers' or vice presidents left the company. Many of the salesmen, unable to cope with the change to selling data processing equipment, left. New salesmen with computer skills were recruited together with a number of systems analysts to develop the necessary software. At NCR's headquarters in Dayton, Ohio, the workforce was cut from 14,000 to 600, while in Dundee, Scotland, the company's UK manufacturing base, the workforce was cut from 6500 to less than 1000.

The changes in physical resources were equally numerous. A new product meant that new machinery was required, but NCR's policy of decentralising production led to the huge complex at Dayton being significantly cut back as manufacturing was moved to several smaller plants. This preference for smaller units also affected the Dundee base where 4 of their 7 plants were closed. Because NCR had changed so rapidly, it was necessary for the company to acquire several small companies to fill the gap in its product range. Companies acquired included Comten, a specialist in communication equipment designed to link into IBM computers, and Data Pathing, a company making data collection systems for large industrial complexes. These acquisitions were financed by selling off some of their existing companies that no longer fitted the new company profile.

The production control systems of the old NCR were not suited to the constantly changing world of data processing equipment, so NCR developed its own on-line manufacturing and control system to co-ordinate production between the many plants.

The effect of these changes on finance was favourable; the debt equity ratio was cut from 50% to 30% and the position was reached where they were able to finance rentals and development of hardware and software entirely out of their own revenues.

Source: Management Today, December 1979, p.74.

* how to originate the new products (R&D strategy);
* how to manufacture them (production strategy);
* how to market them (marketing strategy);
* how to finance the development (financial strategy);
* how to obtain the required manpower and skills (manpower strategy).

The sections that follow discuss the operational issues that will be important in resouce planning. The aim is not to give an exhaustive checklist of the ramifications of strategic decisions but to indicate the nature and importance of the relationship between a change in corporate strategy and the operational strategies of an organisation.[2] The main points from the discussion are summarised in Fig. 9.3 where they are set out against the planning steps raised by the first three questions discussed in Section 9.2

9.3.1 Production Strategy[3]

Some important questions as far as production strategy is concerned are these:

* *What level of production capacity* is desirable? At least three levels[4] can be considered. 'Demand matching' entails attempting to match levels of demand with levels of production and is therefore likely to involve high costs through short production runs. 'Operation smoothing' involves producing to average demand, building up stocks in low demand periods, and drawing off these in high demand periods. 'Subcontracting' entails producing at a minimum level and buying in the remainder.
* *Where should plant be located?* Influences on this might include the proximity of markets, the cost of transport and access to supplies, and the cost, availability and skills of labour or the extent to which there are government incentives to move to an area. So too may economies of scale: for example, a choice between a large, single with the benefit of economies of scale, or several smaller sites nearer to local markets or raw materials.
* *What should be the timing of investment in plant?* Whilst demand may rise smoothly, costs of investment do not; they take place in a stepwise fashion resulting in periods of costly excess capacity: so the timing of investment becomes important. Choices on timing are problematic. Whether to be first with new plant and run the risk that later competitors will invest in improved plant; or to invest above levels of demand and accept overcapacity as the price of moving down the experience curve faster; or to introduce new plant later and run the risk of higher unit cost because of uncompetitive plant or being unable to meet demand.
* Given a change in production process, *is it more sensible to convert existing plant or build new plant?* There may be arguments in favour of each. Conversion may be less costly in terms of capital investment but mean that the down-time of plant during conversion is high. New plant

	Production	Supplies	R & D	Marketing	Finance	Manpower
Identification of required resources	Production capacity Location of plant	Sources of supply Spread of supplies Cost of supplies	Specification of skills Focus of R & D	Marketing mix (product distribution, promotion and price)	Current and capital requirements (over time)	Skills identification Required manpower levels
Fit with existing resources	Convert existing plant or build new Replacement of existing plant	Suitability of existing suppliers	Resource availability	Compatibility with influence patterns Suitability of marketing skills Additional resource requirement	Sources of capital finance: - retained earnings - equity capital - loan capital Sources of working capital: - margins - overdraft	Training needs Policies on manpower reductions or recruitment
Fit between required resources	Level of investment in manufacturing (make or buy) Flexibility of plant Manning and de-manning	Make or buy Supplier image/ reputation	Compatibility with other operations Support availability	Compatibility of: - production levels - cost - parity levels	Effects of: - debt level on profits & earnings per share - share issue on control - dividend policy - asset management	Union consultation Financial implications Team development

Figure 9.3   *Some operational implications of strategic change.*

may be more expensive to build but provide more efficient production on completion.

* *Should the company make or buy the products?* If it makes or if it buys, to what extent should it do so? The issue is whether or not a company is well advised to tie up its funds in manufacturing when it could be investing in something else - more extensive marketing operations for example.

* *Is the production resource flexible enough?* As companies follow paths of increasing replacement of capital equipment for labour there is the danger that expensive plant will need to be utilised to the full;[5] if this plant is not flexible enough to handle different product ranges or variants then the only way full utilisation can be achieved is by seeking extra volume of sales, usually at low margins resulting in lower profits.

* *What manning levels and skills are required* for the production resource? Will this mean increasing or decreasing the workforce?

9.3.2 Supplies Strategy[6]

Using as an example a company seeking to implement a product development strategy, the sort of issues of supplies strategy that might well arise include:

* *What sources of supply* are available for new or changed products? Where are the locations of such supplies and what sort of suppliers are they? Are the sources able to provide regular and reliable delivery?

* *To what extent should there be a spread of supply?* There may be advantages such as high levels of service and continuity of supply in establishing a long term relationship with a limited number of suppliers. This has to be set against the possibility that the organisation may become so linked to that supplier that new ideas from other suppliers are overlooked or more competitive prices ignored.

* *Cost of supplies* is likely to be a major problem for new product initiatives. In its early stages of growth the sales volume may be too low to achieve benefits of low costs through bulk buying. How are costs to be reduced?

* *To what extent are existing suppliers suitable?* The decision to change a supplier is important: for example, a new model of a product may call for a component which could be made more cheaply by a different supplier; but a company may still be very reliant on their existing supplier for other components or for spares for existing models and, as such, would wish to retain their goodwill.

* The *make or buy* issue is again important, this time as far as supplies is concerned. To what extent is it advantageous to own sources of supply as distinct from buying them from elsewhere? This closely relates to the issue of vertical integration, and its advantages and disadvantages of integration have already been covered in Chapter 7.

* To what extent is the *image or reputation of a supplier* important to other

aspects of the business? A new product could benefit (or suffer) considerably in the market if customers know of the use of a component manufactured by a particularly well known supplier.

9.3.3 Research and Development Strategy[7]

R&D strategy is a particularly good example of an area in which consistency with more general levels of strategy and with other functional strategies is very important. It is easy to be seduced by the development of new ideas and products without paying enough attention to the practical considerations of the likelihood of pay-off.[8]

Some of the typical issues to be considered are as follows:

*   *What are the R&D skills required to* put into effect the desired strategy? Is a 'maintenance'[9] role required, concentrating on the updating and improving of existing products and consistent with a 'follower' type product strategy? Is an 'expansion' role needed, seeking for innovations ahead of competitors and consistent with market and product leadership strategies? Or is an 'exploratory' role important in which R&D includes a pure research role?

*   *Is the identified required R&D resource available?* There is little point in a company forging ahead with innovative product development strategies if it currently has a 'maintenance' type R&D department. Either the company has to change the nature of its R&D skills or adopt a more realistic strategy.

*   *What should be the R&D focus?* Should the firm concentrate on product development or process development and at what time should the emphasis switch? Product development will be of crucial importance during the development stage of a product life cycle; and process development and cost reduction as maturity approaches. But when should a company switch its R&D focus from one to the other? Too early and it runs the risk of a competitor developing significant product advantages; too late and it runs the risk of an uncompetitive cost position.[10]

*   *Is the R&D capability compatible* with the other operations areas of the organisation? Is R&D effort being put behind a project that can be marketed, financed and produced effectively, for example?

*   *Is there sufficient support from other areas* of the operation? One of the major reasons for the failure of R&D activity is the lack of resources due to current business pressures or problems of short term profitability.[11]

9.3.4 Marketing Strategy

Often, marketing strategy and the business (and indeed corporate) strategies of organisations are closely intertwined. So marketing strategy is likely to have been considered in general terms at least with regard to issues[12] such as:

* *Market focus,* which is concerned with the strategic posture an organisation seeks in terms of its market. For example, it is important to be sure that in seeking to implement a strategy of product development the company is clear as to exactly which market segments it is concentrating on.

* *What is an acceptable market share?* Upper and lower share limits might usefully be thought of by market segment. What are the share expectations by country, by distributor type or by customer type, for example?

* What is the *expected and acceptable customer spread?* Is the strategy likely to be dependent on one or two major customers or is the market highly fragmented?

* *Competitive edge* is concerned with answering the most basic of questions: "Why should anyone want to buy or use my product?" Certainly this question should have been addressed in the formulation of strategy. To implement strategy this, competitive edge needs to be turned into operational reality. So, for example, the fact that a new technological breakthrough has been achieved will be of no consequence if the potential buyer of the product does not recognise its utility.

However, a more detailed level of planning is also required. For example:

* *Product planning:* what will the range of products be, what level of quality and level of after sales services as far as the emphasised customer benefit is concerned?

* *Distribution channels:* through which channels will the product be distributed to which customers and who within the channel will be responsible for which aspects of marketing.[13] In terms of *physical distribution,* where will products be stocked, in what quantity and how will they be transported?

* *Sales promotion:* what will be the emphasis between the different means of promoting sales - personal selling versus advertising, for instance -which products will receive most emphasis and what will be the expenditure? How many salespeople are required in what territories? What media is most appropriate and at what times?

* *Pricing:* what price levels are appropriate given both required profits and the marketing strategy being adopted? What will the policy be on discounting and credit according to types of customer?

* A strategy may call for a switch from one market segment (e.g. an industrial market) to another (e.g. retail market). Are the *marketing skills* in the company compatible with this switch in emphasis?

* *Provision of marketing resource:* what numbers of additional salespeople or vehicles are needed? Are different product sizes required? Is the sales office provision or depot network adequate?

* Can the marketing requirements be met in terms of levels of *production,* at the *required quality and cost* so as to market the product successfully and make it sufficiently profitable to be financially acceptable?

9.3.5 Financial Strategy[14]

A corporate planner from a major UK company once complained to one of the authors that a major problem he faced was that the financial director of the company did not accept that there was any such thing as financial strategy. The corporate planner was concerned because he recognised that there is little point in developing strategies if there is no clear, long term idea of how they are to be financed. Some of the key issues of financial strategy that are likely to arise are:

* What are the financial requirements of the proposed strategy in terms of *current and capital expenditure?* To examine this sensibly it may require an exercise in both cash and capital budgeting (discussed later in the chapter) since the timing of financial support is of key importance. The identification of these requirements leads on to considerations of the way in which such finance is to be obtained.
* *Is the project to be financed, over time, from retained earnings?* There are indications that management prefer this to be the case, if possible[15], and particularly in small firms.[16] If this is impossible or not seen as sensible, then where are funds to be obtained? There may be a need for further equity capital for example. Is this to be raised through a new share issue or by raising further equity from existing shareholders through a rights issue? Alternatively or in addition, *loan capital* may be more attractive. If so, from where is this to be obtained and on what basis?
* It may also be that there will be an increase in current expenditure - perhaps an increase in stocks or as a result of increased marketing expenditure. How is an increase in *working capital* to be financed? There are two likely sources: tightening up the operation to provide increased profit margins through increased productivity, decreased wastage rates or credit control for example; or negotiating an increase in overdraft facility with the bank.
* An examination of *sourcing of funds* may give rise to a need for change in the financial structure of the organisation. When the company's profits are growing a high level of debt may be advantageous since it increases earnings per share and retained earnings; but when profits are declining, high debt worsens the situation, both for earnings per share and retained earnings. Since the ability of a firm to generate funds for growth is likely to depend largely on the confidence of shareholders and the funds available for reinvestment from retained earnings, decisions on *levels of debt* become of critical importance.
* A company that decides to raise capital by issuing new shares may also have its problems: there may be further dilution of control, particularly

for a private company or the share price may be such that it would be more sensible to achieve an increase in share price before an issue of shares; there may even be fears that a failure to sell the shares might affect confidence in the company.

* What *dividend policy* is to be followed? Management may see the possibility, and regard as desirable, the financing of new developments from retained earnings, but they have to set against this the importance of dividend payout to retain the confidence and support of shareholders. If the company is not showing signs of growth and it cuts its dividend, then shareholders are likely to look for other companies in which to invest.

* In terms of both fixed and current assets, what policies will guide the *asset management* of the company? For example, what levels of cash are to be held? If the levels are too high then questions will be asked both by shareholders and potential buyers as to why the company is not using or distributing the cash.

* Another important aspect of the management of assets is the *deployment of funds* within the enterprise. If funds are to be allocated to one division for a product development strategy, are there other divisions for which funds are not to be made available or curtailed? Here the concern is with investment in the portfolio of the enterprise itself; and a useful model for guiding policy in this area is the product portfolio as discussed in the Appendix.

9.3.6 Manpower Strategy[17]

In the end, the success of a strategy is likely to depend very heavily on the people required to put it into effect. Some of the issues which need to be considered are:

* *What skills are required* to implement a course of action? These skills may be at a managerial or operative level. For example, a decision to move to a capital intensive, automated plant will need quite different skills from a labour intensive plant.

* Associated with this may be the actual *size of the manpower requirement* of the organisation. In the case of a switch to automated plant, for example, the total numbers of staff may be reduced but the numbers required in specific skills increased.

* The *identification of training needs* is important. Which individuals need what sort of experience to develop general management and operating abilities.

* In terms of changes is manning levels, how are numbers to be increased or reduced? In the case of reductions, will this be through *natural wastage, redundancy* or *redeployment*. Will skills that are needed be met from within the organisation or by recruitment?

* To what extent and on what matters is *consultation with unions* and

employee representatives important? A failure to do so could result in expensive industrial action and an uncooperative workforce.

* What will be the *financial implications* of an extensive redundancy programme? In the short term, redundancy payments can reach such high levels that they may mean the difference between relatively healthy overall profits and a loss.

* Increasing emphasis is being placed on *team development* for managers and staff that are capable of working together productively.[18] Has sufficient consideration been given to the teams of managers or staff needed to implement strategic change?

9.4 AIDS TO RESOURCE PLANNING

It is not the intention to deal in this section with all possible approaches that might be used in the planning of resources. Many such aids - break even analysis, funds flow analysis, sensitivity analysis and simulation - have already been discussed in Chapter 8 and readers are encouraged to consider these in the context of resource planning. Rather, this section concentrates on two aids to planning not already discussed and which help to advance the planner's thinking towards two questions discussed in 9.2.4 and 9.2.5 above, namely:

* What are the priorities and key tasks?
* What should be the plan of action?

9.4.1 Financial Planning and Budgeting

Financial planning is concerned with translating the resource implications of decisions or possible decisions into financial statements of one sort or another. This is most commonly done through the various forms of budgets[19] that managers use. Budgets have many uses and perform different roles in organisations. The concern here is with budgets as plans and as models.

A budget may take the form of a consolidated statement of the resource position required to achieve a set of objectives or put into effect a strategy. To achieve such a statement it is necessary to identify and think through the required resource position of the organisation. A budget expresses these in a monthly or yearly form, perhaps split down by departments in the organisation. As such it represents a plan of action stated in resource terms for an organisation. Illustration 40 is an example of a budget's role as a plan. The process of budgeting also involves the thinking through of the resource implications of action and so has a useful role to play in forecasting the impact of decisions on the resources of an organisation or part of an organisation. For example, the planned launch of a new product might mean increased demands on the R&D department. It is likely that that department would then undertake

ILLUSTRATION 40

A Budget's Role as a Plan

• A local council's budgets are both a means of planning and an expression of planned resource allocation to implement policies.

In 1982 a metropolitan council's new controlling party promised to reduce council expenditure and thus reduce the rates. The planning and budgeting process that followed is an example of budgeting's role in the planning process, and how a budget expresses the policies of an organisation.

The planning process required that committees of council officers and councillors achieve a reduction in total expenditure of between 4% and 5% per annum - a reduction which was reflected in the final agreed budget, a summary of which is shown below.

Committee	1983/84		1984/85		1985/86	
	£'000	%	£'000	%	£'000	%
Education	44,520	68.3	40,000	63.9	37,290	62.1
Environment	4,560	7	3,750	6	3,363	5.6
Housing	990	1.5	3,220	5.2	3,903	6.5
Leisure	3,650	5.6	3,380	5.4	3,122	5.2
Social Services	8,970	13.8	9,820	15.7	10,088	16.8
Policy	2,460	3.8	2,380	3.8	2,282	3.8
Total	65,150	100	62,550	100	60,048	100

The above budget expresses the policies which were finally agreed by the council after weeks of negotiation. The two key elements were: an overall reduction in the level of expenditure and the identification of areas that would receive an increased share of the funds and those that would be cut back.

It was decided to change the relative shares of funding between committees. Cuts were seen as possible in Education, because of a decrease in the school age population, and in Environment and Leisure which, it was agreed, were of lower priority. It was felt that Environment and Leisure could raise their own funds by increasing the charges for the services they provided.

On the other hand, the increasing proportion of elderly persons in the borough demanded greater expenditure on domestic help through Social Services and the building of more suitable homes. The increase in the proportion of funds for Housing was to allow for renovation of the council's housing stock.

Within each of the areas of expenditure, individual committees were then faced with planning their own use of funds through a secondary budgeting exercise; which programmes would be cut and which developed? What funds would be needed by whom for this and by when? Each committee's plans were then expressed as budgets by month and by programme.

The budgeting mechanism allowed the council to examine the impact of policy changes on its resources and management. The drawing up of the budget was not just the outcome of a plan but also a model which provided a means of planning.

Source: Rate Fixing and the Budget Process in a Metropolitan District, Case Study from the Education and Training Panel, The Chartered Institute of Public Finance and Accounting.

a budgeting exercise to forecast the resource implications for themselves and may, as a result, come up with requests for additional resources.

Whether at an organisational or departmental level, a budget is in effect a *model of required resources.* A model can be examined, tested and adjusted to see the implications of change in assumptions about the future or changes in the progress that might be achieved in a project. Can the resources needed be sensibly coordinated or are there incompatibilities? Especially useful is the facility to examine the implication of changes in expected performance, or a failure to meet required target deadlines and thus identify key tasks and priorities within the plan.

There are different sorts of budgets. It is always risky to say exactly which sorts of budget are most needed for resource planning, but the following might typically be used:[20]

(i) Capital budgeting is concerned with generating a statement of the cash flows related to a particular project or decision. A company may decide to invest in new plant or acquire a new business. A capital budgeting exercise might well seek to determine: (a) what the outflow and inflow of funds associated with that project will be; (b) what the implications of different means of financing the project would be (for example, how an acquisition financed by increased loan capital would differ from one financed by increased equity capital); or (c) some assessment of how worthwhile the project is through some measure of return of investment (discussed in Chapter 8).

(ii) Working capital budgets seek to show the expected outcome of decisions in terms of changes in stocks, cash, debtors and creditors. Underlying such an exericse would be decisions on expenditure about the management of working capital: it might be that a working capital budgeting exercise might examine different policies on cash, stock or creditor management.

(iii) Departmental budgets may be important if strategic changes are likely to affect parts of the business differently. As mentioned earlier, a decision to adopt a more aggressive product development programme might well mean a much larger allocation of resources to departments such as R&D and a cut-back in others.

(iv) Consolidated budgets and projected profit and loss accounts may well be useful in projecting, perhaps over a period of years, the implications of decisions on an organisation's overall performance. For example, a new venture might reduce a company's overall profits for many years before its benefits at an organisational level are apparent. This may, in turn, highlight as a key task the need to convince shareholders of the wisdom of the venture and the need for patience.

9.4.2 Network Analysis[21]

Network analysis, also known as critical path analysis, has been a widely used management technique since World War II. In fact it was developed for the purposes of military planning during the War and has been adapted for management use since. It is a technique for planning projects by breaking them down into their component activities and showing these activities and their inter-relationships in the form of a network. By considering the times and resources required to complete each of the activities it is possible to locate the critical path of activities which determines the minimum time for the project. The network can also be used for scheduling materials and other resources and for examining the impact of changes in one sub-area of the project on others. The technique is particularly relevant to projects which have a reasonably definite start and finish.

It has been used very effectively in new product or service launches, construction of plant, acquisitions and mergers, relocation and R&D projects - all the sort of activities relevant to strategy implementation. Figure 9.4 is an outline network analysis diagram for the launch of a new car. In fact the analysis would probably be a great deal more detailed, but as an example it can be seen how this sort of analysis can help in resource planning.

* It demands the breakdown of the programme of implementation into its constituent parts by resource area.
* It helps identify priorities because it identifies activities upon which others depend. For example, the network identifies that pilot-building cannot take place before the development of tooling: and since the runout of the old model is not scheduled to start before the pilot-build, and may well need to be fitted into the selling and promotional calendar, it places an emphasis on the priority of tooling that might not have been obvious at the outset.
* A network represents a plan of action. It enables the analyst to examine the implications of changes in the plan or deviations from the plan. He can ask questions and follow through the implications on the whole programme of development of tooling, engineering design, or the pilot-build programme taking a longer, or shorter, time than expected. So a network is of particular value in thinking through the timing implications of a plan.

The network itself may be drawn up at several levels. The sort of network shown in Fig. 9.4 may be fine as a generalisation of a plan of action: however, there would need to be much more detailed planning at a departmental level for example. There might be subnetworks for marketing and production or, indeed, a much more detailed overall network. A common alternative or

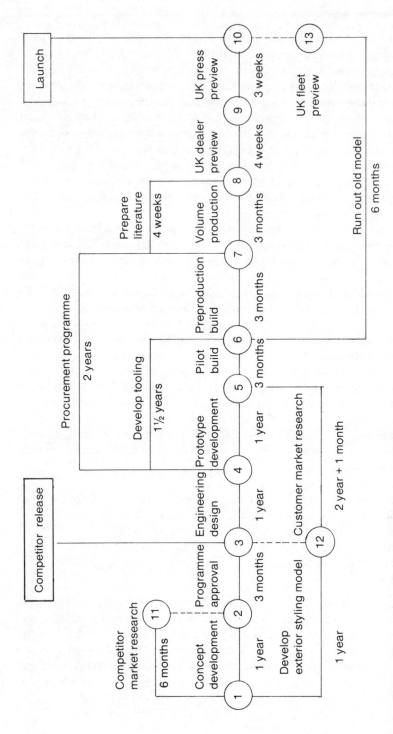

Figure 9.4 *A network analysis for the launch of a new car.*

addition to a network is some form of departmental or project plan which details activities within the network, sets target dates for completion and allocates clear responsibilities for completion of specific tasks.

There are a number of developments of network analysis methods[22] which readers may find of interest. 'Programme evaluation review technique' (PERT) allows uncertainty about the times of each activity in the network to be taken into account. For example, in Fig. 9.4 steps 4 to 6 would be so dependent on the outcome of the market research that, in reality, it may be difficult to make a precise estimate of the time needed for these activities. PERT would be a useful refinement in such circumstances.

9.5 SUMMARY

This book is not just concerned with understanding the problems of, and developing skills in, the formulation of general levels of strategy. It is also concerned with providing material by which readers can think through how strategies can be put into effect. This chapter has begun to do this by looking at the resource planning process. The point has been made that general levels of strategy take effect through the operational activities of an organisation but also that an inability to plan effectively at an operational level can place in jeopardy more general strategic intentions. The chapter has also emphasised that it is not sensible to think of resource planning solely in terms of the functional departments of an organisation because there are problems which transcend these functions. To help planning in this context a number of questions central to resource planning have been identified, together with some aids drawn from management practice and science to deal with the issues raised by the questions.

Underlying the whole area of resource planning is perhaps the single most complex issue in the implementation of strategy, the management of people. In the end, successful strategy implementation depends on the organisation, motivation and control of those who have to make strategies work at both management and operational levels. The next two chapters look at these problems.

REFERENCES

1. It was explained in Chapter 2 that the notion of the recipe as proposed by J-C. Spender, 'Strategy Making in Business', (a doctoral thesis, University of Manchester), is to do with the 'received wisdom' in an industry and expressed in terms of how an organisation should be operated. In this sense the recipe is likely to encapsulate views about which resource requirements are particularly important. Also see P. H. Grinyer and J-C. Spender, 'Recipes, Crises, and Adaptation in Mature, _Intl Studies of Management and Organisation,_ Vol. IX, No. 3, p.113. 1979.

2. R.G. Murdick, R.H. Eckhouse, R.C. Moor and T.W. Zimmerer, *Business Policy: A Framework for Analysis* (Grid Inc: 1976) takes a highly operational perspective on strategic planning and is worth referring to for perspectives on the strategic ramifications at that level.

3. A more extensive checklist of production and operations policy issues is to be found in Chapter 14 of C.J. Constable and C.C. New, *Operations Management* (Wiley: 1976). A more conceptual treatment is provided in Chapter 7 of R. Wild, *Operations Management: A Policy Framework* (Pergamon Press: 1980).

4. These three levels are proposed for consideration by R. Tellier, *Operations Management - Fundamental Concepts and Methods* (Harper and Row: 1978).

5. The problem of utilisation of high levels of capital plant has already been mentioned in the discussion on consolidation strategies in Chapter 7. Readers were referred, then, to articles based on the PIMS data base such as B.T. Gale, 'Can More Capital Buy Higher Productivity?' *(Harvard Business Review:* Jul.-Aug. 1980) and S. Schoeffler, 'Capital-Intensive Technology vs ROI: A Strategic Assessment' *(Management Review:* Sept. 1978).

6. Supplies strategy, important though it is, is not extensively discussed in the literature. However, there is some useful discussion of the area in a chapter by D.F. Cooper called 'Corporate Planning and Purchasing Strategy' in *Corporate Planning and Procurement* edited by D.H. Farmer and B. Taylor. D.H. Farmer (Heinemann: 1975) also discusses supplies strategy in *Insights in Procurement and Materials Management* published by the Institute of Purchasing and Supply.

7. R.E. Burridge, *Product Innovation and Development* (BusinessBooks: 1977) widely covers this field. Readers may also refer to G. Randall, 'Managing New Products' *(BIM Management Survey Report,* No. 47, 1980) which is a survey of activity and problems in the area, as is W.P. Sommers, 'Improving Corporate Performance Through Better Management of Innovation' *(Outlook,* Fall/Winter, 1981).

8. The collapse of Rolls Royce is a very good example of the concentration and reliance on a new development. It is particularly well analysed in a most readable book by John Argenti entitled *Corporate Collapse* (McGraw-Hill: 1976).

9. These terms and the role of R&D are discussed more fully in J.T. Cannon, *Business Strategy and Policy* (Harcourt, Brace & World Inc: 1968).

10. Those wishing to follow up research into the problems of the development of technology as it relates to market conditions might refer to A. Cooper and D. Schendel, 'Strategic Responses to Technological Threats', *Business Horizons* (Feb. 1976).

11. These findings are substantiated by the survey reported in the article by Sommers in *Corporate Planning and Procurement* (see (6) above).

12. The discussion of marketing strategy in P. Kotler, *Marketing Management* (Prentice-Hall: 1976) is useful at this level. In particular, Chapter 3 relates marketing strategy to corporate strategy.

13. Implementing marketing strategy through a channel of distribution can be particularly problematic because of the different perceptions of marketing responsibilities held by channel members. This is discussed more fully in G.N. Johnson, 'The Dilemma of Channel Management' *International Journal of Physical Distribution and Materials Management,* Vol. 11, No. 7, 1981.

14. A sound general discussion of financial strategy and planning can be found in Chapter 5 of John Sizer, *An Insight into Management Accounting,* 2nd ed.,

(Pitman: 1979). More detailed discussion of financial management as it relates to financial strategy is to be found in books on managerial finance: for example, J.F. Weston and E.F. Brigham, Managerial Finance (The Dryden Press: 1978) or L.J. Gitman, *Principles of Managerial Finance* (Harper & Row: 1976).

15.   A number of managerial economists, notably A. Wood in *A Theory of Profits* (Cambridge University Press: 1975), have pointed to the way in which managers will design strategies for growth in such a way as to utilise retained earnings for reinvestment in the firm.

16.   J. Boswell, *The Rise and Decline of Small Firms* (George Allen & Unwin: 1973) points to the reluctance shown by small businessmen to raise finance from outside the firm either by borrowing or share capital.

17.   G. McBeath, *Organisation and Manpower Planning,* 2nd edn.(Business Books: 1969) is still one of the most thorough treatments of manpower planning in relation to strategic change.

18.   Reference has already been made in Chapter 4 on Resource Analysis to the work of Belbin on the importance of managerial teams. See R.M. Belbin *et al.,* 'Building Effective Management Teams', *Jnl of General Management,* Vol.3, No.3, 1976.

19.   As a general introduction to budgets and budgetary control see John Sizer, *An Insight into Management Accounting,* 2nd edn. (Pitman: 1979).

20.   Readers who are not familiar with these techniques should read any good book on management finance. For example, see L.J. Gitman, *Principles of Managerial Finance* (Harper & Row: 1976) or J.M. Samuels and F.M. Wilkes, *Management of Company Finance* (Nelson: 1980).

21.   Network analysis is explained in almost any text on management science or operations management. So, for example, readers could refer to R. Wild's explanation in Chapter 13 of *Production and Operations Management* (Holt, Rinehart & Winston: 1979), K.G. Lockyer, *An Introduction to Critical Path Analysis* (Pitman: 1967) or K. Howard in *Quantitative Analyses for Planning Decisions* (McDonald and Evans: 1975).

22.   Again these derivatives of network analyses are well covered elsewhere (reference 21).

RECOMMENDED KEY READINGS

*   For readers wishing to follow through the ramifications of strategic decisions on functional and operational management: R.G. Murdick, R.H. Eckhouse, R.C. Moor and T.W. Zimmerer, *Business Policy: A Framework for Analysis* (Grid Inc: 1976).

*   As a guide to the sort of financial planning necessary: L.J. Gitman, *Principles of Managerial Finance* (Harper & Row: 1976) or J.M. Samuels and F.M. Wilkes, *Management of Company Finance* (Nelson: 1980).

*   For an explanation of the techniques of network planning: Chapter 13 of R. Wild, *Production and Operations Management* (Holt, Rinehart & Winston: 1979).

10

ORGANISATION STRUCTURE

10.1 INTRODUCTION

One of the most important resources of an organisation is its people: strategy is decided and implemented by them, so how they are organised is crucial to the effective implementation of strategy. This chapter deals with questions which are concerned with the ways in which enterprises are organised.

There are perhaps two main ways in which the form an organisation takes is important. First, it does appear that certain organisational forms may be more capable of dealing with certain problems than others, and conversely that some may give rise to problems that others do not. A highly centralised organisational form may be very good at ordering its internal procedures but may not be so good at coping with a highly complex environment. A highly decentralised company may be better at dealing with a complex environment but bad at getting certain sorts of decision taken. Second, it should be realised that organisational structures are not easy to change. They may well be in part the manifestations of the philosophies, prejudices or ambitions of management or owners, and changing them may be perceived, therefore, as very threatening. This is, then, an area of strategy implementation which is, at one and the same time, important and difficult.

This chapter is concerned with structural problems - it discusses forms of structure such as functional, divisional, holding company and matrix types and the issue of decentralisation or centralisation of decision-making. The next chapter continues the discussion of how strategy is implemented through the people in the organisation in terms both of issues concerned with the management of people at a more individual level, and of the systems employed by organisations to manage people.

10.2 STRUCTURAL TYPES

Managers asked to describe their organisations usually respond by drawing an organisation chart, thereby attempting to map out its structure. It is this aspect of organisational design that concerns the first part of the chapter. It is important to emphasise at this stage that a structure is but one aspect of organisational design and it may tell little about some other vital aspects. The sorts of structures described first are like skeletons: they define the general shape and facilitate or constrain certain sorts of activity; but they are incomplete in themselves without the sort of 'flesh' that is dealt with later in this chapter and the next. It is also worth noting that the categories used to define structures, although common, are not unique. For example, in some texts[1] a separate category of 'holding company' is omitted: it is included here because it is still in common usage, particularly in the UK. Other writers[2] split down the general category of 'multi-divisional' into several subcategories.

10.2.1 The Simple Structure

A simple structure could really be thought of as no formal structure at all. It is the type of organisation common in many very small businesses. There is likely to be an owner who undertakes most of the responsibilities of management, perhaps with a partner or an assistant. However, there is little division of management responsibility and probably little clear definition of who is responsible for what if there is more than one person involved. The operation is then run by the personal control and contact of one individual.

The main problem here is that the organisation can only operate effectively up to a certain size of operation, beyond which it becomes too cumbersome for one person to control. What this size is will, of course, depend on the nature of the business. An insurance broker may personally handle a very large turnover, whereas a similar sized business (in terms of turnover) manufacturing and selling goods, may be much more diverse in its operations and therefore more difficult to control personally.

10.2.2 The Functional Structure

In a functional structure the organisation is based on the primary tasks it has to carry out such as production, finance and accounting, marketing and personnel. Figure 10.1 represents a typical organisation chart for such a business. This structure tends now to be found in smaller companies or those with narrow, rather than diverse, product ranges. However, within a multi-divisional structure, the divisions themselves are likely to be split up into functional management areas. The functional structure has some advantages.[3] If the operation is not too large it enables the chief executive to keep directly in touch with the operations and it is likely to reduce problems of management control because the natural flow of information is vertical and lines of

communication short. It also means that there are likely to be specialists in
senior and middle management positions which, it is argued, improves the
quality of the management of the functions. In functional structures job roles
are likely to be clearly understood and easy to define because they are based on
the tasks the organisation has to carry out.

There are some disadvantages too, particularly as organisations become
larger or more diverse in their interests. Senior managers may become over-
concerned and over-burdened with routine matters, neglecting the strategic
concerns which face the organisation. If the organisation's interests have
become diversified then the functional structure may not cope easily with the
different competitive environments in which it is operating. Suppose, for
example, a one-produce company operating in one market develops a new
product for a different market. Not only are the managers faced with
understanding the demands of different markets, they may also have to cope
internally with different technologies of production for the new products. It
may be difficult for the organisation to deal with these differences by
continuing to manage on a functional, task-based structure since the environment and technology are no longer of the same kind. A further problem which
often arises is where cooperation between functions is required, such as the
planning of new products which may need the coordination of marketing,
production and the finance and accountancy functions. If this has to be done
by referring problems continually up vertical lines of authority for decisions
then cooperation may become a difficulty. Advantages and disadvantages of
functional structures are summarised in Fig. 10.1.

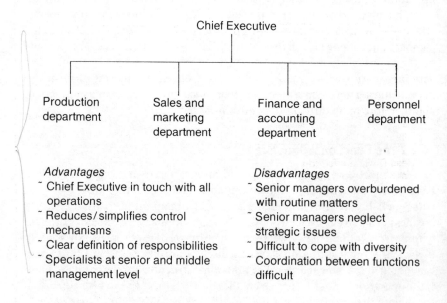

Figure 10.1   *A basic functional structure.*

ILLUSTRATION 41

Bases of Multi-divisional Structures

- Organisations may be divisionalised on different bases, amongst which are included product market, geography and processes.

Product Market Divisionalisation
Lucas Industries (Joseph Lucas Ltd) 1982

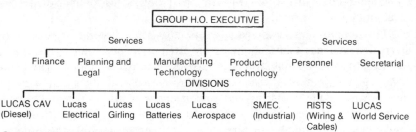

Geographical Divisionalisation
Chef & Brewer Ltd. 1982

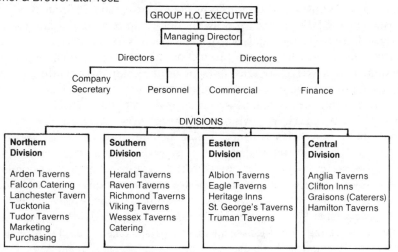

Process Divisionalisation
Aurora Holdings PLC 1981

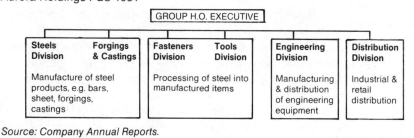

Source: Company Annual Reports.

10.2.3 The Multi-divisional Structure

The main characteristic of a multi-divisional structure is that it is subdivided into units which are usually responsible for defined market or product areas of the enterprise. These divisions may be formed on the basis of products, as for example in Fig. 10.2. There are, however, other bases for divisionalisation such as geographical areas, or the processes of the enterprise. For example, a vertically integrated company might have manufacturing, wholesaling and retail divisions. Illustration 41 shows some common divisional forms employed by firms.

Divisionalisation has increased as operations have become larger or more diversified and has come about as an attempt to overcome the sorts of problems that functional structures have in such circumstances. The main advantage of the multi-divisional structure is that each division is able to concentrate on the problems and opportunities of its particular business environment. The company in Fig. 10.2 might find great difficulty in employing a functional structure throughout its operations: the product markets in which it operates may be so different that it would be impractical to bring the tasks together in a single body. For example, suppose Product Group A is a range of DIY products for distribution to the retail trade and Product Group B is magazines and newspapers - a mix of products that Reed International has. The tasks of production, distribution and marketing are dissimilar. It makes more sense to split up the company according to the different product markets and then ensure that the needs of each division are met by tailoring the operations within the division to the particular needs of that product market. A division will, then, very likely have within it functionally based departments dealing with the specialist tasks of the enterprise. Other advantages arise. Because each division addresses itself to one business area it is possible to measure the performance of that division as a business unit. It becomes clear if it is performing up to expectations or below par. So the company as a whole is able to measure more easily its performance in its diverse areas of activity. Moreover, because these activities are set up as separate operating units, they are the easier to divest if necessary. Divisionalisation also facilitates the passing of profit and general management responsibility down the line. This has two benefits: first it means that the senior management in the parent company are more able to concentrate on strategic matters, and second it helps to develop general management ability at a lower level.

There are, however, disadvantages and difficulties with the multi-divisional structure. One is to do with this issue of devolution of responsibility. To what extent should what sort of responsibility be passed to the divisions? It may be accepted by all for example, that operating responsibility to meet the profit objectives or the deadlines for new product launches should be devolved. But who decides on strategic objectives? Who decides if new product development should take place at all and in what areas? Who decides on levels of expenditure or borrowing? What about the responsibility for acquisition programmes? If immediate action is required to counter a major competitive attack and that action could mean short or even long term reversals, at what level is the decision to be made? So a problem that divisionalised organisations face is defining the extent and nature of decentralisation. This is returned to in Section 10.3.

Another problem is conflict between the divisions for the resources of the parent organisation. On what basis should financial resources be allocated? How will the management of one division react if, despite meeting their budgets, some other division, deemed to have greater growth prospects, is favoured more? Yet further problems occur if there is inter-trading between the divisions; how should transfer prices be fixed and what should the trading relationships be? The same sorts of problems occur if the divisions, based on different product markets, use common plant. Who controls it, who has first call on it, on what basis are the costs of raw material allocated? So, problems of operation and control are often far from straightforward in a multi-divisional firm. These issues of control will be dealt with more fully in Chapter 11.

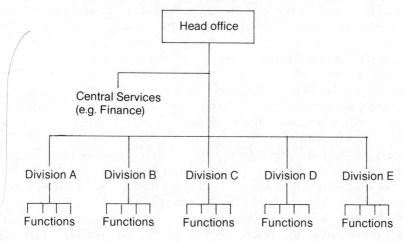

Advantages
- ~ Concentration on business area (e.g. product market)
- ~ Facilitates measurement of unit performance
- ~ Ease of addition and divestment of units
- ~ Facilitates senior management's attention to strategy
- ~ Encourages general management development

Disadvantages
- ~ Possible confusion over locus of responsibility
- ~ Conflict between divisions
- ~ Basis of intertrading
- ~ Costly

Figure 10.2 *A multi-divisional structure.*

Another disadvantage often cited is that divisional structures are costly because they replicate management functions in each division and, with the addition of a central head office staff, this leads to high overheads. This argument is only valid if the cost of the overhead is greater than the cost of inefficiency that could result from an inappropriate structure: it is a matter of management judgement. Figure 10.2 summarises the advantages and disadvantages of a multi-divisional structure.

10.2.4 The Holding Company Structure

In its most extreme form a holding company is really an investment company. It may simply consist of shareholdings in a variety of individual, unconnected, business operations over which it exercises little or no control. However, the term also applies to an enterprise which, itself, operates a portfolio of virtually autonomous business units. Although part of a parent company, these business units operate independently and probably retain their original company names. The role the parent company takes for itself may be limited to decisions about the buying and selling of such companies with very little involvement in their strategy. The logic behind such a structure is one of two kinds. It may be that the holding company is simply a portfolio of interests (or investments) for the parent board (arguably, this is the situation as far as Lonrho is concerned and was certainly the case of the Slater Walker operation). A holding company may also come about in the interests of the member companies: for example, Norcros was established in 1956 as a sort of club of independent companies which could offset their independent profits against others' losses.

An example of a holding company structure is given as Fig. 10.3: the business interests of the parent company are likely to be varied, some of them may be wholly-owned and some not. To a large extent, the business units retain their own identity and perhaps their own individual structures. Comparing this structure with that of other companies with very diverse interests, such as Trafalgar House, the question has to be raised, 'when is a holding company a holding company and when is it a multi-divisional corporation?' Trafalgar House has very diverse interests, including construction, shipping, hotels, air freight, mining and engineering, and the businesses retain their names: but here they are allocated to divisions - property, construction, shipping and hotels - and, more importantly, the centre of the company plays an important role in the formulation of business unit strategy. The essential differentiating feature for a holding company is, then, the extent of the autonomy of the business units particularly over strategic decisions.

The advantages a holding company can offer are based on the idea that the constituent businesses will operate to their best potential if left well alone. So, these businesses will not have to carry the burden of a high central overhead since the head office staff of the parent is likely to be small. However, the business units can benefit from their membership of the group in such ways as the offsetting of profits against others' losses, the benefits of cheaper finance for investment from the parent company and, arguably, in bad times, from the protection of the group. The holding company itself may also claim benefits such as the spreading of risk across many business ventures and the ease of divestment of individual companies. However, some of these advantages are theoretical rather than real. The facts are more likely to be that the businesses run the risk of being sold off to make room for businesses that can perform better. There simply may not be the skills at the centre to provide help since the aim is to keep the centre as slim as possible. Perhaps the greatest weakness of this structure is, however, its lack of internal strategic cohesion. There may be duplication of effort between business units or there may be very little synergy between the business interests. It is one thing to say that business units operate better if they are given the profit responsibility to do so on their own: but in a large, perhaps multi-national operation there are likely to be very considerable pay-offs from having some sort of overall 'logic' to the actions - some sort of internal synergy in the group as described in Chapter 8. These advantages and disadvantages are summarised in Fig. 10.3.

10.2.5 The Matrix Structure

A matrix structure is a combination of structures. It usually takes the form of product and geographical divisions or functional and divisional structures

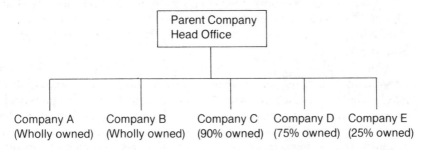

| Parent Company Head Office | | | | |
| Company A (Wholly owned) | Company B (Wholly owned) | Company C (90% owned) | Company D (75% owned) | Company E (25% owned) |

Advantages
- Low central overheads
- Offsetting of individual business losses
- Availability of cheaper finance for individual businesses
- Spreading of risk for holding company
- Ease of divestment for holding company

Disadvantages
- Risk of divestment by holding company for individual business
- Unavailability of skills at group level to assist individual businesses
- Lack of synergy

Figure 10.3 *A holding company structure.*

ILLUSTRATION 42

Matrix Structure at Philips

- In order to control its highly complex activities, Philips, the Dutch-based multinational, adopted a matrix structure -but found there were problems.

The complexity of Philips' activities was demonstrated by the fact that by 1978, the group was involved in over 125 countries and organised its production via some 70 to 80 business units grouped into 14 product divisions. As the group expanded, changes in the group structure were made culminating in a matrix structure being adopted after the Second World War.

The matrix structure allowed for joint responsibility for the group's activities between the national 'selling' organisations and the product divisions. The idea was to maintain 'local' involvement while capitalising on corporate strengths. For example, should a manager in a product division have wanted to develop a pricing policy for a particular product, the matrix would have required him to do this in consultation with the managers in the various national organisations. The advantage was that the 'national' managers would know what price levels their particular market would stand and could advise the manager in the product division accordingly.

Initially this type of structure worked well for Philips. However, a drop in profits in 1971 caused management to question the suitability of the structure. A report reviewing Philips' structure stated that while joint responsibility sometimes gave rise to 'constructive friction', it could also lead to operational inefficiencies in that management become slow in responding to problems.

Various control systems were introduced in 1972/73 to try and improve the situation, although the basic matrix structure remained.

Although the matrix facilitated some activities, for example, corporate planning where the strategies of the various national organisations and product division could be brought together to develop a unified corporate strategy, it was problematic for others. Marketing was one such area where the division of responsibility between the national organisation and product division was unclear. Jan Kavel, who was manager for personal care products, highlighted the problems.

> 'We feel the disadvantages of the matrix acutely here in Groningen (Holland). For one thing, we definitely feel it is a disadvantage not to be responsible for sales - we have people who don't feel the need to sell the product tomorrow, and yet have part of the responsibility for profits. The matrix is slow - we are in a very turbulent market with great potential, and we have far too many low cost competitors. We need very short communication lines, quick decisions, alertness - we've got to be able to act fast. At the moment we are having to spend a vast amount of money on advertising - about 10% of our sales turnover - to compensate for these disadvantages.'

Source: Management Today, August 1978, p.35.

operating in tandem. Figure 10.4 is an example of such a structure and Illustration 42 shows how it operates together with the sorts of problems that are associated with it.

Matrix structures most often come about because an operation is involved in two distinct types of operation, both of which require substantial amounts of management emphasis so that 'pure' divisional structures would be inappropriate. For example, suppose a company increasingly extends its operations on a multi-national scale and develops new product interests. It may regard geographically defined divisions as the operating units for the purposes of local marketing and product divisions as responsible for the central world-wide coordination of product development, manufacturing and distribution to the geographical divisions. Or a group with a number of product divisions may argue that there is no benefit (and may be positive disadvantages) in having all functions in all divisions. It may make sense to have centrally organised selling (with a company-wide sales force), and manufacturing operations (particularly if different divisions use common manufacturing plants) with product development and marketing planning lodged in product divisions.

It is not necessarily the case that a matrix structure as such will result if there are two distinct types of operation in multi-national firms. There are other ways of dealing with this situation which are discussed in Subsection 10.2.6. Also, matrix structures do not only arise in large, highly complex organisations, they are sometimes used in quite small, apparently straightforward organisations but which have distinct types of operation or interest in them. For example, a matrix structure may exist in some public sector organisations: indeed university departments sometimes have matrix structures, one arm of which is responsible for academic, subject-based work and the other for course administration and development.

The benefits claimed for matrix structures[4] are:

*   Quality of decision-making is improved in situations where there is a risk of one vital interest of the enterprise (e.g. the interests of a geographical area) dominating considerations of a problem at the expense of other vital interests (e.g. world-wide coordination of manufacturing).
*   Formal bureaucracy is replaced by direct contact between individuals; the structure encourages informal exchanges of views across responsibilities.
*   Linked with this, it is supposed to increase managerial motivation, because of its participative nature, and managerial development because of the extent to which all levels of management become involved in activities.

However, many of these claims may not be borne out in reality. Matrix structures appear to have some very real problems associated with them:

*   The time taken for decisions to be made may be much longer than in more

'conventional' structures simply because the structure is designed to encourage debate between potentially competing interest groups.

* It is often difficult to be clear who is responsible for what; whilst the idea of joint responsibility may conceptually be laudable, it can give rise to problems. What happens, for example, in a multi-national operation when the division responsible for Africa wants to reformulate a product and the central functions of manufacturing and world-wide marketing coordination insist on product uniformity? Who is actually responsible for marketing?

* This raises another problem. Exactly where does profit responsibility lie? The African division could argue that it cannot be held profit accountable if it does not control its own products. On the other hand, the central functions are not profit responsible because they are not responsible for selling and distribution.

* In fact, matrix structures have to bear a good deal of conflict because of the lack of clarity of role definition and responsibility.

It may be that organisations facing increasing complexity have to choose between bearing costly duplication in a multi-divisional structure and elegant but inefficient matrix structures. These advantages and disadvantages are summarised in Fig. 10.4.

10.2.6 Intermediate Structures

Changes in organisation may be seen as threatening. People may fear the loss of their job, the loss of status or may fear that they will be put into a job they cannot do. So it should not be assumed that changing an organisation structure is an easy matter. It is not surprising then that there exists a whole range of 'shades of grey' between types of structure: these intermediate structures represent ways of coping without a wholesale change in structure. Suppose a company with a functional structure starts to follow new product/ market strategies which increase the diversity of products and the uncertainty which the company faces. How might they cope with this without re-organising on a product division basis? The following are some possible steps:

* Problems will first arise as the new products/markets compete for resources. Initially these conflicts will be resolved by pushing the decision upwards until a sufficiently senior executive makes the decision.

* When too many conflicts need to be resolved in this way new rules, guidelines and procedures may be developed to advise people on how resources are to be shared between products.

* The next step may be to formalise these procedures in the planning process by, for example, allocating a budget to the new product/markets. So, up to now the problem has been dealt with by manipulating methods of control and operation rather than by any structural changes.

*   As the new products/markets become even more important the competition structure create for resources becomes more intense and it may prove necessary to create inter-departmental liaison roles. For example, marketing priorities may not be clear within the production function, so some sort of committee may be set up with representatives from both departments.

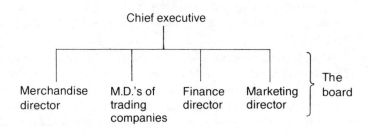

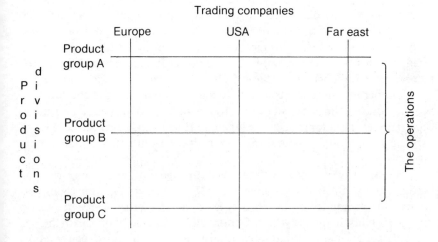

Advantages
~ Quality of decision-making where interests conflict
~ Direct contact replaces bureaucracy
~ Increases managerial motivation
~ Development of managers through increased involvement in decisions

Disadvantages
~ Length of time to take decisions
~ Unclear job and task responsibilities
~ Unclear cost and profit responsibilities
~ High degrees of conflict

Figure 10.4 *A matrix structure.*

*   Sometimes the problem can become so great that a temporary task force is set up to advise on priorities.
*   The next stage may be to create either permanent teams of coordinators or special coordinating jobs (the product manager is a good example).
*   The last step which may prove necessary to maintain the functional is the creation of departments with the sole function of coordination. Centralised planning departments are common for example.

Ultimately, as the diversity increases, the organisation may be forced to divisionalise since the costs of maintaining the functional structure will be unacceptably high or the administrative difficulties might become too great.

As well as these methods of maintaining the existing structure when there are events which reduce its utility, there are some quite common intermediate structural answers to the problem. For some companies it might be more appropriate to describe their structure as 'functional with subsidiaries'.[5] Such companies are sometimes referred to as 'diversified majors'; their main business which employs by far the majority of employees could be a straightforward functional structure; the more peripheral business interests are the divisions. The converse of this is the company which is divisionalised except for certain key functions which remain at the centre and have responsibilities across all the divisions. Channon[6] calls this a 'critical function' structure and found it quite common in insurance companies where investment departments often remain a central function. In many divisionalised retail operations, too, there is a central function responsible for cross-divisional property dealings.

Another intermediate structure often arises when there are development activities outside the responsibility of any one function or division, say a major capital project or new product development. Here it might make a lot of sense to set up a temporary full-time project team drawn from different functions or divisions.

Another way of coping with the need for organisational change without fundamentally affecting what already exists, is to 'externalise' the change by moving the responsibility for it to outside the enterprise. There are many examples of this. In the early 1980s Conservative controlled Councils in the UK decided to offer what were traditional local authority operations, such as refuse collection, to private companies rather than maintain the operational side of the service within their own structure. Franchising is, of course, another means of structuring externally. Here the functions of marketing services, some elements of finance and accounting and perhaps manufacturing are retained within the franchise operation whilst the local selling and cash collection may be dealt with by franchisees.

10.2.7 Structural Types in the UK and USA

A good deal of work has now been done on the way in which structures of businesses in the USA and Europe have evolved.[7] These studies have shown fairly consistent patterns of development throughout the 1940s, 1950s and 1960s, though rather less work has been done on more recent developments in the 1970s. The most authoritative work on UK industry is by Channon who has studied both the manufacturing and service industries.[8]

Figure 10.5 summarises Channon's findings as far as structural change is concerned in UK manufacturing industry between 1960 and 1970. This period showed a marked swing away from functional and holding company structures towards multi-divisional structures. In 1960 just one-third of major manufacturing companies had a divisional structure. By the end of the decade over two-thirds had such a structure. This dramatic change coincided with a major programme of diversification by these firms, many of which were involved in extensive acquisition programmes at that time. Figure 10.6 summarises this increasing diversification for the same period and shows how the same businesses tended to move progressively from businesses with a single product or reliant on a dominant product interest towards more diversified - though product related interests. So, as Channon concludes, divisionalisation has, in large measure, been a response to the need to manage diversity.

	1960 (%)	1970 (%)
Functional	23 (24)	8 (8)
Holding company	41 (43)	20 (21)
Multi-divisional	32 (33)	68 (71)
Total of sample	96 (100)	96 (100)

Figure 10.5 *Structural types of major British manufacturing industries 1960-1970 (derived from: D.F. Channon, The Strategy and Structure of British Enterprises (London and Basingstoke: Macmillan, 1973) p.74).*

Product spread	% in each category	
	1960	1970
Single product	20	6
Dominant product	35	34
Related product	41	54
Unrelated product	4	6
	100%	100%

Figure 10.6 *The extent of product spread in major British manufacturing industry 1960-1970 (derived from: D. F. Channon, The Strategy and Structure of British Enterprise (London and Basingstoke: Macmillan, 1973) p.67).*

Channon found similar, though less developed, trends in the UK service industry sector. Figure 10.7 shows how structural types changed in this sector from 1960 to 1974. There is again a move away from functional and holding company structures towards divisionalisation and, in this sector, 'critical function' structures. Again this trend is associated with increasing diversity, although in service industries this happened later than for manufacturing industry. Up to 1965 62% of the service firms studied by Channon were dependent on a single or dominant product base. Within the last five years of that decade the corresponding figure was 42%.

	1960 (%)		1970 (%)	
Functional	31	(38)	18	(18)
"Critical function"	9	(11)	17	(17)
Holding company	38	(47)	27	(27)
Multi-divisional	3	(4)	37	(37)
Total of sample	81	(100)	99	(100)

A "critical function" structure is defined by Channon as one with semi-accountable geographic or product based operating units but with key functions fully centralised and therefore outside the responsibility of these operating units.

Figure 10.7 *Structural types of British service industries 1960-1970 (derived from: D.F. Channon, The Service Industries: Strategy, Structure and Financial Performance (London and Basingstoke: Macmillan, 1978) p. 31).*

10.2.8 Structural Types in Multi-national Companies[9]

The growth in size and the importance of multi-national businesses warrants some special mention of the structural implications for such organisations. Since multi-national activity usually involves some form of divisionalisation the discussion will also usefully point out that any one divisional type may have several variations. The most basic from of structure for a multi-national is the retention of the home structure and the management of whatever overseas subsidiaries exist through direct contact between the manager of the subsidiary and the chief executive or some other manager in the parent company. In effect there are no changes to the overall structure. This is most common in single-product companies or where the overseas interests are relatively minor, so it cannot be described as typical of the larger multi-nationals.

One of the most common forms of multi-national structure is the *international division.* Here the home-based structure may be retained at first - whether functional or divisional - but the overseas interests managed through a special international division. In turn it is quite possible that within an overall international division there will be other geographic divisions: or indeed it could be that there are several geographically based international divisions each reporting to a home-based head office. The international subsidiaries may draw in the products of the home company or, if large enough, may manufacture for themselves.

Such structures tend to work best where there is a wide geographical spread but quite closely related products. They tend to emphasise local responsibility rather than central control and so may be particularly useful where local knowledge is important. The problems which emerge are of two sorts. First there are problems of coordination if the product interests are diverse or if it is not clear who should be responsible for manufacture or marketing. Suppose, for example, that the overseas interests become, in total or in part, larger than the home based activity; then it may make sense for the home activity to become one geographic division of many in a geographically divisionalised multi-national. In such circumstances, which divisions are responsible for which management tasks? Is manufacturing, for example, to be carried out separately for every product in each division; or are some divisions to be responsible for world-wide manufacturing of certain products? If the former option is selected there is extensive resource duplication; if the latter, coordination becomes a major problem.

There has been a move away from the international divisional structure to what has become known as a *global product* structure. Here the multi-national is split into product group divisions which are then managed on an international basis. The logic of such an approach is that it should promote cost efficiency (particularly of production) on an international basis and provide enhanced transfer of resources (particularly technology) between geographical regions. There is also a tendency for companies to move to global structures as foreign product diversity increases and as foreign sales, as a percentage of total company sales, increase.[10] There should also be better strategic planning on an international basis through the centralised product focus. There are some problems with this structure, however. Although cost efficiency is improved it does not appear that technology transfer is enhanced: indeed technology transfer seems to be better achieved through international divisions than in a global product structure. Also, whilst the structure is well suited to promoting defensive or consolidation strategies, it does not seem to meet the expected benefits of heightened strategic planning and is not suited to the promotion of aggressive or expansion strategies.[11] These difficulties may be accounted for in part by the almost inevitable separation of senior management of the global division from local problems; they are mainly concerned with central coordination and this reduces the sensitivity to local needs, particularly in terms of marketing needs and competitive activity. The tendency to move to global product structures is probably associated with attempts to rationalise the increasing diversity and problems of control within international divisional structures. Such rationalisation has often taken place through some sort of portfolio planning which has tended to emphasise concentration on a more limited product range.

Matrix structures are also common in multi-national organisations. Most typically the matrix is based on a head office responsibility for product and manufacturing planning and geographical divisions for local administration, including selling and distribution. The argument for a matrix structure is that a multi-national is just not suited to an hierarchical structure; decisions are better made through a 'contractual' arrangement between central coordinators and local management. It certainly appears that the structure is better at promoting technology transfer, for example, but this has to be set against the sorts of costs of coordination and conflict discussed above.

Davison and Haspeslagh's[12] research in 180 USA-based companies in 1980 showed that the most common structure (in 32% of the companies) was the global product structure followed by the international divisional structure. This differs from the findings of Stopford and Wells[13] in the late 1960s when 52% of the multi-nationals they researched had international divisions and 18.5% global product structures.

10.3 CENTRALISATION AND DECENTRALISATION

When planning the implementation of strategy in organisational terms, structure is important because it creates what has previously been described as 'the skeleton' which facilitates - and sometimes limits - the activities that need to occur. However, it is a mistake to think it is enough to design an organisation in terms of the 'bones' of a structure. One divisional structure may be much the same as another in name and the sort of organisation chart that may be used to describe it: but that does not in itself help with some other vital aspects of organisational design. One of these other aspects is what sort of decisions should be taken at what level in the organisation, and how this affects the ability to implement (and decide) strategy? This is to do with the issues of centralisation and decentralisation. It is important to be clear what is meant by decentralisation: it is to do with the extent to which decision-making power is devolved in an organisation. This raises the question: 'power over what?' Does it mean power to take decisions on operational issues - the scheduling of production or the hiring of executives for example - or the power to take decisions about the strategic direction of the firm - to diversify or consolidate for example. Decentralisation may mean both, which is one of the reasons why there has been confusion over its use: managers and consultants have too often assumed that decentralisation of strategic and operational decisions necessarily go hand in hand when in fact they need not - and often do not. For example, there is very considerable decentralisation of operational decisions in companies such as Unilever and Proctor & Gamble. A product marketing group in one of Unilever's subsidiaries would make decisions about substantial amounts of advertising expenditure and the scheduling of production in large manufacturing plants. But these decisions would be taken within the context of a strategic framework for the subsidiary approved by Unilever itself. It would be highly unlikely, for example, that Walls Meat or Lever Brothers could take a decision to move outside their existing product market scope without the approval and active involvement of Unilever, who might well decide that such a new venture would be better lodged in some other subsidiary. On the other hand, it is quite possible that a business unit within a company such as Lonrho might take decisions about such a move much more independently and even have the facility to raise funds to do it from outside the parent group. In the case of the Unilever subsidiary *operational decentralisation* is high and *strategic decentralisation* much more restricted: in the case of the Lonrho subsidiary both operating and strategic decentralisation are high. This distinction is important because there are indications that performance characteristics of firms may be influenced by the nature of decentralisation.

It is argued that decentralisation allows and encourages rapid managerial response to local or product specific problems. So, for example, if sales or profits drop in a particular market it is not necessary to refer the matter along hierarchical chains of decision-making; a decision can be made by the manager responsible for that market. However, it is important to point out that the speed of response may well depend on how well defined are the responsibilites for strategic and operational decisions at different levels of management. For example, if the decision is to do with a local distribution problem, then the local manager will probably have the authority to deal with it. But suppose the problem has important strategic implications: perhaps a product requires major redesign and its reformulation requires major funding. Local management may not have this authority. It may mean that the decision has to be referred to more senior levels in head office. There is nothing unusual in this and nothing necessarily wrong with such a process; but it is important for that company to be clear as to what sort of decision-making is to be decentralised and what is to remain centralised. Illustration 43 describes one company that tried both centralised and decentralised systems of management and made quite clear the extent to which it eventually decentralised both strategic and operational decision-making.

Perhaps the most powerful reason for strategic decentralisation is that it is necessary and beneficial when the complexity faced at the top of the organisation is too great to be handled by senior management alone. Take the extreme example of a multi-national operation with interests as diverse, dynamic and complex as micro-electronics, oil exploration and communications technology. It is not conceivable that all strategic decisions could be made at the most senior level. They would certainly be decentralised to strategic business units such as divisions.

There are, of course, arguments for centralisation. Coordination of activities may be facilitated by centralisation. Senior management know what

---

ILLUSTRATION 43

Dawson International

• Dawson International tried both centralisation and decentralisation in its attempt to find the right formula.

By 1970 Dawson, the Bradford-based cashmere dehairing company, had completed its process of vertical integration having acquired a variety of up-market knitwear manufacturers. The increased size of the group meant that Alan Smith, the chief executive, was unable to maintain his customary personal control, leaving many of the newly acquired companies under the control of their original management teams. A slump in the market for luxury knitwear, however, led Smith to seek tighter control through a policy of centralisation.

The Centralisation Phase. Centralisation measures included: the appointment of manufacturing and personnel executives at head office, the grouping of the organisation into divisions, each with a divisional director, and for formation of 'task forces' to undertake cost-cutting assignments.

After initial success, which saw profits rise from a lowly £380,000 in 1970-71 to £3.1 million in 1973, problems began to occur. As one executive explained: 'There were enormous delays in getting decisions made..... There were a lot of people not taking responsibility for anything. There was a lot of information around, but it wasn't being used'. Another executive summed up the individual company's position: 'About 70% of management's time was spent trying to get around the (head office) restrictions'.

When the extent of the mid-70s recession became apparent, one of Dawson's responses was to reduce stocks. However, flooding the market with cashmere garments only served to lower its price, requiring a write-down of raw material stock value by some £3m. Dawson's large stocks were very much the result of the centralisation policy as an executive later acknowledges: 'Centralisation was one of the main causes ..... There was no local responsibility for stocks'.

The Move to Decentralisation. In 1974-75 having written down stock and with a £10m. bank overdraft, Dawson was in a crisis situation. Smith's solution was to pass control of each subsidiary to its managing director, while a heavily reduced head office staff undertook a monitoring role of critical factors such as stock and finance.

Decentralisation allowed the managements of the individual companies to respond quickly to fluctuations in market demand as well as maintain strict control over stock levels. For example, the knitters were able to respond quickly to the UK tourist boom of 1977-78, a move that boosted profits by 50%. Similarly, when the boom had subsided in 1980, the knitters were able to replace home sales by heavy promotion overseas.

As a result of decentralisation, group profits have soared from £500,000 in 1975 to £18.2 m by the early 1980s, but perhaps more significantly the knitters, once a constant drain on cash, started contributing to group profits.

Source: Managment Today, March 1981, p.74.

is going on in all parts of the organisation if decision-making is routed through them so there is less need for complex control systems. Centralisation of major strategic decisions could be important because it is only at the most senior level that an overall perspective of strategic implications can be appreciated so as to decide the overall aims and core strategies of the *whole* organisation and allocate funds between competing claims. Another argument for centralisation is that it provides for speedier decision-making. It is apparently the opposite claim to the first argument in favour of decentralisation. Yet this may not be such a contradiction if the distinction between strategic and operational decentralisation is remembered. In certain circumstances centralis- ation of strategic decisions can be speedier than their decentralisation. Decentralisation speeds up strategic management only if there is effective devolution of power to take strategic decisions and they do not need to be referred up and down management hierarchies for agreement. In Dawson International (Illustration 43) this appeared to be the case after their reorganisation. However, this may not occur for many reasons. For example, really effective strategic decentralisation would presumably involve the authority to allocate funds to major projects, yet the sums of money required for major projects may well be in excess of those under the control of the business unit concerned. In such an event it has to go to the parent group for funds where it will be competing with other business units. What has happened is that the responsibility for making strategic proposals rather than decisions has been devolved, and the authority to take the decisions has been centralised. In such circumstances the danger is that the process of proposal, discussion and agreement or rejection is institutionalised into a lengthy formal process which slows down strategic responses.

It might be more realistic to recognise that strategic decisions, though originating as ideas or proposals lower down, may have to be taken centrally because of such problems as the allocation of group funds. In such cir- cumstances it can be sensible to speed up the process by, for example, minimising the delays in the referral process, keeping the levels of management to a minimum or simply recognising that all such decisions are the perogative of one or two key executives.

It should be clear by now that there is an important distinction between decentralisation and divisionalisation: yet the two terms are often used synonomously both by managers and management writers. The distinction is made clear by the Unilever example. Unilever is a divisionalised operation; certainly it has decentralised operating decisions but it has retained a large element of central control over strategic decisions. Compare this to an advanced electronics company, for example, which could well be small and perhaps functionally organised yet where considerable strategic power may be decentralised to specialists. The lesson is that, whilst divisionalisation may make decentralisation easier, the two do not necessarily go hand in hand.

10.4 STRUCTURAL TYPES AND FINANCIAL PERFORMANCE

There are indications that types of structure and the performance of firms are related. The study of Rumelt[14] of the strategy and structure of industry in the USA and the study on the same issue for UK service industries by Channon[15] are worth comparing because some discernible patterns emerge.

Measures of performance	Means of performance (%)*		
	Functional	F with subsids.	Multi-div.
Growth in earnings/share	5.08	8.22	8.63
Earnings growth	6.76	9.57	10.66
Return on investment	10.28	9.49	10.75
Return on equity	12.28	11.09	12.90
Sales growth	8.55	6.49	9.77
P/Earnings ratio	14.86	16.60	18.73

*Except for P/E which is a ratio

Figure 10.8 *Financial performance by structural type in the USA 1960-1969 (from: Richard P. Rumelt, Strategy, Structure and Economic Performance, Boston, Mass.: Division of Research, Harvard Business School, 1974 (Table 3.3, p. 93). Used with permission.)*

Rumelt's findings are summarised in Fig. 10.8: they show that multi-divisional structures consistently out-perform other structural types. However, underlying this general finding are other important points. It is noticeable, for example, that divisionalised firms perform much better than functional firms on measures of growth than they do on measures of rate of return; the gap between the two types for measures of return on investment and equity are marginal when compared to measures of growth in earnings and sales. But since divisionalisation tends to occur when firms expand and diversify, it might be expected that firms with divisional structures show higher growth figures. Rumelt's data also show that firms which are content to manage through a functional structure perform virtually as well on measures of return as those which opt for divisionalisation. If Channon's study of the UK service industry is examined, a similar but even more marked pattern emerges. The data are summarised in Fig. 10.9 and show that multi-divisional firms certainly perform better on most measures of growth, but that when it comes to measures of return it is the functional companies that perform better. It is also noticeable that on all measures the holding company structure performs worse than the others. Channon argues that this indicates the need for rather more central direction and control, at least at a strategic level, over a firm's activities than holding companies exercise.

Measures of performance	Means of performance (%)		
	Functional	Holding company	Multi-divisional
Growth in earnings/share	19.22	10.01	32.39
Growth in assets/share	15.38	9.41	14.40
Return before interest & tax	18.22	14.71	16.23
Return after tax	9.01	6.23	8.71
Growth in sales	14.6	16.0	30.62
Growth in assets	14.06	15.99	32.57

Figure 10.9 *Financial performance by structural type in the UK service industry 1964-1974 (from: D.F. Channon, The Service Industries: Strategy, Structure and Financial Performance (London and Basingstoke: Macmillan, 1978) p.44).*

There is support for the general implications of the studies of Rumelt and Channon from other researchers. Work by Horovitz and Thietart[16] gives further weight to the finding that companies emphasising high growth best achieve this by divisionalisation and informal management styles[17] whilst those that emphasise profit performance are more likely to be functionally structured with specialist senior managers and more formal management styles. Their findings on levels of decentralisation are also interesting. They found that high growth companies certainly decentralised more than those emphasising profits: however, they also found that high performing companies, whether on measures of growth or profits, tended to retain fairly high degrees of central control on matters of general strategic direction of the company.

There is, finally, strong evidence to suggest that a major and overriding influence is the extent to which the design of the organisation is internally consistent.[18] Child shows how, within the aircraft industry, companies operating in the same environment had varying levels of performance which could be explained in terms of the extent to which the various aspects of their organisational structure were compatible. Of the four airlines he discusses, two performed better than the others and were competitors. However, their structures were quite different. One was divisionalised, relatively decentralised (at least for operational decisions) and formalised in terms of its control and planning, which was on a long time horizon basis. The other successful airline was not divisionalised, operated on much shorter time horizons, remained centralised with top managers meeting regularly to take the major decisions speedily. The point is that both organisations, though structured differently, operated a structure which was internally consistent and enabled them to handle the environment they faced effectively. The poorer performing airlines, on the other hand, had inconsistent structures. For example, though nominally decentralised they severely restricted authority for decision-making, failed to monitor the project performance of divisions and had cumbersome decision-making procedures. They were then unable to respond as effectively to their trading environment.

10.5 INFLUENCES ON ORGANISATIONAL DESIGN

Why are organisations designed the way they are? Why do some organisations have functional structures and others divisional structures? Why are some centralised and others decentralised? And what influences other aspects of organisational decision? This part of the chapter draws on some of the research done in an attempt to answer such questions and also refers readers to further work in the area.

10.5.1 An Evolutionary Perspective

In 1962 Chandler[19] published his study of seventy of the largest firms in the USA. Chandler studied the historical development of these firms in the 1940s and 1950s and drew a number of conclusions which proved to be of central importance in the study of organisations. He found that structure is affected by the strategy followed by an organisation. A change in strategy is likely to result in structural changes. Unfortunately, this finding has given rise to something of an oversimplification of Chandler's work which has often been reduced to the premise that 'structure follows strategy' as though this is some sort of natural inevitability. In fact Chandler found that the process was usually highly problematic for companies. A change in strategy is likely to give rise to administrative problems because the existing organisational structure is not adapted to cope with the new strategy. What usually happens is, given that strategic change occurs, there is an intermediate step between strategic change and structural change, and that step is often the sort of resistance to change that was mentioned earlier in the chapter in discussing intermediate structures. Resistance to structural change to meet the needs of the changed strategy is likely to result in a decline in company performance. It is this decline in performance that triggers structural change. The decline in performance may well result in a change in senior management who will then institute the structural changes that are required.

The sort of pattern of evolution that Chandler found and described is shown in Fig. 10.10. The firms he studied began as single unit operations such as a small manufacturing plant, a warehouse or retail shop; they had a single function (manufacturing or distribution, for example) and they operated in one industry. Their early development was through volume expansion; they simply sold more. This early volume expansion then developed into geographical expansion. A manufacturer might spread the area in which he is selling his product for example. Here is the first change in strategy, one of market development. The problems that ensue are likely to be problems of co-

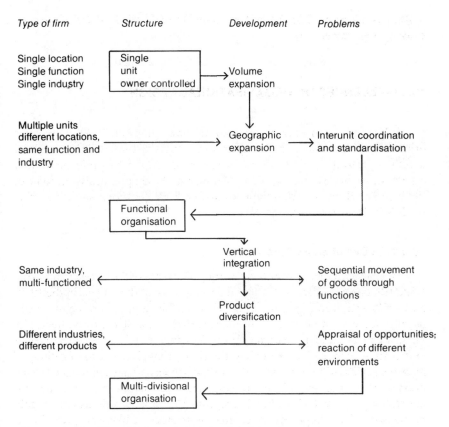

Figure 10.10   *Chandler's model of structural development.*

ordination between the different operating locations or areas. The manufacturer who was doing most of the selling himself in the original limited
geographical area in which he traded finds this impossible with a wider market
and loses touch with what is going on. It is the resultant administrative
problems from this that give rise to the need for a functional organisation. In
such a structure the owner becomes the general manager coordinating the work
of the various functions.

The next strategic step is likely to be vertical integration. Firms are likely
to stay in the same industry but develop or acquire other functions. So the
manufacturer who has expanded into new markets might decide that it would
be as well to have some sort of distribution facility. The sorts of problems he is
likely to face are to do with the balancing of the flow of goods. How much of
what sort of stock should be held and where, for example? This sort of problem
could still be handled by a functional structure but it would require increasing
specialisation: so there is the need for forecasters, inventory controllers and
soon - the birth of the service functions.

Company characteristics	Stage 1	Stage 2
Product line	Single product or single line	Single product line
Distribution	One channel or set of channels	One set of channels
Organisation structure	Little or no formal structure, one-man show	Specialisation based on function
Product/service transaction	Not applicable	Integrated pattern of transactions A → B → C → Markets
R & D organisation	Not institutionalised; guided by owner-manager	Increasingly institutionalised search for product or process improvements.
Performance measurement	By personal contact and subjective criteria	Increasingly impersonal, using technical and/or cost criteria
Rewards	Unsystematic and often paternalistic	Increasingly systematic, with emphasis on stability and service
Control system	Personal control of both strategic and operating decisions	Personal control of strategic decisions, delegation of operating decisions through policy.
Strategic choices	Needs of owner versus needs of company	Degree of integration; market share objective; breadth of product line

Figure 10.11 *Four stages of organisation development. (From Brùce R. Scott, Stages of Corporate Development, 9.371-294, Harvard Business School, Boston. Copyright © 1971 by the President and Fellows of Harvard College, Adapted by J.*

Stage 3	Stage 4
Multiple product lines	Multiple product lines multiple geographical markets
Multiple channels	Multiple channels
Specialisation based on product/market relationships	Grid structure based on product market relationships and regions
Non-integrated pattern of transactions	Non-integrated product and market transactions

Stage 3	Stage 4
Institutionalised search for new products as well as for improvements	Institutionalised search for new products as well as for improvements
Increasingly impersonal using market criteria (return on investment and market share)	Increasingly impersonal, using market criteria (return on investment and market share) but considerations of regional political development also used as criteria.
Increasingly systematic with variability related to performance	Increasingly systematic, with variability related to performance
Delegation of product-market decisions within existing businesses, with indirect control based on analysis of 'results'.	Delegation of product-market decisions within existing businesses, with indirect control based on analysis of 'results' and area control of business also delegated
Entry and exit from industries; allocation of resources by industry; rate of growth	Entry and exit from industries; allocation of resources by industry and by region; rate of growth.

Child, Organization: A Guide to Problems and Practice (London: Harper and Row, 1977, pp. 150, 151). Reprinted with permission.)

The next stage is that of product diversification. As original markets decline or plateau, firms move into different product or service areas. The manufacturer who had previously operated exclusively in the manufacture of, say, textiles moves into plastics perhaps. But the markets for textiles and plastics are likely to be very different. The problems that emerge are to do with the familiarisation and appraisal of very different industries and markets and the translation of these conditions into operating requirements for the different interests of the firm. Chandler suggests that it is this product/market based set of problems that gives rise to divisionalised structures. Firms with a functional structure cannot expect to operate efficiently in very different sorts of market or industry contexts. It makes more sense to have different divisions, each concentrating on its own environment and building the expertise to deal with it. So the structure that is now most common in larger organisations evolves - the multi-divisional structure.

These stages of development are summarised by Scott[20] in terms of the different organisational characteristics demonstrated by each structural type. This summary is shown in the first three columns of Fig. 10.11: the final column is that added by Child[21] to represent and describe the emergence of more complex structures of a matrix nature.

10.5.2 The Influence of Size and Diversity

The evolutionary perspective suggests that structural forms are greatly influenced by size and diversity: the larger that corporations grow, the more there is a move towards divisionalisation and eventually some sort of matrix structure.

It also seems that size and diversity are important influences on organisational structure in other ways. The extent to which internal tasks are specialised is greater: there is an increase in the separation or *differentiation* of tasks.[22] In turn this gives rise to a need for increased coordination (or integration). For example, in a smaller organisation the tasks of production scheduling and stock control are likely to be part of the manufacturing function whereas in a larger organisation there may be a separate department for them. Furthermore, this department may have explicit responsibility for the problems of conflicting demand made by the different functional areas of marketing and production - it may have a coordinating role. So in very large organisations there tends to emerge a proliferation of specialist departments or roles dealing with particular aspects of that organisation. It is inconceivable that all aspects of a large and diverse company could be organised except by splitting up the tasks of management in such a way.

In terms of decision-making, the proliferation of departments and roles leads to a situation where decisions are made by groups of managers: it is this 'management by committee' that so many managers find frustrating but which is so difficult to overcome. In such circumstances a critical organisational design issue is the level at which discussion and referral ends and a decision is taken. The danger is that this level is not clear or is so high up the organisational structure that the decision-making process is very lengthy. In this sense, a critical issue for very large companies is the extent and nature of decentralisation of decision-making (discussed earlier in the chapter).

Diversity is linked to size since very diverse organisations tend to be large. Diversity is one important reason why organisations will choose to move to a structure where decision-making is devolved to smaller units. There are obvious advantages in this since the greater the variety of the company's activities the more difficult is the task of centrally controlling the situation whilst maintaining an ability to respond quickly to the different environments in which the various parts of the company are operating. Hence, central control over detailed policy decisions is sacrificed to capitalise on the greater knowledge which managers at the 'sharp-end' possess about the recipe for success in their part of the business.

10.5.3 The Influence of Product and Technology

There are different ways in which product and technology influence structure. When products are manufactured by a sequence of separate, technical processes, companies may choose to forego the possible economies of continuous production and create separate divisions to deal with each process of manufacture as a means of developing the highest quality of product. Conversely, where there is a highly integrated process, divisionalisation is more difficult simply because the process is difficult to split up.

Similarly, assembly and component manufacture which are quite different in nature, allow components to be manufactured in separate divisions or subcontracted to other companies, as in the motor industry.

In terms of decentralisation, there is much evidence to show that technology influences the ways in which decisions are taken and the levels at which they are taken. As long ago as 1965 Woodward's[23] research showed that there are links between the types of production process and the nature of management. Mass production systems required the standardisation of process and seemed to result in greater direction and control by senior managers: in short, there was a tendency towards centralisation. Firms with less standardised manufacturing processes were more likely to have more decentralised and informal decision-making processes. Woodward's findings have subsequently come under a good deal of critical scrutiny. In particular, it has been argued that the claim that standardised production systems result in formalised and centralised control is really only true within the production side of the company: other departments and the company as a whole may not be organised in the same way.

There is evidence that the more sophisticated and complex the technology of an organisation the more the need for coordination between managers and specialists to deal with the complexity.[24] What emerges is a greater proportion of staff rather than line roles and a greater degree of decentralisation of authority, particularly to middle management. But again the question remains as to what extent this occurs for an organisation as a whole or within the manufacturing and technological areas alone.

10.5.4 The Influence of Competition

The level of competition appears to affect structure in two mains ways. The greater the competition the more likely that decentralisation (measured in terms of discretion over expenditure) will increase, thus providing the means whereby speedy action can be taken to counter competitive action. However, it also seems to be the case that increased competition is likely to encourage more formal methods of management and control - a point returned to in the next chapter. Presumably this is so that senior management are more able to monitor and regulate competitive responses.[25]

10.5.5 The Influence of Accountability and Ownership

In addition to market forces and competition another aspect of the external environment which is a particularly important influence in the UK for example, is the level of government intervention which is well illustrated by nationalised industries and other public sector bodies. Where government involvement is high the issue of public accountability becomes an important influence in deciding structure and it has seemed easier to impose public scrutiny through a centralised structure of decision-making where both power and accountability are in the hands of an easily identifiable team or individual at the centre. Higher levels of decentralisation would disperse authority more widely and make public accountability more difficult - or at least more difficult to demonstrate to the public. However, the price that has often been paid for this ease of public accountability has been an inability to respond quickly to market and other environmental changes and also the need for an unwieldy level of bureaucratic information and control in order to maintain this centralised structure.

It is not just in public bodies with government involvement that centralisation of authority and decision-making occur. In commercial enter-prises where there is pronounced dependency on some external body such as a parent company or a powerful shareholder group, the same sort of result comes about.[26] There is a tendency towards centralisation of decision-making and, because external standards of performance are imposed, a more mechanistic style of management.

Owner control may also be an important influence on structure. For example, many companies which are owner-controlled retain a high degree of centralisation even when they grow quite large. Some of the successful retail operations of the 1960s and 1970s, Dixons and Mothercare, for example, remained highly centralised when private, and continued to do so after going public. The influence of the owner-manager continued. It is also often difficult for a conglomerate built on a holding company basis, with the owners of the businesses remaining as executive chairmen of those businesses, to be restructured into divisions: the original owners understandably see this as a threat to their position and are likely to resist structural change. So whilst it may be logical in market or production terms to move to a divisional structure for example, there is the likelihood that a holding company structure may persist.

10.5.6 The Influence of the Nature of the Environment

Chapter 3 introduced the idea that environmental complexity and dynamism affect the organisation. The important organisational implications of this (mentioned in Chapter 2) are now discussed. However, readers do need to remember what is meant by complexity and dynamism. Dynamism is to do with the amount of change that is going on in the environment of the organisation; complexity is to do with the amount of information an organisation needs to deal with, or the range of inputs it is necessary to absorb, in decision-making. For a fuller explanation readers should refer back to Section 3.3 in Chapter 3.

The main point is that dynamic or complex environments increase uncertainty in decision-making. An organisation can be thought of as a means of facilitating the processing of information or inputs for decision-making purposes, so the form the organisation takes is important as a means of handling uncertainty. Mintzberg[27] argues that the form of organisations is likely to differ in important respects according to these different environmental conditions. His argument can be summarised as follows:

* In an environment which is essentially simple, organisations tend to gear themselves to operational efficiency. Because they are not faced with high degrees of change they can standardise their ways of operating, for example in terms of production, but also in their modes of management. So management and operational styles tend to be mechanistic[28] (or bureaucratic). Because the environment is simple there is also likely to be fairly centralised management: the inputs to decisions are just not complex enough to demand extensive devolution of authority. Mintzberg calls this type of organisation 'centralised bureaucratic'. They are exemplified by some mass production companies or raw material producers which, historically at least, faced fairly simple, stable environments. The great danger, of course, for such organisations is that their environments cease to be so benign and begin to place them under threat which they find difficult to handle, partly because they are not structured to do so.

* Increasing complexity is handled by devolving the responsiblity to specialists. This usually means that organisations in complex environments tend to be more decentralised at least for operational decisions.

Organisations such as hospitals and universities are good examples of those that traditionally have been in fairly stable or predictable environments but of a complex nature. They are what Mintzberg calls 'decentralised bureaucractic' organisations. The ongoing operational tasks - the operations management of a hospital, for example — are done in a standardised way, often with a highly bureaucratic management style. The complexity of some of the aspects of the patient care are then devolved to the specialist skills of the physicians, surgeons, psychiatrists and so on.

* In dynamic conditions, on the other hand, the main problem is one of change and the organisation must adjust to cope with this. The need is to increase the extent to which managers are capable of sensing what is going on around them, identifying change and responding to it. It is unlikely that bureaucratic styles of management will encourage such behaviour, so as the environment becomes more dynamic so it becomes more likely that bureaucracy will be reduced. Management is more likely to adopt an 'organic' style.[29] So retailers operating in fairly simple but often dynamic circumstances tend to be more organic in their management styles. This is not to say that they will necessarily devolve authority for major decisions to lower management. In a simple but dynamic environment it may make a lot of sense to retain fairly centralised management decision-making as a means of ensuring speed of decisions in important matters - which can be achieved provided the systems of management are not littered with bureaucratic procedures and lengthy referral processes. And, in a simple environment, there should be much less need for extensive departmentalisation and layers of management: the organisation can itself be kept simple. This type of organisation Mintzberg calls 'centralised organic'.

* There is some counter-evidence to what Mintzberg argues. High levels of competition require the same sort of speed of response as in a dynamic environment. This can be achieved by retaining centralised decision-making but ensuring that information reaches the decision maker fast with the minimum of bureaucratic hold-ups (which is what Mintzberg suggests is appropriate). Or it could be achieved by decentralising decision-making but ensuring that overall control of what happens at a strategic level is monitored and planned through systematic, more formal, systems. So a 'decentralised bureaucratic' form may also applicable in such conditions.

* What then happens where the environment is both *complex and dynamic?* These are the conditions in which Mintzberg suggests that 'decentralised organic' organisations occur. Some of the firms operating at the frontiers of scientific development are in these conditions. Their environment is changing so fast that they need the speed and flexibility that organic styles of management provides; and the level of complexity is such that they must devolve responsibility and authority to specialists. It is here, then,

that real decentralisation of authority - operational and often strategic -to units within the organisation takes place. These units may be in the form of divisions or they may be specialist departments, but it is they that must respond to the change that is occurring so fast around them. These sorts of environmental conditions, so uncommon in the past, are becoming more and more common. Yet they are the most difficult conditions to cope with, particularly if they are faced by organisations with a structural history of centralised bureaucracy.

The typology of organisations according to these dimensions of uncertainty are summarised in Fig. 10.12.[30]

	Stable	Dynamic
Complex	Decentralised bureaucratic e.g. Hospitals	Decentralised organic e.g. Advanced electronics
Simple	Centralised bureaucratic e.g. Mass production	Centralised organic e.g. Retailing or Decentralised bureaucratic

Figure 10.12 *Environmental influences on organisation structure (adapted from: Henry Mintzberg, The Structuring of Organizations: A Synthesis of the Research, 1979, p.286. Reprinted by permission of Prentice-Hall, Inc., Englewood Cliffs, N.J.). See reference 30.*

10.5.7 The Influence of Managerial Values and Ideologies

It is not just influences from the environment or the strategy being followed that affect organisational design. The values and ideologies of those who run the company are likely to have a major impact too. This is well demonstrated by Miles and Snow[31] who show how the ideologies of owners and senior managers in industrial and public service concerns influence both the choice of strategy and structure.

The *defender* organisation tends to show certain characteristics. Strategically, such organisations tend to specialise rather than diversify. In terms of organisation they are likely to have a functional structure which permits an emphasis on specialisation at most managerial levels and emphasises functional efficiency. Within the functional units an extensive division of labour is likely to help keep down costs by minimising cross-functional or cross-task training. There is likely to be a mechanistic style of management, coordination of activity through the standardising of activities and the scheduling of operations and resolution of conflict by referral of problems through hierarchical levels of management. There will also be a high degree of influence from functions which are concerned with the maintenance of efficiency such as finance and production and lower levels of influence from marketing or R&D. Miles and Snow make the point that such organisations may be very profitable and very efficient providing they are able to find a stable market niche.

The second type is the *prospector,* seeking actively for new opportunities so as to be first in the market. There is, then, much less emphasis on control and efficiency and much more on innovation. Strategically, there is likely to be a greater diversity of interests and more risk ventures. In terms of organisation there will be a product divisional structure perhaps overlaid by a use of project teams to develop opportunities and a tendency to decentralise with the minimum of top-down control. There will be a less extensive division of labour than for a defender because of the need for a transfer of management and expertise between tasks, an organic style of management to encourage flair and risk-taking, and complex systems of coordination with, for example, specialist coordinating roles. Organisational conflict may be high because there is no clear definition of tasks. Influence and power is lodged primarily in development areas of the business such as marketing and R&D. These sort of organisations may not be as efficient and profitable as the defender, but they have chosen to operate in more dynamic environments and seek for innovation, so the yardstick of success may, rather, be adaptation and innovation.

The *analyser* seeks to innovate and change in a changing environment by watching carefully what happens in the market and what competitors do. Miles and Snow argue that these organisations will both maintain an efficiency emphasis through some functional areas whilst pursuing innovation through some divisional emphasis: this may lead to a matrix type organisation or the use of project teams. The functional areas are those that carry out the roles of control and efficiency with specialist managers and mechanistic styles of management, whereas the product divisions or project teams are more likely to be more entrepreneurial.

Whilst no-one would suggest that managerial ideologies will determine structure, they are an important influence. It is also important to realise that trying to make significant shifts in strategy or structure which run counter to the underlying philosophies could well be problematic. For example, the management consultant is often faced with the dilemma of choosing between recommendations on the structure of an organisation which take into account, on the one hand, environmental and business performance pressures for change and, on the other, conservative pressures for the maintenance of the

ILLUSTRATION 44

John Home Ltd.*

- New strategies may require structural changes which conflict with the approaches of the management.

John Home Ltd. was a D.I.Y. retailer concentrated in the North West of the UK. It had been founded by John Home himself in the 1950s and he had steadily increased the number of shops but, until the early 1970s, had remained mainly as a retailer of paint and wallpaper. However, in the 1970s John Home's son, Chris, entered the business and initiated some changes. The acquisition of new retail outlets increased, some of which were in other geographical areas. The product range widened and the company began a wholesaling venture which serviced other retailers. This took place within a highly centralised decision-making system. Apart from the new products introduced by the son, all buying decisions were made by the father or his assistant, there was just one sales manager to control what, by 1978, was a total of 31 shops and, each morning, John Home insisted on seeing all the mail except that which went direct to branches. John did not object to the expansion initiated by Chris, which he recognised had brought extra business, but he was not prepared to devolve any of his authority to others in the organisation.

By late 1978 it was clear the situation was getting out of hand. The operation was getting too diverse for John to control in his personalised and centralised way. A consultant was called in to recommend what should be done: but the consultant faced a dilemma. Retention of the present structure and management style would mean a strategy of further expansion would be unworkable: the pursuit of the evolving strategy would mean the existing structure had to be changed. Yet a change in structure would be resisted by John Home, and a change in strategy by Chris.

The consultant's attempts to persuade John to devolve responsibility met with little success. And Chris argued that the only way his father would 'see reason' was to increase the speed of geographical and product expansion. The declining performance of the business as a result of the ensuing management inefficiency was exacerbated by a decline in sales as the economic recession decreased customer buying power.

In 1981, John Home Ltd. was acquired by a large national retailer who incorporated most of the shops into its geographically divisionalised structure.

Source: Author (G.J.).

* This company's name is disguised to preserve the anonymity of the company.

status quo from those who are in senior positions in the firm, perhaps who have asked for his help. Illustration 44 shows just this problem.

10.6 COPING WITH THE PROBLEM OF ORGANISATIONAL DESIGN

Choice of organisational design may not be at all straightforward. It is clear that there can often be conflicting influences on structure. So, as with strategic choice, there are likely to be several alternative structural designs and many influences on which of them is to be adopted. One or two examples may help make the point.

A common problem of the 1970s was the conflict between the influences of an increasingly turbulent environment and traditional technology. Some examples have already been mentioned of companies with highly routine mass production core technologies which had previously been a major influence on the structure and nature of the organisation. The company would very likely be fairly centralised and bureaucratic in its mode of operation. However, faced with a dynamic environment the company may well have attempted to diversify away from its core technology. This strategic decision might argue for divisionalisation and increased decentralisation at least of operational decision-making, whilst the nature of the environment itself might demand much more organic styles of management. Yet the business may still be highly dependent on the traditional core technology and managers perhaps unwilling to decentralise authority. In such circumstances the structural choice is not straightforward; there are different influences pulling in different directions. Illustration 45 shows how one organisation changed its organisation structure given different pressures and influences.

There are, then, likely to be conflicting influences on organisational design. How then is it sensible to set about dealing with the problem. There is no formula for doing this, no 'right answer'. It is again a question of analysis and in the end, judgment. However, it might be useful to ask these questions:

*   What are the influences inside and outside the organisation which affect how it should be structured? The influences discussed in this chapter should provide a basis for this.

*   From these, which are the critical influences (that is, those that will either affect performance more than the others or those that simply override all others)? Readers might consider that from the example above, the critical influence on the mass producer has become the dynamic nature of the environment; if the company does not cope with this, then its performance will continue to deteriorate.

*   Given the identification of these critical influences, it may be that some clear structural implications emerge, or it could be that there are options. If there are options then it is sensible to consider the advantages and

ILLUSTRATION 45

Nipont

- As the circumstances it faced changed, Nipont changed its organisational structure to divisional and then back to functional

In the years following the Second World War, up the 1970s, Nipont grew to become Japan's largest manufacturer of synthetic textiles, operating from twelve plants in the centre of Japan. Over the years, the company had found opportunities for its business interests to grow over a whole range of related products in the fields of fibres, plastics and chemicals. Despite this spread of activity, Nipont had retained its original functional organisational structure.

By 1970, however, it was clear that if growth was to continue, the company would need to take initiatives in several fields of activity at the same time in order to cope with the rapid changes that were occurring on all fronts of its business. For this reason, product divisions were created which allowed managers to become attuned to the particular needs of their product base so they could best manage the growth that was taking place. Because of the specialisation that occurred in each product area, there was also a need for decision-making to be decentralised to each division.

In the mid-1970s, Japan was subjected to a series of economic shocks; oil price rises, the forced revaluation of the yen, a world-wide shortage of commodities, inflation and then recession. Nipont, in common with the rest of Japanese industry, was faced with rapidly rising material and labour costs and decreasing demand. This resulted in intensified price competition and reduced demand which led to the deterioration of Nipont's financial operations.

In order to restore profitability and to cope with a more uncertain future, the Company decided to revert to a more centralised and functional structure which increased top management's control and afforded a more unified perspective of the Company's activities as it struggled through a difficult period. Consequently, each functional element of the three product divisions was regrouped into a new common functional division. The new Manufacturing Division, for example, was composed of the combined production elements of the previous three product divisions. This 'combined force' was able to concentrate on optimising short-run costs throughout the company, and thus help it to respond more effectively to increasing price competition and factor cost pressures.

Nipont has therefore used the type of organisational structure most suited to its needs at the time - the product-based divisionalised structure helped the company to reinvest and expand in several areas at the same time within existing product fields. But, given a more hostile environment and the need for an emphasis on cost reduction and efficiency, a functional and centralised structure was reintroduced.

Source: 'Regaining Control at Nipont' by Lex Donaldson, Journal of General Management, Summer 1979.

disadvantages of each in the context of the strategy that the organisation wishes to follow.

* The final point is too often overlooked. No matter how elegant a structure is, the most important point is that it has to be workable. How will the structure be put into effect? If divisionalisation of a holding company is recommended then exactly what is going to happen to the chairmen of the many virtually autonomous businesses that are to be rationalised into a few divisions? Who is to report to whom in this new organisation? Where will decisions of what sort be taken? If substantial decentralisation is to take place in the divisions, will more senior management accept it and will more junior management be able to handle it? Part of the evaluation of structural alternatives just as for strategic alternatives, is to consider feasibility.

10.7 SUMMARY

This chapter has concentrated on structural implications of organisational design. It has been argued that strategic implementation is effected through the people in the organisation, and that of key importance is the way in which those people are organised. To help readers understand how this might be accomplished, the chapter has reviewed the various forms of structure in common use, together with their advantages and disadvantages. It then examined the sorts of influence from within the organisation and from outside that may affect structure. The chapter concluded by discussing how consideration of the most appropriate structure might take place.

However, this chapter has only touched on a second, equally vital aspect of organisation: how the people within the structure are to be managed. It is this issue that is turned to in the next chapter.

REFERENCES

1. For example, R. Rumelt does not include the category 'holding company' in his book on American industry *Strategy, Structure and Economic Performance* (Harvard Press: 1974).
2. P. Grinyer and J-C. Spender *Turnaround - Managerial Recipes for Strategic Success* (Associated Business Press: 1978), use sub-categories of the term 'multidivisional' which they describe as 'diversified majors' and passive or acquisitive conglomerates. These are terms we return to later in the chapter to differentiate between the nature of different multi-divisional organisation. Also see P.H. Grinyer and J-C. Spender, 'Recipes, Crises and Adaptation in Mature Businesses', *Intl Studies of Management and Organisation,* Vol.IX, No.3, p.113, 1979.

3. A good summary of the advantages and disadvantages of different structures is given in an article by M. Davis in 'Current Experiments in Management Structure' in *Reviewing the Management Structure* (BIM: 1972).

4. The benefits and problems of matrix structures are discussed more fully by K. Knight in 'Matrix Organisation: A Review' in the *Journal of Management Studies*, May 1976.

5. 'Functional with subsidiaries' is a term used by R. Rumelt, reference 1.

6. D.F. Channon uses the description 'critical function' structure in his study of structure and performance in the UK service industry: *The Service Industries: Strategy, Structure and Financial Performance* (Macmillan: 1973).

7. There is a growing number of such studies, the main ones of which, by country of study, are:
   USA: Alfred Chandler, *Strategy and Structure* (MIT Press: 1962) which is a seminal work and is discussed later in the chapter. Also R. Rumelt, reference 1.
   UK: D.F. Channon, *The Strategy and Structure of British Enterprise* (Macmillan: 1973) and his book on the service industries referred to in reference 6.
   Germany: Heinz Tanaheiser, *Strategy and Structure of German Enterprise.*
   Italy: R. J. Pavan, *Strategy and Structure of Italian Enterprise.*
   France: G. Pooley-Dyas, *Strategy and Structure of French Enterprise.*
   The last three of which are all unpublished doctoral dissertations of the Harvard Business School.

8. The references to Channon's studies are given in (6) and (7) above.

9. For a more extensive treatment of the structure of multi-national companies see:
   M.Z. Brooke and H.L. Remmers, *The Strategy of Multinational Enterprise* (Pitman: 1978, Ch. 2).
   J.M. Stopford and L.T. Wells, Jnr., *Managing the Multinational Enterprise* (Longman: 1972, Chs. 2 and 5).

10. J.M. Stopford and L.T. Wells, reference 9, found this tendency. However, it should be noted that their findings are based on 1968 data.

11. These findings are from research published by W.H. Davidson and P.C. Haspeslagh, 'Shaping a Global Product Organisation', *Harvard Business Review*, Jul.-Aug. 1982.

12. See reference 11.

13. See reference 9.

14. The reference to R. Rumelt's book is given in reference 1.

15. The references to Channon's study on the UK service industry is given in reference 6.

16. J. H. Horovitz and R. A. Thietart's research is summarised in 'Strategy, Management Design and Firm Performance', *Strategic Management Journal*, Vol. 3., 1982.

17. For further support of this finding see J. Child, 'Managerial and Organisational Factors Associated with Company Performance: Part II: A Contingency Analysis', *Journal of Management Studies*, Vol. 12, No. 1, 1975.

18. Both P.N. Khandwalla, 'Viable and Effective Organisational Design of Firms', *Academy of Management Journal*, September 1973; and J. Child, *Organisation: A Guide to Problems and Practice* (Harper & Row: 1977) have found this relationship between the consistency of an organisation's structure and its performance.

19.   A. Chandler's work, *Strategy and Structure* (MIT Press: 1962) began a whole series of investigations into the relationship between strategy and structure. It is a fine study of the historical development of American industry but, in drawing conclusions about organisations in the 1980s it should be remembered that the period being studied was the 1940s and 1950s, a time when the influences on business were somewhat different from the 1980s.

20.   B.R. Scott's summary of A. Chandler's stages appears in, 'The Industrial State: Old Myths and New Realities', *Harvard Business Review,* State: Old Myths. Mar.-Apr. 1973.

21.   See J. Child, *Organisation: A Guide to Problems and Practice* (Harper & Row: 1977, pp.150-151).

22.   A major study highlighting this is that of P. Lawrence and J. Lorsch, *Organisation and Environment* (Irwin: 1969) reprinted regularly since. Similar findings are, however, reported by D. Pugh *et al.* as a result of their research programme which has become known as the Aston Studies (see for example, 'Dimensions of Organisation Structure', *Administrative Science Quarterly,* 1968). More recently P.N. Khandwalla discusses relationships of size and structural characteristics in *The Design of Organisations* (Harcourt Brace: 1977).

23.   See J. Woodward, *Industrial Organisation: Theory and Practice* (Oxford University Press: 1965).

24.   A number of writers and researchers have examined and developed the work of Woodward. In particular the studies which show how the level of sophistication and complexity of technology influences the locus of decision-making are J.W. Hunt, *The Restless Organisation* (Wiley: 1972) and D.J. Hickson *et al.,* 'Operations Technology and Organisation Structure: An Empirical Reappraisal', *Administrative Science Quarterly,* 1969.

25.   This association between high levels of competition and decentralisation combined with formalisation is supported empirically by studies by C. Perrow in 'The Bureaucratic Paradox: the Efficient Organisation Centralises in Order to Decentralise', *Organisational Dynamics,* Spring 1977.

26.   This has been found to be the case in several studies: Mintzberg, *The Structuring of Organizations* (Prentice-Hall: 1979, pp.288-291); D. Pugh *et al.,* 'The Context of Organisation Structures', *Administrative Science Quarterly,* 1969, pp.91-114, and B.C. Beimann, 'On the Dimensions of Bureaucratic Structure: An Empirical Reappraisal', *Administrative Science Quarterly,* 1973, pp. 462-476.

27.   See H. Mintzberg, *The Structuring of Organizations* (Prentice-Hall: 1979, pp. 285-287).

28.   Mechanistic management is a term used by T. Burns and G.M. Stalker in their book, *The Management of Innovation* (Tavistock: 1961) to describe a management system which is fairly regulated and prescribed. Managers are likely to have clearly defined job roles with specified reporting relationships and a clear idea about who takes decisions about what sorts of things.

29.   Again it is T. Burns and G.M. Stalker (see 28 above) that use this term. Organic styles of management are much less formal with less clearly defined job roles, responsibilities and reporting relationships. There may, then, be a good deal more conflict and apparent confusion, but the likelihood is that managers will be more likely to be aware and sensitive to changes outside their immediate day-to-day jobs.

30.   Although Fig. 10.12 builds most directly on H. Mintzberg's typology in, *The Structuring of Organizations* (see 27 above), similar matrices have been used by other writers. In *Organisational Analysis: A sociological View* (Tavistock: 1970, p.78), Perrow's matrix uses independent variables of comprehensibility (how analysable are decision search procedures) and predictability (how many exceptions the organisation encounters). Perrow names organisations in the lower left quadrant 'routine', those in the upper left 'craft', those in the lower right 'engineering', and those in the upper right 'non-routine'. He then fleshes out his matrix with a number of examples from the manufacturing and service sectors. Van de Ven and Delbecq, 'A Task Contingent Model of Work Unit Structure', *Administrative Science Quarterly:* 1974, pp.183-197, present a similar but more elaborate matrix with many other examples and citations of support from the literature.

31.   The work and findings of R.E. Miles and C.C. Snow, *Organizational Strategy, Structure and Process* (McGraw-Hill: 1978), have been discussed earlier in Chapters 2 and 5 and readers should refer to this discussion for a more detailed explanation of their organisational types.

RECOMMENDED KEY READINGS

*   A clear exposition of the different basic organisational structures together with a summary of a good deal of research on the structure is in *Strategy Implementation: The Role of Structure and Process* by J.R. Galbraith and D.A. Nathanson (West Publishing: 1978)

*   The most extensive and thorough treatment of influences on organisational design is H. Minztberg, *The Structuring of Organisations* (Prentice-Hall: 1979). It is also an excellent work of scholarship and readers with an interest in the subject are urged to read it.

*   On structural development in UK companies: D. Channon, *The Strategy and Structure of British Enterprise* (Macmillan: 1973).

*   On financial performance associated with strategy and structure:
        - in the USA, R. Rumelt, *Strategy, Structure and Economic Performance* (Harvard Press: 1974).
        - in the UK and for service industries, D. Channon, *The Service Industries: Strategy, Structure and Financial Performance* (Macmillan: 1973).

11

PEOPLE AND SYSTEMS

11.1 INTRODUCTION

Implementation of strategic change requires the identification of the key tasks needed to effect that change as discussed in Chapter 9, and a proper consideration of the organisational structure and design which will best facilitate those changes. However, the success with which the key tasks are actually performed is determined by the way in which the *people* within and around an organisation are managed and controlled.

Management of people and systems requires an understanding of both the personal and political implications of strategic change and this chapter addresses both these issues. At a personal level people's ability and willingness to implement changes is related to a variety of issues such as personality, capability, motivation and the provision of suitable training. In addition, the systems of reward and control will affect the behaviour of individuals and, as a result, either help or hinder strategic change.

However, people operate in groups within (and around) organisations and the success or failure of new strategies is also governed by the skill with which the political situation within and between these groups is managed. The chapter discusses how the uncertainty generated by strategic change triggers political activity and how the reward and control systems will need to take account of the frictions which can arise between groups when changes are being made.

The relationship between these various factors is represented in Fig. 11.1 which also provides a framework for this chapter.

The performance of people, and the resultant success or failure of strategic implementation is determined by a number of factors:

* Firstly, there are the factors concerned with people as individuals - the *personal factors.* The extent to which people have the capability to perform the necessary tasks, are willing to provide sufficient effort and the degree of satisfaction which they obtain from their jobs.

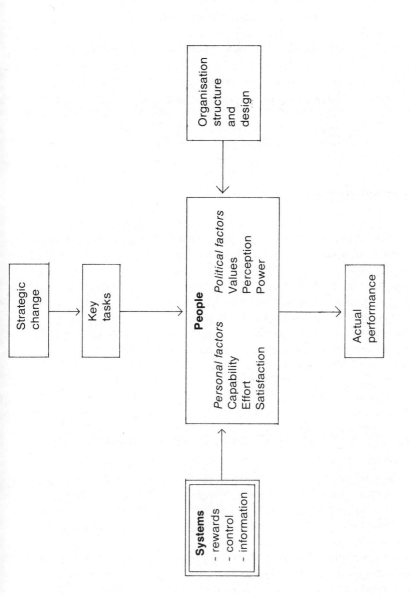

Figure 11.1 *Strategic implementation: the influence of people and systems.*

* Secondly, there are *political factors* in the company situation which will influence the performance of people. The extent to which the values of people are in accord with the proposed changes, the perceptions which people have of the likely consequences of change, and the power which individuals or groups hold which can help them assist or resist strategic change. Many of the difficulties which can arise during the implementation of strategic change are due to the natural tendency of people to resist change and to fight for the *status quo*. This has been called 'dynamic conservatism'.[1]

* Thirdly, there are the *systems* within and around organisations which will shape the attitudes of individuals and groups towards strategic change. In particular the reward, control and information systems can be powerful forces for facilitating (or preventing) change within organisations. Later sections of the chapter will look at how the design and management of these systems can contribute to the success or failure of strategy.

* Fourthly, the *nature of the strategic change* itself will affect people's attitudes. For example, whether the change is familiar or novel, whether it is seen as threatening or opening up new opportunities will determine the willingness and ability of individuals to contribute to successful implementation.

* Lastly, the *organisational structure* and design will influence people's attitude to strategic change. This was discussed in Chapter 10 and will, therefore, not be repeated in this chapter. Readers can usefully refer back to Fig. 10.11 to see how the organisational structure influences the type of reward and control systems within companies.

11.2 PEOPLE - THEIR IMPORTANCE IN IMPLEMENTATION

The influence of people on strategy is a central theme of this book. It has already been seen how they are an important resource (Chapter 4) and a significant influence on choice of policy through their values and power (Chapters 5 and 6). It has also been seen how people outside the company can determine the destiny of those within (Chapters 3 and 5) and how the willingness of people to cooperate with strategic change can be influenced by structural considerations (Chapter 10). Later in this chapter there will be a consideration of how systems of reward, control and information will affect people's attitudes to strategic change.

This section will, therefore, be confined to exploring how the readiness of people to accept and implement change should determine the specific actions which management need to undertake to ensure successful implementation of the key tasks previously identified.

11.2.1 Managing the Political Implications of Change

Strategic changes take place over a fairly long period of time and can make a considerable difference to the way in which an organisation operates. As a result of this the process of implementing strategic change generates a great deal of uncertainty within the organisation which, in turn, triggers off political activity as groups and individuals try to cope with the consequences of change. Mumford and Pettigrew[2] have provided a useful model of how this uncertainty 'cascades' down through the organisation, triggering off more uncertainty as a consequence. This process is illustrated in Fig. 11.2 and Illustration 46. Chapter 5 has already discussed how the values of individuals, groups, and whole organisations form a political system within and around an organisation which determines the extent to which any individual or group is likely to influence strategy.[3] Strategic change upsets this balance and the ability to manage this process is a key part of implementation.

The traditional view[4] has been that the political implications of change are *short-lived* but nonetheless important, however, in many (perhaps most) organisations strategic change does not occur as neat big events but is occurring steadily all the time as was seen in the discussion of incrementalism in Chapter 2. Therefore, the political implications must be seen as a *permanent* feature of organisational life. Although political activity can be thought of as a constraint on implementing rational strategic decisions, perhaps a more helpful view would be that the political process is an important means of implementing strategic change.[5] For example, it helps resolve difficult issues of resource allocation (although opponents of this view would argue that the consequences are not always the best). The practical implications are that managers involved in planning strategic change should in fact be paying as much attention to understanding the political context of implementation as they would expect to spend on resource and financial planning. All too often the latter becomes dominant with the result that implementation can fail or throw the company into disarray.

From the point of view of strategic implementation, the important issue is how management can improve the chances of successful implementation against this background of political activity. A political analysis (for example, see Chapter 5) can identify how individuals and groups are likely to respond to proposed changes. The management of these changes will then require one or more different types of action which are summarised in Fig. 11.3.

Very often the reason for resisting change is the feeling of insecurity or threat which the change engenders in people. Moscow[6] has suggested that this can be a particular problem if people feel either very insecure or very secure. In both cases they are likely to resist change by either rejecting, suppressing or distorting information concerning the proposed changes. In contrast, when people feel moderately secure they tend to react constructively since they are more likely to accept the need to change and not feel threatened by it. One of the skills involved in organisational development (OD) is to create the

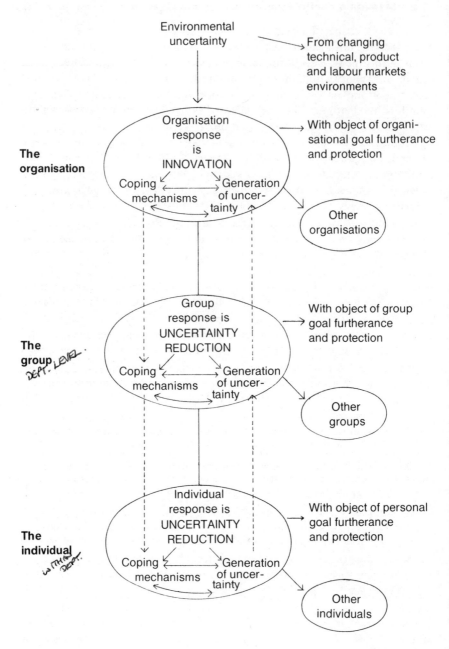

Figure 11.2 *Uncertainty and strategic change (source: E. Mumford and A. Pettigrew, Implementing Strategic Decisions (Harlow: Longman Group Ltd., 1975) p.209).*

ILLUSTRATION 46

Cascade of Uncertainty

- The rapid development of microcomputer technology during the late 1970s caused a considerable amount of political activity at one university.

For many years the provision of computer facilities had been an important strategic issue for universities due to their high cost and their importance to teaching and research. Up until the late 1970s a main frame computer provided the only source of computing. However, by 1978 microcomputers had reached a level of development where senior management in one university had to consider whether they should begin to make use of this new technology. Being a recent innovation, most of the microcomputers did not have a proven track record, leaving senior management uncertain as to whether they needed micro-computers at all and if they did need them, which system would be most appropriate.

At departmental level there was uncertainty as to the outcome of senior management's deliberations, triggering off political activity amongst groups. The computer services department, who operated the university's main frame computer, pressed for its upgrading, realising that the widespread introduction of microcomputers would erode their power. Their main weapon was their expertise, and as senior management was lacking in this area, the computer services department were able to get representatives onto the committee advising on computer provision. The other tack of their argument was that there would be government funding for the upgrading of the main frame computer resulting in an improved facility with no direct cost to the university.

The other groups involved in the political activity were the user departments. They faced the uncertainty brought about by the seemingly impregnable position held by the computer services department and the fear that the decision to upgrade the main frame would be pushed through quickly. The user departments (who preferred microcomputers) attempted to delay the decision to allow departmental members to improve their knowledge of computer systems and so enable them to challenge the computer services' arguments. They also tried to discredit the quality of service provided by the main frame computer, suggesting that departmental micro-computers would provide the type of service the users required. The various user departments also formed alliances in order to create a more powerful lobbying force within the university's formal decision-making structure.

The user departments' response, (the pursuit of greater computing knowledge and a justification for departmentally-based microcomputers) in its turn led to uncertainty for the individual members of the departments who responded in differing ways. Those who were familiar with computers realised the opportunity to enhance their own position within the department, while others, who were previously uninterested in the role of computers in teaching, saw the need to gain such knowledge quickly. The course leaders encouraged the use of micro-computers as a means of enhancing the image of their particular course. However, a minority responded by suggesting that microcomputers were a 'passing fad', and sought to emphasise the traditional role of the teacher.

The response of senior management to this political activity was to permit the purchase of a limited number of microcomputers, partly as a result of the users' arguments, but also because not buying them may have jeopardised the university's claim for a large sum of money from the government to upgrade the main frame computer. To some extent this could be regarded as a 'side-payment' to allow the main decision to proceed.

Source: Authors.

A. The political implications of change

Acceptance of strategic change can be gained by:
1. *providing information* to very secure groups to convince them of the need to change
2. *reassuring* very insecure groups about the consequences of change
3. *widening involvement* of people during strategic choice as a means of ensuring easier implementation
4. implementing those *parts* of the strategy where agreement can be found and deferring other parts (incremental approach).
5. *waiting* until circumstances make particular strategies more politically acceptable

B. The personal implications of change

The following actions may be taken to ensure a match between strategy and people's personality and capabilities:
1. a re-assessment of people's *roles* within the organisation
2. people's capabilities may be a *constraint* on certain strategies, other strategies may better suit their capabilities
3. *training* programmes may be needed
4. *recruitment* of new people may be the best means of acquiring new skills
5. *redeployment* or *redundancy* may be the only means of coping with certain people within the organisation
6. a *settling down period* may be required before more changes are contemplated

Figure 11.3   *Managing the impact of strategic change on people.*

conditions where people feel moderately secure: resistance to change is lowered rather than pressure to change being increased. For individuals and groups who feel very secure about their present position it will be essential to provide *information* which helps them recognise the problems and difficulties which their present position actually holds. For example, unions who are unaware of the pending collapse of a major market may be less resistant to changes in strategy if the situation were explained more fully. In contrast individuals and groups who feel insecure will require *reassurances* concerning the likely consequences of change.

One of the most significant differences between Japanese companies and those in the USA and UK is the extent to which the political process of implementation is handled overtly and thoroughly.[8] Western managers often accuse the Japanese of taking a long time to arrive at important decisions. However, since the typical Japanese decision-making processes ensure the political acceptability of the outcome by a much wider involvement of people in strategic decisions, successful implementation is almost guaranteed once the decision is taken. In contrast, many Western managers are keen to take decisions which subsequently prove difficult to implement.

In many situations it is impossible to obtain complete political viability of a scheme. Nevertheless, there could be *partial viability* in the sense that the major groups are agreed on certain aspects of the proposed changes. Then a more incremental approach to the proposed changes might be possible with some aspects being implemented whilst others are kept open to reconsideration.[9] Sometimes this partial implementation may not involve the most important aspects of strategy. It may be that the various parties are prepared to work together in a very limited way as a basis for testing out the likely success or failure of the main strategy. This is quite a common approach to relationships with outside parties when, for example, two companies are considering a joint venture (as discussed in Chapter 7). Such an approach to strategic implementation is one reason why companies might proceed in an incremental fashion as discussed in Chapter 2.

There are some circumstances where the most rational course of action is so politically unviable that only subsequent *failure* of another strategy can create conditions where the preferred strategy can be implemented.

11.2.2 Managing the Personal Implications of Change

One of the most difficult aspects of implementing any strategic change is ensuring that the employees are able to undertake the key tasks which that change requires. In particular it is important to ensure that people will actually perform at an adequate level. During strategic change the nature of people's jobs might change, with the result that their *capability* may be in question and/or the *satisfaction* they derive from their job may alter. Either of these may, in turn, influence the level of *effort* which people put into their job. Much of the study of work performance has come from behaviourists and the emphasis has tended to be on how individual personality suits people (or otherwise) to particular types of work. Since different strategies inevitably result in different types of work this background can be used to look at the link between choice of strategy and the type of people who will be best suited to it.

Traditionally, the most popular measure of people's suitability for certain types of work has been tolerance of ambiguity.[10] In other words, the extent to which an individual needs work to be highly prescribed as against being very loosely defined and full of ambiguity. An example would be the contrasting situations faced by the factory manager working to weekly output targets and the manager of a newly created subsidiary faced with the task of establishing a new product in a new market area. Certain aspects of personality will make individuals more or less resistant to the adoption of new strategies.[11] These range from some features like habit which may be relatively easy to change, to others like insecurity in new situations, which may prove to be major obstacles. In Chapters 2 and 5 it was mentioned that Miles and Snow [12] categorised organisations into different types which are not easy to change since suitable personality types tend to be selected into the organisation which perpetuates the *status quo*. Some authors[13] argue that it is the stage of development of a company and the degree of diversity in its activities which dictate the types of personalities which are most suitable. Managers who are skilful at establishing new ventures may be very poor managers of static or declining companies.

There are several important conclusions which can be drawn from these observations which should help managers to cope better with the personal aspects of performance during strategic change. These are summarised in Fig. 11.3. Firstly that most strategic changes will require a reassessment of the *roles* and responsibilities of people within the organisation. Equally, it may require new relationships to be made with people outside the company - the traditional suppliers or customers may not be capable of responding to new ways of operating. A proper understanding of the capabilities of people to operate in different ways is essential during implementation of change. This underlines the need for an analysis of an organisation's human resources as discussed in Chapter 4.

Few organisations would be willing or able to change too many of their people at any one time. Therefore people are perhaps better viewed as a *constraint* on the choice of strategy - a reason for not pursuing certain ventures - rather than something that can be moulded to fit a new strategy. In order to manage the people within the organisation it may be necessary to evolve a particular strategy which best utilises their capabilities rather than assuming that they can be changed to fit other strategies. Illustration 47 shows how this strategy may actually come about as a means of utilising the talents of individuals.

Training[14] is an important means of coping with strategic change. Significantly different skills might be needed at all levels in an organisation when new strategies are followed. Some of the larger, diverse companies have highly planned career paths for managers to ensure that they gain the breadth of experience needed at higher levels whilst undertaking line responsibilities in their own specialist area. For example, a financial manager may be moved around within the finance function (e.g. dealing with costing, credit control, capital investment appraisal), but also between divisions or companies to gain experience of the variety of products and markets and geographical locations. In Japanese companies the development of such a breadth of experience is seen as essential to the development of a cooperative spirit within the company.[15]

New strategies may require a type of person who does not exist within the organisation, and recruitment may be the only route to solving this people/ strategy mismatch. A manufacturing company developing by forward integration into retailing will almost certainly need to buy-in managers with a retailing background. Development into overseas markets normally requires people with experience of overseas marketing either as employees or agents. *Redeployment* or *redundancy* of staff is of central importance during many strategic changes. Development by acquisition invariably requires changes of that type. When two organisations are to be pulled together then the new entity

---

ILLUSTRATION 47

Trafalgar House

- Victor Matthew's talent for turning companies around and his need for a succession of challenges had a considerable impact on Trafalgar House's acquisition policy.

The success of Trafalgar House Ltd. in the 1970s was much to do with the close managerial understanding between Nigel Broakes, who as chairman, decided upon the future direction of the company, and Victor Matthews whose task it was to turnaround the acquired companies. However, this process was by no means one-way as Nigel Broakes suggests when discussing the acquisition of the Beaverbrook newspaper group:

> 'Before I describe the acquisition itself let me revert to Victor and his state of mind at the time. He was morbid and morose, and yearned for the days when we had both run individual operations ... and I had to face the possibility that we might lose Victor altogether. I do not want to sound flippant, and there were several other good reasons to want to buy a newspaper group which, whatever its problems, sold more than 20 million papers per week, but I must admit that, at the forefront of my mind, was the desire to see Victor once again engrossed with a challenge -something that would gratify and occupy him, leaving free part of his time for all the rest of Trafalgar ...'

Having acquired Beaverbrook, Matthews, installed as chairman, was immediately involved in an industrial dispute with the Fleet Street unions. Nigel Broakes:

> '... Victor produced a list of 18 conditions without accepting which, those men who had been sacked, would not be re-engaged. The crisis reached its peak on a Saturday, by which time we had lost several hundred thousand pounds. Victor telephoned me four times; the third call was just after lunch and I asked him where he was: "At home, doing the washing up", he told me...
> "They seem to have agreed to everything', he said, in doleful tones.
> "Then why do you sound so depressed", I asked.
> "Because it's been too easy", he replied.'

Clearly, Trafalgar House's acquisition strategy was, at least in part, designed to provide a challenge to Victor Matthews.

Source: Trafalgar House, case study by D.F. Channon, from 'Cases in Strategic Management' by J.M. Stopford, D.F. Channon and J. Constable.

---

needs shaping and pruning to make it effective. People may need to take on different roles to achieve the right number of people in each part of the new company. Figure 11.4 is a checklist of points which need considering when looking at the training, recruitment and redeployment implications of proposed strategies. In addition to these very practical questions it has been the experience of many companies that a good deal of thought needs to be put into the process of settling down a company after a major change.[16] In the case of acquisition the need to establish a new corporate identity with which employees can identify is often of paramount importance.

> **A Checklist**
> 1. What are the objectives of training, recruitment or redeployment?
>   - improving performance?
>   - updating?
>   - developing new skills?
> 2. How many people will be involved and how many different skills?
> 3. Will there be movement between different locations?
> 4. How much will it cost?
> 5. How long will training, recruitment or redeployment take?
> 6. Who will be responsible for managing the process?
> 7. Will there be resistance to the proposals?
> 8. Are training schemes or job descriptions properly worked out?

Figure 11.4 *The training, recruitment and redeployment implications of change.*

11.3 REWARD SYSTEMS

Reward systems[17] are an important influence on strategy since they influence the attitudes of people towards strategic change. There are a variety of rewards including money (payment systems, bonus schemes, profit sharing), promotion, and increased status. In addition the possible use of punishments and sanctions needs to be considered. This section will look at how reward systems affect the behaviour of people during strategic implementation. This will occur both through the influence which rewards have on the behaviour of individuals (personal effects) and also on the relationship between groups and individuals within the organisation (political effects). Both of these will affect the ease with which the key tasks of the strategic change are undertaken.

11.3.1 Rewarding Individuals

At the personal level, the important issue is how different reward systems can or should reflect *capabilities, effort* and *job satisfaction.* A wide variety of opinions have been expressed as to what constitutes a good reward system. The Human Relations movement of the 1930s[18] saw job performance as primarily related to job satisfaction. Others[19] have seen rewards, and particularly payment, as a major stimulus to effort, and emphasis has been placed on payment by results (piece-work, sales commission). In many organisations rewards reflect capability, e.g. where skilled workers are paid more than unskilled. From a strategic viewpoint, it is important that reward systems can somehow take account of all three elements (capability, effort, satisfaction).

Although all three aspects are unlikely to be viewed as being of equal importance at any one time, it should be remembered that reward systems which are geared to only one aspect such as effort may well have a negative effect on people's performance in other ways. For example, the satisfaction of a departmental manager may be undermined by a productivity scheme (effort-related reward system) which results in his operatives earning higher wages than himself. The need to reward capability has often been cited as a reason why differentials between skilled and unskilled jobs need to be maintained. The satisfaction of skilled workers is, to some extent, dependent on their skill being recognised and rewarded. Once again effort-related reward systems may cut across this and result in demotivation of skilled workers.

Figure 11.5 illustrates the range of reward systems commonly available to organisations deciding how best to stimulate the individual performance. The figure indicates which of the three aspects each reward system is designed to deal with. For example, graded pay systems in many organisations are designed to reward capabilities even to the extent of giving increments of pay to those who possess certain qualifications irrespective of their job performance. In contrast, non-monetary rewards are a more common method of improving job satisfaction. The use of status symbols such as cars or large offices are commonly used. Sometimes a change in strategy requires a different method of operating which, in turn, will need a reconsideration of the reward systems being used. Many companies moving from craft-based production systems to light-engineering methods have found this to be so, as Illustration 48 indicates.

Reward systems also need to be considered from a negative point of view, namely the extent to which punishments or sanctions are necessary. Many organisations will specify the circumstances in which employees can be dismissed as a result of their actions or performance.

Type of reward	Factor being rewarded or stimulated		
	Capability	Effort	Satisfaction
Monetary	Graded job/pay system Bonuses (e.g. for qualifications)	Piece-work Productivity schemes Profit-sharing	Differentials important
Non-monetary	Promotion (dependent on qualifications)	Promotion Dismissal	Promotion More autonomy Bigger budget Status symbols (car, office, carpet, etc.)

Figure 11.5 *Types of reward systems.*

11.3.2 Individual or Group Rewards

Rewarding individuals for effort and performance can prove difficult unless the organisational structure and the systems of control allow an individual's performance to be isolated from the efforts of others. From a strategic point of view, therefore, it is, often a very important consideration as to whether reward systems should seek to influence the behaviour of individuals or groups. Illustration 48 shows how the division of labour within the production system of a company manufacturing tea-sets required the maintenance of quality to be dealt with at a group rather than an individual level. Organisations choosing to introduce incentive schemes for managers face similar problems in deciding whether the scheme should be based on the performance of each individual manager or on the management team as a whole.[20] Figure 11.6 summarises the pros and cons of each system. This list is useful in choosing reward systems since it helps in matching the conditions described in the table with the type of strategic change being undertaken. For example, individual incentive schemes are clearly more appropriate for strategies which are highly independent of other company activities and where performance can be easily measured. In contrast, a group incentive would be better where a high level of overlap exists between activities, or where many (perhaps specialist) managers are involved, or where performance is difficult to assign to individuals.

11.3.3 The Political Impact of Rewards

The planning of rewards during strategic implementation also needs to take into account who will control the rewards and sanctions given to individuals. This is the political dimension of reward systems since the ability to give rewards to individuals is an important source of power for certain individuals or groups. Sometimes individuals or groups are allowed to create some of their own resources within the system. So, for example, medical doctors operating within the NHS are often given opportunities to undertake private work alongside their normal duties. The rewards from this private practice provides the doctors with some measure of autonomy from the system which can make strategic changes very difficult to implement if resisted by these doctors.

A common consequence of reward systems can be seen in profit-sharing schemes in divisionalised companies. It is often felt that the profit-earning potential of one division is being impaired by the activities of another. Perhaps one division is the major supplier of another and, as a result, the profit potential of each division is dictated by the price charged for these supplies. This issue of transfer pricing will be discussed more fully later in the chapter.

11.3.4 Rewards to Outsiders

The management of certain rewards to outsiders could be critically

---

ILLUSTRATION 48

Executive Holloware

• Executive Holloware ran into product quality problems when they changed its production process without considering the implications for its reward systems.

By 1975 Executive Holloware, a manufacturer of high quality silver-plated tea-sets, found itself under considerable economic pressure from a generally competitive environment. In an attempt to become more cost efficient the company decided to move away from a craft-based production process, in which each craftsman performed virtually all the stages in the production process, to a 'light engineering' process where groups of workers specialised in different stages of production.

Traditionally, the craftsmen had been paid by piece-rate, but when a similar system was introduced for the new production process, the number of sub-standard products increased alarmingly. By rewarding the 'output' of each stage of production there was no incentive to maintain high quality. Although the old system of piece-work for craftsmen was also output-related, there were two important ingredients that were lost in the new system.

First, in the past the craftsman had complete control of the whole process and could therefore be held responsible for the quality of the output. Second, the level of job satisfaction and pride was considerably higher under the old process. Many craftsmen were de-motivated by the change, indeed several left the company.

The company's solution to the quality problem was to phase-out individual piece-rates and introduce a 'factory bonus' which rewarded the output of good quality work.

Executive Holloware's experiences highlight the importance of having a reward system that is compatible with the production process. Failure to achieve this may jeopardise key aspects of a company's strategy which in this case was the maintenance of high quality products.

Source: Executive Holloware Case Study. Available from the Case Clearing House, Cranfield.

---

important to the successful implementation of policy. For example, the management of rewards for agents and distributors can be a key element of strategy. Catalogue mail order companies, for example, are dependent on motivating several thousand part-time agents over a wide geographical area, many of whom have little time to devote to the job (housewives). Very often short-term incentives such as special prizes for sales performance are used to keep agents motivated.

The relationship with suppliers may need to be managed by the use of rewards and sanctions. If the completion of a complex aero-engine is critically dependent on the arrival of certain components at particular times, then it might be quite appropriate for the organisation to have a legally binding penalty clause in its agreement with suppliers. Looking at the issue in a more

Aspects to be considered	Schemes based on individual performance	Schemes based on group performance
Managerial contribution to company performance	(a) Appropriate where individual's contribution is relatively independent	(a) Appropriate where individuals' contributions are relatively interdependent
	(b) Appropriate where performance standards are relatively variable i.e. some managers at much higher standard than others	(b) Approriate where performance standards are relatively uniform
Type of behaviour	Encourages entrepreneurial, self-reliant or creative types of behaviour	Encourages greater cooperation, coordination and team management
Flexibility of scheme	Scheme can be negotiated individually; or can be uniform	Scheme can be negiotiated individually, but is more likely to be standard or uniform
Administration	Administrative requirements relatively great	Administrative requirements relatively slight
Discrimination	Relatively easy to achieve high discrimination between different levels of performance	Discrimination can be achieved between different groups or teams, but not so easily between individuals

Figure 11.6 *Managerial rewards - individual and group incentives
(Source: Angela M. Bowey, ed., Handbook of Salary and Wage Systems, 2nd edn.,
(Aldershot: Gower Publishing Company Limited, 1982) p. 254).*

positive way, incentives may be provided to suppliers if they meet deadlines
(perhaps by a bonus payment). There is a useful link here with the planning of
resources which was discussed in Chapter 9. The building of an aero-engine is a
complex project and will require the use of resource planning techniques like
network analysis to plan the sequencing of work. This would identify those
supplies and components whose arrival is critically important (i.e. lie on or
near the critical path) and where a selective use of rewards and sanctions

towards suppliers might be sensible. This is preferable to a blanket approach which might unnecessarily alienate suppliers whose deadlines are not so important.

All these considerations are important in the planning of reward systems and involve a great deal of detailed consideration; the key strategic issue is the extent to which any system of rewards is likely to encourage individuals to accept change. The reward system must help create the right climate for strategic changes to be made. This will require managers to decide what the most important issues are for the reward system to deal with. Figure 11.7 is a checklist of the most important issues which need to be considered when planning how reward systems will assist strategic change.

A Checklist
1. Which aspect(s) of the strategy will the reward be most concerned with? E.g. - Quantity
                 - Quality
                 - Cooperation between divisions.
2. Should groups or individuals be rewarded?
3. Should the systems reward effort or capability?
4. Should rewards be mainly monetary, promotion or status?
5. What types of sanctions and punishments are needed?
6. Are important outsiders (suppliers, agents, etc.) properly motivated by the company's rewards?
7. Are the political consequences of the reward systems likely to help or hinder the strategic change?

Figure 11.7 *Reward systems and strategic change.*

11.4 CONTROL AND INFORMATION SYSTEMS

The successful implementation of strategic change invariably involves steering the organisation into areas where there is little previous experience. Even strategies of consolidation which were discussed in Chapter 7 may require modified production systems, changed incentive schemes, or relocation of sales people. Chapter 7 also emphasised the need to view the process of evaluation as one of mapping out the future rather than simply identifying the one best strategy. The implication of this statement is that when the organisation becomes involved in the real problems of implementing strategic change management will need some means of identifying how well the implementation process is proceeding. More importantly they will need to understand what to do if, as is invariably the case, the company strays from the expected best strategy.

It is in this context that this part of the chapter looks at how information and control are important elements of the implementation process.[21] It is intended to review how control and information systems influence the behaviour of people at both a personal and political level so that the relationship between these systems and strategic implementation can be best understood.

11.4.1 Controlling Individual Performance

In looking at the importance of control in strategic implementation care must be taken not to define control too narrowly. In particular, it is important to recognise that a great deal of control exists outside the formal, institutionalised, control systems. In fact, many small companies may have few, if any, formal systems and yet a great deal of control is still exerted over individuals during strategic implementation. Dalton[22] provides a useful way of looking at control by identifying three different types of control as shown in Fig. 11.8.

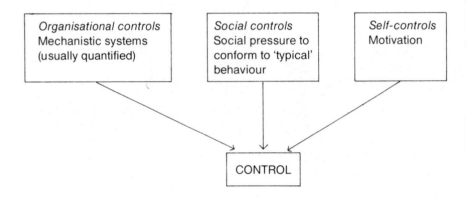

Figure 11.8 *Three types of control on individuals.*

Organisational controls are the formal control systems and often referred to as mechanistic or bureaucratic control. They are usually quantitative and measure performance in a number of ways such as profit, market share, cost variances. The management accounting system of companies is usually responsible for many of these control systems.

Social controls are not explicit or written down but are very powerful forces within organisations. Social control often operates through pressures on individuals to conform to group norms. For example, production operatives often collude on their speed of work and, in this way, resist attempts to change production targets.

Self control, which is often call motivation, is an important way in which individuals regulate their own effort and performance. Highly motivated people will control themselves through their own standards and need for job satisfaction. The manager's involvement in control then becomes one of steering people in the right direction.

In most organisations all three forms of control will be operating simultaneously. Control is likely to be greatest when all three types are pulling in the same direction so that individuals do not feel over-controlled.

During strategic implementation it is often necessary to change the behaviour or performance of individuals through modifications to the control systems. Care must be taken to consider the extent to which changes are likely to affect the capabilities, effort, or satisfaction of individuals, any one of which can influence performance. People's intrinsic capabilities are unlikely to be changed by new systems of control. However, individuals are most likely to spend their time and talents pursuing activities which bring personal recognition or avoid sanctions within the control systems. So a production manager may boost his volume of output by varying the product mix towards the easiest mix despite the fact that this may reduce production of the more profitable lines.

The effort which individuals put into their jobs can be strongly influenced by control (and reward) systems. However, there are dangers in relying on highly mechanistic controls to increase effort particularly if standards are difficult to set. A company entering a new market or line of production could be ill-advised to draw up tight controls too early since that could reduce the freedom to make changes in the light of experience. The standards may have been set too low - reducing motivation - or too high - causing frustration or rejection of the standards. Job satisfaction can be an important form of control. Some individuals can be demotivated by the tightening of mechanistic controls if they are used to performing at a high level whilst regulating their own activities.

11.4.2 The Political Impact of Control and Information Systems

In addition to the influence of control systems on the performance of individuals, there can be a number of political consequences of changing control and information systems which could help or hinder strategic change. Individuals or groups may manipulate information to seek outcomes which are more favourable to them. Modern data processing systems are making information more widely available at different levels in organisations so managers are forced to have more consultation with well-informed groups during implementation of strategic change. Information may also be a means of educating certain groups or individuals and reducing their feeling of insecurity towards proposed changes.

Control is often exerted by dividing an organisation into smaller units such as departments, sections or divisions. Although this might be an important means of dealing with the complexity of strategic implementation it can result in sub-optimal performance if these smaller units pursue their own

---

ILLUSTRATION 49

Pepsi

* The desire to appear impressive in the eyes of head office management lead a number of Pepsi-Cola's executives to 'invent' profits.

The following appeared in a newspaper article in 1982:

'The pressures for rising profits in the highly competitive world of soft drinks were so great for Pepsi-Cola managers in the Philippines and Mexico that they apparently decided to invent them.

The company has announced from its New York Headquarters that it has sacked four executives involved with its Philippine and Mexican bottling plants after accountants discovered that they had over-reported profits by $85 million.

Although the Securities and Exchange Commission has been called in to look for any wrongdoing, the company has put the 'accounting irregularities' down to over-zealous management. The object of the $85 million falsification - which began in 1978 - was 'to improve the apparent performance of their operations,' Pepsi said in a statement.

Pepsi, after dominating the Philippine market for several years has been in strong competition with Coca-Cola over the last two years. With Coca-Cola making big inroads into its foreign markets, Pepsi managers may have felt the need to keep putting on an ever-more impressive performance.

A great deal of hard work was involved. According to the company, profit was inflated by a number of devices, 'including false invoices representing sale of soft drinks, inflated receivables and inventories and legitimate expenses that were deferred'. Its statement talks of 'extensive collusion, creation of false documentation and evasion of company internal controls.'

Although an extreme case, Pepsi's experience highlights a potential problem that can arise when a company's strategy includes devolving responsibility to a large number of divisions. The problem is that dividing an organisation into smaller units without installing an appropriate control system, can provide the 'smaller units' with the opportunity to pursue their own self interest at the expense of the group as a whole.

Source: 'Lies made Pepsi top of the pops', by Alex Brummer, The Guardian, 9th Nov. 1982.

---

narrow self-interest at the expense of the overall company, as Illustration 49 shows. Overlap between the activities of different parts of the organisation can cause internal friction. If different parts of a company inter-trade and the performance of parts is measured in terms of profit then there are invariably disagreements about transfer pricing. If one division provides an important input to another then the profitability of each division is determined by the price at which the input is transferred. Overlap can also occur because different parts of the organisation are in competition with each other. It needs to be decided how far control procedures should discourage this competition by, say, designating sales territories or forcing specialisation of product range.

Sharing of resources can be a major source of friction if, for example, there is disagreement on how overheads for centralised services are apportioned. Often the argument is heard at divisional level that they are profitable 'really' -meaning without the overhead allocation. No mention is made of the contribution of these services to this 'real' profit nor who is expected to foot the bill. Where production or marketing resources are shared by divisions responsible for different products there are often arguments about whether each product is receiving its fair share of resources.

11.4.3 Guidelines for Effective Control of Strategy

Having reviewed the ways in which control and information systems are likely to influence the behaviour of individuals and groups, it is now possible to consider how these systems can be designed to best facilitate strategic change. The following guidelines should be useful (see Fig. 11.9).

*   *Distinguish between various levels of control.* Anthony[23] has suggested that control needs to take place at three levels which he calls the strategic, management, and operational levels. Implementation of new strategies requires control at all these levels, each of which will have a quite different purpose and require different information. For example, a

1. Distinguish levels of control
     e.g. strategic control/management control/operational control.
2. Identify responsibility centres
         revenue centres
         cost centres
         profit centres
         investment centres
3. Identify key factors and control them.
4. Allow diversity of control
     e.g. avoid temptation to have universal standards such as
         sales volume.
5. Use a sensible time period
     e.g. where investment is involved use a realistic measure of
         pay-back period.
6. Avoid misleading measurement
     e.g. the use of surrogate measures can be misleading.

Figure 11.9   *Guidelines for the effective control of strategy.*

venture into a new overseas market would require controlling at a *strategic* level through an overall budget, at the *management* level by monitoring expenditures and motivating employees, and also at the *operational* level by ensuring that routine tasks are properly performed. If strategic implementation is to be successful the control systems need to take these different levels into account. Operational control will normally require more detailed information and should be dealt with by line managers. In contrast strategic control may consist of a few global measures monitored by senior management.

*   *Create responsibility centres.* The complexity of strategic change usually requires the sub-divison of control within a company. These smaller units are often called responsibility centres.[24] They are identifiable parts of the whole organisation and are responsible for a certain aspect of the business; their performance is measured and controlled accordingly. There are a number of bases on which this responsibility can be apportioned as shown in Fig. 11.10.

Type	Examples	Control exerted over	Typical controls
1. Revenue centre	Sales department	Income	Sales targets
2. Cost centre: a) Standard cost centres b)Discretionay expense centres	Production dept. (manufacturing) R & D Administrative dept.	Cost of labour, materials, services,etc. Total expenditure	Detailed budgeting. Standard product costing Budget
3. Profit centres	‾ Internal services (e.g. design) ‾ Product or market division - subsidiary company	Profit	P & L accounts
4. Investment centres	- Subsidiary company	Return on capital	Complete financial accounts

Figure 11.10 *Different types of responsibility centre.*

In terms of previous discussions, the limited devolution of responsibility represented by revenue or cost centres has the advantage that senior management are more able to control the political activity between groups; but the disadvantage that the degree of motivation which the control system provides to individuals or groups may be quite limited. In contrast, the creation of profit or investment centres may provide motivation to perform but create political tensions within the company which may be difficult to control.

*   *Select key factors.* Since strategic implementation is very complex, it is crucial to identify and control those aspects which are critically important to the success or failure of the strategy. These should have been identified during resource planning (Chapter 9). There are often cases where companies recognise the need to be selective but do not select the key factors. A good example of this situation is an organisation which becomes obsessed with a single measure of performance like volume of output or sales without assessing how this fits the overall objective of the company. This can be a severe constraint when new strategies are introduced which do not neatly fit this yardstick. A company wishing to introduce a low volume, high profit product into its traditional range of high volume, low profit lines would have great difficulties if they continued to measure the performance of the sales staff entirely by volume.

* *Allow diversity in control.* The previous example also illustrates the danger of assuming that all an organisation's activities can be controlled by a single, all-embracing system of control. Not only is this not achievable in practice, but it is not desirable when attempting to control strategic implementation. The fact that strategic decisions are long term and made in conditions of uncertainty is in itself sufficient reason for requiring the more liberal application of control.

The continued evolution of new strategies requires this diversity of control. The most obvious example is the lack of profitability of new products during their early days. Chapter 8 explained the importance of a balanced portfolio of products or activities. The profitability of Cash Cows and Stars would not be expected to be the same since the strategic purpose of those two groups of products is different. Their contribution to the company may have to be measured and controlled differently.

* *Avoid misleading measurement.* Control relies heavily on measurement, but many aspects of strategy are difficult to measure quantitatively. This can lead to situations where the pressure to produce quantitative measures may well distort the process of control and, in some cases, lead to poor performance. The police force has a problem in this respect as the assessment of how well law and order is being maintained is very difficult. In the absence of any precise measures there is a tendency to develop surrogate measures, i.e. those things which are measurable. In the case of the police, surrogate measures might be the number of arrests, convictions, or proportion of cases solved. A police force which had extremely good relations with its local community might score badly by these measures.

11.4.4 Analyses for the Control of Strategic Implementation

It is not the intention of this chapter to discuss the detailed use of control techniques.[25] However, there are important links between control techniques and discussions in previous chapters. The analytical techniques used to provide information for control are essentially those which have been discussed fully in the chapters on strategic analysis and evaluation. For example, *market analysis* to establish the size and growth of various market segments and the company's market share is needed during evaluation of strategy but also forms the basis of control of strategic implementation. *Management by objectives* (MBO)[26] is a way of planning the implementation of strategy through the various levels of an organisation (by producing a hierachy of related objectives). MBO also controls the same strategy by measuring performance against these objectives at all levels of the company.

One of the major problems of strategic change is the reallocation of resources. Therefore, techniques of resource planning (Chapter 9) are equally relevant to the process of controlling strategic implementation. For example, *budgets* are useful in planning detailed resource requirements but they are also central to the control process and influence people's motivation.[27] Techniques like *network analysis* help in planning how resources can be scheduled but also provide an on-going means of monitoring and controlling implementation.

Figure 11.11 summarises some analyses which can be used for controlling strategic implementation. In addition, readers are encouraged to re-read the relevant parts of previous chapters.

Type of analysis	Used to control
1. Financial analysis	
˜ Ratio analysis	Elements of profitability
˜ Variance analysis	Cost or revenue
˜ Cash budgeting	Cash flow
˜ Capital budgeting	Investment
2. Market/sales analysis	
Demand analysis	Competitive standing
Market share analysis	
Sales targets	Sales effectiveness
Sales budget	Efficiency
3. Physical resource analysis	
Capacity fill	Plant utilisation
Yield	Materials utilisation
Product inspection	Quality
4. Human resource analysis	
Work measurement	Productivity
Output measurement	
Labour turnover	Work force stability
5. Analysis of systems	
Management by objectives	Accountability
Network analysis	Resource acquisition/task sequencing

Figure 11.11 *Some analyses for controlling strategic implementation.*

11.5 MANAGING PEOPLE AND SYSTEMS

The final part of this chapter is concerned with how the management of people and systems needs to take account of the circumstances facing the organisation during strategic implementation. For example, the type of strategic change envisaged, the size and style of the company, the extent to which the company is specialised or diversified all influence the way that people and systems are managed. In the same way, the type of environment which the company faces and any important changes, such as in information technology, need to be taken into account. All of these factors have been discussed earlier and so this last section is mainly concerned with pulling together these various strands and looking at people and systems as a whole. Figure 11.12 provides a summary of the major points and can be used as a checklist against which to match an organisation's circumstances and how people and systems might best be managed.

11.5.1 The Nature of the Strategic Change

Different strategies require different blends of people and systems. For example, the decision to extend market coverage of a company's products by the use of freelance agents relies heavily on performance-related rewards and less on direct supervision than if the company's own salaried staff were to be used. Equally, the type of person who would make a good agent is not necessarily the same as a good company-based salesperson. Some strategic changes, although major in scale may be of a similar nature to the company's present activities. Strategies of consolidation or product development, for example, may require fewer changes to systems and people's behaviour than would unrelated diversification. This, of course, raises another issue, namely the extent to which new developments can be isolated from other parts of the business. Sometimes it may be desirable to pursue strategies of unrelated diversification by creating new, independent divisions or acquiring separate companies, and in this way the people and systems of the new venture can be operated quite independently of the established business. In contrast, many strategic changes, by their very nature, will be intimately tied up with the current business and, therefore, the people and systems must be planned as a whole.

11.5.2 Size of Organisation

Many of the ideas discussed in this chapter have been based on the premise that organisations are large enough to have structured control and reward systems. The discussion of responsibility centres, for example, assumed that the organisation was of a size whereby strategic implementation would benefit from division of responsibility. Many organisations, of course, are not big

Situation	Appropriate method of managing (examples)		
	People	*Rewards*	*Control*
1. Nature of strategic change			
– related	Redeployment, promotion	Promotion. Use present reward systems	Use present systems (with care)
– unrelated	Recruitment, retraining, redundancy	Separate reward systems can be used	Separate systems can be used e.g. create new profit centre
2. Company size			
– large	Use of specialists	Structured pay systems Promotion as a reward	Formal systems important Extensive use of responsibility centres
– small	Need for general managers	Promotion difficult to use. Often highly personalised payment	Formal systems minimal dependent on social control and motivation Sub-division of control is limited
3. Variety of activities			
– specialised	Career patterns within specialisms	Uniform pay structure	Few different control systems
– diverse	Recruitment, retraining, more important	Several systems of reward	Several separate systems

4. History and culture of the organisation			
~ formal systems	If require more creativity may need to slacken systems	Could be tied to performance e.g. incentive schemes	May benefit from slackening controls but may take time to readjust
~ informal systems	Often creative and independent but some will abuse the system. Systems must fit the style of management	Personalised systems may be appropriate e.g. commission royalties, etc.	Motivation important method of control
5. Nature of the environment			
~ static	Stable workforce, little training, etc.	Formal, detailed, payment systems and job grades are possible	Formal systems probably work
changing	Recruitment, redeployment, training, etc., very important	Ad hoc arrangement may be necessary	Looser systems will be needed until situation stabilises
~ complex	Many specialists required	Several different systems may be needed	A number of different systems needed

Figure 11.12 *Matching people and systems to the company's situation.*

enough for these concerns to be real - or even if there are, changes could not be introduced in a cost-efficient way. Some ways of organising control systems require duplication of activities which could not be borne by smaller companies. Very often organisations have to subcontract certain activities (such as transport, servicing, etc.) because they are not big enough to run these services economically. This may result in less control over strategic implementation than is perhaps desirable. Managers in small companies need to have a wide range of skills. Equally, small companies cannot use promotion as an important reward since there is nowhere to be promoted to.

11.5.3 Diversity of Activities

It has already been mentioned that there is often a natural tendency within companies to search for a single unified system of control and equal simplicity in its reward systems. Whereas simplicity should not be underrated as a virtue, it is unlikely to be achievable in situations where the company's activities are very diverse. This diversity may arise internally, e.g. different technologies or production systems, or externally, e.g. different market areas. The need to recognise and reflect the diversity of a company's activities was one of the guidelines for good control of strategic change.

Similar arguments apply to the 'people' aspect of implementation. Organisations with a great variety of activities will need to reflect this in their recruitment, promotion, training and management development policies. Equally, the search for an all-embracing pay structure may prove fruitless. In contrast, uniformity may be achievable, and perhaps desirable, in an organisation which is highly specialised.

11.5.4 History and Culture of the Organisation

The successful implementation of strategic change must take account of the history of an organisation and the dominant values or culture which exists. Very often these two factors are related. The behaviour of individuals within a company is strongly conditioned by the way in which systems have been operated in the past. Although it might be highly desirable to give more freedom and responsibility to a particular division of the company to ensure success of a new strategy, it may in fact be difficult for the people concerned to respond. Often the reverse situation is the case: management feels the need for tighter control over groups who have in the past enjoyed a high level of autonomy (such as designers, scientists or super-salesmen). Sometimes the solution to this dilemma can be found in the system of rewards which may be related to royalties, commissions, or a limited tenure contract of employment.

Cammann and Nadler[28] have very usefully extended this discussion into the area of management style. They argue that implementation of strategy is often unsuccessful not because the systems do not fit the overall culture but because they do not fit the style of the managers who have to operate the systems. For example, managers who have always relied heavily on informal relationships as their form of control may be in difficulty if forced to introduce highly formalised systems (e.g. work measurement). Their conclusion is that problems during the implementation of strategy which at face value point towards poor systems are better solved by improving the match between these systems and the management style. This can be done in one of two ways: changing the systems or retraining the management to change their style.

11.5.5 The Nature of the Environment

It has already been suggested that organisations operating in environments with high diversity will require different people and systems than those coping with less diversity. Similarly, in highly complex environments (e.g. aerospace) there will be a greater need for specialists and the systems of control and reward will need to reflect this.

The degree of change in the environment will also be very influential on the choice of people and systems. Organisations operating in highly dynamic environments will have a special need for people who can tolerate ambiguity -mechanistic control systems will tend to be ineffective and highly institutionalised reward systems may prove very constraining.

Advances in information technology affect strategic implementation in a number of ways. The greater availability of information at many levels changes the balance of power within the company and usually necessitates greater consultation concerning strategic change. Information may be a key resource for opening up new opportunities such as with international speculation in money or strategic resources. It is the ability to operate good systems of information and control which make such strategies possible. The improved communication within companies is a real opportunity which should facilitate strategic change. There is evidence[29], however, that these opportunities are not necessarily grasped by management who tend to use better data processing to extend the traditional bureaucratic control systems.

11.6 SUMMARY

This chapter has been concerned with the issue of managing strategic change through the management of people and the use of systems. The range of issues included are closely related to the other aspects of implementation discussed in Chapters 9 and 10. In a similar way there are strong links with the earlier sections of the book concerned with strategic analysis and strategic choice. A proper analysis of an organisation's environment, resources, and the values of people in and around it is an invaluable background against which the details of strategic implementation can be planned. Equally, the choice of strategies will have an overriding influence on how easily the changes can be implemented. However, in the final analysis it is the skill with which managers (and others) actually implement strategic change which determines the success or failure of strategy. 'A strategy which is not implemented is no strategy at all'.[30]

REFERENCES

1. 'Dynamic conservatism' is a useful idea since it is a reminder that people will actively fight to maintain the *status quo* rather than simply be indifferent. For a fuller discussion see: C. Argyris and D.A. Schon, *Theory in Practice: Increasing Effectiveness* (Jossey-Bass: 1974).
2. E. Mumford and A. Pettigrew, *Implementing Strategic Decisions* (Longman: 1975), is a report on the research into the introduction of large scale computer systems in four large organisations. The process of implementation was monitored over a period of two to five years.
3. Readers should look back to Chapter 5 or one of the key references for that chapter. For example: B.D. Reed and B.W.M. Palmer, *An Introduction to Organisation Behaviour* (Grubb Institute: 1972).
4. A.V. Johnston, 'Consulting Skills Manual', unpublished, 1970, argues that an essential attribute of consultants (which would include managers within companies) is their ability to understand the political realities of the situation which they face. We have taken this view in earlier chapters of this book (particularly Chapter 5).
   J. Pfeffer, *Power in Organizations* (Pitman: 1981) is a most interesting discussion of why the importance of political activity has been consistently underrated in management literature. Most treatments have tended to view political behaviour as a hiccup in an otherwise rational and tidy situation.
5. I.C. Macmillan, *Strategy Formulation: Political Concepts* (West: 1978, Ch.5) considers strategy from a political perspective and provides some very useful insights into why the political process needs to be seen as a means of implementing strategy.
6. D. Moscow, 'Consulting Skills Manual', unpublished, 1970, emphasises the importance of how individuals will react to proposals for change in determining the political feasibility of change. He proposes that the key issue is the degree of security which people feel.
7. The value of lowering the resistance to change is argued in a number of books and papers. For example: G. Watson, 'Resistance to Change', in W. Bennis, K. Benne and R. Chin, *Planning of Change* (Holt, Rinehart, 2nd Edn: 1969). An early classic is K. Levin, *Field Theory in Social Science* (Harper & Row: 1951).
8. W. Ouchi, *Theory Z - How American Business Can Meet the Japanese Challenge* (Addison-Wesley: 1981) is a very interesting review of the major differences in approach of American and Japanese management. It is particularly relevant to Chapter 11 since it compares the attitudes towards a number of aspects of implementation such as reward systems, management development, decision-making processes, and control.

9. In a private communication (1982) D. Tranfield of Sheffield City Polytechnic, argues for the need to be realistic in an assessment of political viability and to proceed on the 'common ground' whilst keeping other aspects open for review. G. Watson (see reference 7) also likes this keeping open of options as an important means of reducing resistance to change.

10. J.R. Galbraith and D.A. Nathanson, *Strategy Implementation: the Role of Structure and Process* (West: 1978, pp.86-87) explain more fully a number of research findings in the link between 'tolerance for ambiguity' and performance.

11. G. Watson (see reference 7) identifies a range of personal characteristics which will affect an individual's resistance to change. Included in his list are habit, depedence, selective perception and self-distrust.

12. R.E. Miles and C.C. Snow, *Organizational Strategy, Structure and Process* (McGraw-Hill: 1978). This work has already been cited extensively in Chapters 2, 5 and 10.

13. J.R. Galbraith and R.A. Nathanson (see reference 10) discuss this point on p.88.

14. Training is discussed in many books on personnel management. In relation to our book the important aspects of training are those which influence strategic capability. There is, therefore, a strong link with Chapters 4 and 9. Readers may care to look at one of the following general references on training: A.C. Hamblin, *Evaluation and Control of Training* (McGraw-Hill: 1974); T. Boydell, *The Identification of Training Needs* (BACIE, 2nd edn.: 1975); M. Armstrong, *A Handbook of Personnel Management Practice* (Kogan Page, 1977, Chs 8 and 9).

15. W. Ouchi, (see reference 8) Chapter 2 explains how such an attitude towards the development of individuals contrasts with many American and UK companies where specialisation is all-important. Again he cites this as an important reason for the success of Japanese companies.

16. S. Majaro, 'The Organisation of Change', *Management Today,* March 1972, argues that the potential economic benefits of mergers are often not achieved because they are not organised in a way which will help a successful merger.

17. Most books about rewards concentrate on wage payment systems. For example: M. Armstrong (see reference 14) Chapters 12 and 13. A useful review of research on the relationship between rewards and strategy can be found in: J.R. Galbraith and D.A. Nathanson (see reference 10) pp.81 and 85.

18. F.J. Roethlisberger and W.J. Dickson, *Management and the Worker* (Wiley: 1964), is an interesting book written by two of the Hawthorn researchers of the 1930s. Pages 517-535 describe how cash incentives are not the prime motivation to perform well.

19. Payment by results is discussed in most texts on rewards, personnel management, and often operations management. A useful discussion can be found in: G.H. Webb, 'Payment by Results Systems' in *Handbook of Salary and Wage Systems,* edited by A.M. Bowey (Gower: 1975).

20. This issue of group versus individual rewards for managers is discussed by: M. White, 'Incentive Bonus Schemes for Managers' (Bowey, ed.) (see reference 19).

21. Two useful reference books on control systems are: R.N. Anthony, *Planning and Control Systems: A Framework for Analysis* (Harvard Graduate School of Business Administration: 1965) and R.N. Anthony and J. Dearden, *Management Control Systems: Text and Cases* (Irwin, 3rd edn: 1976).

22. G.W. Dalton and P.R. Lawrence, *Motivation and Control in Organisations* (Irwin: 1971) have contributed to bridging the gap between a narrow view of control

systems and a much more useful view of the whole process of control including motivation of individuals and groups.

23. Anthony (see reference 21) has provided a model of control which is found useful by many people, namely the three levels: strategic, management, and operational.
24. Responsibility centres are a useful means of dividing control systems. They have been discussed by many authors, for example: Anthony & Deardon (see reference 21) and R.F. Vancil, 'What Kind of Management Control Do You Need?', *Harvard Business Review,* March 1973.
25. Anthony (reference 21) can be used as a general reference on control techniques.
26. J. Humble, *Management by Objectives in Action* (McGraw-Hill: 1970).
27. D.T. Otley, 'The Behavioural Aspects of Budgeting' (Institute of Chartered Accountants: 1977). This paper explains the many different and often conflicting purposes for which budgets can be used.
28. C. Cammann and D.A. Nadler, 'Fit Control Systems to Your Managerial Style', *Harvard Business Review,* Jan. 1976. In this paper the authors explain the importance of managers using systems of control which suit their own style and personality as well as the situation.
29. B. Hedburg and S. Jönsson, 'Designing Semi-confusing Information Systems for Organisations in Changing Environments', *Accounting Organisations and Society,* 1978. The authors argue that control and information systems tend to be used to protect the *status quo* and can inhibit the company's chances of capitalising on new opportunities.
30. A.J. Rowe, O.R. Mason and K.E. Dickel, *Strategic Management and Business Policy: A Methodological Approach* (Addison-Wesley: 1982) looks at a number of different approaches to strategic implementation and underlines its importance.

RECOMMENDED KEY READINGS

* A useful book which concentrates on problems of strategic implementation is P.J. Stonich, *Implementing Strategy: Making Strategy Happen* (Ballinger: 1982).

* For further discussion of reward systems and their links with strategy see: M.S. Salter, 'Tailor Incentive Compensation to Strategy' (*Harvard Business Review,* Mar.-Apr., 1973).

* For a discussion of the way in which aspects of control and structural design need integrating see Chapter 6 of J. Child, *Organisation: A guide to Problems and Practice* (Harper & Row: 1977).

* Control systems are well discussed in the writings of R.N. Anthony. Particularly: *Planning and Control Systems: A Framework for Analysis* (Harvard Graduate School of Business: 1965) and R.N. Anthony and J. Dearden, *Management Control Systems: Text and Cases* (Irwin: 1976).

EPILOGUE

By necessity, textbooks need to be structured and written in a way which allows the reader to systematically develop an understanding of the subject. However, there are dangers in this since the reader may gain an insight into the 'building blocks' which make up the subject but fail to appreciate its 'wholeness'. This is a particular concern with the study of corporate strategy since the essence of the subject is that of 'wholeness' rather than intensive study of the parts.

The point was made at the beginning of the book that the adopted focuses of analysis, choice and implementation may not take the form of a step-by-step process in practice. They are likely to be inter-related and, indeed, it is likely that the emphasis placed upon each will differ according to the organisation and its circumstances.

The simplest way to understand this is by looking at some of the examples which have been discussed in various parts of the book. The purpose of doing so is to show that corporate strategy in all organisations is concerned with managing strategic change but that this process may be achieved in different ways.

* In a large conglomerate or divisionalised company, those employed at the centre or head office may be primarily concerned with *analysis,* trying to understand the company's position, its balance of activities, and the opportunities which exist, perhaps through a corporate planning department. In contrast managers in each division may spend most of their time on *resource planning* and implementing new strategies.

* In a multi-national company the corporate management may be absorbed in aspects of *company structure.* For example, whether the company strategy will be more effective if lines of responsibility are shifted from global product divisions to international divisions.

* In contrast the owner of a small fast growing company may be mainly worried about obtaining the *resources* to capitalise on the opportunities which have been opened up. At a later stage as growth slows the search for new *strategic options* may dominate the strategic thinking in the company.

341

* Many industrial companies need to spend large sums of money on capital equipment and therefore, pay a great deal of attention to the *analysis* and *evaluation* of capital expenditure projects. Retailing companies, however, may have little money tied up in fixed assets (properties are, after all, saleable) and may develop new strategies by a series of small incremental steps where the company learns through *implementation* of ideas.
* In public sector organisations there may be a special need to understand the *political environment* within which decisions are made and implemented.
* In Japan the process of *strategic evaluation* is much more overtly political in the sense that acceptability of proposed changes tends to be tested out much more fully during evaluation than tends to be the case in Europe and North America.

In all of these situations the development of strategy will depend on the development of an understanding of the strategic position (strategic analysis), choosing between possible options (strategic choice) and planning and executing the strategy (strategic implementation). But where the process begins and what the focus of attention is, is likely to change over time, or depend on the position in the organisation from which corporate strategy is viewed.

There is, of course, a danger associated with these differences in emphasis or focus. The danger is that an organisation, or a manager, may come to see strategy in too limited a way, that some of the 'building blocks' will be emphasised at the expense of the 'wholeness' of the problem. A theme throughout this book has been that strategic decision-making will depend on the interaction of many management issues and activities, but that above all, it is necessary for management to be sensitive to, and develop an understanding of, the overall nature of strategic problems. It is common for managers to fail to do this. They become so familiar with their own functions, or the particular way they have been used to approaching problems, that they find it difficult to conceive of wider issues. Communication on matters of strategic importance is often difficult between different levels of management or between different functions for example. Managers cannot be expected to conceive of problems or opportunities in strategic terms unless they are familiar with concepts and practices of strategic management wider than their own particular experience. The view expressed in this book is that the sort of flexibility, sensitivity and imagination required of managers today at all levels in an organisation can be enhanced by their 'exploring corporate strategy'.

APPENDIX

THE PRINCIPLES OF THE EXPERIENCE CURVE AND PORTFOLIO ANALYSIS

The Boston Consulting Group (BCG) is a world-wide business consultancy operation which has conducted studies of company performance which have shown a direct and consistent relationship between the aggregate growth in volume of production and declining costs of production. This Appendix summarises their findings. However, the reader should realise this is a cursory glance at a study of very wide implications and those who wish to understand the subject in any detail must read further.[1] We are aware that the ideas discussed in the paper have been questioned by other writers and we suggest that readers also refer to them.[2] It is not the intention here to present the models as a panacea for strategic management, and we advise those with only passing familiarity with the ideas to avoid taking an over-literal view of their implications. However, we do regard them in the context of this book as a most useful stimulus for the conceptualism of strategic issues.

The Experience Curve

The premises of the BCG findings are these:

* that in any market segment of an industry, price levels tend to be very similar for similar products;
* therefore what makes one company more profitable than the next must be the levels of its costs.

It is the key determinants of low cost levels that the BCG attempted to unearth. Their arguments can be summarised as follows:

1.   The relationship between unit costs and total units produced over time resembles that shown in Fig. A. It is this curve that the BCG calls the experience curve. It is important to note that:

*   by total units produced, the BCG means cumulative units over time;
*   the growth of total costs therefore tend to plateau with cumulative production.

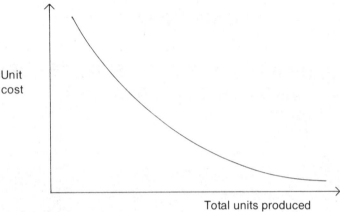

Figure A *The experience curve.*

2.   the BCG's studies in both the USA and Europe show that each time experience (i.e. cumulative production) doubles, costs decline between 20% and 30% net of inflation.

3.   Some of the reasons for this suggested by the BCG[3] are:

(a) *The learning function:* anyone doing a job learns to do it better over time and given increased experience: labour costs should in fact decline by about 10 - 15% each time cumulative experience doubles.

(b) *Specialisation:* as scale of production increases so it becomes possible to split jobs into more and more specialist jobs. 'Doing half as much but twice as often equals the same amount of effort but twice the experience with the task. If the scale doubles simultaneously with total experience, then ..... costs decline 10 - 15% because of learning plus 10 - 15% because of specialisation'.[4]

(c) *Scale:* the capital costs required to finance additional capacity diminish as that capacity grows. The BCG suggests that an approximate scale effect in process industries is that 'Capital cost increases by the six-tenths power of the increase in capacity'. The reader should, however, note that this is a phenomenon which has been questioned as a generalisation.

4.   Since cost is, in general, a function of experience then cost is also a function of market share. If competitors A and B launch similar products at the same time and their relative market shares remain constant at say 20% for A and 40% for B, then over the same period of time B will gain twice the experience of A and should then have reduced costs 20 - 30% more than A. If this is true then the importance of gaining and holding market share becomes very important indeed.

5.   Market share does not necessarily relate to the overall market. If a product is differentiated so that it is competing in a definable, relevant market segment, then it is the market share of that segment that is important.

   The overall implication of the BCG's findings is that successful companies make almost all their profits from products in which they dominate their market segment. This view has become a very strong influence on many companies' choices of strategy.

The Product Portfolio

   In order to dominate a market, a company must normally gain that dominance when the market is in the growth stage of the product life cycle. In a state of maturity, a market is likely to be stable with customer loyalties fairly fixed. It is therefore more difficult to gain share. But if all competitors in the growth stage are trying to gain market share competition will be very fierce: therefore only those companies prepared to invest in order to gain share will gain dominance. This might well mean that a company following the principles suggested by the BCG will need to price low and spend high amounts on

Figure B *The product portfolio.*

advertising and selling in order to dominate. Such a strategy is one of high risk unless such low margin activity is financed by higher profit earning products. This leads to the idea of a balanced product mix. The BCG have suggested the model of the product portfolio or the growth share matrix as a tool by which to consider product strategy. This product portfolio is shown as Fig. B.

The matrix combines market growth rate and market share and thus directly relates to the idea of the experience curve.

A *star* is a product (or business) which has a high market share in a growing market. As such the company may be spending heavily to gain that share but the experience curve effect will mean that costs are reducing over time and hopefully at a faster rate than competition. The product (or business) could, then, be self-financing.

The *question mark* (or problem child) is also in a growing market but does not have a high market share. Its parent company may be spending heavily to increase market share but, if they are, it is unlikely that they are getting sufficient cost reductions to offset such investment because the experience gained is less than for a star and costs will be reducing less quickly.

The *cash cow* is a product (or business) with high market share in a mature market. Because growth is low and market conditions more stable the need for heavy marketing investment is less. But high market share means that experience in relation to low share competition continues to grow and relative costs reduce. The cash cow is thus a cash provider.

Dogs have low share in static or declining markets and are this the worst of all combinations. They are often a cash drain and use up a disproportionate amount of company time and resources.

The implications for the analysis and evaluation of strategy are discussed in the relevant chapters of the book, in particular Chapters 4 and 8.

REFERENCES

1.   Further reading on the BCG models are:
      P. Conley, 'Experience Curves as a Planning Tool', available from the Boston Consulting Group as a pamphlet.
      B. Hedley, 'Strategy and the Business Portfolio', *Long Range Planning,,* Vol. 10, Feb. 1977.
      J.H. Grant and W.R. King, 'Strategy Formulation: Analytical and Normative Models' in *Strategic Management: A New View of Business Policy and Planning,* D. Schendel and C. Hofer (eds) (Little Brown 1979).
2.   Readers may care to refer to the following:
      S.P. Slatter, 'Common Pitfalls in Using the BCG Product Portfolio Matrix', *London Business School Journal,* Winter, 1980.
      R. Wensley, 'PIMS and BCG: New Horizons or False Dawn', *Strategic Management Journal,* Vol. 3, No.2, 1982.
      John Thackeray, 'The Corporate Strategy Problem', *Management Today,* Oct. 1979.

3.   For a fuller account of their reasons see: 'The Experience Curve Reviewed: Why
      Does it Work', pamphlet from the BCG (1974).
4   From A.Silberston, 'Economies of Scale in Theory and Practice' *The Economic
      Journal,* Vol. 82, 1982.

INDEX